WORDPERFECT®
OFFICE 2000
FOR
DUMMIES®

WORDPERFECT® OFFICE 2000 FOR DUMMIES®

by Julie Adair King

IDG BOOKS WORLDWIDE

IDG Books Worldwide, Inc.
An International Data Group Company

Foster City, CA ◆ Chicago, IL ◆ Indianapolis, IN ◆ New York, NY

WordPerfect® Office 2000 For Dummies®

Published by
IDG Books Worldwide, Inc.
An International Data Group Company
919 E. Hillsdale Blvd.
Suite 400
Foster City, CA 94404
www.idgbooks.com (IDG Books Worldwide Web site)
www.dummies.com (Dummies Press Web site)

Copyright © 1999 IDG Books Worldwide, Inc. All rights reserved. No part of this book, including interior design, cover design, and icons, may be reproduced or transmitted in any form, by any means (electronic, photocopying, recording, or otherwise) without the prior written permission of the publisher.

Library of Congress Catalog Card No.: 99-63109

ISBN: 0-7645-0429-0

Printed in the United States of America

10 9 8 7 6 5 4 3 2 1

1B/QZ/QW/ZZ/IN

Distributed in the United States by IDG Books Worldwide, Inc.

Distributed by CDG Books Canada Inc. for Canada; by Transworld Publishers Limited in the United Kingdom; by IDG Norge Books for Norway; by IDG Sweden Books for Sweden; by IDG Books Australia Publishing Corporation Pty. Ltd. for Australia and New Zealand; by TransQuest Publishers Pte Ltd. for Singapore, Malaysia, Thailand, Indonesia, and Hong Kong; by Gotop Information Inc. for Taiwan; by ICG Muse, Inc. for Japan; by Norma Comunicaciones S.A. for Colombia; by Intersoft for South Africa; by Eyrolles for France; by International Thomson Publishing for Germany, Austria and Switzerland; by Distribuidora Cuspide for Argentina; by Livraria Cultura for Brazil; by Ediciones ZETA S.C.R. Ltda. for Peru; by WS Computer Publishing Corporation, Inc., for the Philippines; by Contemporanea de Ediciones for Venezuela; by Express Computer Distributors for the Caribbean and West Indies; by Micronesia Media Distributor, Inc. for Micronesia; by Grupo Editorial Norma S.A. for Guatemala; by Chips Computadoras S.A. de C.V. for Mexico; by Editorial Norma de Panama S.A. for Panama; by American Bookshops for Finland. Authorized Sales Agent: Anthony Rudkin Associates for the Middle East and North Africa.

For general information on IDG Books Worldwide's books in the U.S., please call our Consumer Customer Service department at 800-762-2974. For reseller information, including discounts and premium sales, please call our Reseller Customer Service department at 800-434-3422.

For information on where to purchase IDG Books Worldwide's books outside the U.S., please contact our International Sales department at 317-596-5530 or fax 317-596-5692.

For consumer information on foreign language translations, please contact our Customer Service department at 1-800-434-3422, fax 317-596-5692, or e-mail rights@idgbooks.com.

For information on licensing foreign or domestic rights, please phone +1-650-655-3109.

For sales inquiries and special prices for bulk quantities, please contact our Sales department at 650-655-3200 or write to the address above.

For information on using IDG Books Worldwide's books in the classroom or for ordering examination copies, please contact our Educational Sales department at 800-434-2086 or fax 317-596-5499.

For press review copies, author interviews, or other publicity information, please contact our Public Relations department at 650-655-3000 or fax 650-655-3299.

For authorization to photocopy items for corporate, personal, or educational use, please contact Copyright Clearance Center, 222 Rosewood Drive, Danvers, MA 01923, or fax 978-750-4470.

Trademarks: All brand names and product names used in this book are trade names, service marks, trademarks, or registered trademarks of their respective owners. IDG Books Worldwide is not associated with any product or vendor mentioned in this book.

is a registered trademark or trademark under exclusive license to IDG Books Worldwide, Inc. from International Data Group, Inc. in the United States and/or other countries.

**IDG
BOOKS**
WORLDWIDE

About the Author

Julie Adair King has been wrestling with computers since 1976, when she stood in line with all the other first-year geeks at Purdue University to type programming commands into now-antiquated keypunch machines. Since then, she has churned out documents using almost every type of word processor, spreadsheet, and office utility program to grace the computer-store shelves.

A longtime writer and editor, King is the author of *WordPerfect Suite 7 For Dummies, WordPerfect Suite 8 For Dummies, Digital Photography For Dummies,* and *Adobe PhotoDeluxe For Dummies.* In addition, she has contributed to many other computer-related books, including *CorelDRAW! 7 For Dummies, Photoshop 4 Bible, Photoshop For Dummies,* and *PageMaker 6 For Dummies.*

ABOUT IDG BOOKS WORLDWIDE

Welcome to the world of IDG Books Worldwide.

IDG Books Worldwide, Inc., is a subsidiary of International Data Group, the world's largest publisher of computer-related information and the leading global provider of information services on information technology. IDG was founded more than 30 years ago by Patrick J. McGovern and now employs more than 9,000 people worldwide. IDG publishes more than 290 computer publications in over 75 countries. More than 90 million people read one or more IDG publications each month.

Launched in 1990, IDG Books Worldwide is today the #1 publisher of best-selling computer books in the United States. We are proud to have received eight awards from the Computer Press Association in recognition of editorial excellence and three from Computer Currents' First Annual Readers' Choice Awards. Our best-selling *...For Dummies®* series has more than 50 million copies in print with translations in 31 languages. IDG Books Worldwide, through a joint venture with IDG's Hi-Tech Beijing, became the first U.S. publisher to publish a computer book in the People's Republic of China. In record time, IDG Books Worldwide has become the first choice for millions of readers around the world who want to learn how to better manage their businesses.

Our mission is simple: Every one of our books is designed to bring extra value and skill-building instructions to the reader. Our books are written by experts who understand and care about our readers. The knowledge base of our editorial staff comes from years of experience in publishing, education, and journalism — experience we use to produce books to carry us into the new millennium. In short, we care about books, so we attract the best people. We devote special attention to details such as audience, interior design, use of icons, and illustrations. And because we use an efficient process of authoring, editing, and desktop publishing our books electronically, we can spend more time ensuring superior content and less time on the technicalities of making books.

You can count on our commitment to deliver high-quality books at competitive prices on topics you want to read about. At IDG Books Worldwide, we continue in the IDG tradition of delivering quality for more than 30 years. You'll find no better book on a subject than one from IDG Books Worldwide.

John Kilcullen
Chairman and CEO
IDG Books Worldwide, Inc.

Steven Berkowitz
President and Publisher
IDG Books Worldwide, Inc.

VIII
WINNER
*Eighth Annual
Computer Press
Awards 1992*

IX
WINNER
*Ninth Annual
Computer Press
Awards 1993*

X
WINNER
*Tenth Annual
Computer Press
Awards 1994*

XI
WINNER
*Eleventh Annual
Computer Press
Awards 1995*

Dedication

This book is dedicated to my grandparents, Irene Harris, Mae King, and the late George Harris and Cecil King. Thank you for a lifetime of love.

Author's Acknowledgments

Thanks to Project Editor Melba Hopper for helping me to avoid editorial missteps and for making sure that everything happened when it should, how it should, in the best and most painless way possible. Thanks also to Technical Editor Lee Musick, who did his usual stellar job in steering me away from embarrassing technical faux pas; and to Acquisitions Editor Steve Hayes for always lending a supportive ear. I also want to acknowledge the book's Production Coordinator, Regina Snyder, and all the people in the IDG Books production department who work so hard to turn raw words and pictures into the polished pages you see here.

Last but not least, a heartfelt word of appreciation to Michelle Murphy-Croteau and Chip Maxwell at Corel Corporation. Your assistance and friendly cooperation is appreciated more than you know!

Publisher's Acknowledgments

We're proud of this book; please register your comments through our IDG Books Worldwide Online Registration Form located at http://my2cents.dummies.com.

Some of the people who helped bring this book to market include the following:

Acquisitions, Editorial, and Media Development

Project Editor: Melba D. Hopper
  (Previous Edition: Robert H. Wallace)

Associate Acquisitions Editor:
  Steven H. Hayes

Copy Editor: Melba D. Hopper

Technical Editor: Lee Musick

Editorial Manager: Mary C. Corder

Editorial Assistants: Donna Love,
  Paul E. Kuzmic

Production

Project Coordinator: Regina Snyder

Layout and Graphics: Linda M. Boyer,
  Thomas R. Emrick, Chris Herner,
  Angela F. Hunckler, David McKelvey,
  Barry Offringa, Brent Savage, Janet Seib,
  Michael A. Sullivan, Brian Torwelle,
  Dan Whestine

Proofreaders: Christine Berman,
  Vickie Broyles, Rebecca Senninger,
  Susan Sims

Indexer: Sherry Massey

Special Help
  Michelle Vukas, Suzanne Thomas

General and Administrative

IDG Books Worldwide, Inc: John Kilcullen, CEO; Steven Berkowitz, President and Publisher

IDG Books Technology Publishing: Brenda McLaughlin, Senior Vice President and Group Publisher

Dummies Technology Press and Dummies Editorial: Diane Graves Steele, Vice President and Associate Publisher; Mary Bednarek, Director of Acquisitions and Product Development; Kristin A. Cocks, Editorial Director

Dummies Trade Press: Kathleen A. Welton, Vice President and Publisher; Kevin Thornton, Acquisitions Manager

IDG Books Production for Dummies Press: Michael R. Britton, Vice President of Production and Creative Services; Cindy L. Phipps, Manager of Project Coordination, Production Proofreading, and Indexing; Shelley Lea, Supervisor of Graphics and Design; Debbie J. Gates, Production Systems Specialist; Robert Springer, Supervisor of Proofreading; Debbie Stailey, Production Control Manager; Tony Augsburger, Supervisor of Reprints and Bluelines

Dummies Packaging and Book Design: Patty Page, Manager, Promotions Marketing

◆

The publisher would like to give special thanks to Patrick J. McGovern,
without whom this book would not have been possible.

◆

Contents at a Glance

Table of Contents

Introduction

*W*hoever said "ignorance is bliss" obviously never had to use a computer. Although it's true that you're better off not knowing some things — for example, exactly *what* you just stepped in — not knowing how to use a computer program can make you decidedly unblissful, especially if someone expects you to actually do some work using that program. Even if you're lucky enough to figure out how to accomplish a certain task without any instruction — which is doubtful, given that most programs are about as self-explanatory as macroeconomics — you most certainly won't be able to do the job quickly, or well, or without a heaping dose of hair-pulling, teeth-gnashing frustration.

The problem is, working your way through the instruction manuals provided by software manufacturers takes time — more time than you've got. On top of that, software manuals are notoriously dull and obtuse. A few minutes with a typical manual not only strips you of any excitement you felt about getting a new program, but also leaves you more confused than you were before.

So how do you solve this dilemma — especially now that you bought WordPerfect Office 2000, which gives you not one, but several major programs to conquer? Wait a minute . . . I think I hear . . . yes, that's definitely the sound of hoofbeats and bugles in the distance. The cavalry, in the form of *WordPerfect Office 2000 For Dummies,* has arrived to rescue you from imminent disaster. (Well, actually, you've been holding the cavalry in your hands all this time, but I didn't want to mention it earlier and spoil the dramatic build-up. Also, I was afraid you were allergic to horses.)

Okay, So What Will This Book Do for Me?

In short, this book will get you up and running with the major programs in WordPerfect Office 2000 in the fastest and most enjoyable way possible. You don't have to wade through pages of technobabble to find out how to do something. You don't have to waste your time reading about features you'll never use in a million years. Instead, you get quick, easy-to-understand how-to's for tackling those tasks you need to do every day, whether you're using your computer at work, at home, or both.

Thanks to the philosophy of the ...*For Dummies* series, you'll also have a pretty good time getting acquainted with your new software. As you probably already guessed, this series is based on the notion that you can give people the information they need and have a little fun in the process. If it's against your principles to laugh while you work, you can feel free to ignore the cartoons and other lighthearted touches throughout this book, though.

What Programs Does This Book Cover?

Like WordPerfect Suite 8, WordPerfect Office 2000 is actually a bundle of programs, known as a *suite* in computer parlance. The suite comes in several flavors: Standard Edition, Voice-Powered Edition, and Professional Edition. The Standard Edition includes WordPerfect 9, Quattro Pro 9, Presentations 9, and CorelCentral 9, while the Voice-Powered Edition offers those core programs as well as Dragon NaturallySpeaking and Corel Print Office. The Professional Edition includes everything in the Voice-Powered Edition plus a database program called Paradox and some additional tools for using the suite in a large office network.

This book covers the Standard Edition and Voice-Powered Edition. Of course, you can also use this book if you bought the Professional Edition, although you don't find coverage of Paradox or the network tools here.

How Is Stuff Organized?

...*For Dummies* books are organized differently from other books in that they're not meant to be read cover to cover, starting with Chapter 1 and continuing in sequence through the last chapter. You can read the book in that fashion, of course, and it will make perfect sense to you. But the book is also designed to work like a reference book. When you encounter a situation that stumps you (or simply interests you), look it up in the Table of Contents or Index and flip to the section that contains information on that subject. You don't have to read the entire chapter to understand what's going on; you can find out what you need to know to tackle the problem at hand quickly and without any messy cleanup.

WordPerfect Office 2000 For Dummies is organized into several parts, with each part focusing on a different aspect of using the suite. The following paragraphs give you a little preview of what's to come.

Part I: The Suite Life

Here's where you shake hands with your new programs and find out what each intends to do to justify its existence in your computer. You also discover how to do some basic things like move around inside programs, use your mouse and keyboard to make the programs actually do something, and get on-screen assistance from the Help system. (Mind you, with this book at your side, you may never need to look up information in the Help system. But the WordPerfect Office 2000 Help system has some tools that actually complete certain computing chores for you — which makes it worth checking out.)

Part II: Good-Bye, Typewriter . . . Hello, WordPerfect!

This part explains everything you need to know to create letters, memos, reports, and other documents using WordPerfect 9. You find out how to enter and edit text, change the type size and style, add graphics to your documents, check your spelling, and do all sorts of other things to produce professional-looking pages. Reading this section causes you to lose all respect for your typewriter.

Part III: Crunching Numbers like a (Quattro) Pro

Part III gives you the lowdown on using Quattro Pro 9 to create budgets, track sales and inventories, and do other number-crunching tasks. You also find out how to create and edit simple tables of information, such as a list of your favorite sports teams, their win/loss records, and the amount you lost betting that they could beat the other guys. And, to help you put your numbers in perspective, you discover how to turn data into colorful charts.

Part IV: Those Other Programs

I probably should have rethought the title for this part, because it sounds as though the programs covered in this section aren't worth much attention — which is anything but the case. Part IV explains how to use Presentations 9, a powerful tool for creating multimedia slide shows; CorelCentral 9, a personal information manager and scheduling tool; Dragon NaturallySpeaking, which enables you to dictate, rather than type, letters and other documents; and Corel Print Office, an entry-level graphics program. (Remember, you get these last two programs only if you buy the Voice-Powered Edition of WordPerfect Office 2000.)

Part IV also explains how to use all the programs in the suite together to get things done more efficiently. You find out how to create text or graphics in one program and then make copies that you can use in other documents, for example. You even discover how to create copies that automatically get updated when the original data changes.

Come to think of it, a better name for this part may be "Don't Miss This Part — Important Stuff Here!"

Part V: The Part of Tens

In this part, you find three top-ten lists of tricks, tips, and techniques. One list describes ten cool features that are fun to try when you have some time to kill. Another lists ten shortcuts that you can use in most of the suite programs to save yourself a little time and energy. And the third offers still more ways to get more done in less time, which is what owning a computer is all about, after all.

In addition, this part includes an appendix that walks you through the steps of installing WordPerfect Office 2000. I'll be the first to admit that the appendix is neither exciting nor entertaining. But seeing as how you can't use any programs in the suite until you install them — except as tax write-offs, maybe — you really ought to read the appendix anyway.

That Symbol Means Something, Doesn't It?

Scattered throughout the margins in this book are little symbols — known as *icons* in the computer universe. The icons flag information that's especially important, interesting, or just plain useful.

A Tip icon alerts you to a secret, easy way of doing something. Well, maybe not secret, exactly, but something that you may not discover on your own.

The Remember icon marks information that you need to tuck away in a corner of your brain for future reference. Trust me, this stuff will come in handy one day.

When you see this icon, you're about to read information that may save you a big headache. Warning icons point out things you need to do to make sure that your day doesn't go horribly awry.

 If you're upgrading to WordPerfect Office 2000 from WordPerfect Suite 8, look for this icon, which indicates information about things that are new or work differently in this version.

This icon highlights technical or background information that you may or may not want to read. If you do take the plunge, you'll be better equipped to hold your own in discussions with computer geeks.

Other Conventions Used in This Book

As you can see if you flip through the pages in this book, many words have a particular letter that's underlined. As I explain in Chapter 2, the underlined letters represent keyboard shortcuts for commands. You can press the Alt key in combination with the underlined letter to choose a command quickly.

When you see two words joined by a little arrow, you're looking at commands that you're to choose in sequence. For example, if I tell you to choose File➪Print, you click the File menu and then click the Print command in the menu. Or, now that you're hip to keyboard shortcuts, you can also press Alt plus F and then press P.

The small button icons — like the one attached to this paragraph — tell you of yet another way to choose a command. These icons represent buttons and tools available on the program's toolbar, Property Bar, or some other on-screen location. You click the button to access the command. To send a document to the printer, for example, you click the Print button shown in the margin here.

By the way, Chapter 2 covers all this stuff (plus other tips for choosing commands quickly) in more detail.

What Now?

That's entirely up to you. Turn the page and begin reading Chapter 1, or pick out a topic in the Index or Table of Contents that strikes your fancy and start there instead. But either way, do commit yourself to reading *something*, even if it's just a few paragraphs a day. I promise that you can acquire the skills you need to be successful with WordPerfect Office 2000 in no time — and it won't even hurt.

Remember, ignorance may be bliss in some areas of life, but when it comes to computers, knowledge is power.

Part I
The Suite Life

The 5th Wave By Rich Tennant

"...AND, AS WE ALL KNOW, SAVE FOR ONE PERSON, SERIOUS DEPARTMENTAL INTEGRATION FOR SUITE SOFTWARE DEVELOPMENT IS PRACTICALLY COMPLETE."

In this part . . .

1 f computing were an athletic event — as it sometimes is — installing WordPerfect Office 2000 would be like stuffing Michael Jordan, Monica Seles, Tiger Woods, and stars from several other sports into your computer. Like these athletic greats, each of the programs in the Office 2000 suite excels in a particular area.

The superstars in WordPerfect Office 2000, though, all play by the same basic set of rules so that you can easily figure out how things work. The programs also know how to play together nicely, so you can get more done in less time. On top of that, they won't hold you up for millions of dollars every time their contracts expire.

This part of the book introduces you to your new team members and explains which player you use in which situations. It also covers the features that work the same way throughout the suite and explains how to get a program to cough up inside information when you run into trouble.

In sporting terms, this part is like spring training camp for your mind: Time spent here helps you avoid brain cramps down the road.

Chapter 1

Browsing through the Big Box

*W*hen I got my first apartment after leaving college, I went to the hardware store and bought one screwdriver, one hammer, and one wrench. Not having had much exposure to tools when I was growing up, I thought that I could handle whatever household projects arose with those three tools.

For years, I struggled to make those three tools work in any situation, which, of course, resulted in lots of frustration. And then one day, confronted by a bolt I couldn't budge with any combination of screwdriver, hammer, and wrench, I splurged and bought a ratchet set. What a revelation! Suddenly, I had the power to overcome any bolt. I was so excited that I went around the house loosening and tightening everything I could find, thrilling to the little click-click-click sound of my new ratchet.

Lest you think that you've wandered into *Hardware For Dummies* by mistake, let me interrupt this little trip down handyman lane and explain its relevance to the topic at hand: using WordPerfect Office 2000. You see, WordPerfect Office 2000 is like a well-equipped toolbox. It contains powerful tools to handle just about every computing chore. But as it is with hammers, wrenches, screwdrivers, and ratchets, the key to success is using the right tool for the job.

This chapter explains which of the many programs in WordPerfect Office 2000 you should use to accomplish various tasks. It also explains how the programs are all designed to work similarly — and work together — so that you can use several tools in tandem to complete one project.

What Do All These Programs Do?

Packing an enormous bang for the buck, WordPerfect Office 2000 includes programs to handle just about every computing chore you can dream up. Carrying the toolbox analogy further — and some may say a step too far — it's as though someone gave you a Sears credit card, headed you toward the Craftsman tools aisle, and told you to go nuts. (Pardon the pun — *nuts,* get it?)

As with previous upgrades of this suite, this incarnation includes new editions of the core programs — WordPerfect, Quattro Pro, Presentations, and CorelCentral. You also get a new bundle of accessory programs. If you purchased the Standard Edition, you're now the proud owner of the following tools:

✔ WordPerfect 9 is the latest version of a very popular and powerful word processor. In WordPerfect, you can create any kind of text document, from a simple letter to an annual report. You can add graphics to your documents, use fancy fonts, put text into columns, and do a whole lot of other stuff that your typewriter only dreams about. Figure 1-1 shows an example of the type of document you can create in WordPerfect. Chapters 4 through 9 explain WordPerfect's many features and commands.

Figure 1-1: In WordPerfect, you can create sophisticated, professional-looking documents such as this one.

✔ Quattro Pro 9, the subject of Chapters 10 through 15, is a leading spreadsheet program. With a spreadsheet program, you can handle accounting tasks from creating a budget to tracking product inventories. Quattro Pro can also crunch any numbers you throw at it, whether you want to calculate your company's annual net profits, perform cost and price analyses, or figure out whether you can save money by refinancing a loan.

Figure 1-2 shows a spreadsheet that I created to calculate the potential profits for stocks bought and sold at various prices. When I see a stock that I'm interested in buying, I plug in the stock price and the estimated sell price, and Quattro Pro calculates the payoff.

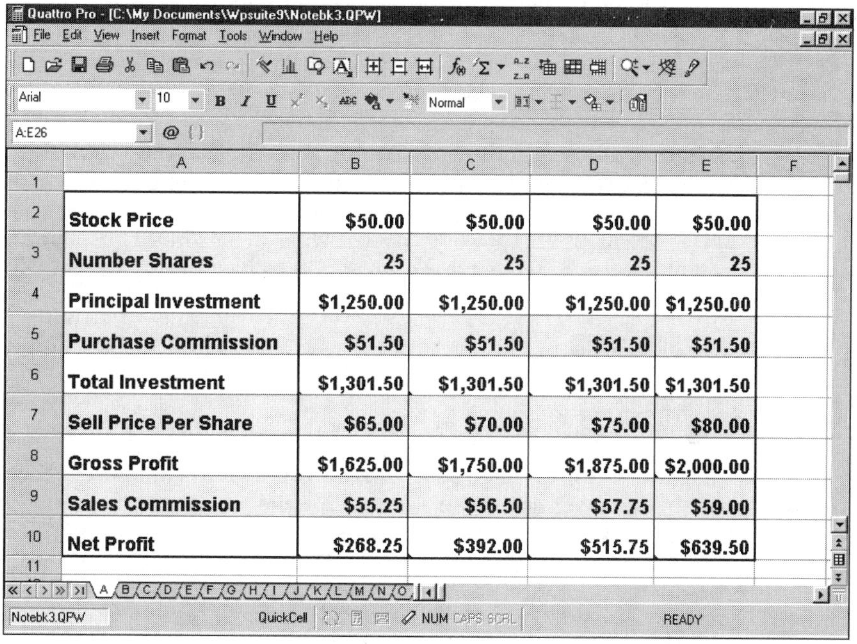

Quattro Pro - [C:\My Documents\Wpsuite9\Notebk3.QPW]
File Edit View Insert Format Tools Window Help

Arial   10   B I U   ABC   Normal

A:E26   @ {}

	A	B	C	D	E	F
1						
2	**Stock Price**	$50.00	$50.00	$50.00	$50.00	
3	**Number Shares**	25	25	25	25	
4	**Principal Investment**	$1,250.00	$1,250.00	$1,250.00	$1,250.00	
5	**Purchase Commission**	$51.50	$51.50	$51.50	$51.50	
6	**Total Investment**	$1,301.50	$1,301.50	$1,301.50	$1,301.50	
7	**Sell Price Per Share**	$65.00	$70.00	$75.00	$80.00	
8	**Gross Profit**	$1,625.00	$1,750.00	$1,875.00	$2,000.00	
9	**Sales Commission**	$55.25	$56.50	$57.75	$59.00	
10	**Net Profit**	$268.25	$392.00	$515.75	$639.50	
11						

A B C D E F G H I J K L M N O

Notebk3.QPW   QuickCell   NUM CAPS SCRL   READY

Figure 1-2:
When you have a complex math problem to solve, don't count on your fingers — use Quattro Pro instead.

✔ Presentations 9 enables you to create multimedia presentations complete with graphics, sound clips, and animation. Presentations also offers a nice selection of tools that you can use to draw and edit graphics and create organizational charts. Chapters 16 and 17 are devoted to Presentations.

✔ CorelCentral 9, covered in Chapter 18, is a personal information manager — that is, it provides tools for tracking your schedule, storing information about business and personal contacts, and generally organizing all the bits and pieces of your overly complicated life. Of the core programs, CorelCentral is the one most radically different from its previous self. The program is no longer integrated with Netscape Navigator, for example, and the user interface has changed dramatically.

If you purchased the Voice-Powered Edition, you also get two additional major programs:

- Dragon NaturallySpeaking is a voice-recognition program. Using this cutting-edge tool, you can dictate letters, memos, and other documents to your computer. As you speak, your words appear on-screen — no more pounding your fingers against the keyboard. Chapter 19 tells all, so to speak.

- Corel Print Office (see Chapter 20) is a publishing package geared especially to home and small-business users. You can use the program's artistic tools to create flyers, brochures, greeting cards, and more. In addition to providing templates that make designing such pieces a snap, Print Office includes Corel Photo House, which provides basic image-editing tools for cleaning up scanned photographs and pictures taken with digital cameras.

Whether you bought the Standard or Voice-Powered Edition of the suite, you also get tons of clip art, a nice selection of fonts, a number of small utilities, and Trellix, a program for publishing long documents on the Internet or a corporate intranet. I don't cover these extras in this book because I think the available page space is better dedicated to programs you're likely to use on a more frequent basis.

Which Program Do I Use When?

Each WordPerfect Office 2000 program specializes in handling certain tasks. But several programs enable you to handle jobs that are unrelated to the program's main function, too. Quattro Pro, for example, is primarily designed for creating spreadsheets, but it also has commands that let you use your spreadsheet data to create a slide show. It's like having a hammer that has a Swiss Army knife attached to the handle. (Okay, okay, I'll give up on the hardware analogy now. But it was really fun while it lasted, wasn't it?)

Just because you *can* do a task in a certain program, however, doesn't mean that you *should*. Yes, you may be able to create a slide show in Quattro Pro, but you get better results if you use the tool specifically designed for creating slide shows — that is, Presentations.

The following list offers some suggestions to help you decide which program is most appropriate for the challenge at hand. Keep in mind that you don't have to use just one program to create a document, though. As explained in the next section (as well as in Chapter 21), the programs in the suite are designed so that you can use them all together to handle a single project.

✔ WordPerfect is the best choice for creating text-based documents, from letters to memos to reports.

✔ If you purchased the Standard Edition, you can also use WordPerfect to create documents that contain clip art, such as advertising flyers or simple brochures. If you purchased the Voice-Powered Edition, turn to Print Office to create such graphics-intensive projects.

✔ Use Quattro Pro for accounting projects such as creating budgets, recording sales, tracking inventories, and doing anything else that involves calculating data.

✔ Also use Quattro Pro for creating tables of data, such as an employee list showing each worker's name, phone number, address, department, and so on. You can create tables in WordPerfect, too, but Quattro Pro makes the job easier.

✔ To create a data chart — for example, a chart that shows your company's annual sales by region — use Quattro Pro. To create organizational charts, use Presentations.

✔ To create slide shows — whether for display on a computer or a regular projector — use Presentations.

✔ Want to edit a scanned photograph or image from a Photo CD? Head for Photo House, if you purchased the Voice-Powered Edition of WordPerfect Office 2000. You can crop away unwanted portions of the image, touch up the image, and adjust things like color balance and contrast. Presentations also offers some image-editing tools for those who own the Standard Edition of the suite.

✔ If you want to create some simple graphics to enliven your documents or slide shows, use Presentations or Print Office. WordPerfect also provides some basic graphics tools, but they're not as easily accessible or flexible as those in Presentations and Print Office.

✔ To create text-based graphics — for example, a company logo that presents the company name in a stylized design — use TextArt, which you can access in Presentations or WordPerfect. See Chapter 22 for a look at TextArt in action; see Chapter 16 for information on some other text effects you can create in Presentations.

✔ Are you a hunt-and-peck typist who requires hours to type even a short document? If you own the Voice-Powered Edition of the suite, you can dictate, rather than type, your document. Turn to Chapter 19 for assistance with getting your computer to listen to what you say.

Hey! These All Look Alike!

If you have a sharp eye, you'll notice right away that most programs in WordPerfect Office 2000 have a similar look. Many of the buttons, tools, and menu commands are the same from program to program. Which means that after you know what a particular button or command does in one program, you can apply that knowledge in all the other programs. You don't have to memorize a different set of buttons and commands for each individual program.

The beauty of the suite is more than skin-deep, however. As discussed in Chapter 21, the programs are designed to interact with each other so that you can use several different programs to handle one computing project. For example, if you need to create a report that includes text, graphics, and a spreadsheet, you can create the text in WordPerfect, the graphics in Presentations or Print Office, and the spreadsheet in Quattro Pro, and then combine the different elements together into one finished product.

The cooperative nature of your WordPerfect Office 2000 programs gives you an important computing advantage. Not only can you get up and running with all the programs quickly, but you also can use their combined strengths to get your work done in less time and with less effort. In fact, I could say that WordPerfect Office 2000 is a little like one of those new, many-tools-in-one power tools that are all the rage in hardware stores these days. But I swore off hardware analogies earlier in this chapter, so I won't.

Chapter 2

Basic Stuff You Need to Know

· ·

In This Chapter

▶ Powering up your programs

▶ Getting acquainted with windows

▶ Using the mouse and keyboard to make things happen

▶ Figuring out which buttons do what

▶ Choosing commands from menus and dialog boxes

▶ Customizing your screen

· ·

*L*ife sure was simpler before computers, wasn't it? You didn't need to endure mind-numbing conversations about such things as operating systems and Internet Service Providers. You didn't need to spend oodles of cash on the latest computer gadget to keep up with the Joneses. And you didn't need to waste precious brain cells mastering the meaning of such cryptic phrases as "logging on to the network server" or "downloading a printer driver."

Well, like the situation or not, computers are here to stay. So you may as well pick up a few tricks to help you communicate with that big, glowing box on your desk — not to mention with the kids in your life. This chapter covers the basics of using Corel WordPerfect Office 2000, from starting up a program to customizing your screen display.

If acquiring this information seems like a daunting (and boring) chore, take heart. First, I promise to keep it simple — telling you just what you need to know and nothing more. Second, mastering these basics not only puts you on friendlier terms with your computer but also enables you to join the legions of folks who've discovered how to use the computer as an excuse for goofing off. Pretty soon, you, too, can sound believable as you stare earnestly at your boss and say, "Sorry, I can't complete that project for you today because the network server is down and I can't download the right printer driver."

Almost everything I cover in this chapter applies to most Windows programs, not only to programs in WordPerfect Office 2000.

Starting Up and Shutting Down

Firing up a program is a cinch. Here's the routine:

1. **Click the Start button on the Windows taskbar to display the Start menu.**

2. **Click Programs in the Start menu.**

3. **Click WordPerfect Office 2000 in the Programs menu.**

4. **Click the name of the program you want to start.**

You can also start some programs by using the DAD icons, as explained in "Using DAD," later in this chapter.

Shutting down a program is just as easy. Simply click the Close button — that little square button marked with an *X* in the upper-right corner of the program window. If you haven't saved your work, the program prompts you to do so.

You can also shut down a program by choosing File⇨Exit from the menu bar or by pressing the Alt key together with the F4 key (Alt+F4). But these methods require two clicks or key presses rather than one. Who needs all that extra work?

Mastering the Mouse

If the mouse is a new entity in your world, here are some terms you need to know. (Keep in mind that this information applies to a traditional mouse. If you're using a trackball, touchpad, or some other tool for sending signals to your computer, check its manual for instructions.)

- ✔ The *mouse cursor* is that little thing that moves around the screen when you move your mouse. Cursors take on different shapes and sizes depending on what program you're using and what you're trying to do.

- ✔ To *click* means to press and release a mouse button. If I tell you to *click* something, move your mouse so that the cursor is pointing to that something and then click the mouse button. To *double-click* is to press and release the mouse button twice very quickly.

- ✔ Usually, the left mouse button is the *primary button* — the one you use to accomplish most tasks. With some brands of mice, however, you can switch the buttons around so that the right button is the primary button. In this book, whenever I say to click or double-click, I mean that you're to push the primary mouse button. If you need to click the secondary mouse button, I tell you to *right-click*. If you switch your mouse buttons, remember that, if I tell you to right-click, you actually left-click — and vice versa.

Right-clicking your way to fame and fortune

Although the left mouse button is the primary clicker, the right mouse button can be extremely useful, too. Right-clicking something on-screen usually displays a menu of commands or options related to that item. Some programs call these menus context-sensitive menus; Corel calls them QuickMenus. To discover what Quick-Menus are available to you, just right-click your way around the screen.

✔ To *drag* is to move the mouse while you hold down the primary mouse button. Dragging is a handy way to move words and objects around. After you have the item where you want it, you release the mouse button to complete the drag. Releasing the mouse button is called *dropping*. The entire operation is known as *drag and drop*.

Saving Time with Keyboard Shortcuts

Sometimes, using the mouse can be cumbersome. Luckily, you have another option. You can perform most common computing tasks without ever taking your hands off the keyboard, as described in the following list:

✔ To open one of the menus at the top of a program window, press Alt plus the menu's *hot key* — the letter that's underlined in the menu name. Then to choose a command from the menu, press the command's hot key — no Alt this time. You can also use Alt+hot key combos to select options in dialog boxes. (I explain dialog boxes in the section "Digging through Dialog Boxes," later in this chapter.)

✔ *Keyboard shortcuts* enable you to choose a command by pressing one or two keys in combination. To open a document in WordPerfect, for example, you press Ctrl+O — in other words, press the Ctrl key along with the O key.

Many programs automatically display the available shortcuts next to the command names in menus. But in WordPerfect Office 2000 programs, you may need to tell your computer to display the shortcuts. For how-to's, see the section "Customizing Your View," later in this chapter.

In most programs, you can determine the shortcut for a command by pausing your cursor over the command name. If you have the QuickTips option turned on (also explained in the section "Customizing Your View"), a little box pops up to provide information about the command and show the keyboard shortcut, if one exists.

Doing Windows

Figure 2-1 shows the window you see after you first start WordPerfect. (Your screen may look slightly different than mine, depending on the default settings on your system, but the essentials are the same.) This window works much like every other window you encounter in the WordPerfect Office 2000 suite — or in any Windows program, for that matter. Here's a rundown of the basic parts:

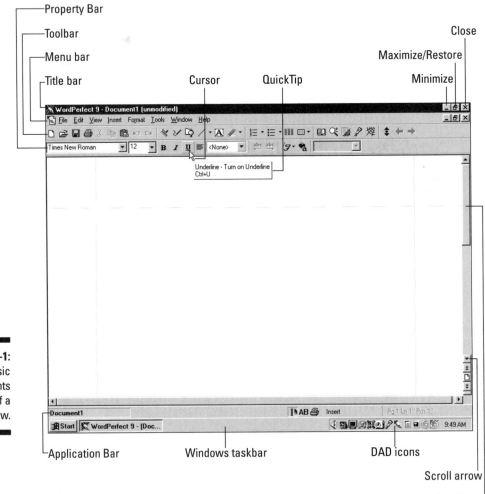

Figure 2-1:
The basic components of a window.

✔ The *title bar* tells you which program you're using. (The title bar is a great reference for the absent-minded.) If you have more than one program open, the title bar of the active program is highlighted, while title bars on inactive programs appear dimmed.

✔ The *menu bar* is simply a row of menus, each of which contains a list of commands. To display a menu, click its name in the menu bar or press Alt plus the hot key (the underlined letter in the menu name).

Whenever you see two commands joined by an arrow in this book, choose the commands in sequence. Format➪Line➪Spacing, for example, means to click the Format menu, choose the Line command in that menu, and then choose the Spacing command in the Line submenu. The underlined letters indicate hot keys for the command.

If a command is *dimmed*, or *grayed out*, it's not available, either because it's not pertinent to the task you're trying to accomplish or because your system doesn't support the command.

✔ The *toolbar* is a strip of buttons that you can click to choose certain commands quickly and efficiently.

✔ The *Property Bar* is a special entity to some WordPerfect Office 2000 programs. Like the toolbar, the Property Bar contains buttons that provide quick access to popular commands. But the Property Bar is *context sensitive* — a nerdy way for saying that the assortment of buttons displayed on the bar depends on what you're doing at the moment. If you're working with text, for example, the Property Bar contains buttons for formatting text.

Property Bar and toolbar buttons that include both an icon and a down-pointing arrowhead have two functions. If you click the arrowhead, you display a drop-down list of options. Click an option to select it. In most cases, the icon for that option then appears on the button face to the left of the arrowhead. If you want to select the same option again, you can simply click the icon — you don't have to select the option from the drop-down list.

✔ Near the bottom of the window, you see the *Application Bar*. If you're familiar with other Windows programs, you may notice that the Application Bar bears a strong resemblance to the feature usually known as a *status bar*. But the Application Bar offers a convenient twist: It displays a button for each open document in the program. You can switch back and forth among open documents by clicking the buttons. (You can also switch to a different document by choosing its name from the Window menu or clicking anywhere in the document's window.)

The Application Bar also contains icons and information about the active document. Sometimes, clicking, double-clicking, or right-clicking an item in the Application Bar enables you to perform actions or commands.

- ✔ Lurking beneath the Application Bar is the Windows *taskbar.* Click the program buttons on the taskbar to switch from one running program to another. (You can also switch to a different program by clicking the program window.) On the right end of the taskbar is the *Desktop Application Director* (DAD), explained in the section "Using DAD," later in this chapter.

- ✔ Click the up- and down-pointing *scroll arrows* in the *scroll bar* on the right side of the window to move the screen display up or down so that you can see a different part of your document. Click the scroll arrows at the bottom of the window to move left or right. Drag the *scroll box* to scroll in bigger increments.

WordPerfect and Quattro Pro offer additional new tools for scrolling through your documents. You can find out more about these handy scrolling options in Chapter 4 (WordPerfect) and Chapter 10 (Quattro Pro).

- ✔ In the upper-right corner of the window are the Minimize button, the Maximize/Restore button, and the Close button. If you have a document open, you get two sets of buttons. The top set controls the program window; the bottom set affects the document window. These controls are covered in the following section, "Resizing, Moving, and Closing Windows."

- ✔ Remembering what all the different elements on your screen do or mean isn't always easy. Luckily, you can find out with a quick move of your mouse. Just place the mouse cursor over a button or item, and a little flag — called a *QuickTip* — unfurls to give you helpful information. If you don't see the QuickTips, follow the information given in "Customizing Your View," later in this chapter, to turn them on.

Resizing, Moving, and Closing Windows

You can shrink, enlarge, reshape, and rearrange your windows until you get them just the way you like them. The keys to this heady power are the Minimize, Maximize/Restore, and Close buttons, labeled earlier in Figure 2-1. Here's how they work, moving from right to left:

- ✔ Click the Close button to close the window and the document or program that the window contains.

- ✔ The appearance and purpose of the Maximize/Restore button alternates depending on the current status of the window. If the button face shows a single box, it's the Maximize button. Clicking this button enlarges the window so that it eats up your entire screen. If the button shows two stacked boxes, it's the Restore button. Clicking this button restores the window to its former size.

✔ Click the Minimize button to hide the window temporarily. After you minimize a program window, a program button appears on the Windows taskbar; click this button to make the window reappear. After you minimize a document window, it shrinks to a tiny bar at the bottom of the program window. This bar offers both a Maximize and a Restore button; click either one to redisplay the window.

You can also resize a window by placing the cursor over an edge of a window. After the cursor becomes a two-headed arrow, drag the window border to enlarge or shrink the window. To move a window, drag its title bar.

Customizing Your View

Resizing and reshaping your windows isn't the only way to customize your view of the computer world. You can also change the way that certain other screen elements appear. Chapters 4, 10, and 16 provide details on changing the screen appearance when you're working with WordPerfect, Quattro Pro, and Presentations, respectively. In addition to the tips provided in those chapters, play around with these general customization tricks:

✔ Many programs offer more than one toolbar; you can choose which ones appear on-screen. Normally, the command regulating the toolbars lies on the View menu. (The exact command and the extent of your options vary from program to program.)

✔ You can alter your toolbars and Property Bar so that they contain buttons for the commands you use most. You can find more information in Chapter 24.

✔ If you don't like the position of the toolbar or Property Bar, place your cursor on an empty spot in the bar until the cursor changes to a four-headed arrow. Then drag the toolbar to a new home. In some cases, the bar turns into a free-floating window, complete with a title bar and Close button. To resize the window, drag a corner of the window.

✔ Most programs offer Zoom buttons on the Property Bar or toolbar. (The button usually looks like a little magnifying glass.) Use these buttons to magnify or reduce the size of your document on-screen. Zoom options sometimes are also found under the View menu, depending on the program you're using.

✔ WordPerfect, Quattro Pro, and Presentations enable you to hide and display shortcut keys on menus and turn QuickTips on and off. In WordPerfect, choose Tools➪Settings and then click the Environment icon. The Environment Settings dialog box appears, as shown in Figure 2-2. Click the Interface tab to access the Shortcut Keys and QuickTips options.

A check mark in the option box means that the option is turned on. In Presentations and Quattro Pro, choose Settings from the Tools menu and click the Display icon or tab in the resulting dialog box to access these options.

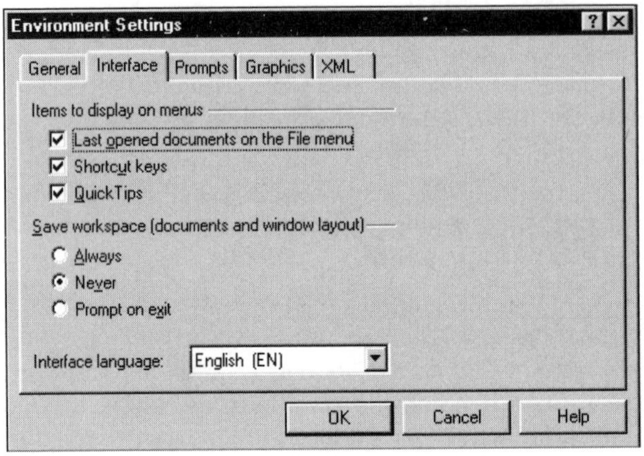

Figure 2-2:
You can control whether keyboard shortcuts and QuickTips appear on-screen.

Environment Settings

General | Interface | Prompts | Graphics | XML

Items to display on menus
☑ Last opened documents on the File menu
☑ Shortcut keys
☑ QuickTips

Save workspace (documents and window layout)
○ Always
● Never
○ Prompt on exit

Interface language: English (EN)

OK | Cancel | Help

Using DAD

The *Desktop Application Director — DAD* for short — places icons for certain programs along your Windows taskbar. You can click an icon to launch the program. If you don't see the DAD icons on-screen, click the Windows Start button and then choose Programs➪WordPerfect Office 2000➪Utilities➪ Desktop Application Director 9.

 To remove an icon from the taskbar, click the DAD Properties icon on the taskbar to open the DAD Properties dialog box. Click the name of the icon you want to remove, click the Delete button, and then click OK.

 To add an icon, click the Add button and choose the program execution file (the one that starts the program) from the Open dialog box. (The filename has the letters EXE tagged onto the end.) Click OK to close the dialog box. You can even add programs that are not in the WordPerfect Office 2000 suite.

To turn off DAD altogether, right-click the DAD Properties icon on the taskbar and then choose Exit DAD from the QuickMenu.

Digging through Dialog Boxes

After you choose some commands, you get a dialog box similar to the one shown in Figure 2-3. By making selections in the dialog box, you tell the program how you want it to carry out a particular command.

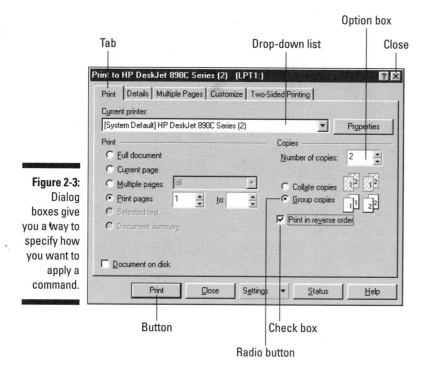

Figure 2-3:
Dialog
boxes give
you a way to
specify how
you want to
apply a
command.

The components of a dialog box work as follows:

✓ To change a value in an option box, double-click the box or press the option's hot key (the underlined letter in the option name). Then enter a new value from the keyboard. In some cases, you can change the value by clicking the little arrows next to the option box.

✓ To display the contents of a drop-down list, click the little downward-pointing arrowhead. Then click the option you want to use.

✓ You can resize some dialog boxes so that you can display more of their contents. Just drag any corner of the box.

✓ To turn a radio button on or off, click the button. The option is on if a black dot appears in the middle of the button. You can turn on only one radio button in a group at a time.

✔ To turn a check box on or off, click the check box. An X or a check mark in the box (depending on the program) means that the option is turned on. You can turn on as many check boxes as you want.

✔ Clicking the rectangular buttons — sometimes called Command buttons — initiates a command or displays a menu or second dialog box of related options.

✔ Some dialog boxes, such as the one shown in Figure 2-3, contain several layers of options. To get to a different layer, click its tab.

✔ You can move from option to option by pressing the Tab key. To move to the previous option, press Shift+Tab.

✔ To close a dialog box and return to your document without making any changes, click the Close or Cancel button.

✔ Some dialog boxes contain a question mark button. Click this button and then click an option in the dialog box to get more information about how the option works.

Chapter 3

Can I Get Some Help, Please?

*A*re you the sort who hates to ask for help from anyone? Do you prefer driving around hopelessly in circles to stopping at a gas station for directions, for example? Is your VCR still blinking "12:00" because you refuse to let your 10-year-old show you how to set the clock?

If so, you probably want to skip this chapter. On the other hand, if you believe that there's nothing shameful about asking for help — and that doing so can save you time and headaches — you're going to find the information on the next few pages invaluable.

This chapter explains the various tools offered by the WordPerfect Office 2000 Help system. You discover where to click to get information about a particular topic, how to display step-by-step on-screen instructions for completing a task, and how to use templates that automatically create common documents with hardly a keystroke or deep thought required on your part.

Not all programs in the suite offer all the advanced Help features covered in this chapter. And some use slightly different command names or hot keys than the ones mentioned here. But the basic aspects of the Help systems work the same way, and even the most simple Help system should provide some guidance if you get stuck.

Getting Help from an Expert

A special help feature available in the major suite programs, PerfectExpert is sort of like having a software service representative built into your computer (only better, because you don't need to wade through a snarl of voice mail commands or cool your heels on hold for 30 minutes before you get your question answered).

PerfectExpert comprises three main components: One sticks close to your side and walks you through the steps in creating a document; one enables you to ask for specific information in plain English; and one provides templates that automate the process of creating common documents. The following sections describe each of these tools.

Keeping an expert by your side

If you choose Help⇨PerfectExpert or click the PerfectExpert toolbar button in WordPerfect, Quattro Pro, or Presentations, the PerfectExpert window appears on-screen, as shown in Figure 3-1. (Don't click the PerfectExpert button on the DAD bar. While the button on the DAD bar looks just like the one on the toolbar, it has another purpose entirely. See Chapter 2 for more information on the DAD bar.)

By default, the PerfectExpert window locks itself into position on one side of the document window. Drag the border between the PerfectExpert window and the document window to resize the two windows.

You can separate the PerfectExpert window from the document window if you want to make it even smaller or move it to a different location. Move your cursor toward the edge of the PerfectExpert window until the cursor turns into a four-headed arrow. Then drag the window to a location you like better. Resize the window by right-clicking the title bar, choosing Size from the QuickMenu, and then dragging one of its corners. To move the window, drag its title bar. Drag the window back to the left edge of the screen to re-anchor it in its default position.

The PerfectExpert helps you work your way through basic tasks. After you first turn on the PerfectExpert, you see the Home page — ground zero for building a document or performing some other task. You take advantage of the various PerfectExpert features as follows:

 ✔ Click a topic button (refer to Figure 3-1) to get help with the task referenced by the button name. For example, in the screen shown in Figure 3-1, you click the Typing button for help with typing documents in WordPerfect.

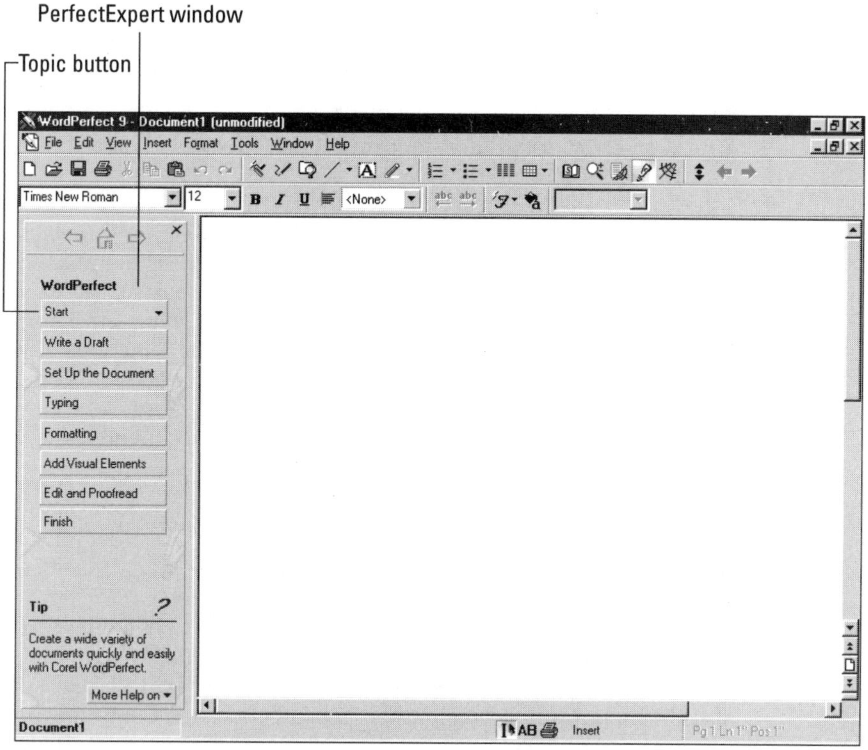

PerfectExpert window

Topic button

Figure 3-1:
The Perfect
Expert
window
gives you
step-by-step
assistance
in creating
documents.

✔ After you click a topic button, you may be presented with another set of related buttons. If you click the Typing button in the WordPerfect PerfectExpert window, for example, you see a new set of buttons: Change the Font, Change Tab Settings, and other topics related to typing. Or you may be taken to the dialog box where you accomplish the task you clicked.

✔ After you click your way into a dialog box, you can get more information about how to use the various options by clicking the Help button in the dialog box or, in some cases, by clicking the More Help On button in the PerfectExpert window. Either way, a Help window opens with information about the topic at hand. (See the section "Navigating a Help Window," later in this chapter, for more information.) Some dialog boxes also include a question mark icon in the upper-right corner; click the icon and then click an option in the dialog box to get an explanation of what that option does.

✔ Click the Home icon at the top of the PerfectExpert window to return to the Home page. (The Home icon is the one that looks like a little house, by the way.)

✔ Click the question mark icon, located near the bottom of the PerfectExpert window, to access the Ask the PerfectExpert panel of the Help window, which I describe in the next section.

✔ To close the window, click the X icon in the upper-right corner of the PerfectExpert window, click the PerfectExpert toolbar button, or choose Help⇨PerfectExpert.

The PerfectExpert window is a good idea, but I find it a little lacking in that you're left to your own devices after you get inside the dialog box related to the topic you clicked. I suppose that the feature may be helpful for folks who can't remember what menu command to choose to perform a specific task, are brand-new to computers and don't know what a menu is in the first place, or weren't clever enough to buy this book. As for you, you savvy book buyer, I suspect that you'll agree that the PerfectExpert window is a perfect waste of screen space, unless, of course, you happen to be traveling and didn't think to tuck this book in your briefcase.

Hey, I have a question!

The Ask the PerfectExpert feature enables you to ask a question of the little information fairy who lives inside the Help system. You can ask your question in plain English, which makes Ask the PerfectExpert the ideal solution for those who haven't yet completed the full course in Computer Babble 101.

This option is available in WordPerfect, Presentations, Quattro Pro, and CorelCentral. Here's how it works:

1. **Choose Help⇨Ask the PerfectExpert.**

   The Ask the PerfectExpert panel of the Help dialog box appears, as shown in Figure 3-2.

2. **Type your question in the top text box.**

3. **Click the Search button.**

   The bottom half of the dialog box displays a list of possible topics to explore, as Figure 3-2 shows. The percentage value indicates how relevant the Help system thinks the topic is to your question. But use your own judgment — the Help system is often off the mark in this regard.

4. **Click a topic and click the Display button.**

   Or just double-click the topic. Either way, you see a Help window containing the information you requested. You can find out about the intricacies of the Help window in the section "Navigating a Help Window," later in this chapter.

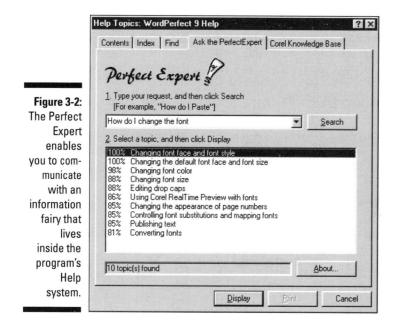

Figure 3-2:
The Perfect
Expert
enables
you to com-
municate
with an
information
fairy that
lives
inside the
program's
Help
system.

That bit about the information fairy isn't for public consumption, by the way. Most people don't believe in things such as fairies that live inside computers. These naysayers insist that computers are nothing more than cold, uncaring machines, a bundle of wires and chips, and such. I say that's nonsense — how else can you explain data that mysteriously disappears and appears without any warning? But until the world comes around to my way of think-ing, you're better off keeping this news to yourself. Look for an episode of *The X Files* focusing on this very subject soon.

Using PerfectExpert Templates

PerfectExpert templates speed up the process of creating common docu-ments, from mailing labels to household inventory worksheets.

To access the templates, take one of these steps:

✔ Click the Corel New Project icon on the DAD bar. (If you're working in WordPerfect, Presentations, or Quattro Pro, be sure to click the icon on the DAD bar and not the one on your toolbar. The toolbar button has another function.)

✔ If you're not running DAD, click the Windows Start button and then choose Programs➪WordPerfect Office 2000➪Corel New Project.

✔ Inside WordPerfect, Quattro Pro, or Presentations, choose the New from Project command from the File menu.

Regardless of which avenue you walk, the dialog box shown in Figure 3-3 appears. Choose a category of documents from the drop-down list at the top of the Create New tab and then double-click the type of document you want to create. The appropriate program for creating the document opens, along with the PerfectExpert window, which contains buttons related to the different steps in creating the document.

Figure 3-3:
Choose a
template
from the
Perfect
Expert
dialog box
to create
common
documents
quickly.

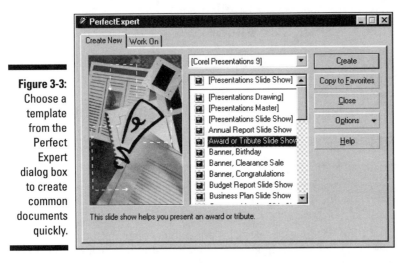

Typically, the templates format the document and create some appropriate text and/or graphics. You can edit the document as you would any other document. Click the different topic buttons in the PerfectExpert window for help in completing the document. (See the preceding section for information about using the PerfectExpert window.) You may also need to put the WordPerfect Office 2000 CD in your CD drive for some templates; the template software lets you know whether the CD is necessary by displaying an alert box.

The first time you open the PerfectExpert dialog box, your computer may gurgle and spit for a minute or two while the system configures the templates for use. And the first time you use some templates, you're asked to enter personal or business information (your name, address, and so on) that helps the PerfectExpert customize your document.

Getting More Help

Here are still more ways to dig up information about a subject that's troubling you:

✔ Choose Help⇨Help Topics or press F1 to display the Help Topics dialog box and then click the Index tab to display the panel of the Help Topics dialog box shown in Figure 3-4. Enter a topic in the top text box or use the scroll bar and arrows to locate the topic in the list below. Double-click the topic you want to explore.

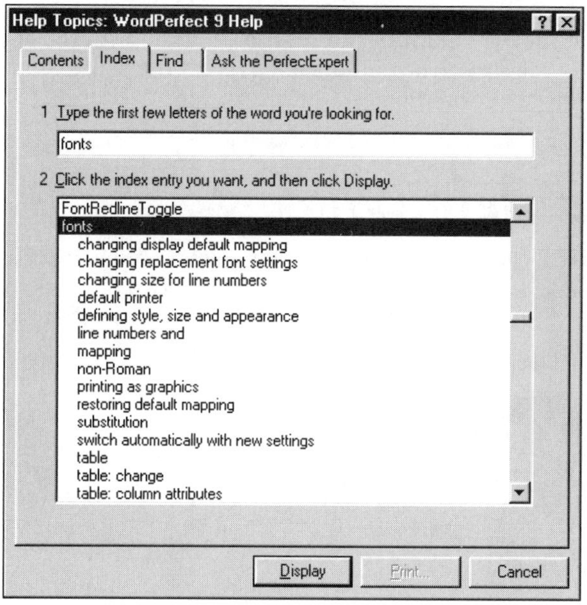

Figure 3-4: Double-click an item in the Index list to display information about that topic.

Help Topics: WordPerfect 9 Help

Contents | Index | Find | Ask the PerfectExpert |

1 Type the first few letters of the word you're looking for.

    fonts

2 Click the index entry you want, and then click Display.

    FontRedlineToggle
    fonts
        changing display default mapping
        changing replacement font settings
        changing size for line numbers
        default printer
        defining style, size and appearance
        line numbers and
        mapping
        non-Roman
        printing as graphics
        restoring default mapping
        substitution
        switch automatically with new settings
        table
        table: change
        table: column attributes

    Display | Print... | Cancel

✔ On the Contents tab of the Help Topics dialog box, Help information is organized by subject. Double-click one of the book icons to display a list of page icons for different tasks. Double-click a page icon to display the Help information for that task.

✔ Some dialog boxes have a little question mark button, usually at the top of the dialog box. For information about a dialog box option, click the question mark icon and then click the option to display a pop-up information box. Click again to get rid of the information box. If the dialog box also has a button labeled Help, clicking the button displays information about that dialog box in a Help window.

- If you have a modem and are hooked into the Internet, you can get online help by choosing Help➪Corel Web Site. Or, from the Windows Start menu, choose Programs➪WordPerfect Office 2000➪Corel.com.

  For a quick way to search for information on a specific topic, click the Corel Knowledge Base tab inside the Help Topics dialog box. From here, you can enter a keyword and search the technical support information that's stored in the Corel Knowledge Base at the Corel Web site.

  In order for these online tools to function, you must be connected to the Internet and have Microsoft Internet Explorer installed on your computer. If you prefer to use another browser, though, you can find all the online help by pointing your browser to www.Corel.com.

- Pause your mouse cursor over a button or other on-screen element to display a QuickTip box with hints about what that button or element does. For more information on QuickTips, see Chapter 2.

Navigating a Help Window

Figure 3-5 shows a typical Help window that appears after you display information about a particular command or task. Here are a few tips for making your way around the Help window and performing some other useful tricks:

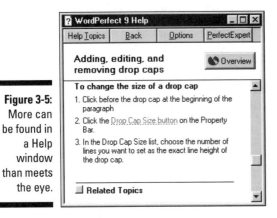

Figure 3-5:
More can
be found in
a Help
window
than meets
the eye.

- Click underlined words or phrases to jump to information about that topic. Clicking a word or phrase that's adorned with little icons or gray squares also jumps you to that topic.

- If you click a term that's underlined with a dashed line, an explanation of the term pops up.

✔ Click the Back button to return to the previous page. (In some Help windows, you instead click the left-pointing arrow button to return to the previous screen and click the right-pointing arrow button to go to the next screen.)

✔ Click the Help Topics button to display the Help Topics dialog box. The dialog box opens with the help tab you last accessed at the forefront.

✔ To print a Help screen, click the Options button and then choose Print Topic from the menu that appears. (In some Help dialog boxes, you instead choose File⇨Print Topic.)

✔ If you want to keep the Help window on-screen as you work in the program, click the Options button and choose Keep Help On Top⇨On Top from the menu that appears. (In some Help dialog boxes, you see an Options menu instead of an Options button; in that case, choose Options⇨Keep Help on Top⇨On Top.)

✔ You can resize the Help window as you would any window — just drag an edge or corner of the window.

Using the Reference Center

WordPerfect Office 2000 comes with its own digital library of reference manuals, contained in a utility called the Reference Center. The suite also includes Adobe Acrobat, the program that you need to view the Reference Center documents. (Acrobat replaces Envoy, the document viewer provided with previous editions of the suite.)

To view a Reference Center manual, first put the CD into your CD-ROM drive. The WordPerfect Office 2000 Setup window may appear automatically, depending on how you have your CD-ROM drive set up in Windows. If the Setup window appears, click Reference Center to launch the Reference Center window. (You must have Acrobat installed on your computer; see the Appendix at the back of this book if you need help installing the program.)

If you don't see the Setup window after putting the CD in your CD drive, click the Windows Start button and choose Programs⇨WordPerfect Office 2000⇨ Setup and Notes⇨Corel Reference Center to display the Reference Center window.

Inside the Reference Center window, click the icon for the manual that you want to see. After a few seconds, the manual opens in an Adobe Acrobat window, as shown in Figure 3-6.

Hand cursor

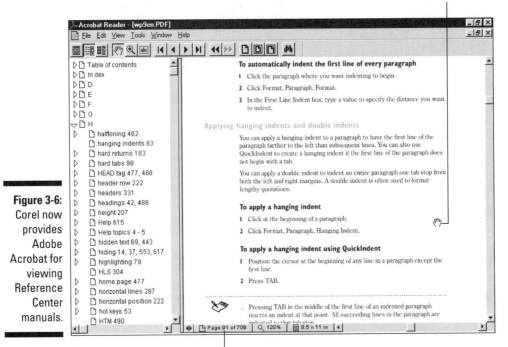

Page button

Acrobat is a commonly used document viewer, so you may already be familiar with its basic operation. But in case you're new to the game, here are the basics:

✔ Click the Next Page or Previous Page toolbar buttons to go forward or backward one page.

✔ Click the First Page or Last Page buttons to, er, go to the first or last page of the manual. You probably didn't need me to tell you that.

✔ To travel to a specific page, click the Page button in the lower-left corner of the screen (refer to Figure 3-6). Or choose View➪Go to Page. The Go to Page dialog box opens. Enter the page number you want to see and click OK.

✔ Click the Hand button to display the hand tool, labeled in Figure 3-6. Drag with the hand tool to "tug" at the on-screen page, moving the area you want to see into view. Of course, you can also drag the scroll box and click the scroll arrows on the right side of the window to shift the display, just as you do in most programs.

✔ Click the Zoom icon and then click the page to zoom in on the text. Ctrl+click to zoom out.

✔ To hunt down a specific topic, click the Find button to display the Find dialog box. Enter the topic in the Find What text box and then click Find.

✔ Some manuals include hypertext links, usually marked by an underscored word or a button or other small graphic. If you are an Internet user, you're familiar with the hypertext notion. You click the link to jump to a page that contains related text. You can tell that you're looking at a link when the cursor changes into a little hand with a pointing index finger. If you see a hand with another finger raised, you may want to speak to whomever used your computer last.

✔ For some manuals, the document viewing window is split into two panes, as in Figure 3-6. In the right pane, you see the document itself. The left pane contains a Table of Contents and Index. Click the right-pointing triangle next to any item to display subentries in that particular category. Each entry acts as a hyperlink; you just click an entry to jump to the related information in the manual.

For example, to see what the WordPerfect Reference Center manual says about hanging indents, click the triangle next to the letter H to display a list of all index entries starting with that letter. Then click the hanging indents item to jump to the pages dealing with hanging indents.

Not all manuals offer this feature. In some manuals, the index page is provided at the beginning of the manual rather than in a separate pane of the window. But regardless of where you find the index, you can usually click an index entry to travel to related information in the manual.

✔ To open another reference center manual, choose File⇨Open. The manuals are stored on the WordPerfect Office 2000 program CD, in the Corel/Shared/Refcntr folder. Manuals have the file extension PDF.

✔ PDF stands for *portable document format,* in case you were dying to know. PDF is a popular format for the creation and distribution of electronic documents.

✔ To print the manual, choose File⇨Print. In the Print dialog box that appears, you can choose to print the entire manual or just certain pages. Keep in mind that if you're printing on an older printer that has limited printer memory, you may have trouble printing manuals that include many graphic elements.

✔ To close a manual, just click the Close button in the document window, as you do for any standard document. Or choose File⇨Close.

I've given you just the basics on using Acrobat; if you want to know more, choose Help⇨Reader Online Guide. You can use the techniques just discussed to explore the online Acrobat manual and pick up other tricks to enhance your document-viewing pleasure.

Part II

Good-bye, Typewriter . . . Hello, WordPerfect!

In this part . . .

*B*ack in the old days (you know, before Bill Gates took over the world), producing reports, letters, and other text documents was no easy feat. Even if you had a really good typewriter, turning out professional-looking, error-free pages often required hours and hours of tedious labor — not to mention gallons of correction fluid.

Thanks to the advent of the word processor, you can now produce flawless pages of text and graphics in minutes. Okay, maybe not minutes, but certainly in a heck of a lot less time than it took using the old Smith-Corona. What's more, you can easily rearrange sentences and paragraphs, fancy up your pages with all sorts of fonts and pictures, and even get the computer to check your spelling.

WordPerfect is one of the more powerful word processors on the market. In fact, the program offers so many features that you'll probably never use them all. This part introduces you to the features you'll use every day to create basic documents — as well as a few fun tricks for producing not-so-basic documents.

Chapter 4

The Process of Processing Words

*I*f you were alive in the precomputing era, when the typewriter was the primary mechanism for producing text, you will have a special appreciation for WordPerfect. No longer do you have to type and retype the same page over and over until you get it just right. No longer do you need to spend hours dabbing at mistakes with correction fluid. And no longer do you need to strain your back hurling a heavy typewriter at the uncaring boss who asks you to add "three tiny paragraphs" to the beginning of a 20-page report that took you days to complete.

WordPerfect gives you the power to churn out page after page of great-looking (and correctly spelled) text in no time. This chapter gets you started on your word-processing adventure by explaining what's what on the WordPerfect screen, showing you how to create and open documents, giving you basic how-to's for entering text and moving around the screen, and describing ways to make the WordPerfect interface behave just the way you want.

Getting Started

 To start WordPerfect, you can just click the WordPerfect DAD icon on the Windows taskbar, if you have the DAD utility enabled. (You can read more about DAD in Chapter 2.) Another way to start the program is to click the Windows Start button and then choose <u>P</u>rograms⇨WordPerfect Office 2000⇨ WordPerfect 9.

After some gurgling by your computer, you see a screen that looks something like the one in Figure 4-1. Your screen doesn't display the text you see in the figure — the Corel folks foolishly declined my offer to use my poetry in the opening screen.

Many elements of the WordPerfect window are the same as you find in any Windows program window. Chapter 2 covers these basic window components. But a few things in the window are specific to WordPerfect. Here's what you need to know:

✔ The white portion of the screen represents the text entry area. Think of this area as your digital typing paper.

✔ The blinking black bar is the *insertion marker*. The marker, labeled in Figure 4-1, indicates where the next character you type will appear. The sections "Entering Text" and "Moving Around in Your Document," later in this chapter, provide more details about this all-important item.

Margin guideline   Inspiring poetry

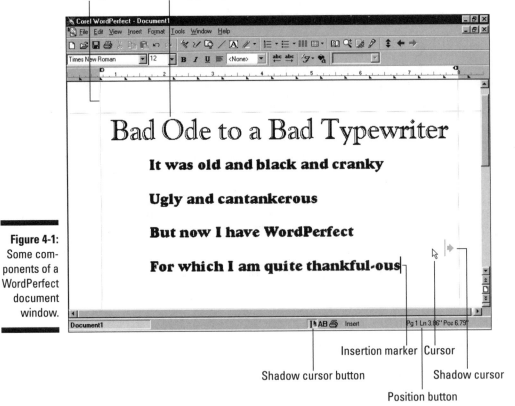

Figure 4-1:
Some components of a WordPerfect document window.

Insertion marker   Cursor

Shadow cursor button   Shadow cursor

Position button

✔ The nonblinking gray bar with the little arrow by its side is the *shadow cursor*. You turn the shadow cursor on and off by clicking its button on the Application Bar (explained in Chapter 2) or by choosing <u>V</u>iew⇨ Shad<u>o</u>w Cursor.

In this book, the term *cursor* refers to the mouse cursor rather than the shadow cursor. If I want you to do something with the shadow cursor, I specifically say "shadow cursor."

The shadow cursor hovers near your mouse cursor and shows you where the insertion marker will appear if you click. The main advantage of the shadow cursor is that it enables you to type anywhere in your document without adding tabs, spaces, or paragraph returns to position the insertion marker.

Try this exercise: With the shadow cursor turned on, type a word at the top of your page. Then click near the center of the page and type another word. WordPerfect automatically adds whatever paragraph returns, tabs, or spaces are needed to place your insertion marker at the spot you clicked. Now try the same thing with the shadow cursor turned off. Whoops, doesn't work, does it? You need to add all the paragraph returns and tabs yourself.

By default, the shadow cursor "snaps to" (aligns with) the nearest tab stop. The little gray arrow next to the shadow cursor changes depending on whether the tab stop is a regular left tab, center tab, and so on. (For more about tab stops, see Chapter 7.) You can change this behavior if you want; see the following section, "Customizing Your Workspace," for details. When the snap-to function is turned on, you can't click with the shadow cursor between tab stops; if you try, the cursor just jumps to the nearest tab stop.

✔ If you turn off the shadow cursor, your mouse cursor looks like the capital letter *I*. This cursor is known as the *I-beam cursor,* for obvious reasons. You also get the I-beam when you move your cursor into a block of existing text. Either way, clicking with the cursor repositions the insertion marker at the spot you click.

✔ The dotted horizontal and vertical lines on-screen indicate page margins. If these *margin guidelines* don't appear on your screen, choose <u>V</u>iew⇨G<u>u</u>idelines to open the Guidelines dialog box, click the Margins check box, and click OK. You can find out how to change the margin settings in Chapter 7.

✔ The *Position button* on the Application Bar indicates the location of the insertion marker. The button displays the current page number, line number, and distance from the left edge of the page.

✔ If you're upgrading from a previous version of WordPerfect, you may have noticed a few new buttons at the bottom of the vertical scroll bar. These buttons provide some additional options for navigating through your documents. The upcoming section "Moving Around in Your Document" tells all.

Customizing Your Workspace

You can control many things about the WordPerfect *interface* (a fancy term for how the program looks and behaves). I could spend hours walking you through all the options, but my guess is that you have neither the time nor inclination for that kind of detail. So the following sections point you toward the most important options for the kinds of tasks that most people are likely to tackle in WordPerfect.

Options HQ: The Settings dialog box

The key to many customization options is the Settings dialog box, shown in Figure 4-2. To open the dialog box, choose Tools⇨Settings or press Alt+F12. Clicking any of the icons in the dialog box opens another dialog box in which you can specify how you want a particular aspect of the program to work.

Figure 4-2: Make WordPerfect bow to your whims via this dialog box.

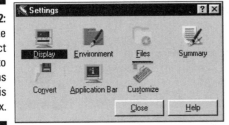

Click the Display icon to open the Display Settings dialog box, shown in Figure 4-3. On the Document tab of the dialog box, you can do all of the following, and more:

✔ **Change the default unit of measure:** To change the default measurement unit used in dialog boxes, choose an option from the Units of Measure drop-down list. To select the measurement unit that you want WordPerfect to use on the ruler and on the Position button (labeled in Figure 4-1), choose one of the options from the Application Bar/Ruler Display drop-down list. You can read more about the ruler in Chapter 7.

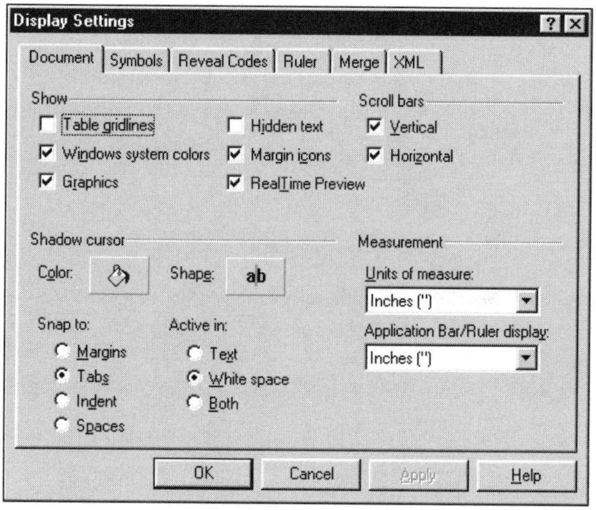

Figure 4-3:
You can
control how
certain
screen
elements
appear by
using
options in
this dialog
box.

✔ **Display or hide certain screen elements:** In the top half of the dialog box, you control whether scroll bars, margin icons, and other screen elements are visible. Click the check box next to the item you want to display or hide; a check mark in the box means the item will appear on-screen.

✔ **Turn RealTime Preview on and off:** WordPerfect 9 includes a new feature that enables you to preview the results of certain edits before you actually make the change. You can preview how your text will look in a certain typeface, for example, or how your document will display at different zoom levels available from the Zoom menu. Corel assures me that RealTime Preview puts no additional strain on your computer's system resources, so there's no reason to turn it off unless it bugs you. Click the RealTime Preview check box to turn the option on and off

✔ **Control the shadow cursor:** Click the Color and Shape buttons in the middle of the Display Settings dialog box to change the appearance of the shadow cursor. Click one of the Snap To radio buttons to specify whether you want the shadow cursor to snap to (align automatically with) spaces, tabs, margins, or indents. The Active In radio buttons enable you to set the shadow cursor to be active in text only, in the white space of your document only, or both.

Still inside the Display Settings dialog box, click the Symbols tab to display the options shown in Figure 4-4. Here you can control whether so-called *hidden symbols* appear on-screen.

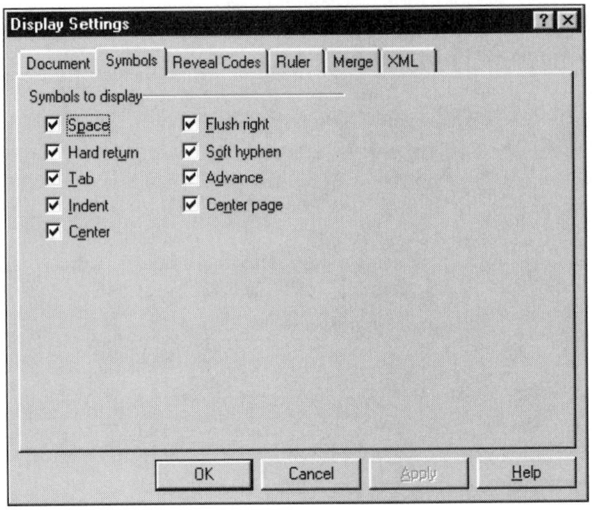

Display Settings

Document | Symbols | Reveal Codes | Ruler | Merge | XML

Symbols to display

- ☑ Space   ☑ Flush right
- ☑ Hard return   ☑ Soft hyphen
- ☑ Tab   ☑ Advance
- ☑ Indent   ☑ Center page
- ☑ Center

[OK] [Cancel] [Apply] [Help]

Figure 4-4:
Travel here
to display
and hide
formatting
symbols.

Hidden symbols are little symbols that show you where spaces, paragraph breaks (also known as *hard returns*), tabs, indents, and other formatting instructions are located throughout your text. Figure 4-5 shows some hidden symbols scattered throughout a famous ode.

You can also turn hidden symbols on and off by choosing View➪Show ¶ or by pressing Ctrl+Shift+F3.

More ways to custom-tailor your view

The Display Settings dialog box discussed in the preceding section isn't the only vehicle for custom-tailoring the WordPerfect interface. Check out these options:

- ✔ **Choose which toolbars are visible:** Choose View➪Toolbars to display the Toolbars dialog box. You get a list of all the available toolbars. Check the box beside a toolbar you want to see; uncheck the box to put the toolbar away.

    If you have a toolbar displayed, you can right-click an empty area in the toolbar to display a QuickMenu that lists all the available toolbars. Click a toolbar name to turn the toolbar on or off. A check mark next to the name means the toolbar is turned on.

- ✔ **Hide or display the Application Bar:** You can turn the Application Bar on and off via the Toolbars dialog box, just discussed. But a quicker method is to choose View➪Application Bar. Or, if the Application Bar is visible and you want to hide it, just right-click the bar and choose Hide Application Bar from the QuickMenu.

✔ **Hide or display the Property Bar:** To put the Property Bar away, right-click it and choose Hide Property Bar. To turn the Property Bar back on, choose View⇨Toolbars and check the Property Bar box in the Toolbars dialog box.

✔ **Change the Application Bar contents:** You can specify what items you want displayed on the Application Bar. To see all your options, right-click the Application Bar and then click Settings to display the Application Bar Settings dialog box. Or choose Tools⇨Settings and click the Application Bar icon.

✔ **Add, remove, and rearrange toolbar and Property Bar buttons:** You can delete buttons you don't use and add buttons for commands you need frequently. For the how-to's, see Chapter 24.

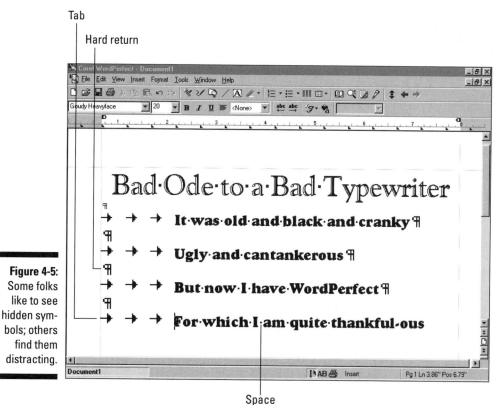

Tab

Hard return

Figure 4-5:
Some folks like to see hidden symbols; others find them distracting.

Space

> ✔ **Hide or display margin guides, column guides, and other nonprinting guides:** Choose View⇨Guidelines and select the guides you want to display from the Guidelines dialog box.
>
> ✔ **Hide or display the ruler:** Choose View⇨Ruler or press Alt+Shift+F3 to hide or display the ruler. (I discuss the ruler in Chapter 7.) Or, if the ruler is visible, right-click it and choose Hide Ruler from the QuickMenu.

Opening and Closing Documents

Before you can type on a typewriter, you need to put a piece of paper in the machine. And before you can do anything in WordPerfect, you need a *document.* The following sections explain how to create a new document, open an existing document, and close documents after you finish working on them.

Creating a new document

When you first start WordPerfect, you're presented with a new blank document. If you need a second blank document, you can get one by doing any of the following:

> ✔ Choose File⇨New.
>
> ✔ Click the New Document button on the toolbar.
>
> ✔ Press Ctrl+N.
>
> ✔ Choose File⇨New from Project.
>
> ✔ Press Ctrl+Shift+N.

If you choose any of the first three options, you get a new blank document, just as you do after you first start WordPerfect. But if you use one of the last two methods to open a new document, WordPerfect displays the PerfectExpert dialog box, shown in Figure 4-6.

The Create New tab of the dialog box contains templates for creating common documents, such as press releases or work schedules. If you use a template, WordPerfect handles basic formatting chores for you and provides sample document text. You simply edit the text and tweak the formatting to your taste. If you want to use a template, click it in the list and then click Create. For some templates, the PerfectExpert window appears to guide you through the process of working with the template. (See Chapter 3 for more information about PerfectExpert.)

If you decide that you don't want to use a template, choose the WordPerfect Document option from the list of templates. WordPerfect then gives you an ordinary blank document.

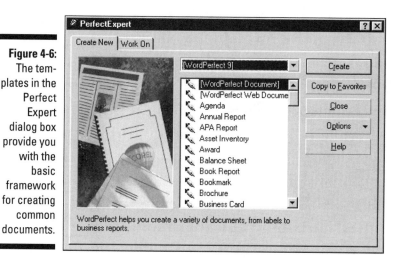

Figure 4-6:
The tem-
plates in the
Perfect
Expert
dialog box
provide you
with the
basic
framework
for creating
common
documents.

Opening existing documents

To open an existing document, you can follow any of these roads:

- ✔ Choose File⇨Open.
- ✔ Press Ctrl+O.
- ✔ Click the Open button on the toolbar.

Whichever method you choose, the Open File dialog box appears. This dialog box, shown in Figure 4-7, works like just about every other Open File dialog box in a Windows program. In case you're new to the game, here are the basics:

- ✔ To open a document, double-click its name in the Document List box (labeled in Figure 4-7). Or click the document name once and then click Open or press Enter.

- ✔ To split your Open File dialog box in two, revealing the Preview box shown in Figure 4-7, click the Preview button in the toolbar. Now, if you click a document name in the list box, WordPerfect displays a preview of the document. Use the scroll arrows along the side and bottom of the Preview box to scroll through your document if the entire document isn't visible in the box.

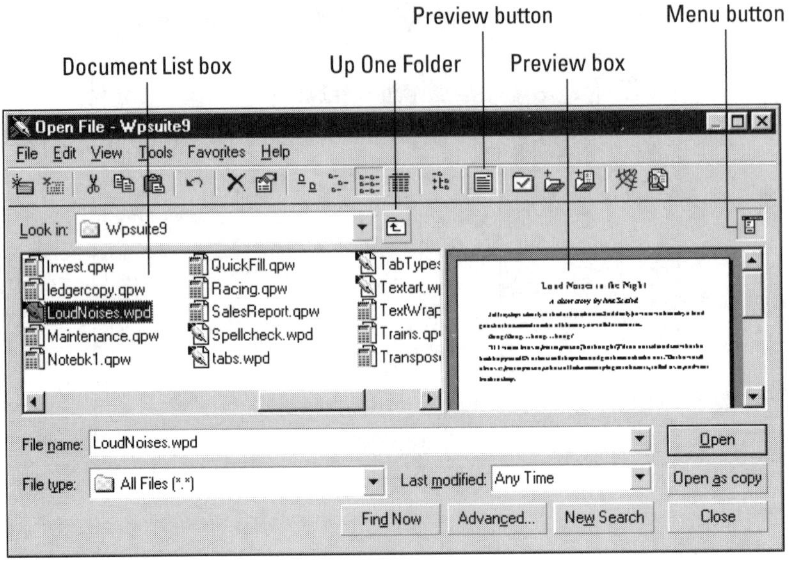

Preview button   Menu button

Document List box   Up One Folder   Preview box

Figure 4-7:
The
imposing
Open File
dialog box
isn't as
complicated
as it looks.

Right-click the Preview box to display a QuickMenu that enables you to change how the document appears in the Preview box. Choose Original Size to see your text at its real size. Choose Size to Height or Size to Width to shrink the display so that you can see the entire page inside the Preview box. If you want to display the preview inside a window that's separate from the Open File dialog box, choose Use Separate Window. (To put the Preview box back inside the Open dialog box, right-click the preview area and choose Use Separate Window again.)

✔ Drag the vertical border between the Document List box and the Preview box to make one box smaller and the other larger. Drag a corner of the dialog box to make the entire dialog box larger or smaller.

✔ Click the downward-pointing arrow at the end of the File Name option box to display a drop-down list of the last ten documents you edited. Click a document name in the list to select that document.

✔ The menu button (labeled in Figure 4-7) toggles a dialog box menu bar on and off.

✔ The menu bar contains many commands that enable you to change how your dialog box works. For example, if you choose View➪Details, you can see detailed information about each file, including the date it was last modified and its size.

✔ If the document you want isn't stored in the folder displayed in the Look In option box above the Document List box, click the downward-pointing arrow to display a drop-down list of folders and drives. After you find the folder you want, click it to display its contents in the document list box. Double-click a folder in the Document List box to display the folder's contents. Click the Up One Folder button, labeled in Figure 4-7, to back up one folder.

✔ *Folders* are little storage compartments on your computer's hard drive. You use them just as you'd use hanging files or file folders in your file cabinet — to store groups of related documents together. Before Windows 95, folders were called *directories*. Many programs still use the old term, but the meaning is the same.

✔ If you still don't see the file you want, you may need to change the file type shown in the File Type option box. If you want to see all types of files, open the drop-down list and select All Files. If you want to see only WordPerfect documents, select the WP Documents (*.wpd) option.

✔ If you click the Open As Copy button rather than the Open button, WordPerfect opens a copy of your original document. This option gives you a way to fool around with a document, secure in the knowledge that if you screw it up, you still have the original available.

You can open any of the last ten documents you edited without opening the Open File dialog box. Just choose the document name from the bottom of the File menu. If you don't see any document names on your File menu, choose Tools➪Settings, click the Environment icon, click the Interface tab, and select the Last Opened Documents on the File Menu option.

Another way to open your recently edited documents is to click the Work On tab of the PerfectExpert dialog box. (Choose File➪New from Project or press Ctrl+Shift+N to open the dialog box.) The right side of the dialog box lists the last documents that you had open. Select the Preview Document check box at the bottom of the dialog box and then click a document name to see a preview in the left side of the window. Double-click the name of the file you want to open.

You're probably wondering what those little boxes that appear to the left of each filename on the Work On tab do (unless, of course, you have better things to do with your time). Well, if you click the little square beside a filename, a check mark appears in the square. The next time you open the dialog box, files that have check marks appear at the top of the file list.

Closing a document

When you're sick and tired of looking at a document, click the document window's Close button — the one marked with an X, at the far-right on the menu bar. (Make sure that you click the Close button on the menu bar and not the one on the title bar, which closes the WordPerfect program.) Alternatively, choose File⇨Close or press Ctrl+F4.

If you haven't saved your document to disk yet, WordPerfect prompts you to do so. For specifics on saving, see Chapter 5.

Whenever you close all your open documents, WordPerfect automatically opens up a new, blank document for you. If you then open an existing document, WordPerfect closes the new document it just created.

Entering Text

Putting your words down on paper is easy: Just bang those keys, and WordPerfect slaps the corresponding letters onto your page. Go ahead, try it: Type **Now is the time for all good men to come to the aid of the party** or one of those other hysterical typing-class goodies.

In a lot of ways, creating text in WordPerfect is the same as creating text on a typewriter. But in just as many ways, the process is quite different. And, if you rely on the same techniques that worked so well on your typewriter, not only can you botch things up, but you're also failing to take advantage of the power that WordPerfect offers. So, unless you want your computer to serve as a $2,000 typewriter, remember the following:

- ✔ **The insertion marker — not the mouse cursor or shadow cursor — controls where the next thing you type appears.** Click at the spot where you want to position the insertion marker. If you have the shadow cursor turned on, you can click anywhere on your page and begin typing. If the shadow cursor is off, you can click inside existing lines of text only.

  Not sure what I mean by insertion marker, mouse cursor, or shadow cursor? See the section "Getting Started," earlier in this chapter. Also see "Moving Around in Your Document," later in this chapter, for other ways to position the insertion marker.

- ✔ **Use Delete or Backspace to erase mistakes.** If you type a character or characters and then change your mind, press the Backspace or Delete key to wipe out your error. The Backspace key gets rid of letters to the left of the insertion marker; the Delete key zaps characters to the right of the insertion marker. For a host of other editing options, see Chapter 6.

- **Don't press the Enter or the Return key when you reach the edge of your page.** WordPerfect automatically wraps the text to the next line whenever necessary. Pressing Enter or Return creates a paragraph break. This rule is important to remember because of the way that WordPerfect applies paragraph formatting such as line spacing, indents, and so on, as you find out in Chapter 7.

- **You can create new pages automatically or manually.** When you fill up a page, WordPerfect creates a new page automatically. Your text then wraps to the new page.

  To create a page break before the end of a page, press Ctrl+Enter or choose Insert⇨New Page.

- **Don't use spaces to indent paragraphs or lines of text.** If you do, you don't get consistent spacing. Chapter 7 explains why and shows you the right way to indent text.

- **Pay attention to the text-entry mode.** You can work in either of two modes for entering text. If you work in _Insert mode,_ whatever you type is inserted between existing text. If, for example, you type _Bob,_ click between the _B_ and the _o,_ and then press _l,_ you get _Blob._

  If you work in _Typeover mode,_ whatever you type replaces existing characters. In the preceding example, the _o_ gets replaced by the _l_ that you type, and you get _Blb._ A button on the Application Bar tells you which mode is active (the button label reads either Insert or Typeover and is located just to the left of the Position button by default). Click the button or press the Insert key on your keyboard to switch modes.

- **A striped line underneath a word means you goofed — maybe.** A red-striped line is WordPerfect's way of telling you that you may have a spelling problem. Similarly, a blue-striped line indicates a potential grammatical error. These two features are called Spell-As-You-Go and Grammar-As-You-Go, respectively. You can find out more about them in Chapter 9.

- **The QuickCorrect feature may change what you type.** If WordPerfect changes the text you type or overrules your formatting instructions, the program's QuickCorrect features are probably enabled. For information about QuickCorrect, see Chapters 6 and 8.

With these basic guidelines in mind, you're ready to start typing your next novel. For information on how to do more advanced stuff, such as using tabs and changing the size and font of your text, see Chapters 7 and 8. Chapter 6 explains how to edit text you've already typed.

Zooming In and Out

You can change the size that your document appears on-screen by zooming in for a close-up look at your work or zooming out to get a larger perspective.

Click the Zoom button on the toolbar to unfurl the Zoom menu, which offers a variety of view sizes. If none of the sizes on the menu appeals to you, click the Other button at the bottom of the menu to open the Zoom dialog box. Then click the Other radio button in the dialog box and enter a zoom value in the corresponding option box. Or click the up and down arrows alongside the option box to change the value.

In WordPerfect 9, pause your cursor over any value in the Zoom menu to preview the results of that option. WordPerfect temporarily displays your document at the chosen zoom value. You must have the RealTime Preview option enabled for this feature to work. To find out how to turn RealTime Preview on and off, see "Options HQ: The Settings dialog box," earlier in this chapter.

Remember that changing the Zoom size *does not* affect the actual size of your document or text — just the size at which WordPerfect displays your handiwork on-screen.

Moving Around in Your Document

Sophisticated programs such as WordPerfect give you lots of different ways to do the same thing. That flexibility is nice, but it can also be overwhelming. Such is the case with the topic of *navigation* — which is geekspeak for moving around in your document. WordPerfect gives you about a zillion ways to move the insertion marker and view different portions of your document.

Scrolling through the scenery

If you simply want to view hidden portions of your document, you can use the scroll arrows and scroll boxes on the horizontal and vertical scroll bars. Chapter 2 gives you all the whys and wherefores of scroll arrows and boxes, but I labeled a scroll arrow and the scroll box in Figure 4-8 to remind you what these gadgets look like. Use the horizontal scroll box/arrows to shift the document display left or right. Use the vertical scroll box/arrows to shift the display up and down.

As you drag the scroll box on the vertical scroll bar, a QuickTip flag appears near the box to indicate the current page number, as shown in Figure 4-8.

When you scroll using the scroll arrows or boxes, you _don't_ move the insertion marker. If you want to reposition the insertion marker, use the techniques outlined in the next two sections.

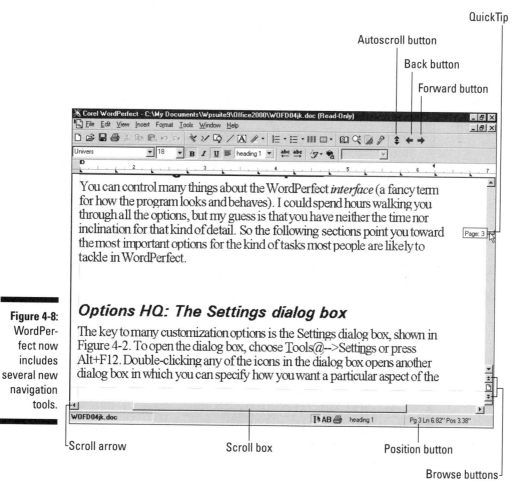

Figure 4-8:
WordPerfect now includes several new navigation tools.

Scroll arrow

Scroll box

Position button

Browse buttons

Moving the insertion marker

You can relocate the insertion marker — that blinking black bar that indicates where the next thing you type will appear — by executing these maneuvers:

✔ **Click at the spot where you want to place the insertion marker.** When you move your mouse cursor into a block of text, your mouse cursor turns into the I-beam cursor — in other words, the cursor looks like the capital letter *I*. Place the I-beam where you want to place the insertion marker and then click.

   If you have the shadow cursor feature turned on, you can click anywhere in your document and begin typing. Just place the shadow cursor where you want to put the insertion marker and then click. For more about this neat trick, see "Getting Started," earlier in this chapter.

✔ **Press the arrow keys on your keyboard.** For example, press the down arrow to move the insertion marker down one line. As long as you hold down the arrow key, the insertion marker keeps moving in the direction of the arrow.

   If an arrow key has a number on it, make sure that the Num Lock feature is off. (Press the Num Lock key to turn the feature on and off.) If Num Lock is on, the arrow keys type numbers instead of moving the insertion marker.

✔ **Use the Back and Forward buttons on the toolbar.** When you're working on a long document, the Back and Forward toolbar buttons, labeled in Figure 4-8, can come in handy. In essence, the buttons undo and redo insertion point moves.

   Say that you type a few paragraphs. You want to delete the first letter of first paragraph, so you place the insertion marker in front of that letter and press Delete. To put the insertion marker where it was before you moved it, click the Back button (the one that looks like a left-pointing arrow). Click the Forward button to put the insertion marker where it was before you clicked the Back button.

✔ **Click the Browse buttons.** At the bottom of the Vertical scroll bar (on the right side of the window), WordPerfect provides a trio of buttons known as the Browse buttons. Using these buttons, which are labeled in Figure 4-8, you can move the insertion marker to a specific portion of your document.

   By default, the Browse buttons are set to enable you to travel page by page through your text. Click the top Browse button (the one with the two up-pointing arrows) to jump to the beginning of the previous page in your document. Click the bottom Browse button (the one with the down-pointing arrows) to jump to the top of the next page.

So what does that middle Browse button do? It changes the browsing function so that you can search for something other than page breaks. For example, if your document contains several tables, you can browse by table. Clicking the top Browse button then takes you to the previous table in the document, and clicking the bottom Browse button takes you to the next table.

You can browse by table, graphic box, endnote, footnote, heading, page, comment, and edit position. The Edit Position option does the same thing as the Back and Forward buttons on the toolbar, so you can do without that function. For most documents, the Page and Heading options are the most useful.

To change the Browse setting, click the middle Browse button to cycle through the available options. With each click, WordPerfect displays a QuickTip banner indicating what option is current. (See Chapter 2 for more information about QuickTips.)

✔ **Open up the Go To dialog box.** If you click the Position button in the Application bar (refer to Figure 4-8), WordPerfect displays the Go To dialog box. Enter a page number in the Page Number option box or select a page position from the Position list. Then click OK to move the insertion marker to that location.

Just for good measure, WordPerfect gives you three — that's right, three — other ways to access the Go To dialog box: Choose Edit➪Go To, press Ctrl+G, or right-click anywhere on the scroll bar and choose Go To.

✔ **Press a few keys.** Instead of reaching for the mouse, you can use keyboard shortcuts to move the insertion marker. Table 4-1 lists some popular marker-moving shortcuts.

✔ **Turn on Autoscrolling.** Check out the next section for information on this hot new tool.

Table 4-1	Keyboard Navigation Shortcuts
Press This Key	*To Do This*
Home	Move to the beginning of the current line.
End	Move to the end of the current line.
Ctrl+Home	Move to the beginning of the document.
Ctrl+End	Move to the end of the document.
Page Up (PgUp)	Move up one screen.
Page Down (PgDn)	Move down one screen.
Alt+PgUp	Move up one page.

(continued)

Table 4-1 *(continued)*

Press This Key	To Do This
Alt+PgDn	Move down one page.
Ctrl+↑	Move to the beginning of the current paragraph or, if you're at the beginning, to the beginning of the preceding paragraph.
Ctrl+↓	Move to the beginning of the next paragraph.

Using the keyboard shortcuts in Table 4-1 can really speed up navigation time. What's more, you can use them to navigate documents in most Windows programs, not just in WordPerfect. So why not dump some of the more useless pieces of information in your brain — for example, maybe you don't really *need* to remember the theme song from *Gilligan's Island* anymore — to make room for these shortcuts.

Autoscrolling from here to there

For a new twist on scrolling, check out the new Autoscroll feature. Autoscroll shifts the document display automatically for you, giving you a click-free way to wander through long documents. If you own a fancy new computer mouse that has a scrolling wheel — the Microsoft Intellimouse comes to mind — you're already familiar with the concept behind the WordPerfect Autoscroll tool.

The following steps give you a trial run of the Autoscroll tool:

1. **Click the Autoscroll button on the toolbar.**

   Your cursor changes into an icon that looks just like the Autoscroll button — just to be wacky, I'll call the cursor the Autoscroll cursor. And the vertical scroll bar display changes, too. In the center of the vertical scroll bar, you see a six-sided, white icon. That icon represents home base for the Autoscroll tool.

2. **Move your mouse up or down to start scrolling.**

   Don't click — just move the mouse a little bit up or down and then take your hand off the little critter. WordPerfect begins scrolling the display up, toward the beginning of your document. Nudge the mouse down to scroll downward. (If you're using a touchpad or other pointing device, use whatever technique you normally use to move the cursor.)

   The Autoscroll cursor changes depending on which direction you're scrolling. You see an upward-pointing arrow when you're scrolling toward the beginning of your document and a downward-pointing arrow when scrolling toward the end of the document.

Scrolling speed depends on how far the up- or down-pointing arrow moves from the Autoscroll home base (that white icon on the scroll bar). If you move the mouse a short distance, the Autoscroll cursor hovers near home base, and the display scrolls slowly. Shove the mouse farther, and the Autoscroll cursor moves farther from the home base icon, and the display scrolls more rapidly. Practically speaking, though, you don't need to keep your eye on that home base icon. Just remember that as you move the Autoscroll cursor toward the top or bottom of the document window, the scrolling speed increases. So, if you want to take a slow scroll, keep the cursor a short distance from the vertical center of the window (the horizontal position makes no difference).

3. **Move the Autoscroll cursor near home base to pause scrolling.**

   The double-headed arrow appears when you move the Autoscroll cursor into vertical alignment with the home base icon. In other words, to pause scrolling, move the cursor to the vertical center of the page. Move the mouse up or down to begin scrolling again.

4. **Click or press a key to turn off Autoscrolling.**

   You can't do any editing or typing while the Autoscroll tool is turned on. So, when you finish looking through your document, click the left mouse button or press any key to turn Autoscrolling off and return to the standard cursor.

Note that if you're using a mouse that has a scrolling wheel, you may or may not be able to use the mouse's scrolling function in WordPerfect (I couldn't make it work on my system, at least). But don't get too bugged, because with Autoscroll, you can scroll your document just by moving your mouse — no more wearing out your finger spinning the mouse's scrolling wheel.

Chapter 5

Save and Print: Dull but Vital Basics

Some chapters in this book are a lot of fun to explore. You discover all sorts of cool things you can do by clicking here, clicking there, and otherwise messing around with on-screen gizmos and gadgets. Other chapters — such as this one — are less action-packed but are vital to getting your money's worth from your software.

This chapter focuses on two of the dull but very necessary aspects of word processing: how to save documents to your computer's hard drive or a removable storage disk and how to print your finished masterpiece. It's not the kind of stuff you can use to titillate your friends (unless you have really geeky friends), but the information is important if you want to stop fooling around and actually produce something in WordPerfect.

The good news is that, after you slog through these yawner topics, you don't need to repeat the process for every program you use. Although this chapter explains concepts in terms specific to WordPerfect, you use virtually the same procedures to save and print documents in all programs in the WordPerfect Office 2000 suite — and in most other Windows programs as well.

Saving Your Work (And Your Sanity)

Here's a little saying to remember while you're working in WordPerfect or in any other computer program: Save your work, save your mind.

Until you choose the Save command, everything you do in a document is temporary. If WordPerfect shuts down for any reason — Windows crashes, you have a power failure, whatever — your document tumbles into the electronic abyss, and all your hard work is gone forever. So learn to save early and save often.

Saving for the very first time

To save a document for the first time, follow these steps:

1. **Choose File⇨Save, press Ctrl+S, or click the Save button on the toolbar.**

   The Save File dialog box appears, as shown in Figure 5-1, unless some text is selected in your document. If text is selected, you see a dialog box that gives you the option of saving just the selected text or the entire file. Click the option you want and then click OK to access the Save File dialog box.

2. **Choose a storage location for your document.**

   Tell WordPerfect where you want to store the document by choosing a drive (hard drive or floppy drive) and folder from the Save In drop-down list.

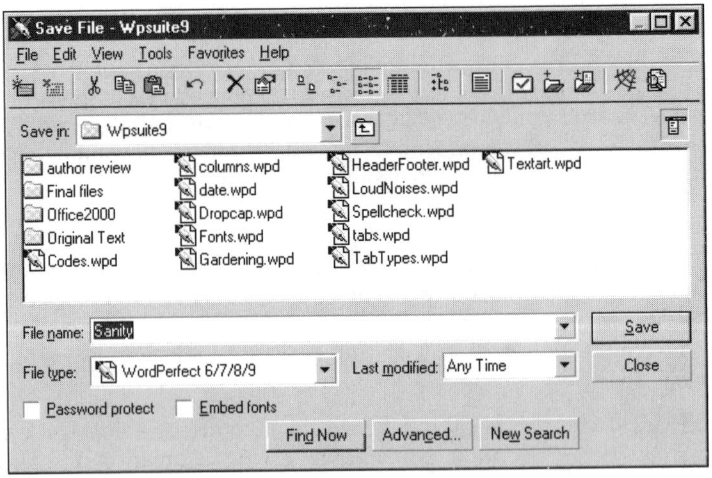

Figure 5-1:
Unless you want to lose all your work, make friends with the Save File dialog box.

Save File - Wpsuite9			_ □ ✕
File Edit View Tools Favorites Help			
Save in: ☐ Wpsuite9			
☐ author review	☐ columns.wpd	☐ HeaderFooter.wpd	☐ Textart.wpd
☐ Final files	☐ date.wpd	☐ LoudNoises.wpd	
☐ Office2000	☐ Dropcap.wpd	☐ Spellcheck.wpd	
☐ Original Text	☐ Fonts.wpd	☐ tabs.wpd	
☐ Codes.wpd	☐ Gardening.wpd	☐ TabTypes.wpd	

File name: Sanity — Save

File type: WordPerfect 6/7/8/9 — Last modified: Any Time — Close

☐ Password protect ☐ Embed fonts

Find Now   Advanced...   New Search

3. Enter a document name in the File Name option box.

For tips on choosing a filename, see the upcoming sidebar "What's in a (Windows 95) filename?"

4. Choose a file type from the File Type drop-down list.

You can choose from many file formats. By default, WordPerfect saves your document in its *native* (own) format, which has the file extension WPD. But if you want to save the document for use in some other program — for example, if you want to share the document with a friend who uses Microsoft Word — choose that program's file format from the drop-down list.

5. Embed your document fonts (optional).

If you're saving a document for use on a computer other than the one you used to create the document, you may want to *embed* the fonts in the document file. *Font,* as you find out in Chapter 7, is a fancy name for typeface. If you open the document on a computer that doesn't have the same fonts as the original computer, alternate fonts are substituted for the missing ones. Depending on the design of your document, the font substitution may throw the page formatting off. In other words, your document may look very different than it did when you saved it.

If you select the Embed Fonts check box at the bottom of the Save File dialog box, all the necessary font files are stored in your document file. That way, you have access to the fonts regardless of what computer you use to work on the document.

Because embedding fonts increases the file size, though, turn off the option if you're not going to use your document on another computer.

6. Click the Save button.

That's it! You're protected — for now.

If you make any changes to your document after you save it, those changes aren't protected until you resave the document. So save often during your computing sessions and also before you close a document. To resave the document, just choose the Save command again — pressing Ctrl+S is the easiest method. WordPerfect saves your document, this time without bothering you with the Save File dialog box.

Saving another copy with the Save As command

You may sometimes want to save a document under a different name than you saved it the first time. Say that you open Document A and make some changes to it. You're not sure whether your client is going to like the changes or prefer the original version. By using the Save As command, you can save the changed document as Document B, which leaves Document A intact.

You can also use the Save As command to save the document to a different folder or drive than where you originally saved it — for example, if you stored the document on your hard drive and now want to save a copy on a floppy disk. Another use for the command is saving a document in a different file format (type of file). If you're giving your document to a coworker who uses a different word processor, for example, you can save it in a format compatible with that program.

To save a document under a new name, in a different format, or to a new destination, choose File⇨Save As or press the F3 key to open the Save As dialog box, which works just like the Save File dialog box (see Figure 5-1). Choose a folder and hard drive from the Save In drop-down menu, choose a file format from the File Type drop-down menu, and enter a name in the File Name option box. Then click the Save button or press Enter.

If you're copying your document for use on another computer, you may want to use the Embed Font option to copy the document fonts along with the rest of the document. For more information, see Step 5 in the preceding section.

In a hurry to get your document onto a floppy? You can save the document without bothering with the Save File dialog box. If the document is already open, choose File⇨Send To and then select your floppy drive (A or B) from the Send To submenu. If the document isn't open, choose File⇨Open to display the Open File dialog box, right-click the filename, and choose the Send To command from the QuickMenu that appears.

What's in a (Windows 95) filename?

In the past, PC users had to follow strict rules in naming files. A correct filename consisted of an eight-character document name, followed by a period, followed by a three-letter file extension. (The extension indicated the type of document — WPD for WordPerfect documents, TIF for a graphics file saved in the TIFF format, and so on.)

The arrival of Windows 95 changed the naming rules. Filenames can now contain as many as 255 characters, although why you'd want such a long name is beyond me. Filenames still have three-letter file extensions, but you usually don't need to add the extension if you're saving a file. You select the file type in the Save File dialog box, and the program adds the appropriate file extension automatically.

If you want to share a document with a coworker who's still using Windows 3.1 or earlier, however, stick with the old eight-character, three-letter-extension naming conventions. Longer filenames may be truncated (cut off) in your coworker's Open File dialog box, making it difficult to tell which file is which.

Getting extra protection through automatic saving

With all the other things you need to remember during a day — your manager's favorite flavor of latté, the date of your next salary review — remembering to save your documents on a regular basis can be difficult. Fortunately, WordPerfect provides an option that offers some protection against a lapse in memory (yours, not the computer's). While you're working in a document, the program can automatically make a backup copy of the file. Should your computer crash while you're working on a document that you haven't yet saved, you can usually open the backup copy and retrieve at least some of your work.

To use this feature, choose Tools⇨Settings or press Alt+F12 to open the Settings dialog box. Then click the Files icon in the dialog box. The Files Settings dialog box appears, as shown in Figure 5-2. Click the Document tab if it's not already at the forefront of the dialog box. Now look for the Timed Document Backup Every check box (spotlighted in the figure). If you don't see a check mark in the box, click the box to turn on the option.

Figure 5-2:
If you
turn on
automatic
document
backup,
WordPerfect
makes a
backup
copy of your
document at
specified
intervals.

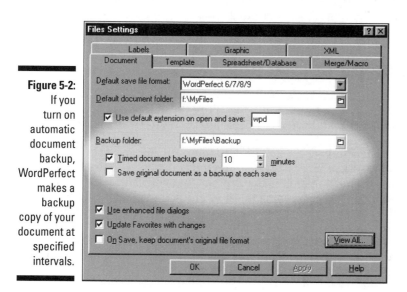

By default, WordPerfect saves the backup copy every ten minutes, saving the copy in the location shown in the Backup Folder drop-down list. You can raise or lower the time according to your individual tolerance for risk. Just change the value in the option box next to the check box. But don't set the backup interval *too* low, as some users have reported that doing so disrupts the program's capability to back up documents successfully. The general consensus suggests five minutes as the minimum backup interval.

Even after you turn on automatic backup, you still need to save your document before you close it. The backup copy that WordPerfect makes is only temporary and is deleted when you close your document. If you close the document without saving it to disk, any changes you made to the document are lost.

Printing Your Pages

Printing is usually a pretty straightforward process — after you get your printer set up to work with your computer, that is. Because different systems require different printer configurations, I can't give you specific instructions for setting up your printer. The printing information I'm about to give you assumes that your printer and computer are on speaking terms. If you have trouble, ask your local printer guru for help (look for the person with ink-stained fingers).

Having expertly dodged that responsibility, I can move on to basic printing guidelines. The following three sections explain how to preview your document before printing, how to send your document to the printer, and how to take advantage of some special printing options.

Previewing before you print

WordPerfect 9 includes a new Print Preview toolbar, shown in Figure 5-3. You can display the toolbar by choosing File⇨Print Preview or by choosing View⇨Toolbars and checking the Print Preview item in the Toolbars dialog box.

The Print Preview toolbar doesn't provide you with any new features or functions; it simply makes accessing some common document formatting controls easier. The toolbar contains buttons that you can click to perform such pre-printing tasks as running the spell checker (explained in Chapter 9), changing the page setup (covered in Chapter 7), and sizing your document to fit the available page space through the Make-It-Fit command (also explained in Chapter 7). To see what the various toolbar buttons do, pause your cursor over each one to display an identifying QuickTip label. (See Chapter 2 for more information about how QuickTips work.)

Print Preview toolbar

Print Preview button

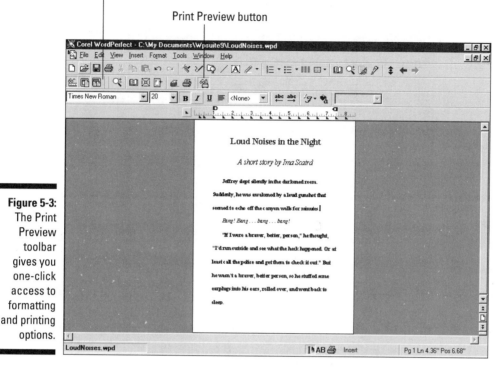

Figure 5-3:
The Print
Preview
toolbar
gives you
one-click
access to
formatting
and printing
options.

 The Print Preview button (labeled in Figure 5-3) toggles the print preview function on and off. With the preview on, you can get a look at your document as it will appear when printed. If you display the toolbar by choosing the Print Preview command from the File menu, the Print Preview button and preview are turned on by default. When the preview is turned on, clicking the Print Preview button again not only turns off the preview, it also hides the Print Preview toolbar.

Sending a document to the printer

Ready to put words on paper? Follow these exhilarating steps:

1. Choose File⇨Print, press Ctrl+P, or click the Print button.

WordPerfect provides a Print button on the standard toolbar, on the Application Bar, and on the Print Preview toolbar. If you use the Print Preview toolbar option, be sure to click the button that looks like the one in the margin next to this paragraph. The button to the left of the printer button sends your document to the printer without giving you the chance to choose any printing options.

However you choose the Print command, the Print dialog box zooms into view, as shown in Figure 5-4.

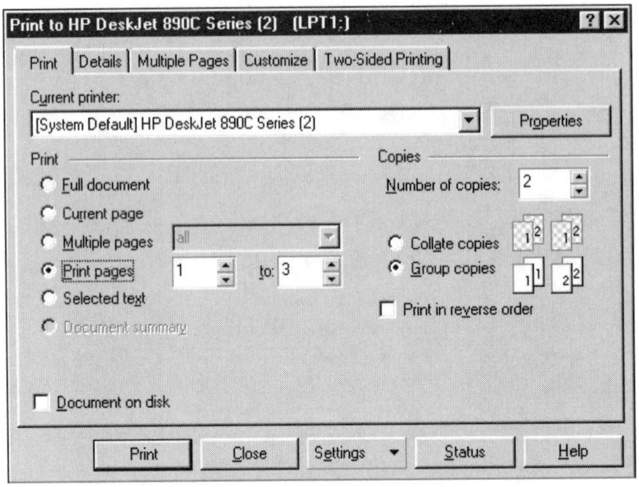

Figure 5-4:
The Print dialog box enables you to establish your print settings.

2. **Choose a printer from the Current Printer drop-down list.**

   Unless you're on a network and have access to more than one printer, you probably don't need to worry about this step. The right printer should already be selected by default.

3. **Specify how many copies you want to print.**

   Enter the number of copies in the Number of Copies option box. (There's a surprise.) If you print more than one copy, the Group Copies and Collate Copies options become available. If you choose Group Copies, the printer prints all copies of page 1, then all copies of page 2, and so on. If you choose Collate Copies, the printer prints the entire document once, prints the second copy of the document, and so on — in other words, it collates the pages for you.

4. **Specify which pages you want to print.**

   Here are your options:

   • To print your entire document, select the Full Document radio button.

   • To print just the current page (the page on which the insertion marker is located), select the Current Page radio button.

   • To print several pages that fall together (for example, pages 1 through 5), select the Print Pages radio button and then enter the first page number and last page number in the adjacent option boxes, as shown in Figure 5-4.

- To print several pages that don't fall in sequence — say, pages 1, 4, and 5 — click the Multiple Pages radio button. Then double-click inside the adjacent drop-down list box and enter the numbers of the pages you want to print. You no longer have to travel to the Multiple Pages tab of the dialog box to enter your page numbers, as in past editions of WordPerfect.

  You can enter page numbers in several ways. You can enter each page number, separated by a comma or space. Or you can indicate a range of pages by entering the first page in the range, a hyphen, and then the last number in the range. For example you can also combine the two approaches by entering *1,4-8.*

- If you select text before choosing the Print command, you can print just the selection by choosing the Selected Text radio button.

5. Click the Print button or press Enter.

Your pages should start shooting out of your printer momentarily. Well, maybe not shooting, exactly — they actually sort of crawl out if you have a printer like mine.

Playing with a few print options

Poke about in the Print dialog box, and you discover a wide range of special printing options. The following list points you toward some printing tasks that you can tackle using these options:

- **Print your document sideways or longways.** You can print your document using *portrait* or *landscape orientation*. In portrait mode, text runs parallel to the short edge of the paper (longways, or the normal printing mode). In landscape mode, the document prints sideways so that text runs parallel to the long edge of the paper.

  To choose the orientation, click the Properties button in the Print dialog box. WordPerfect opens the Properties dialog box. The dialog box varies depending on your printer, but you should find an option that enables you to choose between landscape and portrait printing. To change the orientation of your document permanently, see Chapter 7.

- **Print pages in reverse order.** Normally, page 1 of a multiple-page document prints first. If you prefer to start printing with the last page, check the Print in Reverse Order check box on the Print tab of the Print dialog box.

✔ **Print a document without opening it.** This feature was available in Version 8, but the process is a little different in Version 9. First, choose File⇨Print to open the Print dialog box. Then click the Document on Disk check box in the lower-right corner of the dialog box. A drop-down list appears next to the check box. Click the little folder icon at the end of the drop-down list to display the Document on Disk dialog box. This dialog box looks and works similarly to the Open File dialog box discussed in Chapter 4. Locate the file you want to print and double-click it to close the Document on Disk dialog box. Then choose your print settings as you would for any document and click Print to express your document to the printer.

✔ **Print without pictures.** Printing graphics sometimes takes a lot of time and printer memory. If you're short on either and are just printing a rough draft of your document, you can print it without graphics by selecting the Print Text Only check box on the Details tab of the Print dialog box.

Another way to limit the strain on your schedule and printer memory when printing documents with graphics is to lower the Resolution setting, also found on the Details tab. Your printed piece doesn't look as good as it would if printed at a high resolution, but the output may be okay for a draft copy. (For some printers, you may not be able to change the resolution.)

✔ **Scale the document for printing.** You can change the size of your document for printing by using the new enlarge and reduce options, explained fully in the next section.

Enlarging or reducing your document

The WordPerfect 9 Print dialog box includes a whole tabful of new options related to enlarging or reducing your document. Click the Customize tab to explore the possibilities, shown in Figure 5-5.

None of the Customize options permanently changes the size of your document; only the current printout is affected. Here's a rundown of what you can do:

✔ To scale (enlarge or reduce) the document, click the Enlarge/Reduce radio button. Then enter a scaling percentage in the adjacent option box. A value of more than 100% enlarges the document; a value of less than 100% shrinks it.

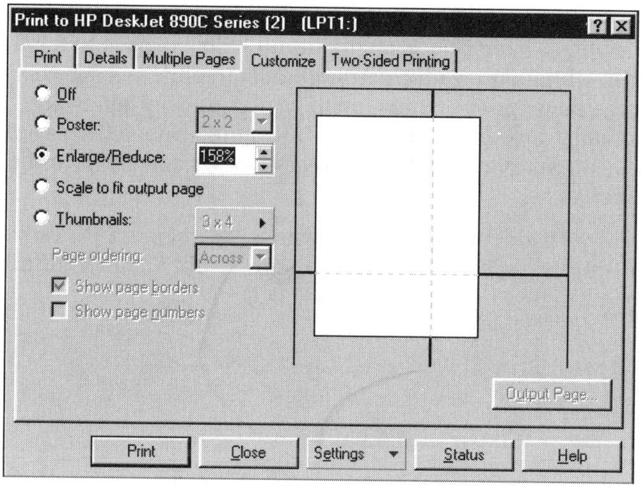

Figure 5-5:
The
Customize
tab provides
options for
resizing
your printed
document.

If you enlarge the document past 100%, WordPerfect *tiles* the printout. That is, your document is printed on several sheets of paper that you then can tape together to create one big document. The preview area on the right side of the Customize tab indicates how many tiles — sheets of paper — are required to print your document at the chosen size. In Figure 5-5, an Enlarge/Reduce value of 158% spread the document across four tiles.

✔ The Poster option enables you to print your document as a poster that contains as many tiles — sheets of paper — as you want. You choose the number of tiles by making a selection from the drop-down list next to the Poster radio button. Select 2 x 2, for example, to produce a poster that's two pages wide by two pages tall.

WordPerfect automatically scales your document to fit the poster size you select. As you change the value in the Poster drop-down list, the Enlarge/Reduce value changes accordingly.

✔ To enlarge or reduce your document so that it automatically fits your paper size, select the Scale to Fit Output Page radio button. Then click the Output Page button to display a dialog box in which you choose the paper size, the paper orientation (landscape or portrait), and the page margins. Click OK to return to the Print dialog box.

✔ If you're printing a long manuscript, you may want to take advantage of the Thumbnails option. Using this feature, you can print tiny versions — thumbnails — of your pages, printing several thumbnails on one page of paper. You can then review the layout and arrangement of your document easily by looking at the thumbnails.

When the Thumbnails radio button is selected, options appear that enable you to specify how many thumbnails you want on each page, the order in which you want the thumbnails to appear, and whether you want the page number and a page border to print along with each thumbnail. Click the Output Page button to choose the paper size, orientation, and margins for the printout; click OK to return to the Print dialog box.

✔ To print your document at its original size, click the Off radio button. All other options on the Customize tab are disabled and your document prints normally.

Chapter 6

Eating Your Words and Other Editing Tasks

. . . .

. . . .

*T*his chapter shows you the basics of editing in WordPerfect. You find out how to delete unwanted text; how to copy and move words, sentences, and entire paragraphs; and how to use the QuickCorrect feature to automatically correct mistakes as you type.

After you become familiar with editing in a word processor, you're forever ruined as far as using a traditional typewriter. Not only do you find the limitations of a typewriter unbearable, but your typing accuracy goes to pot. WordPerfect enables you to fix mistakes so easily that you soon find yourself typing with far less regard for hitting the right keys than you used to have. You can type as fast as your thoughts take you, knowing that you can come back later and quickly clean up any blunders.

Don't mourn the loss of your typing accuracy, however. Look at it from the positive side: If the computer's down and someone asks you to type that letter or memo on a typewriter, you can honestly say, "Gee, I'd like to, but now that I'm a word-processing expert, I'm just no good on the typewriter. We pay a heavy price for this advancing technology, don't we?"

Make sure that you walk away quickly, before the other party has a chance to get over the shock and question your sincerity.

Selecting Stuff You Want to Edit

Before you can perform many editing and formatting tasks, you must first *select* the characters or paragraphs you want to change. Figure 6-1 shows an example of how selected text looks on-screen.

You can select text in countless ways. Here are just a few:

- ✔ Drag over the characters or words you want to select. By default, WordPerfect selects the entire word when you drag quickly over any portion of the word. You can turn off this feature if you have trouble dragging slowly enough to select single characters. Press Alt+F12 to open the Settings dialog box, click the Environment icon, and deselect the Automatically Select Whole Words When Dragging to Select Text check box on the General tab.

- ✔ To select a single word, double-click that word.

- ✔ To select a sentence, triple-click anywhere within the sentence. Or, to select the first sentence on a line of text, move the cursor into the left margin of the sentence and click once.

- ✔ To select a paragraph, quadruple-click anywhere within that paragraph. Yikes! Who thought up that one? If this maneuver is beyond you, move the cursor to the left margin of the paragraph and double-click.

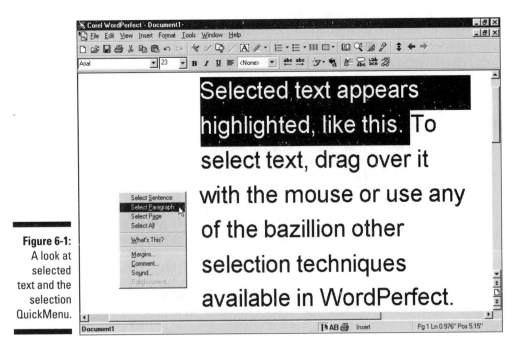

Figure 6-1: A look at selected text and the selection QuickMenu.

✔ Click anywhere in the word, sentence, or paragraph that you want to select. Move the mouse cursor to the left margin until the pointer becomes a right-pointing arrow and then right-click to display the QuickMenu, as shown in Figure 6-1. Click the selection option you want to use.

✔ You can access the same selection commands found on the QuickMenu by choosing Edit➪Select. If you ask me, this method is the hard way to do things, but you may like doing things the hard way.

✔ To select everything in a document, press Ctrl+A (A for all).

✔ Here's one of my favorites: Place the insertion marker at the beginning of the text you want to select. Press Shift and then use the arrow keys and other cursor movement keys that I describe in Chapter 4 (End, Home, and so on) to extend the selection to the rest of the text you want to select. For example, click and then press Shift+End to select everything from the insertion marker to the end of the current line.

✔ If you select something and then decide that you want to add to the selection or subtract from it, just press and hold the Shift key as you use the arrow keys to move the end of the selection. Or press Shift and then click to set the new end of the selection.

✔ To cancel a selection entirely, click anywhere inside your text.

After you select text, you can wreak all kinds of havoc on it. You can copy it, delete it, move it, and replace it, as I cover throughout the rest of this chapter. And, as I discuss in Chapters 7 and 8, you can change the font and type size, change the line spacing and paragraph spacing, indent the text, capitalize it, number it, and make it do a little clogging dance to "Rocky Top." Oh, sorry, got a little carried away — in WordPerfect 9, text clogs only to "Orange Blossom Special."

If you begin typing while text is selected, the selected text is replaced by the new text you type.

Deleting Selected Stuff

To get rid of unwanted text, select the text and press Delete or Backspace. You can also use Delete and Backspace to get rid of unselected text. Delete erases characters to the right of the insertion marker; Backspace erases characters to the left.

If you zap something into oblivion and then realize that you didn't want to get rid of it after all, don't panic. You can usually get it back by using the Undo command, explained in the section "Undoing Changes," later in this chapter.

Moving and Copying Text

Being able to erase unwanted text with a click of the mouse or press of a key is pretty cool. But it's nothing compared with the editing power you gain after you discover how to cut, copy, and paste text. By using these techniques, you can quickly move and copy text from one place to another.

The cut, copy, and paste techniques described in this section work similarly in all Windows programs. You can use them to copy and move graphics as well as text. (You find more information about editing graphics in WordPerfect in Chapter 8. Make sure that you also check out Chapter 21, which discusses some special ways to move and copy data between documents and programs.)

Using the Copy, Cut, and Paste commands

You can copy a piece of text and place the copy in a new location by using two methods. You can drag and drop the text, as explained in the following section, "Dragging and dropping," or you can use the Copy and Paste commands, as outlined in this section.

Which method is better depends on your dexterity with the mouse and the type of copying or moving you're doing. If you're copying a large block of text or copying from one document to another, using the Cut, Copy, and Paste commands is often easier. For small bits of text, dragging and dropping is more convenient.

To copy text by using the Copy command, follow these steps:

1. **Select the text that you want to copy.**

   Use any of the selection techniques discussed in the section "Selecting Stuff You Want to Edit," earlier in this chapter.

2. **Press Ctrl+C or click the Copy button on the toolbar.**

   If you prefer, choose Edit⇨Copy. WordPerfect sends a copy of your text to the Windows Clipboard, a temporary storage shed for copied and cut data.

3. **Click at the spot where you want to place the copy.**

   You can put the copy in your current document or in another open document. You can even put the copy in a document you created in another program.

 4. **Press Ctrl+V or click the Paste button.**

   Alternatively, you can choose Edit⇨Paste. Whichever method you pick, WordPerfect places your copy at the new location.

The process for moving selected text is the same as for copying text except that you use the Cut command rather than the Copy command. You can choose the command from the Edit menu, click the Cut button on the toolbar, or press the keyboard shortcut Ctrl+X.

 After you cut or copy something to the Clipboard, that text stays on the Clipboard until you cut or copy something else. So you can paste the cut or copied text as many times as you want in your document. Just keep pressing Ctrl+V.

Notice that the three shortcut keys, X, C, and V, lie right next to each other on your keyboard. Why were these keys chosen for the Cut, Copy, and Paste shortcuts? Well, maybe because *X* sort of looks like a pair of scissors (for Cut), *C* is the first letter in *Copy,* and *V* . . . well, maybe it's supposed to bring to mind the word *Viscid,* which means sticky (like paste). Then again, maybe not.

Dragging and dropping

If you're handy with a mouse — or touchpad or whatever pointing device you use — dragging and dropping provides a quick way to cut and copy text. Try using the technique described in the following steps to move a piece of text:

1. **Select the text that you want to move.**

2. **Place the mouse cursor on the selected text.**

3. **Press and hold the left mouse button as you drag the text to its new home.**

   As you drag, the insertion marker moves along with your mouse cursor. A little box appears next to the cursor to show that you grabbed the text. Position the insertion marker at the spot where you want to place the text.

4. **Release the mouse button.**

   The text appears at its new location.

If you want to copy a piece of text rather than move it, press Ctrl anytime before you release the mouse button. A plus sign appears next to the cursor to tell you that you're copying instead of cutting the selected text.

 In addition to dragging and dropping text within the same document, you can drag and drop between two open WordPerfect documents. To move a piece of text, just drag it from the first document to the Application Bar button for the second document. Wait until the second document comes to life and then drop the text into the document. To copy the text instead of moving it, press Ctrl before you release the mouse button.

You can also drag and drop stuff from a WordPerfect document into a document created in another program. Check out Chapter 21 for the details.

Undoing Changes

If you're upgrading to Version 9 from a previous version of WordPerfect, you may have noticed that one of the program's commands, Undelete, didn't make the cut for Version 9. Undelete enabled you to bring back text that you erased using the Delete command.

Don't grieve too much for the loss of the Undelete command. In fact, don't give it another thought. The Undo command can accomplish the same thing as Undelete — and much, much more.

Undo can reverse almost any editing action, not just deletions. Undo is like having a magic wand that makes all your bonehead moves disappear. (Don't you wish you had an Undo command in real life?)

The following list reveals the secrets to using Undo:

✔ To undo the last editing change you made, choose Edit➪Undo, click the Undo button, or press Ctrl+Z or Alt+Backspace.

✔ Change your mind about that undo? Choose Edit➪Redo, click the Redo button, or press Ctrl+Shift+Z to put things back the way they were before you chose the Undo command.

Help! Everything got screwy when I moved stuff around!

If everything goes kablooey after you rearrange text — for example, all your plain text suddenly becomes bold and vice versa — you've messed up WordPerfect's hidden codes. You see, any time that you give WordPerfect a formatting instruction, whether you want to set a tab, make text bold, or change a paragraph indent, the program inserts little hidden codes into your text. And, if you accidentally grab a code as you select a piece of text — or you don't grab a code that should be moved along with that text — WordPerfect gets all perplexed.

If this situation occurs, you have a couple options: One, you can reformat the text as needed. Two, you can choose View➪Reveal Codes or press Alt+F3 to display the Reveal Codes window. In this window, you can see and edit the hidden formatting codes.

The problem with editing codes is that the process can be confusing, especially for beginners. If you like puzzle-solving, however, and you want to become a code-cracker, check out *WordPerfect 9 For Windows For Dummies,* by Margaret Levine Young, David C. Kay, Jordan M. Young, and Kathy Warfel (published by IDG Books Worldwide, Inc.), which dedicates an entire chapter to the subject.

✔ You must choose Redo immediately after choosing Undo. If you type new text or make any other changes, Redo becomes unavailable.

✔ If you want to go further back in time than your last editing action, you have two options: You can keep choosing the Undo command, or you can choose Edit➪Undo/Redo History to display the Undo/Redo History dialog box, as shown in Figure 6-2. The Undo list box shows your recent editing changes — albeit in rather cryptic terms. Click the action that you want to undo from the Undo list and then click the Undo button.

Figure 6-2:
Reverse a
series of
edits via the
Undo/Redo
History
dialog box.

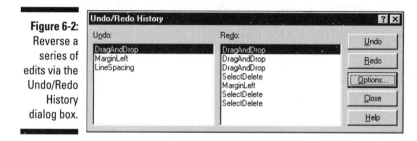

After you select an action in the Undo list box, all actions above it in the list are automatically selected and are also undone. You can't select the third action in the list, for example, without undoing the first and second actions as well.

After you click Undo, the actions you reversed appear in the Redo list box. WordPerfect makes the changes in your document, but nothing's set in stone until you click Close to exit the dialog box. If you change your mind and want to restore an action, select it from the Redo list box and click the Redo button.

✔ By default, WordPerfect enables you to undo your last ten editing changes. But if you click the Options button in the Undo/Redo History dialog box, WordPerfect displays a second dialog box, where you can raise or lower the number of undos by adjusting the Number of Undo/Redo Items value. You can raise the value to a maximum of 99 (down from past years, when you could undo up to 300 edits). Keep in mind that the higher the number of undos you can perform, the more you tax your computer's memory.

✔ Undo can't undo all actions. You can't, for example, undo saving a document. You can, however, print your document and then undo edits you made before you chose the Print command.

Letting WordPerfect Correct Mistakes for You

Wouldn't it be nice to have a servant that trailed around after you all the time, cleaning up your messes for you? What — you say that you're a mom, and *you're* the servant? Well, now's your chance to be the mess-maker and have someone else — namely WordPerfect — pick up after you.

WordPerfect's QuickCorrect feature, which is turned on by default, provides as-you-type error correction. Type a word incorrectly, and WordPerfect corrects it for you as soon as you hit the spacebar. Try typing **teh,** for example, and pressing the spacebar. WordPerfect assumes that you really meant to type *the,* so it automatically changes *teh* to *the.* It doesn't even bother you with a dialog box, beep, or other whiny complaint — it just goes quietly about its cleanup business.

Adding words to the QuickCorrect list

To access options that control QuickCorrect, choose Tools⇨QuickCorrect or press Ctrl+Shift+F1 to display the QuickCorrect dialog box, as shown in Figure 6-3. The Replace Words as You Type option determines whether WordPerfect corrects your spelling as you type, as just described. If the option is selected, your little typing buddy is at your service.

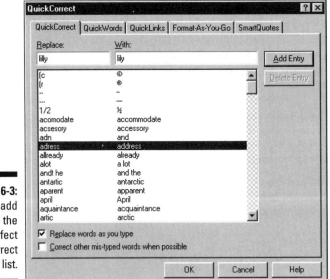

Figure 6-3:
You can add words to the WordPerfect QuickCorrect list.

To determine which words need correcting, WordPerfect consults an internal list of commonly misspelled and mistyped words. The list appears in the QuickCorrect dialog box. If you want to add a word to the QuickCorrect list, type the misspelled version in the Replace option box and enter the correct word in the With option box. Click Add Entry and click OK.

If you turn on the Correct Other Mis-typed Words When Possible option at the bottom of the QuickCorrect dialog box, WordPerfect goes beyond the bounds of the QuickCorrect list in automatically correcting words. If you type any word that's misspelled according to WordPerfect's spell-checking dictionary, the program automatically corrects the word for you. WordPerfect doesn't make the correction, however, if it finds two or more possible ways to correct the mistyped word. If you type *knowledgable,* for example, WordPerfect automatically inserts an *e* before *able.* But if you type *thier,* no correction is made, because WordPerfect doesn't know whether you meant to type *their, thief, tier,* or some other variation of those letters.

Fixing other flubs on the fly

In addition to fixing spelling and typing errors, WordPerfect can make sure that the first letter in a sentence is capitalized, change two uppercase letters in a row into an uppercase letter followed by a lowercase letter (changing *THe* to *The,* for example), eliminate double spaces between words, and convert two spaces at the end of a sentence to a single space.

To turn these features on and off, choose Tools⇨QuickCorrect and click the Format-As-You-Go tab in the QuickCorrect dialog box, as shown in Figure 6-4. The sentence-correction options are located in the top half of the dialog box. (Other options relate to formatting features that you can explore in Chapter 8.)

Click the Exceptions button to enter words or phrases for which you don't want WordPerfect to automatically capitalize the first letter following a period or other end-of-sentence punctuation. For example, if a product name includes such punctuation — as in Microsoft Picture It! — you may want to enter the product name as an exception. Otherwise, the first letter after the punctuation mark is automatically capitalized, as in "Microsoft Picture It! Is designed for the novice photo editor."

Overruling unwanted corrections

As helpful as QuickCorrect can be, it can also get in the way sometimes. Suppose that you want to use the word *august* in its adjectival sense rather than referring to the month — as in, "The king had an august nature." WordPerfect plows right ahead and changes your lowercase *august* to *August.*

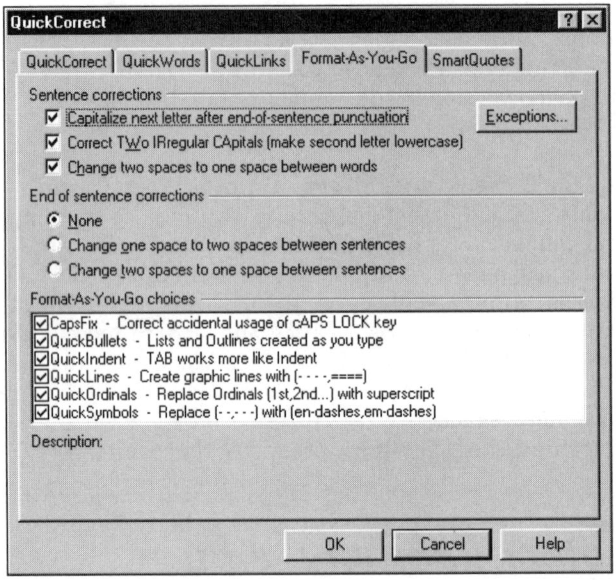

Figure 6-4:
WordPerfect
can also
make
automatic
corrections
to
sentences
with the
options in
this dialog
box.

You can overrule WordPerfect by deleting the word that it's correcting from the QuickCorrect list. Choose Tools⇨QuickCorrect (or press Ctrl+Shift+F1) to open the QuickCorrect dialog box, select the word in the list on the QuickCorrect tab, and click Delete Entry.

If you want WordPerfect to substitute different text after you type a particular word or set of characters, select the original word in the QuickCorrect list, enter the new replacement text in the With option box, and click the Replace Entry button. (This button becomes available after you click the With option box.) Click OK to make your wish the law of the land.

To turn off QuickCorrect altogether, deselect the Replace Words as You Type check box on the QuickCorrect tab of the QuickCorrect dialog box.

Chapter 7

Making Your Text Look Pretty

Creating professional-looking text is an artistic endeavor. And the task involves more than just turning a fancy phrase. You also need to think about things such as type style and size, the amount of spacing between words and letters, and how much to indent lines and paragraphs from the margins.

These design considerations — known collectively as *formatting* — play a significant role in whether people take the time to read your documents. Eye-catching, easy-to-read pages draw in readers and make them more receptive to your message. Poorly designed, difficult-to-read pages become receptacles for used chewing gum (or worse).

This chapter shows you the ins and outs of getting your text ready for public consumption. You find out how to make characters bold and italic, how to control text spacing, and how to perform other feats of formatting magic. In other words, this chapter gives you a chance to explore your artistic side.

 After you get a block of text formatted just the way you like it, you can use the QuickFormat command and paragraph styles to automatically copy the formatting to other text. See Chapter 9 for details.

Playing with Fonts

One of the most noticeable ways to dress up your text is to change the font, type style, and type size.

The *font* — sometimes called *typeface* — determines the shape and design of the characters. Each font has a distinct name, such as Times New Roman, Helvetica, and so on. Figure 7-1 shows a few different fonts for your amusement.

Type style refers to any special formatting attributes applied to the text — boldface, italics, underline, and so on. *Type size* determines, uh, well, how big the characters are. Sorry to insult you.

The following sections explain how to deal with each of these character formatting issues.

Choosing a font

WordPerfect Office 2000 comes with a bunch of fonts, and you may have other fonts installed on your system, too. By default, WordPerfect uses the Times New Roman font, a time-honored, traditional serif font.

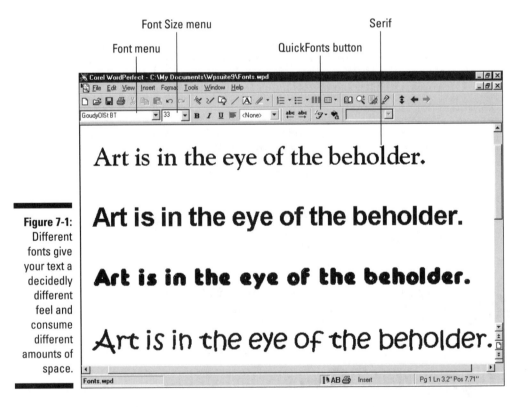

Figure 7-1: Different fonts give your text a decidedly different feel and consume different amounts of space.

A *serif* font is one that has serifs — little lines decorating the upper and lower ends of the strokes of the letters. A *sans serif* font has no serifs (*sans serif* means "without serifs" in French). The top example shown in Figure 7-1 is a serif font; the other three are sans serif fonts.

For long blocks of text, use a serif font, which is easier to read. Sans serif fonts are best used for headlines, subheads, and other short blocks of text.

Notice that characters in different fonts can be markedly different not only in design, but also in the amount of space they take up. All four lines in Figure 7-1 use 33-point type, but the first line is significantly shorter than the other three. The line isn't shorter because it's set in a serif font, but because of the thickness of the characters in that particular font. Character widths vary greatly from font to font, sans serif or serif aside.

Most people love to play with fonts. But keep in mind that the more fonts you install, the more you tax your computer. So be selective, and install only those fonts that you're really going to use.

Now that you've completed Fonts 101, you're ready for the exciting part — actually applying a font. The following list serves as your font-changing manual:

 ✔ If you select a piece of text before choosing a font, the new font is applied to the selected text only. If you don't select text, the font is applied to all text from the insertion marker forward, up to the point where you previously applied a font change.

 ✔ To change the font for a single word, just click anywhere in the word and then select the font.

 ✔ So how do you pick a font? The easiest method is to click the arrow at the end of the Font menu (refer to Figure 7-1), which lives on the Property Bar. WordPerfect displays a list of all fonts installed in your system. Click the font you want to use.

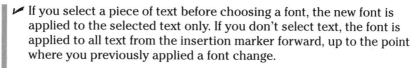

 As you pass your cursor over each font name, WordPerfect displays a preview to the side of the drop-down list to show you what the font looks like. This feature was available in Version 8, but Version 9 goes one step farther. If you have the RealTime Preview option enabled, WordPerfect also temporarily displays your actual document text in the font. For details about enabling RealTime Preview, see Chapter 4.

 ✔ The Font Properties dialog box, revealed in Figure 7-2, provides another method of applying fonts. To display the dialog box, choose Format⇨Font, press F9, or right-click in the document window and choose Font from the QuickMenu. Select the font from the Face list in the upper-left corner of the dialog box. While in the dialog box, you can also apply a variety of text formatting attributes, including type size, style, color, and shading. See the next section for the inside scoop on these formatting attributes. Note that although WordPerfect displays a preview of the font at the bottom of the dialog box, you don't have the advantage of the RealTime Preview feature using this method of choosing fonts.

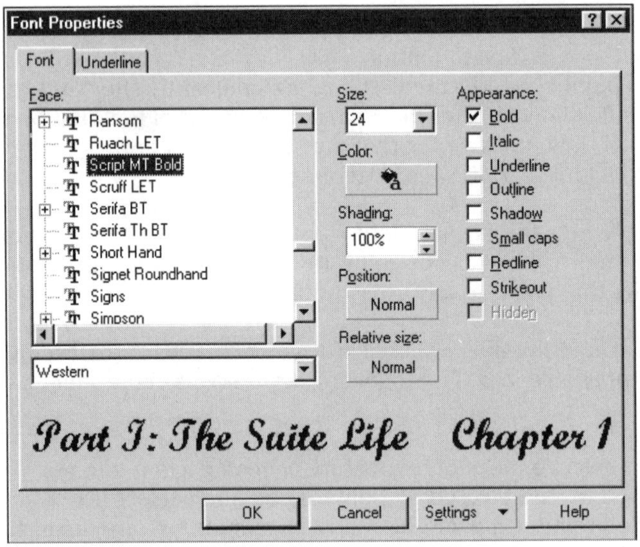

Figure 7-2:
The Font
Properties
dialog box
gives you a
way to set
several type
options at
once.

✔ To quickly apply a font that you recently used, click the QuickFonts button on the Property Bar. WordPerfect displays a list of the most recent font combinations (font, size, and style) you've used. Click the font combination you want to apply.

✔ The default font is applied to all text unless you choose another font. As in past versions of WordPerfect, you can change the default font and type size. But the process is different in Version 9: First make sure that no text is selected. Then press F9 to open the Font Properties dialog box and choose your font and font size. Then click the Settings button to display a small menu of options. Select the Set Face and Point Size as Default for All Documents option to use your settings as defaults for the current document and for any new documents you create. If you select the Set Face and Point Size as Default for This Document option, the defaults apply to the current document only, and the previously set defaults are used for any new documents.

Whichever option you choose, WordPerfect applies the new defaults to all text in the current document that used the original defaults. If you previously applied a different font, size, or style to a piece of text, however, WordPerfect leaves that formatting intact.

Changing the type size and style

As with font changes, changes to type size and style affect any text from the insertion marker forward *except* for text you previously formatted. If you want to change the size or style for a specific portion of text, select the text and then apply your formatting changes.

With that piece of news implanted in your mind, you're qualified to fool around with the following text attributes:

✔ **Type size:** For quick size changes, use the Font Size menu on the Property Bar (refer to Figure 7-1). Click the down-pointing arrow to display a menu of type sizes and then click the size you want to use. If you want to use a size not on the list — for example, 12.5-point type — double-click the option box to the left of the arrow, enter the size you want, and press Enter. Alternatively, you can change the type size in the Font Properties dialog box (press F9 or choose Format⇨Font). Select a size from the Size menu, which works just like the Font Size menu on the Property Bar.

You can use the Relative Size button in the Font Properties dialog box to make your text proportionally larger or smaller than the current font size. Click the button to display a menu of choices — options at the top of the list make the font proportionally smaller; options at the bottom, proportionally larger. The option stays in effect until you change the font back to Normal. You probably aren't going to have much use for this option.

Type size is measured in *points.* A point is roughly equivalent to ¹⁄₇₂ inch. If you want people to be able to read your text easily, don't use type smaller than 10 points.

✔ **Bold, Italics:** These type style options are available via the Property Bar. Click the **B** button to make text bold, the *I* button to make it italic. The Property Bar buttons *toggle* the styles on and off — click the button once to turn the style on; click again to turn the style off. You can also use the shortcut keys for these styles: Ctrl+B, Ctrl+I, respectively. Pressing the shortcut once turns the style on; pressing the keys a second time turns the style off.

You can also apply these style options by choosing them from the Appearance options inside the Font Properties dialog box (press F9 to open the dialog box).

You may see a plus sign to the left of some font names in the Font dialog box. If you click the plus sign, you can access bold, italic, or bold italic versions of the font (and sometimes, all three). Font designers often provide these special versions of their typefaces because not all programs apply boldface and italics the same way. By choosing the special version of the font, you know that you're seeing the font as the designer intended. You don't need to worry about the distinction unless you're sending your document to a service bureau for professional printing. In that case, use the special version of the font, because applying the program's bold and italics attributes instead may cause problems.

✔ **Underline:** Click the U button or press Ctrl+U to underline text; click or press the shortcut keys again to turn off the underlining.

Want to get fancy with your underlining? Press F9 to open the Font Properties dialog box and then click the Underline tab to display a slew of underlining options. You can choose a different line style, change the color of the line, and specify whether you want to underline text only, both text and the spaces between words, text and spaces between tab stops, or all of the above. You can even establish a new default underline style by clicking the Settings button. WordPerfect then uses the new underline style when you add an underline via the Property Bar button or keyboard shortcut. See the last bullet point in the preceding section for information on setting the default.

✔ **Special text effects:** Several of the Appearance attributes available in the Font Properties dialog box apply special effects to your type. You can create shadowed type, outlined type, double-underlined type, and more. You can apply as many attributes as your conscience allows; just check the boxes of the ones that strike your fancy. (***Hint:*** Unless you want people to run away screaming after taking one look at your text, use these effects sparingly.)

✔ **Superscript and subscript:** Click the Position button in the Font Properties dialog box to reveal the superscript and subscript options. Click the option you want to use. Leave the setting on Normal for normal text. (Did you guess that one already?)

✔ **Font color:** You can change the font color quickly by clicking the Font Color button on the Property Bar. WordPerfect displays a selection of color swatches; click the swatch that you want to use. Click the More button to access a color wheel that enables you to create a custom color. Drag the little square in the color wheel to choose the basic hue; drag the square in the neighboring slider bar to make the color darker or lighter. Inside the Font Properties dialog box (press F9 to display the dialog box), click the Color button to access these same color options.

✔ **Shading:** For this option, which changes the translucency of your text, you must open the Font Properties dialog box (press F9). Set the Shading value lower than 100% to make your text partially transparent so that whatever is behind the text becomes visible. Set the value at 100% for fully opaque (non-transparent) text.

✔ **Highlighting:** Ever had one of those neon yellow highlighter pens? The kind people use to mark important stuff in reports, textbooks, and such? You can create a similar highlighting effect in WordPerfect by clicking the Highlighter button on the toolbar or by choosing Tools⇨Highlight⇨ On. The cursor changes to a little highlighter pen. Drag across the text you want to highlight. To change the color that the pen applies, click the down-pointing arrow on the Highlighter button to display a bunch of

Why won't WordPerfect do what I tell it to?

If you can't get a particular formatting command to work the way it's supposed to — or applying a formatting command gives you unexpected results — it's probably because you've messed up your document's *hidden codes.* You see, any time that you give WordPerfect a formatting instruction, the program inserts little hidden codes into your text. Moving text around, deleting text, and removing and reapplying formatting can sometimes mess up these hidden codes.

If things get screwy, one solution is to open the Reveal Codes window shown in the following figure. Press Alt+F3 or choose View⇨Reveal Codes to display the window. (Choose the command again to hide the window.) If you're familiar with WordPerfect's codes, you can take a stab at sorting out the formatting codes to

figure out what went wrong. If you want to become a hidden-code guru, check out *WordPerfect 9 For Windows For Dummies,* by Margaret Levine Young, David C. Kay, Jordan M. Young, and Kathy Warfel (IDG Books Worldwide, Inc.), which offers an in-depth explanation of the subject.

If playing in the Reveal Codes Amusement Park makes you queasy, however, simply try selecting the text you want to format and reissuing the formatting command. If you still don't get the results you want, check the style applied to the text. (Chapter 9 discusses styles.) Try applying the None style and then applying your formatting again. If things still don't work right, you need a WordPerfect guru to help you clean up your hidden codes.

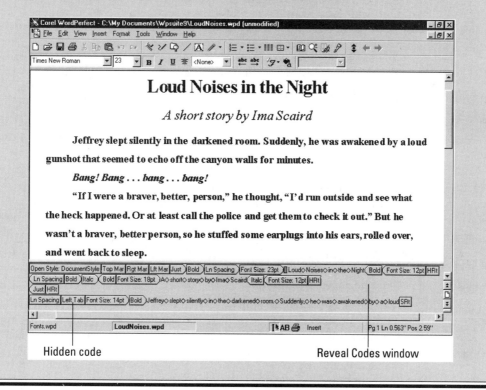

Hidden code   Reveal Codes window

color swatches. Click the color you want to use. Or choose Tools➪Highlight➪Color to display a dialog box where you can adjust both the color and transparency of the highlight.

Turn on the Print/Show option on the Tools➪Highlight submenu to see the highlighting on-screen and in your printed document. (If you see a check mark next to the Print/Show command, the option is turned on. Click the command to toggle the feature on and off.) Click the highlighter button or choose Tools➪Highlight➪On again to put the pen away.

Choosing a Page Size and Orientation

When you create a standard new document, WordPerfect gives you an 8½-x-11-inch page size, with text oriented in *portrait* position — that is, with text running parallel to the short edge of the paper. This position is called portrait, by the way, because portraits normally use this same orientation. If you turn the page on its side, you get *landscape* orientation — so named because landscape paintings typically use this layout.

If you choose one of the PerfectExpert templates to create your document, WordPerfect selects a page size that's appropriate for the document. You can change the page size and/or orientation at your whim, however. Here's how:

✔ To change the page size, choose File➪Page Setup or press Ctrl+F8. The Page Setup dialog box opens. On the Size tab, shown in Figure 7-3, choose a page size and orientation (known collectively as a *page definition*) by making a selection from the Page Definition list box. Click the Portrait or Landscape radio button to set the page orientation.

Select the Following Pages Different from Current Page check box to display a second set of page size and orientation options. These options affect the pages following the current page, just as the name implies.

✔ If one of the preset page definitions isn't sufficient, click the Options button near the lower-right corner of the dialog box. Choose the New option to create a new page definition or choose Edit to edit an existing page definition.

✔ All page definitions that you apply take effect from the insertion marker through the end of your document or to the point where you previously set a new page definition.

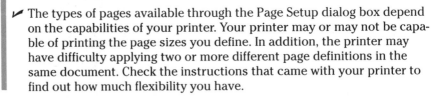

✔ The types of pages available through the Page Setup dialog box depend on the capabilities of your printer. Your printer may or may not be capable of printing the page sizes you define. In addition, the printer may have difficulty applying two or more different page definitions in the same document. Check the instructions that came with your printer to find out how much flexibility you have.

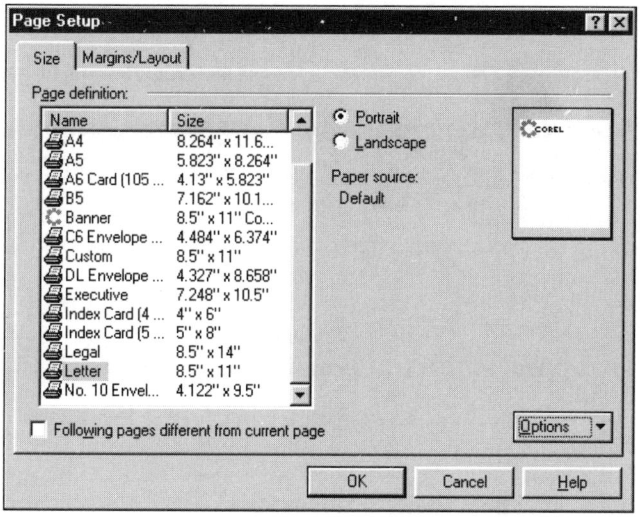

Figure 7-3:
Choose your
page size
and orienta-
tion on the
Size tab of
the Page
Setup dialog
box.

> If you want to create and print labels or envelopes, bypass the Page Setup dialog box and instead turn to Chapter 9, where you find information on a quicker option.

Setting Page Margins

See those dotted lines running across the top, bottom, left, and right sides of your page? Those are *margin guidelines*. (If the guidelines don't appear on-screen, choose View⇨Guidelines, select the Margins check box in the Guidelines dialog box, and click OK.) To change a margin, all you need to do is move your cursor over the guideline until it changes into a two-headed arrow, as shown in Figure 7-4. Then drag the guideline to a new position. As you drag the guideline, a little box appears to show you the cursor's distance from the edge of the page.

If you prefer, you can use the following methods for setting margins instead:

✔ Press Ctrl+F8 to open the Page Setup dialog box with the Margins/Layout tab active. Enter your margin settings into the Left, Right, Top, and Bottom option boxes and click OK.

To set equal margins all the way around the page, enter a value into any option box and then click the Equal button to put the same value in the other three option boxes. Click the Minimum button to set each margin to the minimum size allowed by your selected printer.

Margin guideline

Left margin control   Ruler   Margin move cursor   Right margin control

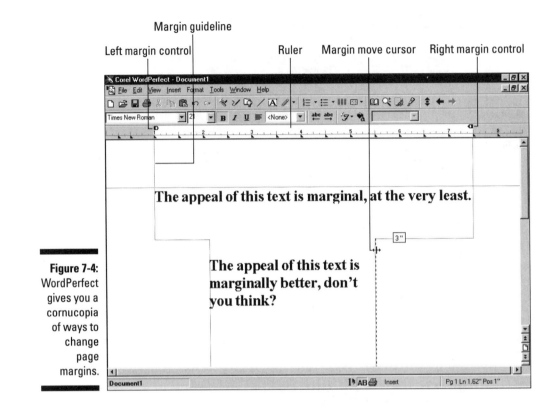

Figure 7-4:
WordPerfect
gives you a
cornucopia
of ways to
change
page
margins.

> Drag the left and right margin controls on the ruler (refer to Figure 7-4). If the ruler isn't visible, choose <u>V</u>iew➪<u>R</u>uler or press Alt+Shift+F3 to display it. Make sure that you drag the margin controls — the left- and right-most black thingies on the ruler — and not the neighboring diamond-shaped black icons, which set indents for individual paragraphs.

Left and right margin settings affect text from the point of the insertion marker forward and remain in effect until you enter new settings or WordPerfect encounters another margin setting that you previously established. Top and bottom margin settings affect the current page and any subsequent pages up to the point where you enter new settings or previously changed the margins. If you want, you can also apply margin settings to selected text only.

Setting Tabs

Please place your left hand on your computer monitor — on the top, not the screen (fingerprints, you know) — and repeat this pledge: "I hereby swear to always use tabs instead of spaces to line things up in columns." Why? Well, for one thing, it's a heck of a lot easier to press the Tab key once instead of hitting the spacebar a zillion times to shove text across the page. But more important, your text may not line up correctly if you use spaces, as Figure 7-5 demonstrates. The entries in the Class, Major, and Age columns are slightly misaligned in the top example.

Figure 7-5:
With spaces between column entries, text doesn't align exactly (top). If you use tabs, everything lines up neat and tidy-like (bottom).

NAME	CLASS	MAJOR	AGE
NAME···············	·······CLASS···············	·····MAJOR···········	·AGE
Bob·Parwood·············	·······Freshman···············	·····History···············	18
Suzannah·Dainings·······	Senior···············	·····Comm.···············	22
Tim·Misi···············	Sophomore···············	Music···············	20

NAME→	CLASS→	MAJOR→	AGE
Bob·Parwood→	Freshman→	History→	18
Suzannah·Dainings→	Senior→	Comm.→	22
Tim·Misi→	Sophomore→	Music→	20

This alignment problem happens because many fonts aren't *fixed-width* fonts — in other words, different characters vary in width. (This kind of font is known as a *proportional* font, by the way.) So if you type *Mary* and press the spacebar four times, you don't end up at the same spot as you do if you type *Jill* and press the spacebar four times. In addition, the width of a space varies depending on the font you're using. Tabs, on the other hand, move the insertion marker to a specific spot on the page, so everything lines up as it should. The bottom example in Figure 7-5 proves the point.

Don't use tabs to indent the first line of a paragraph, however. Instead, use the first-line indent option explained in the section "Indenting the first line of your paragraphs," later in this chapter.

If you're new to tabs, here's how they work: Each time you press the Tab key, WordPerfect moves the insertion marker to the next available tab stop to the right. Press Shift+Tab and you move the insertion marker to the previous tab stop — a procedure known in WordPerfect clubs as *back tabbing*.

By default, WordPerfect gives you a tab stop every half inch across the page. In many cases, you need to override the default tab stops and set your own custom tab stops. The following sections tell you what you need to know to work with tabs.

Adding, moving, or deleting a tab stop

If you add, move, or delete a tab stop, the new setting takes effect from the current paragraph forward to the end of the document or to the point where you change the tab settings again or previously changed tab settings. If you select a paragraph before changing a tab stop, the change affects the selected paragraph only.

The easiest way to set a tab is to use the ruler. (If the ruler isn't visible, choose View➪Ruler or press Alt+Shift+F3.) The little black triangles at the bottom of the ruler represent the tab stops. For a look at a tab stop, check out Figure 7-6.

You can add, move, and delete tab stops with one swift click or drag, as follows:

- By default, WordPerfect adds a standard left tab when you click the ruler. (Click in the bottom half of the ruler, not the top.) To set a different type of tab, right-click the bottom half of the ruler, choose the tab type you want from the QuickMenu that appears, and then click the ruler at the spot where you want to add the tab stop. (The following section explains your options in more detail.) After you select a new tab type, that type becomes the default tab style. So you can add more tab stops of the same type by simply clicking the ruler.

- To move a tab stop, drag it along the ruler.

- To delete a tab stop, drag it down off the ruler.

You can also set tab stops in the Tab Set dialog box, shown in Figure 7-7. To open the dialog box, choose Format➪Line➪Tab Set or right-click the ruler and choose Tab Set from the QuickMenu. In the dialog box, enter the tab stop position in the Tab Position option box and click Set and Close to close the dialog box. To enter more than one tab stop, enter Set instead of Set and Close. Keep entering tab positions and clicking Set to establish each tab stop. Click Set and Close after you enter all your tab stops.

To remove a tab stop inside the Tab Set dialog box, enter the position of the stop you want to remove in the Tab Position box. Then click Clear. (But really, dragging the tab stop off the ruler is easier.)

Here's some more stuff you need to know about changing your tab stops:

- You can choose from four major tab types, each of which aligns and formats tabbed text differently, as explained in the following section.

- Normally, WordPerfect measures tab stops from the left margin of your page. But you can tell the program to measure them from the left edge of the page, if you prefer. WordPerfect calls tabs measured from the left margin of the page *relative tabs*; tabs measured from the edge of the page are *absolute tabs*. You can specify which option you want by selecting one of the Tab Position radio buttons in the Tab Set dialog box.

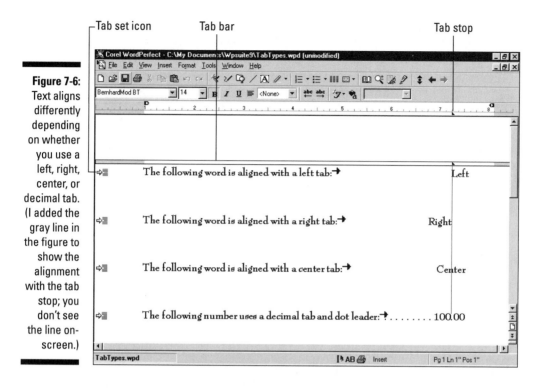

Tab set icon   Tab bar   Tab stop

Figure 7-6:
Text aligns
differently
depending
on whether
you use a
left, right,
center, or
decimal tab.
(I added the
gray line in
the figure to
show the
alignment
with the tab
stop; you
don't see
the line on-
screen.)

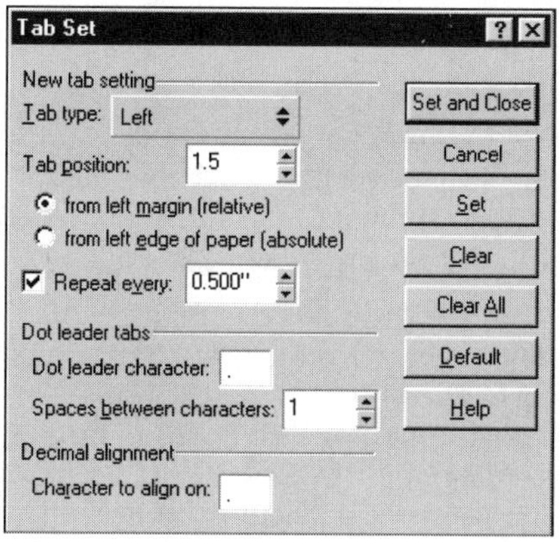

Figure 7-7:
The Tab Set
dialog box
lets you get
specific
about how
you want
tabbed text
to appear.

✔ After you add, delete, or move a tab stop, WordPerfect displays an icon in the left margin of the screen (refer to Figure 7-6). If you click the icon, you get a *tab bar,* which is a miniature version of the ruler. You can use the tab bar to change the tab settings for the paragraph just as you do on the ruler bar.

Click outside the tab bar to hide it again. (If the tab stop icons don't appear, choose Tools⇨Settings or press Alt+F12 to open the Settings dialog box, click the Display icon to open the Display Settings dialog box, and turn on the Margin Icons check box on the Document tab.)

✔ If you see a little balloon with quotation marks instead of the normal tab set icon, you've inserted more than one formatting instruction or another element, such as a sound clip (as explained in Chapter 22). Click the icon to display the individual formatting icons and then click the tab icon to display the tab bar.

✔ You can tell WordPerfect to space tabs at a specified increment across the page — for example, setting a tab stop every 3 inches. To do so, set the position of the first tab in the Tab Position option box of the Tab Set dialog box, check the Repeat Every check box, and specify the distance between tabs in the adjacent option box.

✔ To clear all tab stops, right-click a tab stop on the ruler and choose Clear All Tabs from the QuickMenu. Or choose the Clear All button in the Tab Set dialog box. Be sure to right-click a tab stop or in the bottom portion of the ruler where the tab stops are located. Otherwise, you get a different QuickMenu that doesn't have all the tab-related options.

✔ To return to the default tab stops — a left tab every half inch across the page — right-click a tab stop on the ruler and choose Default Tab Settings from the QuickMenu. Or choose the Default button in the Tab Set dialog box.

✔ If the QuickIndent feature is turned on, pressing Tab creates a paragraph indent instead of an ordinary tab in some situations. For more information about this feature, see the section "Indenting entire paragraphs," later in this chapter.

✔ The Tab key functions differently in Typeover mode than it does in Insert mode. (See Chapter 4 for an explanation of these editing modes.) In Typeover mode, pressing Tab moves the insertion marker across a line of text from one tab stop to the next but doesn't insert a tab. If no text is present, pressing Tab does insert a tab.

✔ By default, you can position a tab stop directly on a tick mark (gray dividing line) on the ruler or exactly between two tick marks. If you want to position a tab somewhere else, you have two options. You can set the tab by entering a specific position in the Tab Position option box of the Tab Set dialog box, or you can change the way the ruler works. Right-click anywhere on the ruler and choose Settings from the QuickMenu to open the Ruler tab of the Display Settings dialog box. Deselect the Tabs Snap to Ruler Grid check box and click OK.

Choosing a tab stop type

WordPerfect gives you four major types of tab stops, which you choose either from the Type drop-down list in the Tab Set dialog box or by right-clicking a tab stop (or the area where the tab stops appear), choosing a tab

REMEMBER

When should I take a paragraph break?

As you enter text, don't press the Enter key after you get to the end of a line, as you do on some typewriters. WordPerfect automatically wraps your text to the next line for you. Pressing Enter inserts a *hard return*.

A hard return tells WordPerfect that one paragraph ends and another begins — which is why a hard return also goes by the name *paragraph break*. If you select a paragraph, WordPerfect grabs everything from the paragraph break preceding the insertion marker to the paragraph break after the insertion marker. WordPerfect also relies on the hard returns to tell it which text to change after you apply certain paragraph-level formatting, such as line spacing, paragraph indents, and paragraph spacing.

The moral of the story: Press Enter at the end of a line of text only if you want to end the paragraph. If you want to break text at the end of a line but don't want to start a new paragraph, press Ctrl+Shift+L.

type from the resulting QuickMenu, and then clicking the ruler to insert the tab. If you want to change an existing tab stop, click the tab stop instead of the ruler after you select the tab type.

Your tab type options, as shown in Figure 7-6, are as follows:

- ✔ **Left:** Text aligns to the right of the tab stop. A left tab stop on the ruler looks like this: ◣
- ✔ **Right:** Text aligns to the left of the tab stop. A right tab stop looks like this: ◢
- ✔ **Center:** Text is centered on the tab stop. A center tab stop looks like this: ▲
- ✔ **Decimal:** The decimal point lines up with the tab stop. This setting is normally used to align columns of numbers. A decimal tab stop looks like this: ▲

    By default, decimal tabs align text by the decimal point (the period). But you can change the character on which text aligns by entering a new one in the Character to Align On option box in the Tab Set dialog box. If, for example, you have a column of numbers that incorporate commas but no decimal points — such as $95,000 — you can set the align character to a comma. If the align character is a decimal point, but your numbers don't have decimal points, the numbers align by the last digit.

- ✔ You can put a *dot leader* into your tabbed text by choosing the Dot Left, Dot Right, Dot Center, or Dot Decimal options from the Tab Type drop-down list of the Tab Set dialog box. On the QuickMenu that appears when you right-click a tab stop, the options appear as ...Decimal, ...Right, and so on.

Dot leaders help guide the reader's eye across columns of text, as you can see in the last example shown in Figure 7-6. You can change the character used for the dot leader by entering a new one in the Dot Leader Character option box in the Tab Set dialog box. You can also vary the amount of space between each dot leader by changing the Spaces Between Characters value.

Indenting and Aligning Text

Pressing the Tab key isn't the only way to shove text across the page. You can also use WordPerfect's indent and justification options to change the way that text fits between the left and right margins of your page.

Indenting the first line of your paragraphs

If you want to indent the first line of each paragraph in your document, use indents instead of tabs. Why? Well, suppose that you use a tab to indent every paragraph in a long document. Then you decide that you don't want to indent those paragraphs after all. If you use tabs, you must remove the tab from every paragraph. If you use indents, on the other hand, all you need to do is change the indent setting to zero.

If you apply a first-line indent without any text selected, WordPerfect indents the first line of every paragraph after the insertion marker, up to the point where you apply another indent or you previously indented a paragraph. If you select text before applying a first-line indent, only the selected paragraphs are affected.

The quickest way to bump in the first line of your paragraphs is to drag the first-line indent control on the ruler. Labeled in Figure 7-8, the control is the top little triangle just to the right of the left margin control.

If you have trouble using the control — grabbing that tiny triangle can be a challenge — follow these steps instead:

1. **Choose Format⇨Paragraph⇨Format.**

   WordPerfect displays the Paragraph Format dialog box, as shown in Figure 7-9.

2. **Enter the amount of the indent in the First Line Indent option box.**

3. **Click OK or press Enter.**

To remove first-line indents, just change the First Line Indent value back to zero.

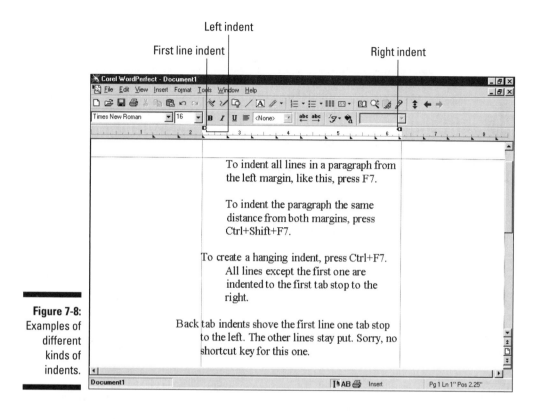

Figure 7-8:
Examples of
different
kinds of
indents.

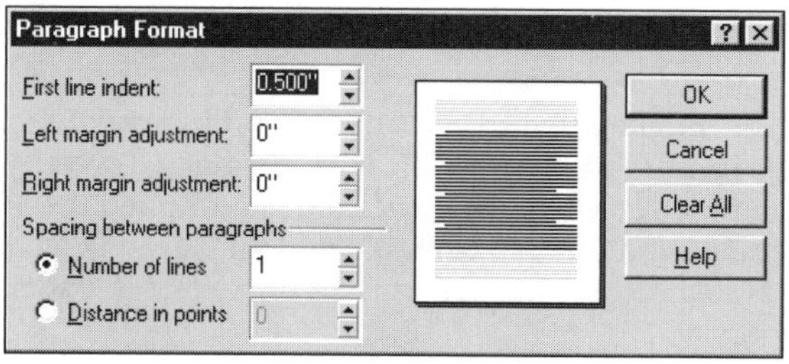

Figure 7-9:
Use the First
Line Indent
option to
indent the
first line of
paragraphs.

Indenting entire paragraphs

As Figure 7-8 shows, you can also indent the entire paragraph from the left margin, indent the paragraph from both the right and left margins (called a double indent), and indent all but the first line of a paragraph (called a hanging indent). In addition, you can create what WordPerfect calls a *back tab,* which shoves the first line of a paragraph one tab stop to the left.

To apply these indents, first select the paragraphs you want to indent. If no text is selected, the indenting is applied from the current paragraph forward, up to the point where WordPerfect encounters any previously set indents or you establish a new indent. Then choose Format⇨Paragraph and choose an indent option from the Paragraph submenu. Or, to bypass the menus, use the keyboard shortcuts listed in Table 7-1 or drag the paragraph indent controls on the ruler bar (labeled in Figure 7-8).

With the exception of the first-line indents, WordPerfect indents your text according to the tab stops you set. To change the amount of indent, you have to change the tab stops, as explained earlier in this chapter.

Table 7-1	Indent Options and Shortcuts	
Indent Type	*Shortcut*	*What It Does*
First Line Indent	None	Indents the first line of a paragraph.
Indent	F7	Indents all lines of a paragraph one tab stop to the right.
Double Indent	Ctrl+Shift+F7	Moves all lines of a paragraph inward one tab stop from the left margin and an equal distance from the right margin.
Hanging Indent	Ctrl+F7	Indents all lines of a paragraph except the first line one tab stop to the right.
Back Tab	None	Moves the first line of a paragraph one tab stop to the left.

You can also use the Tab key to create standard and hanging indents if the QuickIndent feature is turned on, which it is by default. (To verify that QuickIndent is enabled, select Tools⇨QuickCorrect to open the QuickCorrect dialog box, click the Format-As-You-Go tab, and look at the QuickIndent check box. A check mark means the feature is turned on; click the check box to turn QuickIndent off.)

To create your indents using QuickIndent, move the insertion marker to the beginning of any line in the paragraph *except the first line*. Whacking the Tab key then delivers the following results:

  ✔ If the first line in the paragraph doesn't begin with a tab, WordPerfect gives you a hanging indent. Press Tab a second time to shove the whole paragraph one tab stop to the right. Press Shift+Tab to shove the hanging-indent lines (all but the first line) one tab stop to the left.

> ✔ If the first line does begin with a tab, the tab is simply converted to a standard indent. Press Tab again to apply a hanging indent, moving all lines but the first line one tab stop to the right. Now the Tab and Shift+Tab combination work as described in the preceding bullet point.

To remove an indent, place the insertion marker at the beginning of the paragraph (press Ctrl+Up Arrow to get there quickly). Press Backspace once to remove a standard indent, double indent, or back tab. Press Backspace twice to remove a hanging indent.

Justifying text

Another way to change the amount of space between the edges of a paragraph and the left and right margins is to change the *justification*, sometimes referred to as *alignment*. Figure 7-10 shows the five available alignment options: Left, Right, Center, Full, and All.

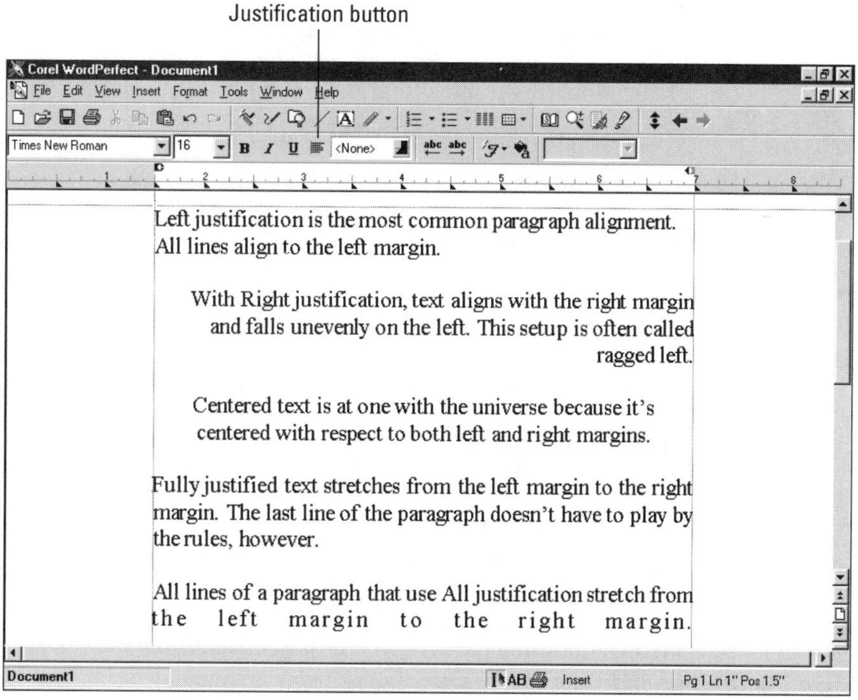

Justification button

Figure 7-10: Use the alignment options to align text in different ways in relationship to the left and right margins.

- ✔ *Left justification* aligns all lines in a paragraph to the left margin. This alignment is sometimes called *ragged right* because the right edge of the paragraph has an uneven look.

- ✔ *Right justification* aligns the paragraph to the right margin and is sometimes known as *ragged left* because of the appearance of the left edge of the paragraph.

- ✔ *Center justification* centers each line between the left and right margins.

- ✔ *Full justification* spaces the text so that all lines align perfectly with both the left and the right margin — except for the last line of the paragraph, which simply aligns with the left margin. Sometimes, WordPerfect needs to add spaces throughout the text in a line to justify it. Other times, text gets crammed closer together.

- ✔ *All justification* is the same as Full justification except that the last line of the paragraph is fully justified along with all the other lines. As you can see from the last example in Figure 7-10, this option can result in awkwardly spaced text.

As with other formatting commands, justification affects all paragraphs from the insertion marker forward through the rest of the document, up to the point where you choose a different justification option or previously changed the justification. If you select text before applying a justification command, the justification affects the selected paragraph only.

Here's a rundown of the various and sundry ways to change the justification:

- ✔ Click the Justification button on the Property Bar and select an option from the drop-down list.

- ✔ Choose Format➪Justification and choose an option from the Justification submenu.

- ✔ Press the justification shortcut keys: Ctrl+L for Left justification; Ctrl+R for Right justification; Ctrl+E for Center justification; and Ctrl+J for Full justification. The fact that there is no shortcut key for the All justification option should be a clue that this isn't a terrific option in most cases.

WordPerfect also enables you to right-justify and center a single line or part of a line of text. You may want to have the name of a document align with the left margin of the page, for example, and have the day's date align with the right margin. This technique works only on single lines; you can't right-justify one line in a multiline paragraph unless you insert a line break (Ctrl+Shift+L) at the end of the line.

Your options are as follows:

- ✔ To right-justify an entire line, place the insertion marker at the beginning of the line (press Home to get there quickly). Then choose Format➪Line➪ Flush Right or press Alt+F7.

✔ To right-justify part of a line, place the insertion marker before the text you want to justify and then choose the Flush Right command.

✔ To add dot leaders before the justified text, choose Format⇨Line⇨Flush Right with Dot Leaders. (I explain dot leaders in the section "Choosing a tab stop type," earlier in this chapter.)

✔ To center a line, choose Format⇨Line⇨Center or press Shift+F7.

✔ If you right-click at the beginning of the text you want to justify, you can choose the Center or Flush Right command from a QuickMenu.

✔ To remove the justification, put the insertion marker at the beginning of the justified text and press Backspace.

Spacing Things Out

The amount of space between lines and paragraphs in your text has a dramatic effect on how readable and attractive your document appears. Text that's all squished together is difficult to read and looks intimidating (just take a look at any legal document). On the other hand, text that's too spaced out is also difficult to read because the reader's eye must work too hard to get from one character to the next. Examples of some too-tight text, too-loose text, and just-right text are shown in Figure 7-11.

Adjusting line spacing

To adjust the amount of space between lines in a paragraph — a value known in typesetting circles as *leading* (pronounced *ledding*)— click at the point where you want the line spacing to change or select the paragraph you want to format. Then choose Format⇨Line⇨Spacing to display the Line Spacing dialog box, as shown in Figure 7-12. Enter the value you want to use in the option box and click OK or press Enter.

Adjusting the space between paragraphs

Just as line spacing sets the amount of space between lines in a paragraph, paragraph spacing sets the amount of space between paragraphs. (Sorry, I probably didn't need to explain that to you, did I?)

Anyhow, paragraph spacing works similarly to line spacing in that, if you select a paragraph before adjusting the spacing, your changes affect only that paragraph. If you don't select anything, your changes apply from the insertion marker forward, up to the point at which you inserted any previous paragraph spacing changes.

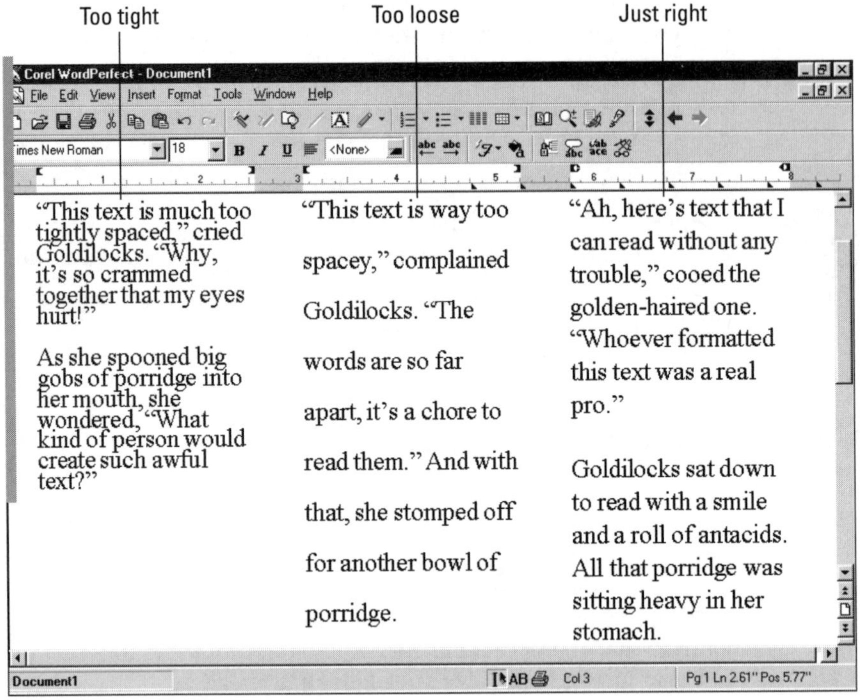
Too tight
Too loose
Just right
Corel WordPerfect - Document1
File Edit View Insert Format Tools Window Help
Times New Roman
18
<None>
"This text is much too tightly spaced," cried Goldilocks. "Why, it's so crammed together that my eyes hurt!"
As she spooned big gobs of porridge into her mouth, she wondered, "What kind of person would create such awful text?"
"This text is way too spacey," complained Goldilocks. "The words are so far apart, it's a chore to read them." And with that, she stomped off for another bowl of porridge.
"Ah, here's text that I can read without any trouble," cooed the golden-haired one. "Whoever formatted this text was a real pro."
Goldilocks sat down to read with a smile and a roll of antacids. All that porridge was sitting heavy in her stomach.
Document1
Col 3
Pg 1 Ln 2.61" Pos 5.77"

Figure 7-11: Text that's spaced too closely together or too far apart can give readers indigestion.

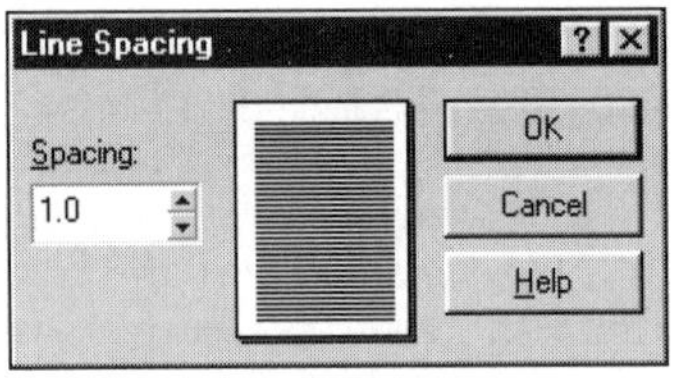
Line Spacing
Spacing:
1.0
OK
Cancel
Help

Figure 7-12: Set line spacing in this dialog box.

After you ponder that bit of news, here's how to move forward to adjust the paragraph spacing:

1. **Choose Format➪Paragraph➪Format.**

   The Paragraph Format dialog box opens. (You probably remember this dialog box from Figure 7-9.)

2. **Enter a value in the Number of Lines option box.**

   TIP: You can enter custom values, such as 1.25, by double-clicking the option box and then typing the number.

If you prefer to make your paragraph spacing measurements in points instead of lines, select the Distance in Points radio button and enter the spacing value in that option box instead.

3. Click OK or press Enter.

Centering text on a page

If you want your document text to be perfectly centered between the top and bottom margins on your page — you perfectionist, you — move the insertion marker to the beginning of the text you want to center. Choose Format⇨Page⇨Center to open the Center Page(s) dialog box and choose a radio button to specify whether you want to center the current page of text or the current page and any subsequent pages. Press Enter to scoot your text smack-dab in the vertical center of the page.

If you later want to remove the centering, choose the Center command again and select the No Centering radio button in the Center Page(s) dialog box.

Making Text Fit on a Page

WordPerfect has a nifty little feature called *Make It Fit* that automatically adjusts your margins, font sizes, and line spacing so that your text fits neatly on the page.

Version 9 offers an enhanced Make It Fit command. In past editions of WordPerfect, the feature affected the entire document. Now you can adjust the settings of selected paragraphs only, leaving the rest of the document alone.

To apply the Make It Fit feature to your whole document, make sure that no text is selected. Then choose Format⇨Make It Fit to open the Make It Fit dialog box, shown in Figure 7-13.

In the dialog box, specify how many pages you want the text to consume and which formatting items WordPerfect can play with in laying out the pages. Click the Make It Fit button to see what WordPerfect can do. If you don't like the results, click the Undo button or press Ctrl+Z to put things back the way they were.

If you want to reformat only part of the document, select the paragraphs you want to adjust before choosing the Make It Fit command. When you go this route, the Top Margin and Bottom Margin adjustment options are unavailable.

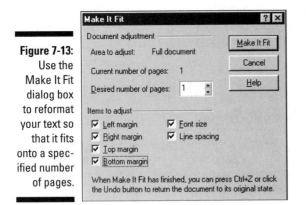

Figure 7-13:
Use the
Make It Fit
dialog box
to reformat
your text so
that it fits
onto a spec-
ified number
of pages.

Chapter 8

Doing the Fancy Stuff

● ●

In This Chapter

▶ Creating bulleted and numbered lists

▶ Inserting page numbers, dates, and special characters

▶ Adding headers and footers

▶ Putting text into columns

▶ Inserting graphics

▶ Creating lines, borders, and fills

● ●

*I*n their earliest incarnations, word processors did little more than, well, process words. You could cut, copy, and paste text, make words italic or bold, and play with margins and paragraph indents — but that was about it. If you wanted to do anything more complicated, such as add a picture to a page or put your text in columns, you turned the work over to the publishing department or sent it out to a printing company.

Today, WordPerfect gives you the power to handle many page layout and design tasks right at your desk. As you find out in this chapter, you can create bulleted and numbered lists, add headers and footers, and get WordPerfect to number your pages automatically. And, if you need even fancier pages, you can insert graphics, put text in columns, and add borders and backgrounds to elements on the page.

Creating Bulleted and Numbered Lists

One of the most common design devices used in everyday documents is the bulleted or numbered list. WordPerfect gives you several ways to create these lists easily.

To add bullets before paragraphs that you've already typed, follow these steps:

1. Select the paragraphs to which you want to add bullets.

2. **Click the arrow on the Bullets button on the toolbar.**

   A menu of bullet styles appears.

3. **Click a bullet style.**

   WordPerfect applies the Bullet formatting style, which inserts the bullet character before each paragraph and indents the text following the bullet.

Now that you have the basic bullet technique under your belt, investigate a few more bullet-making options — presented in a bulleted list, of course.

✔ After you select a bullet style from the Bullets menu, you can simply click the face of the Bullets menu button to apply that same style of bullet again. No need to display the menu.

✔ If none of the styles on the Bullets menu suits you, click the More option to open the Bullets and Numbering dialog box, shown in Figure 8-1. Or choose Insert⇨Outline/Bullets & Numbering to open the dialog box.

   Inside the dialog box, click the More Bullets button, which in turn opens the Symbols dialog box. Click a symbol to use as your bullet and click Insert and Close. (See "Tracking Down Special Characters," later in this chapter, if you need help navigating the Symbols dialog box.)

   The symbol you choose appears as an option in the Bullets and Numbering dialog box. Click OK to close the dialog box. WordPerfect adds the bullet before your selected paragraphs and also adds the new bullet style to the Bullets menu on the toolbar. The menu can hold only eight bullet styles, so the new bullet style kicks one of the former occupants off the menu. (Note that if you use a special symbol as a bullet, the symbol may look different on the Bullets menu than it does in "real life." A fancy symbol may appear as a plain square or slash, for example.)

✔ To create a bulleted list on the fly — that is, before you begin typing your text — choose your bullet style from the Bullets and Numbering dialog box or from the toolbar. WordPerfect inserts a bullet and then creates a hanging indent for the bulleted text. (I explain hanging indents in Chapter 7.) Type the text for the first bulleted item and then press Enter to create the next bullet. After you type the last item in the bulleted list, press Enter and then press Backspace to discontinue the bullets. Or click the Bullets button on the toolbar.

✔ For a quick way to create a standard round bullet, just press Ctrl+Shift+B.

✔ You can apply a few other bullet styles via keyboard shortcuts if you have the QuickBullets feature enabled. To turn on QuickBullets, choose Tools⇨QuickCorrect, click the Format-As-You-Go tab, and select the QuickBullets check box. Now you can apply the bullet characters shown in Table 8-1 by pressing the key listed in the first column of the table followed by the Tab or Indent key.

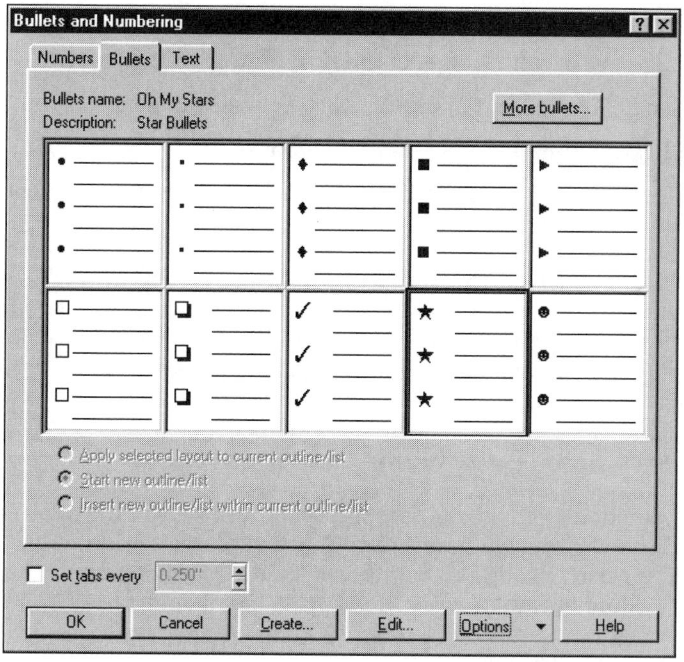

Figure 8-1:
Open the
Bullets and
Numbering
dialog box
to go
beyond the
default
bullet
options.

Table 8-1	QuickBullets Shortcut Keys
Press These Keys	*To Create This Bullet Character*
>	▶
o or *	•
0	●
^	◆
-	—
+	★

Numbered lists

The steps for numbering items in a list are pretty much the same as for adding bullets to a list. To apply numbers to existing text, follow these steps:

1. **Select the paragraphs that you want to number.**

2. **Click the arrow on the Numbering button on the toolbar.**

   A menu of different numbering style options appears.

3. **Click the number style you want to use.**

   WordPerfect inserts the numbers and indents text following the numbers.

If you add or delete an item in the list after you create it, WordPerfect renumbers the list automatically. To add an item, click just before the paragraph break for the preceding item and press Enter to get the number for the new item. To delete a numbered item, just delete the paragraph as you normally would.

You should be aware of a few other numbering options:

✔ If you don't like the numbering styles available on the Numbering menu, choose Insert➪Outline/Bullets & Numbering to open the Bullets and Numbering dialog box and then click the Numbers tab. Or just choose the More option from the Numbering menu on the toolbar. Scroll through the available numbering style options, click the one you want to use, and click OK.

✔ After you select a numbering style from the Numbering menu, you can apply that same style again by simply clicking the Numbering menu button face. You don't need to go through the tedious process of choosing the style from the menu every time.

✔ If QuickBullets is turned on, as explained in the preceding section, you can create a numbered list by typing the first number and a period and then pressing Tab. You can type letters (a, b, c) or Roman numerals (I, II) instead of regular numbers, if you prefer. WordPerfect automatically formats your paragraph for a numbered list. After you type the first item in the list, press Enter, and WordPerfect presents you with the next number. After you type the last item in the list, press Enter and then press Backspace to return to regular paragraph formatting.

More news about bullets and numbers

Just for good measure, here are a few other juicy tidbits about creating bulleted and numbered lists:

✔ By default, WordPerfect places the bullet or number at the left margin and indents the bulleted text to the first tab stop to the right. To change the amount of space between the bullet and the text, move the tab stop. To indent the entire paragraph without changing the amount of space between the bullet or number and the text, change the first-line indent, as explained in Chapter 7.

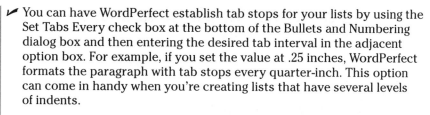

✔ You can have WordPerfect establish tab stops for your lists by using the Set Tabs Every check box at the bottom of the Bullets and Numbering dialog box and then entering the desired tab interval in the adjacent option box. For example, if you set the value at .25 inches, WordPerfect formats the paragraph with tab stops every quarter-inch. This option can come in handy when you're creating lists that have several levels of indents.

✔ To move an item up or down in a list, click at the beginning of the paragraph and then click the Move Up or Move Down button on the Property Bar.

✔ To shove a list item one tab stop to the right, click the Demote button on the Property Bar. To move it one tab stop to the left, click the Promote button. In numbered lists, WordPerfect may change the item's number to reflect its new position in the list, depending on the numbering style you selected.

✔ If an item in a list is more than one paragraph long, press Ctrl+Shift+L to separate the paragraphs instead of pressing Enter. Otherwise, you get a bullet or number at the start of each paragraph.

✔ To delete a bullet or number from a paragraph, click before the first letter in the paragraph and press Backspace. If you want to remove bullets or numbers from a whole bunch of paragraphs, select the paragraphs you want to reformat and choose the None style from the Styles menu on the Property Bar. (For more information about styles, see Chapter 9.) Note that even if the None style appears to be selected in the menu, you must display the menu and click the style again to apply it to your paragraphs. And by applying the None style, you apply paragraph formatting related to that style, replacing any indents and other formatting created when you added bullets or numbers.

Numbering Your Pages

WordPerfect can automatically number the pages in your document — and renumber them if you add or delete pages. To turn on automatic page numbering for a document, walk this way:

1. **Click anywhere in the page on which you want the page numbering to begin.**

2. **Choose Format⇨Page⇨Numbering.**

   The Select Page Numbering Format dialog box appears, as shown in Figure 8-2.

3. **Select the placement and format of the page numbers.**

   Choose the placement from the Position drop-down list and the format from the Page Numbering Format list box. The preview at the side of the dialog box shows you how and where the page numbers will appear.

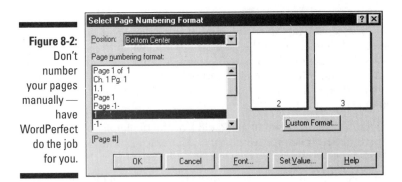

Figure 8-2:
Don't
number
your pages
manually —
have
WordPerfect
do the job
for you.

4. **Choose the font and size for your page numbers.**

   Page numbers appear in the same font as the default document font. If you want to use a different font, click the Font button to open the Page Numbering Font dialog box, which contains many of the same options as the Font Properties dialog box discussed in Chapter 7. After you specify the font, size, style, and other font attributes, click OK.

5. **Set the starting page number.**

   Normally, WordPerfect numbers pages according to their positions in your document. In Step 1, suppose that you click the third page of your document to tell WordPerfect that you want page numbering to begin on that page — maybe pages one and two are your title page and table of contents. If you want that third page to be numbered Page 1, you need to click the Set Value button to open the Values dialog box. Enter the starting page number in the Set Page Number option box of that dialog box and click OK.

6. **Click OK.**

   The page numbers appear as you requested. (You must be working in Page view or Two Pages view, however, to see them. Choose either view from the View menu if necessary.)

To remove page numbers from your document, click the first numbered page, choose Format➪Page➪Numbering and choose No Page Numbering from the Position drop-down list.

To prevent a page number from printing on a particular page, click that page, choose Format➪Page➪Suppress, select the check box for the Page Numbering item, and click OK.

Inserting the Current Date and Time

Here's a tool you're going to love if you're never sure what day it is, let alone what the time is. WordPerfect can automatically insert the current date and/or time into your text and even update the information each time you open or save the document. You may, for example, want to use this feature to add the date to form letters that you use frequently. Just follow these steps:

1. **Place the insertion marker at the spot on the page where you want to insert the date/time.**

2. **Choose Insert⇨Date/Time from the menu bar.**

   WordPerfect opens the Date/Time dialog box.

3. **Select a date and time format.**

   Just click on a format in the scrolling list. You can select from a wide range of formats, from the traditional month/date/year style (for example, August 30, 1999) to the downright odd (30Aug99). You can also choose to insert just the date, just the current time, or the date and time together.

   If you want the date and time to update automatically every time you open or save the document, select the Keep the Inserted Date Current check box.

4. **Click OK or press Enter.**

   WordPerfect inserts the date and time according to your computer's system clock. If the date or time is incorrect, update it in the Windows Control panel.

To insert the date or time in the format currently selected in the Date/Time dialog box, just press Ctrl+D. Press Ctrl+Shift+D to insert the date/time and have it automatically updated whenever you open or save the document.

Tracking Down Special Characters

You're typing up your annual holiday letter to friends and relatives, thoughtfully recounting the details of your two-week vacation in France, and you realize with horror that your computer keyboard doesn't have any of those little accent marks you need to type foreign words. How ever will you tell that hilarious story about that quaint café in Chalôns, let alone mention your upcoming second honeymoon in Curaçao?

Relax — all those foreign accent marks and other special typographical symbols are yours for the taking. They reside in the Symbols dialog box, as shown in Figure 8-3. To grab a symbol and put it in your document, follow these steps:

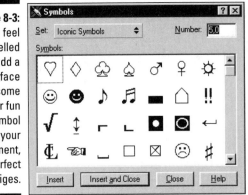

Figure 8-3:
If you feel compelled to add a smiley face or some other fun symbol to your document, WordPerfect obliges.

1. **Position your insertion marker where you want the symbol to appear.**

2. **Choose Insert⇨Symbol or press Ctrl+W to open the Symbols dialog box.**

3. **Locate the character you want to insert from the Symbols list.**

   Each of the symbol sets in the Set drop-down list offers a different selection of special characters. (***Hint:*** For foreign characters, choose the Multinational option. For monetary symbols, look in the Typographic Symbols category.)

   Use the scroll arrows alongside the Symbols list box to hunt through the available characters in the current character set. After you find the one you want, click to select it.

4. **Click Insert.**

   Or just double-click the character. WordPerfect inserts the character in your document where your insertion point is located.

You can leave the Symbols dialog box on-screen as long as you need it. The dialog box operates the same as any other open window — click it to make it the active window; click your document to make the document the active window. After you finish inserting your special characters, click the Close button.

You can insert some commonly used symbols, such as em dashes (—) and the registered trademark symbol (®), by using the keyboard shortcuts listed in Table 8-2. For these shortcuts to work, the Replace Words as You Type option box must be selected in the QuickCorrect dialog box. (Press Ctrl+ Shift+F1 to open the dialog box and turn on the option.) Remember that WordPerfect doesn't change your keystrokes into the corresponding symbol until after you press the spacebar.

QuickCorrect can also automatically replace so-called straight quotes (") and straight single quotes (') — otherwise known as apostrophes — with curly quotes (" ") and curly single quotes (' '). This substitution is a good thing — straight quotes are considered gauche in professional typesetting circles. But if you're typing measurements, such as 9'5", you need those straight quotes. No worries — if you type a number, WordPerfect uses the straight quotes instead.

All this quotation-mark-substituting depends, however, on the settings in the QuickCorrect dialog box. Press Ctrl+Shift+F1 to open the dialog box, click the SmartQuotes tab, and select all three check boxes on that tab to turn on these options.

If you use a special symbol frequently and WordPerfect doesn't offer a QuickCorrect shortcut for it, you can create your own. Here's how: Go to the QuickCorrect tab of the QuickCorrect dialog box. Then, in the Replace option box, enter the shortcut you want to use — for example, you may want to use the shortcut _tm_ for a trademark symbol. Then, click the With option box and press Ctrl+W to open the Symbols dialog box. Find the symbol you want and click Insert and Close to put the symbol in the With option box. Click Add Entry in the QuickCorrect dialog box and then click Close.

Table 8-2	Shortcuts to Common Symbols
Symbol	_Shortcut_
©	(c
®	(r
— (em dash)	- - - (three hyphens) or m- (m, hyphen)
– (en dash)	- - (two hyphens) or n- (n, hyphen)

Creating Headers and Footers

Headers and footers provide a quick and convenient way to create text that repeats on every page (or almost every page) in your document. A _header_ contains text that appears at the top of every page — for example, the document title or chapter title. A _footer_ contains text that appears at the bottom of your pages. The current date and the page number are two common footer elements.

The advantage of using headers and footers is that you don't need to retype the same text, page after page. You create the text once and use the Header/Footer command to place it automatically on every page.

Before you create a header or footer, make sure that you're working in Page view (which you access by choosing View➪Page or pressing Alt+F5) so that you can see what you're doing on-screen. Then follow these steps:

1. **Click at the top of the first page on which you want the header/footer to appear.**

2. **Choose Insert➪Header/Footer to open the Headers/Footers dialog box, as shown in Figure 8-4.**

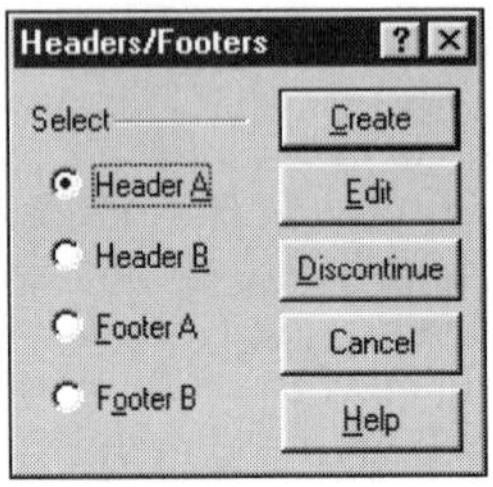

Figure 8-4:
Choose the header or footer you want to create from this dialog box.

Headers/Footers	? X
Select	Create
◉ Header A	Edit
○ Header B	Discontinue
○ Footer A	Cancel
○ Footer B	Help

3. **Select the header/footer you want to create by clicking the appropriate radio button.**

   If you need only one header/footer for your document, select Header A or Footer A. If you need two different sets of headers/footers — as you do if you want a different header/footer for your left-hand pages than for your right-hand pages — select A for one header and B for the other.

4. **Click Create.**

   WordPerfect displays several header/footer buttons on the Property Bar, as shown in Figure 8-5. (More about what those buttons do in the list that follows these steps.) The name of the title bar also changes to display the name of the current header/footer.

5. **Create your text.**

   You can enter as much text as you want and even add graphics (as I explain later in the section "Adding Graphics"). Figure 8-5 shows the header text that I created for my next blockbuster screenplay.

 6. **Click the Header/Footer Close button on the Property Bar.**

   Or just click anywhere in your main document. You're now back in the regular document-editing mode, as you can see by the changes to the title bar and the Property Bar.

Header margin guideline   Header/Footer close button

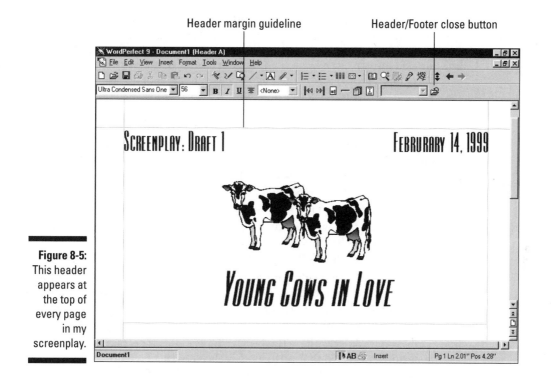

Figure 8-5:
This header
appears at
the top of
every page
in my
screenplay.

Here's some additional info about headers and footers:

✔ To change the left, right, top, and bottom margins of the header or footer, just drag the header or footer margin guidelines (a header guideline is labeled in Figure 8-5). If you don't see the guidelines, choose View➪Guidelines and select the Margins option in the resulting dialog box. The header/footer margin guidelines work just like the standard document margin guidelines, covered in Chapter 7.

✔ To place a specific amount of distance between the header/footer and the main document text, click the Distance button and set the distance value in the dialog box that appears. The result is the same as dragging the bottom margin guideline for a header or the top margin guideline for a footer, but you get more precise control over the spacing.

✔ You can edit a header/footer by clicking it on any page on which it appears. The title bar of the document window changes to show that you're working on the header/footer. Click outside the header/footer to return to your main document.

✔ To move from one header or footer to another quickly, use the Previous Header/Footer and Next Header/Footer buttons on the Property Bar.

✔ If you want to include the page number on pages that have a header/footer, the best way to do so is to insert them in the header/footer instead of using the Numbering command covered earlier in this chapter. Otherwise, your header/footer text may overprint your page numbers. To insert the page number, click the Page Numbering button on the Property Bar and choose Page Number from the drop-down list.

✔ You can specify whether you want a header/footer to appear on every page, on every even page, or on every odd page. Choose the Header/Footer Placement button on the Property Bar to open the Placement dialog box, click the radio button for the option you want to use, and click OK or press Enter.

✔ Click the Horizontal Line button to insert a line that stretches from the left margin to the right margin. If you click on the line to select it, you can then drag it to a different position if needed. Drag the selection handles to change the width or length of the line.

✔ If you don't want a header/footer to print on a particular page, click the page (click the main body of the page, not the header or footer). Choose Format⇨Page⇨Suppress to open the Suppress dialog box. Then select the check box for the header or footer that you want to suppress.

✔ If you want to discontinue the header/footer after a certain page, put the insertion marker on that page, choose Insert⇨Header/Footer to open the Headers/Footers dialog box, select the radio button for the header/footer that you want to discontinue, and click the Discontinue button. To get rid of the header/footer on all pages in the document, do the exact same thing, but put the insertion marker at the beginning of the first page where the header/footer appears.

Putting Your Text in Columns

WordPerfect enables you to divide your pages into columns — as you may want to do if, say, you're creating a newsletter article. Here are the steps:

1. **Put the insertion marker at the point in your document where you want the columns to begin.**

   If you want to format just certain paragraphs in columns, select the paragraphs instead.

2. **Choose Format⇨Columns.**

   Or click the Columns button on the toolbar and choose Format from the menu that appears. Either way, the Columns dialog box appears, as shown in Figure 8-6.

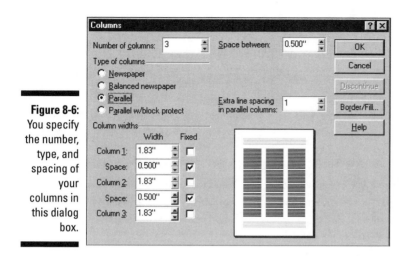

Figure 8-6:
You specify
the number,
type, and
spacing of
your
columns in
this dialog
box.

3. **Specify the number of columns you want in the Number of Columns option box.**

4. **Choose a column format by clicking one of the Type of Columns radio buttons.**

Your options are:

- *Newspaper* fills the first column on the left all the way to the bottom of the page, fills the next column to the bottom of the page, and so on, until all the text is placed in columns.

- *Balanced Newspaper* fills the columns the same way that Newspaper does, except that WordPerfect attempts to make all the columns the same length.

- *Parallel* groups text across the page in rows, similar to what you find in a table. You may want to use this option if you're creating a script, for example, in which you want the video portion of the scene to run down the left side of the page and the audio to appear on the right side, as shown in Figure 8-7.

- *Parallel w/Block Protect* works the same way as Parallel does, except that WordPerfect makes sure that no row of text is split across two pages. If the text in one column in the row is too long to fit on the page, the entire row moves to the next page.

As you make your choices, the preview page in the dialog box changes to show you how your columns are going to appear.

Columns button

Column guide

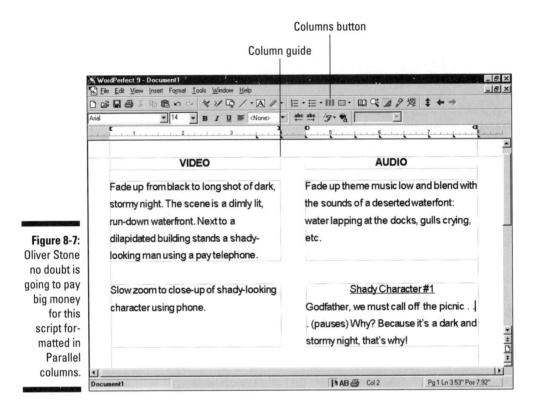

Figure 8-7:
Oliver Stone
no doubt is
going to pay
big money
for this
script for-
matted in
Parallel
columns.

5. If necessary, adjust the column width and spacing.

By default, WordPerfect spaces your columns evenly across the page and puts a one-half-inch space between each column. If you want some other spacing, change the values in the Space Between and Column Widths option boxes. If you're not sure what spacing or width values you want, don't sweat it; you can easily change the values later.

Use the Extra Line Spacing in Parallel Columns option to add more space between the rows of text in parallel columns.

6. Add a border or fill if you want.

Clicking the Border/Fill button takes you to the Column Border/Fill dialog box, where you can add a border and/or background to your columns. The options in this dialog box are explained in the section "Adding borders and fills," later in this chapter. After adding your border or fill, click OK to return to the Columns dialog box.

7. Click OK or press Enter to create your columns.

You can also create newspaper columns by clicking the Columns button on the toolbar and choosing the number of columns you want from the drop-down list. WordPerfect creates your columns based on the default settings in the Columns dialog box.

As you see in Figure 8-7, WordPerfect displays dotted guidelines to indicate the boundaries of each column. (If you don't see the guidelines, choose View➪Guidelines and turn on the Columns option in the Guidelines dialog box.) You can resize your columns by dragging the guidelines or by dragging the space between columns (in publishing terms, that space is called a *gutter*).

Entering and editing text in columns involves a few special techniques:

✔ If you're typing text in a Newspaper column, WordPerfect automatically moves the insertion marker to the next column after you fill up the current column. To break the column before that point, press Ctrl+Enter or click the Columns button and choose New Column from the drop-down list.

✔ If you're typing text in Balanced Newspaper columns, WordPerfect continually shifts text back and forth between the columns to balance the column length. Press Ctrl+Enter to begin a whole new block of balanced columns.

✔ In Parallel and Parallel with Block Protect columns, Ctrl+Enter moves you across the row to the next column. If you press Ctrl+Enter at the end of a row, WordPerfect creates a new row and moves the insertion marker to the leftmost column in that row.

✔ To move from one column of text to another column of text, just click the mouse to reposition the insertion marker. You can also use the following keyboard shortcuts: Alt+Home moves you to the top of the current column; Alt+End moves you to the end of the current column; Alt+← takes you to the previous column; and Alt+→ takes you to the next column.

✔ To change the column type, put the insertion marker where you want the different column formatting to begin. Then choose Format➪Columns (or click the Columns button and choose Format) and establish your new column settings as outlined in the preceding steps.

✔ If all you want to do is change the number of columns, you can click the Columns button and choose a number from the drop-down list. (Notice that the last item on the toolbar's Columns drop-down list shows you the type of columns you're creating. The button doesn't actually do anything.)

✔ To turn off column formatting, put the insertion marker at the point where you want to get rid of the formatting, choose Format➪Columns, and click Discontinue in the Columns dialog box. Or click the Columns button on the toolbar and choose Discontinue from the drop-down list.

Adding Graphics

Ah, here's the really fun part: adding pictures to your pages. WordPerfect Office 2000 comes with a bunch of clip art — pictures, borders, and other graphic elements — that you can use to add zest to your documents. You can also create your own drawings using a variety of drawing tools.

Inserting an existing graphic

To place a graphic from the WordPerfect Office 2000 clip-art collection on a page, follow these steps:

1. **Position the insertion marker at the spot in the document where you want to put the graphic.**

2. **Click the Scrapbook button on the toolbar or choose Insert⇨Graphics⇨ Clipart.**

   WordPerfect opens the Scrapbook, which provides you with thumbnail views of the available graphics. Click the Clipart tab to see simple drawings; click the Photos tab to see photographic images. Chapter 17 offers more details about the Scrapbook, which has been refined in Version 9.

3. **Click the graphic and click Insert.**

   Or, even easier, simply double-click the graphic. WordPerfect closes the Scrapbook and plops the graphic onto your page and surrounds the graphic with little black boxes. These boxes are *selection handles,* and they indicate that the graphic is selected and ready to be moved or edited. (See the upcoming section "Editing graphics" for details.)

You aren't limited to just the pictures you see in the Scrapbook. You can use graphics from any source, as long as they're stored in a graphics format that WordPerfect can handle. To insert a graphic not in the Scrapbook, choose Insert⇨Graphics⇨From File. WordPerfect displays the Insert Image dialog box, which looks suspiciously like the Open File dialog box discussed in Chapter 4 — and works just like it, too. After you locate the graphic you want, double-click it to place it in your document.

If you don't get the Insert Image dialog box but instead get a little hand cursor, choose Tools⇨Settings to display the Settings dialog box, click the Environment icon to open the Environment Settings dialog box, and click the Graphics tab. Then deselect the Drag to Create New Graphics Boxes option and click OK. This option enables you to set the size of your graphic before you insert it by drawing a box to hold your picture. (WordPerfect creates the box for you automatically if the option is turned off.) You can always resize your graphic later, however, even if you don't use this option.

Drawing your own pictures

WordPerfect 9 gives you access to a new batch of drawing tools that simplify the process of creating basic shapes. These tools are the same drawing tools found in Presentations 9, and because I cover them fully in Chapter 17, I won't go into much detail here.

To pick up a drawing tool, click the down arrow on the Draw Shapes button on the toolbar. WordPerfect displays a menu of icons representing the different drawing tools. Click an icon to use that tool.

The tools on the menu represent only a small assortment of the available tools, however. To find more tools, choose Insert⇨Shapes to open the Draw Object Shapes dialog box. Click the radio button for the category of tools you want to see. WordPerfect displays icons for all the tools in that category. Click the icon for the tool you want to use and click OK. You can then begin drawing in your document.

As you can see, the process for accessing all the drawing tools in WordPerfect is a bit cumbersome. So, if you want to do more than create a few simple shapes, I suggest that you do your drawing in Presentations, where all the tools are conveniently located on flyout menus — you don't have to keep opening a dialog box to use a certain tool. Presentations also offers many more ways to enhance your drawings than WordPerfect does. After you create your drawing, you can copy and paste it into your WordPerfect document using the techniques outlined in Chapter 21. Of course, if you purchased the Voice-Powered Edition of the suite, you can also create your artwork in Print Office and then copy it into WordPerfect.

Alternatively, you can open up the Presentations window inside WordPerfect by clicking the Draw Picture button on the toolbar or by choosing Insert⇨ Graphics⇨Draw Picture. For more information on using Presentations inside WordPerfect, see Chapter 21.

Editing graphics

If you want to do very much editing to a graphic, use Presentations or Print Office, which offer better drawing and editing tools. In fact, if you double-click a clip-art graphic, the Presentations window opens inside WordPerfect, making all the Presentations tools available. (For more about using Presentations, see Chapters 16 and 17. Also check out Chapter 20, which introduces you to Print Office, and Chapter 21, which explains how this program-within-a-program stuff works.)

Move cursor

Draw Shapes menu   Selection handle

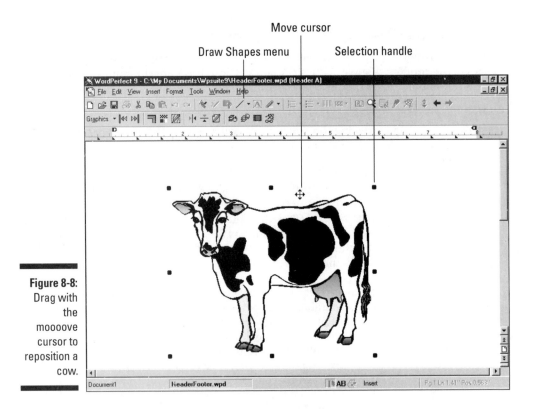

Figure 8-8:
Drag with
the
moooove
cursor to
reposition a
cow.

But you can perform some simple editing tricks by using WordPerfect's own artistic capabilities. First, click the graphic to select it. Black boxes — *selection handles* — appear around the graphic, and a batch of graphics-related buttons appear on the Property Bar, as shown in Figure 8-8. Now you can do all the following to your graphic:

✔ To resize a graphic, drag a selection handle. Drag a corner handle to retain the graphic's original proportions as you resize. If you want to get specific, click the Graphics button on the Property Bar, choose Size from the resulting menu, and enter new height and width values in the Box Size dialog box.

✔ If you're working with a scanned photograph or other bitmap image, rather than a piece of clip art or shape drawn with the Draw Shapes tools, be careful about resizing. When you enlarge this type of graphic too much, it gets all fuzzy and unattractive, like that four-week-old bagel in your bread box. See Chapters 17 and 20 for more scoop on working with photographs and other bitmap images.

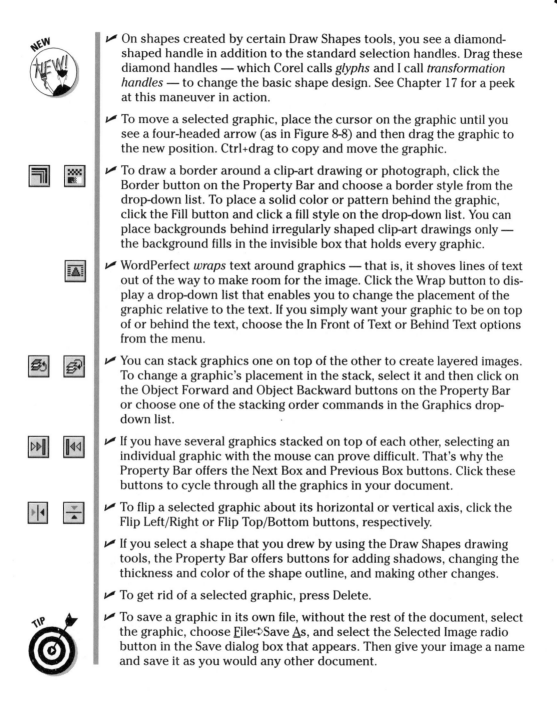

✔ On shapes created by certain Draw Shapes tools, you see a diamond-shaped handle in addition to the standard selection handles. Drag these diamond handles — which Corel calls *glyphs* and I call *transformation handles* — to change the basic shape design. See Chapter 17 for a peek at this maneuver in action.

✔ To move a selected graphic, place the cursor on the graphic until you see a four-headed arrow (as in Figure 8-8) and then drag the graphic to the new position. Ctrl+drag to copy and move the graphic.

✔ To draw a border around a clip-art drawing or photograph, click the Border button on the Property Bar and choose a border style from the drop-down list. To place a solid color or pattern behind the graphic, click the Fill button and click a fill style on the drop-down list. You can place backgrounds behind irregularly shaped clip-art drawings only — the background fills in the invisible box that holds every graphic.

✔ WordPerfect *wraps* text around graphics — that is, it shoves lines of text out of the way to make room for the image. Click the Wrap button to display a drop-down list that enables you to change the placement of the graphic relative to the text. If you simply want your graphic to be on top of or behind the text, choose the In Front of Text or Behind Text options from the menu.

✔ You can stack graphics one on top of the other to create layered images. To change a graphic's placement in the stack, select it and then click on the Object Forward and Object Backward buttons on the Property Bar or choose one of the stacking order commands in the Graphics drop-down list.

✔ If you have several graphics stacked on top of each other, selecting an individual graphic with the mouse can prove difficult. That's why the Property Bar offers the Next Box and Previous Box buttons. Click these buttons to cycle through all the graphics in your document.

✔ To flip a selected graphic about its horizontal or vertical axis, click the Flip Left/Right or Flip Top/Bottom buttons, respectively.

✔ If you select a shape that you drew by using the Draw Shapes drawing tools, the Property Bar offers buttons for adding shadows, changing the thickness and color of the shape outline, and making other changes.

✔ To get rid of a selected graphic, press Delete.

✔ To save a graphic in its own file, without the rest of the document, select the graphic, choose File➪Save As, and select the Selected Image radio button in the Save dialog box that appears. Then give your image a name and save it as you would any other document.

Creating Borders, Fills, and Lines

Another way to jazz up your pages is to add borders, lines, and fills to selected text. *Fill,* by the way, is a computer-art term that refers to the color or pattern inside a selected area, such as a page.

Adding borders and fills

You can add a border or fill to a page, paragraph, or column. To do so, select the text you want to dress up. Or, if you want to apply the effects to all your pages, paragraphs, or columns, don't select any text. Your formatting then affects all text from the insertion marker forward.

To apply borders or fills to paragraphs or pages, choose the Border/Fill command from the Format➪Paragraph or Format➪Page submenu. To apply a border or fill to columns, click the Border/Fill button inside the Columns dialog box (which you access by choosing Format➪Columns), as I discuss in "Putting Your Text in Columns," earlier in this chapter. Regardless of where you choose the Border/Fill command, you open a Border/Fill dialog box that looks something like the one shown in Figure 8-9. (The dialog box name and options change slightly depending on whether you're formatting columns, paragraphs, or a page.)

You can probably find your way around the dialog box on your own, but here are a few pointers to guide you:

✔ Border options are found, appropriately enough, on the Border tab of the Border/Fill dialog box. Click a border style in the Available Border Styles list and then play around with the Color and Line Style options. If you're applying a border to a page, you can choose from two different border categories by making a selection from the Border Type drop-down list. As you mess with the options, the preview box shows you how your border is going to look.

✔ To add a drop shadow, use the options on the Shadow tab. Note that the Shadow tab, as well as all other tabs except the Border tab, disappear if you select Fancy as your Border Type when applying a border to a page.

✔ Apply a solid color or patterned fill behind your text by using the options on the Fill tab. When applying fills to pages, you must choose the Line option from the Border Type menu to access fill options. You can create solid-colored backgrounds or wacky-patterned backgrounds, as shown in the preview box in Figure 8-9.

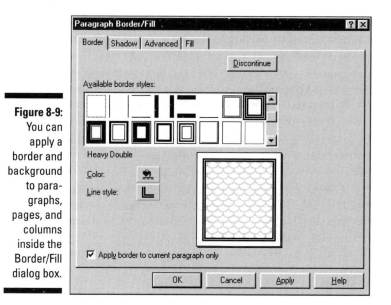

Figure 8-9:
You can apply a border and background to paragraphs, pages, and columns inside the Border/Fill dialog box.

✔ The options on the Advanced tab of the Border/Fill dialog box are available only after you select certain options on the other tabs. If you select a fill from the Fill tab, for example, you can use the options at the bottom of the Advanced tab to create a *gradient fill* — that is, one that blends from one color to another in a geometric pattern. Choose any option but None from the Gradient drop-down list to create a gradient fill.

✔ After you change the settings on any tab, click Apply to put your most recent changes into effect. If you want to apply the effect to more than the current paragraph/page/column, make sure that the check box at the bottom of the Border tab isn't selected. After you're satisfied with how things look, click OK.

✔ To remove a border from selected text, choose the Border/Fill command to open the Border/Fill dialog box and then click the Discontinue button. To delete a fill, choose the blank (white) fill on the Fill tab instead of using the Discontinue button.

Adding lines

In addition to the line-drawing tools available from the Draw Shapes menu, WordPerfect gives you a few other quick ways to create a line:

✔ To draw a straight line from the left margin to the right margin, click at the spot where you want the line to appear and choose Insert⇨Line⇨ Horizontal Line or press Ctrl+F11.

✔ Type four hyphens or four equal signs and then press Enter to create a single or double horizontal line, respectively. (The QuickLines check box on the Format-As-You-Go tab of the QuickCorrect Options dialog box must be selected. Choose Tools⇨QuickCorrect to open the dialog box.)

✔ To create a vertical line from the top margin to the bottom margin, click the spot where you want to position the line and then choose Insert⇨ Line⇨Vertical Line or press Ctrl+Shift+F11.

✔ Choose Insert⇨Line⇨Custom Line to display the Create Graphics Line dialog box. Here, you can create a custom-tailored line, choosing a line style, color, length, thickness, and other line attributes in one fell swoop.

✔ To move a line, click it to display its selection handles (little black squares) and then drag it to the new position.

✔ Drag a selection handle to resize the line. Depending on which handle you drag, you can make the line fatter, skinnier, longer, or shorter.

✔ After you select a line, buttons for changing the color, thickness, style, and orientation of the line appear on the Property Bar.

✔ To delete a line, click it to display the selection handles and then press Delete.

Chapter 9

Tools to Save You Time (And Embarrassment)

. . . .

In This Chapter

▶ Using styles to speed up formatting

▶ Copying character and paragraph formatting

▶ Finding and replacing words and phrases

▶ Checking your spelling

▶ Using QuickWords

▶ Creating labels and envelopes

. . . .

*H*ave you heard the expression, "The hurrieder I go, the behinder I get"? No? Well, my Grandma King says it all the time, and she's nobody's fool. Loosely translated, this time-honored saying means that, if you rush to get a job done, you make mistakes that put you even further behind schedule than if you had taken a slow, methodical approach. At least, I think that's what it means.

At any rate, going slow isn't always possible in our speed-it-up, get-it-done-yesterday world. Your boss wants that report now, your client wants that project done yesterday, and the IRS wants all your money *this very minute* — with a hefty interest penalty for any delay whatsoever.

Fortunately, WordPerfect has some tools that not only help you work faster, but also help make sure that your documents don't contain any embarrassing spelling or formatting mistakes. This chapter shows you how to use these tools so that you can go hurrieder without getting any behinder.

Using Styles to Speed Up Formatting Chores

You can save yourself an enormous amount of time by using *styles* to format your documents. Styles are like templates that you can use to quickly apply character and paragraph formatting to your text.

Here's how it works: You create a style that contains all the formatting instructions for a specific text element — for example, a headline style that uses 14-point, bold Helvetica type; centered alignment; and double line spacing. To format your headlines, you just select the headline text and apply the headline style. WordPerfect applies the right font, type size, alignment, and line spacing in one fell swoop.

Using styles not only saves you time, but it also ensures that your formatting is consistent throughout your document. You don't need to worry about what font, type size, or spacing you're supposed to use each time you create a new headline — all the formatting information is contained in the style. And, if you want to change the formatting of your headlines (for example, you decide to use 13-point type rather than 14-point type), you don't need to search through your document looking for headlines and changing them manually. You just edit the style, and WordPerfect automatically applies the new formatting to any paragraphs that use the style.

Choosing a style type

You can create three types of styles in WordPerfect:

- ✔ *Character styles* contain formatting related to individual characters of text — font, type size, type style, and so on. They can't contain paragraph-level formatting, such as indents and line spacing.

- ✔ *Paragraph styles* contain paragraph-level formatting plus character-level formatting.

- ✔ *Document styles* can contain paragraph-level formatting, character-level formatting, plus document-level formatting such as page size. I don't cover this option because, frankly, creating and editing document styles is complicated, and you probably won't have much reason to use them, anyhow.

WordPerfect assigns a standard document style, called *DocumentStyle*, to every document you create. You can't delete this style, although you can edit it if you're a WordPerfect hidden codes aficionado (or know someone who is), as I explain in the section "Editing a style," later in this chapter. You really shouldn't need to delete or edit the DocumentStyle style, however, because formatting you do inside the document overrides the style's formatting instructions.

Creating character and paragraph styles

WordPerfect comes with some prefab styles that you can select from the Styles menu on the Property Bar (labeled in the upcoming Figure 9-3). But you probably want to define your own styles because the prefab styles aren't likely to meet your specific formatting needs. You can create styles from scratch, but an easier method is to create some text, apply the formatting you want to use, and then use the QuickStyle feature to create a style based on your formatted text.

To create a character or paragraph style in this fashion, follow these steps:

1. **Format and select the text you want to use as the basis for the style.**

   If you want to create a paragraph style, you can simply click anywhere inside the paragraph. To create a character style, select the actual character or characters by dragging across them.

2. **Choose QuickStyle from the Styles menu on the Property Bar.**

   If you need help locating the Styles menu, flip ahead to Figure 9-3, where it's labeled. After you choose the QuickStyle item from the menu, the QuickStyle dialog box appears, as shown in Figure 9-1.

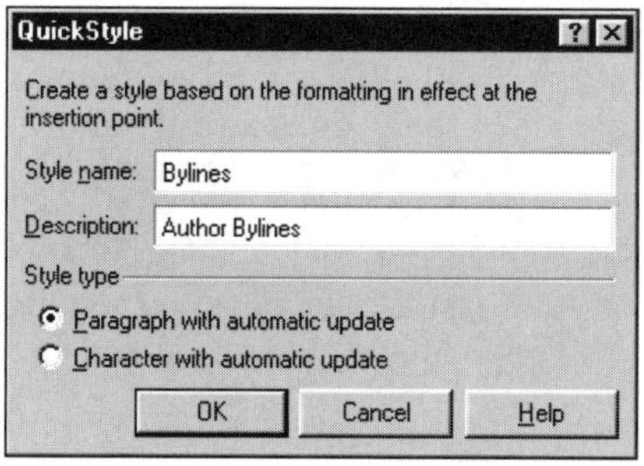

Figure 9-1: Use the QuickStyle command to create a style based on existing text.

QuickStyle	? X

Create a style based on the formatting in effect at the insertion point.

Style name: Bylines

Description: Author Bylines

Style type
- ⦿ Paragraph with automatic update
- ○ Character with automatic update

[OK] [Cancel] [Help]

3. **Give your style a name and a description.**

   Enter the name into the Style Name option box. (You can't use a style name that already exists.) In the Description box, enter some descriptive text that reminds you what sort of text you plan to format with the style.

4. **Choose a Style Type radio button.**

   The differences between the style types are explained in the preceding section.

5. **Click OK or press Enter.**

   You should see your new style listed on the Styles drop-down list.

Applying styles

Applying styles to your text is easy:

- ✔ To apply a character style, select the text you want to format and choose the style name from the Styles menu.
- ✔ To apply a paragraph style, click the paragraph you want to format and select the style.
- ✔ To apply a style to several paragraphs, select the paragraphs before selecting the style.

If you're not sure what style you applied to a particular paragraph, click the paragraph and then take a look at the Styles drop-down list. The current style is displayed. If no style is applied, you see the word <None>.

Editing a style

Suppose that you create a paragraph style named Bylines for all the author bylines in your monthly newsletter. You originally specify that you want the bylines to be left-justified. You later decide that you want them to be centered instead. All you do is click one of the bylines and change the justification, as I explain in Chapter 7. WordPerfect automatically makes the same change to all text that uses the Bylines style.

If you don't want WordPerfect to perform this automatic updating, you can turn off the function inside the Styles Editor dialog box, as I describe in the upcoming steps.

By default, character styles are created with automatic updating enabled as well, which means that, if you click or select a word that uses the style and change the font or other character formatting, WordPerfect changes the formatting for all other text that uses that style as well.

If you select just a portion of a word or paragraph before reformatting it, your changes apply to that text only, regardless of whether automatic updating is enabled.

To turn off automatic updating for a style, head for the Styles Editor dialog box. This dialog box is also the place to go if you have disabled automatic updating but want to make a particular formatting change to all text that uses the style. To access this dialog box and change your styles, follow these steps:

1. **Choose Format⇨Styles or press Alt+F8 to open the Styles dialog box.**

2. **Click the style you want to edit and then click the Edit button.**

   WordPerfect displays the Styles Editor dialog box, as shown in Figure 9-2.

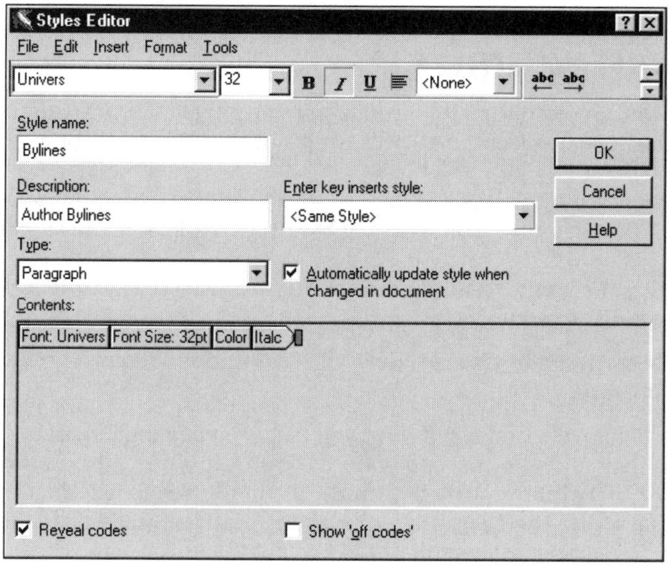

Figure 9-2:
You can make changes to a style by using the Styles Editor dialog box.

3. **Make your edits to the style.**

   The dialog box has a menu bar and a mini-toolbar that offer many of the same commands as the regular WordPerfect window. If you want to add a formatting attribute, choose the appropriate command from the menus or toolbar. (If you click the little up- and down-pointing arrows at the end of the mini-toolbar, you display a few hidden toolbar buttons.)

   To delete a formatting attribute, drag its code out of the Contents window at the bottom of the Styles Editor dialog box. To get rid of the italic attribute in the Byline styles, for example, you'd drag the Italc code (at the end of the Contents line in Figure 9-2) out of the window. Make sure that the Reveal Codes check box is selected at the bottom of the dialog box, or the codes aren't displayed.

If you want to *replace* a formatting attribute — say, to substitute 10-point type for 12-point type — drag the old code out of the window before you set the new attribute.

To disable automatic style updating, deselect the Automatically Update Style When Changed in Document check box.

4. **Click OK or press Enter to return to the Styles dialog box.**

5. **Click the Close button.**

WordPerfect closes the Styles dialog box and applies the updated formatting to any text that uses the style.

Removing styles

If you want to remove a style from a paragraph, click inside the paragraph and select <None> from the Styles drop-down list on the Property Bar.

Removing character styles is dicier — it requires deleting hidden codes in the Reveal Codes window. So take a big breath and follow these steps:

1. **Click the space to the left of the first character in the text that you want to "destyle."**

2. **Press Alt+F3 or choose <u>V</u>iew⇨Reveal <u>C</u>odes to open the Reveal Codes window.**

In the Reveal Codes window, you can see your document text along with all the hidden formatting codes. To the left of the first character in the text that you want to unformat, you should see a code that begins with Char Style (the character style code), as shown in Figure 9-3. A similar code appears at the end of the text that uses the style.

3. **Drag either of the Char Style codes out of the Reveal Codes window.**

Deleting one code deletes both.

If things don't look right after you remove the style code, press Ctrl+Z to undo your edit. Then go make nice with the WordPerfect guru in your office to get some help sorting out your codes.

Alternatively, you can simply select the text and apply new formatting without deleting the original character style code. But leaving in old formatting codes can lead to hidden-code buildup, which can occasionally cause problems if you move or otherwise edit text. So deleting the code entirely is a good idea.

Styles menu

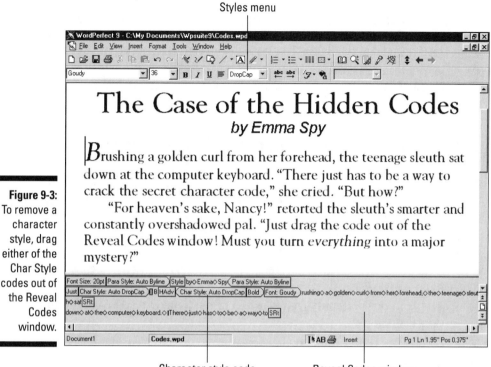

Figure 9-3:
To remove a character style, drag either of the Char Style codes out of the Reveal Codes window.

Character style code   Reveal Codes window

Another trick for removing character style codes is to click just to the left of the text you want to reformat and then press Backspace. No change? Press Ctrl+Z and then press Delete. See, the hidden character style code resides somewhere in the space between the first character in the text and the preceding character. But determining exactly where the code is hiding is difficult. Your cursor may look like it's poised to wipe out the first character in the text, but it may actually be on the code — something to remember if you really want to delete the character but you end up destroying formatting instead. Try this procedure a few times with the Reveal Codes window open to get a feel for how WordPerfect does things.

To completely remove a style from the document, follow these steps:

1. **Press Alt+F8 or choose Format⇨Styles to display the Styles dialog box.**

2. **Click on the style you want to remove, click the Options button, and select Delete from the drop-down list.**

WordPerfect presents the Delete Styles dialog box, which contains two radio buttons: Leave Formatting Codes in Document and Including Formatting Codes. If you want to delete the style but leave the formatting it applied intact, choose the former. If you want to erase both the formatting and the styles, choose Including Formatting Codes.

3. To complete your mission, click OK and then click Close.

Copying Formats with QuickFormat

WordPerfect offers another tool to speed up your formatting life: *QuickFormat*. QuickFormat copies the formatting from one chunk of text to another. You can copy the formatting of a selected word, block of text, or paragraph. To see how it works, follow these steps:

1. Select the text that has the formatting you want to copy.

If you want to copy paragraph formatting, you can just click inside the paragraph.

 2. Choose Format⇨QuickFormat or click the QuickFormat button on the toolbar.

The QuickFormat dialog box appears, as shown in Figure 9-4.

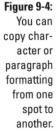 **Figure 9-4:** You can copy character or paragraph formatting from one spot to another.

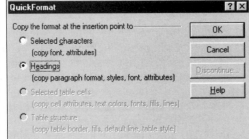

3. Choose a copy option from the group of radio buttons in the dialog box.

If you choose the Selected Characters radio button, you copy the formatting of the selected characters only — font, type size, type style, and so on. If you choose the Headings button, you copy both the text formatting and the paragraph formatting (styles, indents, borders, and so on).

4. Click OK or press Enter.

Your cursor turns into a little paint roller.

5. Drag the cursor over the text you want to format.

If you're copying paragraph formatting to a single paragraph, you can just click inside the paragraph instead. The paint roller cursor remains visible, and you can keep "painting" the formatting onto as much other text as you want.

6. After you finish painting your text, turn off QuickFormat.

For the fastest results, just click the QuickFormat button again.

If you copy formatting by using QuickFormat — whether character or paragraph formatting — WordPerfect creates a QuickFormat style based on your formatting. (I explain styles in the preceding section.) The style then appears on the Styles menu, just as a regular style does. The first QuickFormat style you create is called QuickFormat1; the second one is called QuickFormat2 — and so on. So, if you want to copy the formatting to any subsequent text after you put away the QuickFormat paint roller, you can just apply the QuickFormat style from the Styles menu. You can also rename the style by changing its name in the Styles Editor dialog box, as I explain in the section "Editing a style," earlier in this chapter.

WordPerfect creates the QuickFormat styles with automatic updating enabled, which means that you can click inside one piece of text that uses the style, make a formatting change, and have that change automatically applied to all other text that uses the style. Note that the automatic updating *doesn't* occur if you select just a portion of a paragraph and change the formatting, so, if you want to reformat just a few words in a paragraph, you don't affect other text. To disable the automatic updating altogether, follow the steps outlined in "Editing a style," earlier in this chapter.

For paragraphs formatted with QuickFormat, you have another option for turning off automatic updating. If you don't want formatting changes to affect a particular paragraph, click anywhere in the paragraph, choose Format➪QuickFormat or click the QuickFormat button to open the QuickFormat dialog box, and click the Discontinue button. Then choose the Current Heading radio button. Now this paragraph remains untouched if you make changes to other paragraphs that carry the QuickFormat style. If you instead choose the All Associated Headings radio button, automatic updating is turned off for all paragraphs that use the style.

Finding and Replacing Errant Text

People seem to have a hard time making up their minds these days. Just as you finish typing the text for your company's 100-page annual report, the board of directors replaces all the top management. You create a catalog touting your client's new product, and just before you send the thing to the printer, the client decides that spelling the product name *ConsumerScam* instead of *Consumer Scam* would be really cool.

When these sorts of unavoidable changes happen, you could scroll through your text, hunt down all instances of outdated or incorrect information, and make the changes manually. Or you could do the smart thing and have the WordPerfect Find and Replace feature do the job for you. To go on your search and destroy mission, follow these steps:

1. **Click at the spot in your document where you want to begin searching for the incorrect text.**

2. **Choose Edit⇨Find and Replace or press Ctrl+F.**

   The Find and Replace dialog box appears, as shown in Figure 9-5.

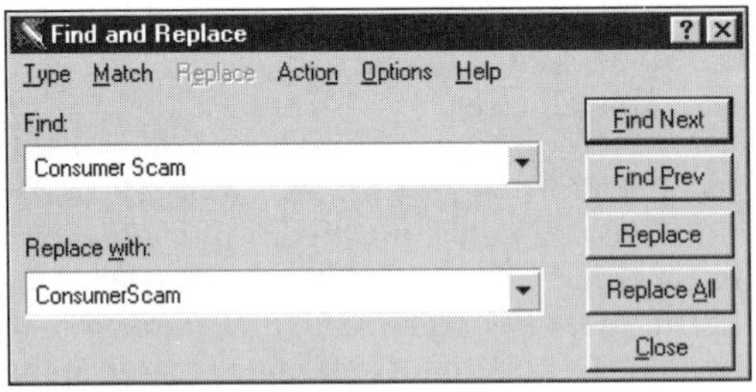

Figure 9-5:
Use the Find
and Replace
command to
track down
and replace
errant text.

3. **Click the Type menu and check the status of the Text option.**

   If you see a check mark next to this option in the menu, the option is turned on, which is what you want. If not, click the option to activate it. Turn off the other options in the menu, if they happen to be checked. (More about what you can do with those options in a bit.)

4. **Type the word or phrase that you want to replace in the Find option box.**

   Or click the arrow at the end of the box to select text that you recently found and replaced.

5. **Type the replacement word or phrase in the Replace With option box.**

   Or click the arrow at the end of the box to select replacement text that you recently used.

6. **Click the Find Next or Find Prev button.**

   Find Next finds the first occurrence of the incorrect text after the insertion marker. Find Prev searches for the first occurrence of the incorrect text before the insertion marker.

After WordPerfect finds the incorrect text, it highlights the text in your document. If you click Replace, WordPerfect replaces that text and moves on to find the next occurrence. If you click Find Next or Find Prev, WordPerfect leaves the current text alone and starts hunting for another occurrence of the text.

If you click Replace All, WordPerfect automatically replaces every occurrence of the text from the insertion marker through the end of the document. (You can change the extent of the search by changing the settings in the Options menu. See the bulleted list later in this section for details.)

If you want to edit the found text instead of replacing it, just click your document to activate it. Then edit as normal. If you want to begin searching again, click inside the Find and Replace dialog box to make it active.

If WordPerfect can't find any more occurrences of the incorrect text, an alert box appears to tell you so. Click OK to get rid of the box.

7. **Click Close to shut the Find and Replace dialog box.**

   If you prefer, you can leave the dialog box open and available for future searches. You can move the dialog box to a different spot, if necessary, by dragging its title bar.

If you replace a word by mistake during your Find and Replace session, double-click your document and then choose Edit⇨Undo or press Ctrl+Z to undo the replacement. Click the Find and Replace dialog box to reactivate it and continue searching and replacing.

Leave the Replace With option box empty if you want to delete every occurrence of a word or phrase. WordPerfect then replaces each occurrence of the incorrect text with, uh, nothing, which is the same as deleting it. Nifty, huh?

Now that you know the basic steps involved in the Find and Replace dance, try out a few variations. The menus in the Find and Replace dialog box offer all sorts of options that enable you to customize your search:

  ✔ If you turn on the Word Forms option in the Type menu, you can search and replace all forms of a word. If you type *fish* in the Find text box, for example, WordPerfect finds the words *fish, fishing,* and *fishes.* WordPerfect also alters the Replace With text to match the form of the word it finds — for example, if you originally used *hare* as the Replace With text, and the search finds the word *fishes,* the Replace With text changes to *hares.* Sometimes, WordPerfect gives you a drop-down list offering several choices of Replace With text.

✔ Normally, WordPerfect finds any word that contains the characters you type in the Find text box. If you tell it to search for *bee*, for example, WordPerfect finds any words that contain those three letters, including *been*, *beer*, *beet*, and so on. If you turn on the Whole Word option in the Match menu, WordPerfect finds only the word *bee*. This option isn't available if the Word Forms option is turned on in the Type menu.

✔ Turn on the Case option in the Match menu to limit the search to text that uses the same case (uppercase or lowercase letters) as the text you type in the Find text box.

✔ The Match⇨Font command enables you to search for text that uses a specific font, type size, and type style. Type the text you want to find in the Find text box and then choose Match⇨Font. WordPerfect displays a Match Font dialog box in which you can specify the specific font characteristics that you want to use in the search.

✔ You can also replace just the font or case of the found text. If you want to make *ConsumerScam* boldface, for example, you can enter *ConsumerScam* in both the Find option box and the Replace With option box, choose Replace⇨Font, and turn on the bold attribute in the Replace Font dialog box that appears. You can use the Replace and Match options together to find text with certain attributes and replace those attributes with other attributes — for example, to find all instances where *ConsumerScam* is italicized and make it boldface instead.

✔ Notice that the Replace menu becomes available only if the Replace With option box is active; the Match menu is available only if the Find option box is active.

✔ The menu options stay active until you turn them off. If you turn on font matching for one search, for example, it's automatically turned on for the next search you do. So check the options before you start each search to make sure that everything's the way you want it. Remember, a check mark next to an option means that the option is turned on. Click the option to toggle it on and off.

✔ The options on the Action menu tell WordPerfect to select the text it finds or to position the insertion marker before or after the text. If you turn on Select Match, for example, WordPerfect selects the text it finds in your document. You can then edit, delete, format, or move the text without needing to select it first. Just click in the document window to make it active; after you finish editing and are ready to continue your search, click inside the Find and Replace dialog box again.

✔ The commands on the Options menu control the direction and extent of the search. The first option on the menu tells WordPerfect to begin searching at the top of the document; the second option tells it to search from the insertion marker to the end of the document and then search from the beginning of the document to the insertion marker. If you don't turn on either option, WordPerfect searches from the insertion marker forward to the end of the document and then stops.

The Options menu contains two additional choices: The Limit Find Within Selection option searches selected text only; the Include Headers, Footers, Etc. in Find option searches the main body of the document as well as in headers, footers, text boxes, and so on.

You also choose Options➪Limit Number of Changes to display the Limit Number of Changes dialog box, which contains one option: Limit Changes To. As you can guess from the dialog box name, this option controls how many replacements WordPerfect makes after you choose the Replace All button. If you enter a value of 3 in the Limit Changes To option box, for example, WordPerfect replaces only the first three occurrences of the text that it finds. If you specify 0 as the limit, WordPerfect replaces all occurrences of the found text.

If all you want to do is find the next occurrence of a particular word or phrase, select the text and then click the Find Next button on the Property Bar or press Alt+Ctrl+N. WordPerfect locates the text and selects it. To find the preceding occurrence of the word or phrase, click the Find Previous button or press Alt+Ctrl+P.

Checking Your Spelling

Remember that kid in grade school who won all the spelling bees? Well, WordPerfect makes that kid's brain cells available to you through its Spell Checker. You can ask the Spell Checker — a.k.a. Mr. Smarty Pants — to look over your document and point out any misspelled or duplicated words.

The Spell Checker knows only whether the words you use are spelled correctly — it doesn't know whether you used the wrong word or the wrong form of a word. The Spell Checker doesn't notify you that you typed *your,* for example, if you meant to type *you're.* The moral of the story: Just like Mr. Smarty Pants in grade school, the Spell Checker isn't nearly as smart as you may have been led to believe. And running the Spell Checker is no substitute for proofreading your document.

Even so, running the Spell Checker before you print or save your finished copy is always a good idea. WordPerfect is likely to turn up some typos or misspellings that you missed. The next two sections explain how to check the spelling after you finish typing your work and how to use on-the-fly spell-checking features, which alert you to mistakes as you type.

Running the Spell Checker

Here's how to give your document a spelling test by using the Spell Checker:

1. **Press Ctrl+F1 or click the Spell Checker toolbar button.**

   You can also choose <u>T</u>ools⇨<u>S</u>pell Checker. The Spell Checker window opens, as shown in Figure 9-6. WordPerfect finds and highlights the first misspelled or duplicated word. The Replace With text box shows WordPerfect's suggested correction, and the Replacements list offers other possible corrections.

   If you want to check only a portion of your document, select it before opening the Spell Checker. Alternatively, tell WordPerfect which part of your document to check by choosing an option from the Check drop-down list in the Spell Checker window.

2. **Select the appropriate options to tell WordPerfect to replace, ignore, or add the word.**

   • To replace the misspelled word with the word in the Replace With text box, click the Replace button. If you want to replace the misspelled word with some other word, type it into the Replace With text box or click it in the Replacements list. Then click the Replace button.

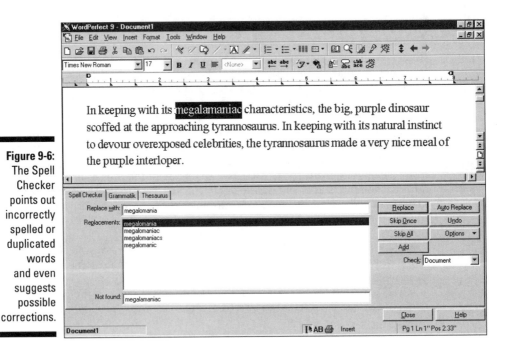

Figure 9-6:
The Spell Checker points out incorrectly spelled or duplicated words and even suggests possible corrections.

- Alternatively, you can click inside your document to make it active again and edit the word yourself. Click back inside the Spell Checker window and click Resume when you're ready to start checking more words.

- WordPerfect knows only the words that are included in its internal dictionary — which means that Spell Checker marks as incorrect many words that are really okay. To tell WordPerfect to ignore a particular word and move on to the next misspelled word, click Skip Once. To tell it to ignore this word throughout the rest of the document, click Skip All. To add the word to the WordPerfect dictionary, click Add.

- By default, WordPerfect checks words that contain numbers, checks for duplicate words, and checks for incorrect capitalization. If you don't want the Spell Checker to check any or all of these things, click the Options button and turn off these options in the drop-down list. (A check mark next to an option means that the option is turned on.)

- The Auto Replace button is, in my opinion, a dangerous little doodad. Click this button, and WordPerfect automatically replaces all occurrences of the misspelled word with the correct word. The misspelled word and its correction are also added to the QuickCorrect list. (See Chapter 6 for information about QuickCorrect.) And any time you type the misspelled word again, WordPerfect automatically replaces the word with the correction if the Replace Words As You Type option is turned on in the QuickCorrect dialog box.

  The problem with the Auto Replace feature is that it's activated even if you never click the Auto Replace button. When you start the Spell Checker, WordPerfect consults the QuickCorrect list, and replaces *any* words on that list with their "correct" spelling and punctuation. Using the same example as I do in Chapter 6, say that you use the word *august* as an adjective, rather than as the month name. Because *August* is listed in the QuickCorrect dialog box as the appropriate replacement for *august,* the Spell Checker automatically makes the replacement in your document. I find this behavior frightening because you have no way of knowing what words are being replaced. To be safe, I recommend that you click the Options button and turn on the Prompt Before Auto Replacement option. That way, the Spell Checker stops on every misspelled word and enables you to decide whether you want to replace it.

If you replace a word by mistake, click on the Undo button inside the Spell Checker window.

After WordPerfect finishes grading your spelling, it asks whether you want to close the Spell Checker window. Click Yes to close the window or No to leave it open and available for your next spelling session. If you leave the window open, click the Start button to check more text.

You can resize the Spell Checker window by dragging its top edge up or down. You can also move it to another position on-screen by placing the cursor near the top of the window until the cursor becomes a four-headed arrow. After you see the arrow, you can drag the window to a new location. Drag any edge of the dialog box to resize it.

Activating your spelling and grammar coach

If you want to be notified of incorrect spellings as you type, turn on the Spell-As-You-Go feature. WordPerfect then underscores any misspelled word with a red striped line after you type it. Right-click the word to display a QuickMenu of suggested spellings. Click the word in the QuickMenu to replace the misspelled word with that word.

Personally, I find this feature distracting, but you may like it. To turn Spell-As-You-Go on, choose Tools⇨Proofread⇨Spell-As-You-Go. Turn the feature off by choosing Tools⇨Proofread⇨Off. If you turn on Grammar-As-You-Go, a related proofreading feature, Spell-As-You-Go is automatically turned on as well.

In addition to Spell-As-You-Go, WordPerfect offers two additional digital writing coaches that nag you about errors in your composition:

✔ Choose Tools⇨Proofread⇨Prompt-As-You-Go to toggle the Prompt-As-You-Go feature on and off. If you click a misspelled word or a grammatically incorrect word while Prompt-As-You-Go is enabled, the Property Bar displays a Prompt-As-You-Go menu that contains a list of corrections. Click a correction to insert it in place of the problem word.

   If you click a word that's spelled correctly and doesn't pose any grammatical problems, the Prompt-As-You-Go menu offers synonyms for the word, acting like a mini-thesaurus. Click a word in the list to replace the original word in your text.

✔ Grammar-As-You-Go, which you access by choosing Tools⇨Proofread⇨Grammar-As-You-Go, is supposed to underline grammatical errors with a blue striped line, just as Spell-As-You-Go underlines spelling errors with a red striped line. You can then right-click the word to choose a suggested replacement word or select a correction from the Prompt-As-You-Go menu, if that featured is turned on.

Unfortunately, WordPerfect appears to be a little lacking in the grammar department. After I typed "Them there fools ain't no better than me," for example, Grammar-As-You-Go underlined only *ain't* as a possible error. Thank goodness we still have them there real-life copy editors to keep us on track because ain't none of us would look too smart if we relied on Grammar-As-You-Go.

Using QuickWords

With QuickWords, a relative of the QuickCorrect feature covered in Chapter 6, you can type a few characters to represent a long word or phrase and then have WordPerfect automatically replace those characters with the expanded version of the text. To use QuickWords, follow these steps:

1. **Type and select the text you want to represent with the abbreviation.**

   For example, say that you want WordPerfect to substitute *IDG Books Worldwide* when you type *IDG*. In your document, you would type *IDG Books Worldwide* and then select the phrase.

2. **Choose Tools⇨QuickWords to open the QuickCorrect dialog box, with the QuickWords tab at the forefront.**

3. **Type the abbreviation you want to use in the Abbreviated Form option box.**

   Continuing with the IDG Books Worldwide example, you would type *IDG* in the box.

4. **Set your expand options, as appropriate.**

   If you want WordPerfect to replace the abbreviation with the full text as you type the abbreviation, check the Expand QuickWords as You Type Them check box. If you don't choose the Expand QuickWords as You Type Them check box, WordPerfect waits until you issue the go-ahead to replace the abbreviations with the full text.

   If you want WordPerfect to use the same formatting as the original text every time it replaces the abbreviation with the expanded text, click the Options button and choose Expand as Text with Formatting. Otherwise, choose Expand as Plain Text.

5. **Click OK.**

If you didn't sign up for as-you-type replacements in Step 4, you can expand an abbreviation by clicking it and pressing Ctrl+Shift+A.

If you forget the abbreviation for a QuickWords phrase, click an abbreviation that looks familiar on the QuickWords tab of the QuickCorrect dialog box. A preview of the expanded text appears in the dialog box. Click the Insert in Text button to put the text in your document.

Although most folks use QuickWords to speed up the process of typing long phrases or names, you can also use it to substitute a graphic for a text abbreviation. First, add the graphic to a document using the standard techniques explored in Chapter 8. Then select the graphic (click it to display the selection handles), open the QuickWords dialog box, enter the abbreviation you want to use, click Add Entry, and click OK. Now you can type the abbreviation to insert the graphic quickly.

Playing Post Office

Want to make sure that your letters and packages make it safely and swiftly from the Post Office to your recipient's mailbox? Decrease the odds of some enroute snafu by creating neatly printed envelopes and labels instead of scrawling the addresses by hand.

WordPerfect offers two features that make creating envelopes and labels a cinch, as well as an option for inserting names and addresses stored in the CorelCentral Address Book into your documents. The remainder of this chapter explains these helpful tools.

Creating envelopes

If you want to print an envelope, you can use the Page Setup command discussed in Chapter 7 to create documents that match the size of the envelope. But, for a more convenient route to glory, choose Format⇨Envelope.

In past versions of WordPerfect, the Envelope command took you to the Envelopes dialog box, where you chose your envelope size and handled various other envelope-creation chores. Now the command formats your document to match the dimensions of a standard No. 10 envelope and displays Property Bar buttons that enable you to change the envelope size, insert addresses from the CorelCentral Address Book, set a specific position for the return and mailing address, and even add a postal bar code to the envelope. (Note that if you change the envelope size, WordPerfect uses that size by default the next time you choose the Envelope command.)

After you choose the Envelope command, the cursor is positioned at the spot where the mailing address should go, so just type your address.

What about the return address? If you previously used a PerfectExpert template that required you to enter your name and address, WordPerfect inserts the name and address as the return address. To change that information, just select the text and edit it as usual. If you haven't yet used such a template, just click at the position where you want the return address to go and type your address. If you like, you can drag the margin guidelines to adjust the distance of the return address from the edge of the envelope.

To create another envelope in the same document, press Ctrl+Shift+Enter, just as you do to start a new page in a regular WordPerfect document.

If you want to design a custom envelope for your business (or pleasure), choose File⇨New from Project and select the Envelope template from the PerfectExpert dialog box. The template provides you with several envelope designs, which you can explore by following the prompts and instructions in the PerfectExpert window (the window appears automatically when you use the template).

Making labels

To create and print labels, point and click this way:

1. **Press Alt+F5 or choose View⇨Page to switch to Page view.**

   If you work in Draft view, you can't see the individual labels as well as you can in Page view.

2. **Choose Format⇨Labels.**

   WordPerfect opens a dialog box that enables you to choose from a slew of preset label types and sizes. (You can also click Create to enter custom label sizes.)

3. **Choose a label size and click Select.**

   Your document changes so that you see one label. (If you select a large label size, the screen may not appear to change, but if you zoom out, you can see that the document is, in fact, formatted for the label.)

4. **Type the first label.**

   To center the text vertically on the label, choose Format⇨Page⇨Center. Use the standard Indent command (Format⇨Paragraph⇨Indent) to position the text horizontally within the label. (See Chapter 7 for more details on both of these commands.)

5. **Press Ctrl+Shift+Enter to create the next label.**

   WordPerfect creates each label as a separate page in your document. So, to start a new label, you use the same shortcut as you do for starting a new page (Ctrl+Shift+Enter).

If you use the CorelCentral Address Book to store your correspondence information, you can insert addresses directly from the Address Book. Rather than typing your label text in Step 4, choose Tools⇨Address Book to open the Address Book. Click the first address you want to insert and Ctrl+click all additional addresses. Then click the Insert button in the Address Book window. WordPerfect creates labels for all of the addresses you clicked. In some cases, you may be asked to specify an address style after you click the Insert button. Click the style you want and click OK.

When you're ready to print your labels, use the File⇨Print command as usual. Keep in mind that because each label is considered a separate page, you can print individual labels by printing just the pages that contain those labels. You can do so by using the Current Page, Print Pages, or Multiple Pages options inside the Print dialog box. And, if you want to print many copies of the same label, just use the Number of Copies option in the Print dialog box, as you would to print multiple copies of any document. For details on printing, see Chapter 5.

Inserting addresses into your documents

To insert a contact address from the CorelCentral Address Book into a WordPerfect document, choose Tools⇨Address Book inside WordPerfect. The CorelCentral Address Book window appears. Click the address you want to insert and then click Insert.

Part III

Crunching Numbers like a (Quattro) Pro

In this part . . .

*I*n the interest of keeping everyone thoroughly confused, computer industry bigwigs like to give things obscure, meaningless names. Take Quattro Pro, for example. Loosely translated, *quattro* means *four* in some long-forgotten language. So it follows that Quattro Pro makes you a professional at . . . four?

The real story behind Quattro Pro's name has to do with a marketing ploy to unseat a rival program, Lotus 1-2-3. (Get it — 4 is one better than 3?) Well, at least that's the rumored reason, and it seems as plausible as any.

As you dive into this part of the book, don't waste another minute worrying about why Quattro Pro was given such a name. Concentrate instead on what this terrific program can do for you: build tables, do mathematical calculations, turn ordinary numbers into impressive charts, and generally help keep track of and calculate any kind of data, from your annual sales figures to your household budget. Come to think of it, that's four things that Quattro Pro does well . . . hmm.

Chapter 10

The Spreadsheet Solution

1 hate math. If you want me to add, multiply, subtract, or divide, you darn well better give me a good reason — and a calculator. Numbers and I just don't get along. Never have, never will.

If you share my aversion to things mathematical, you're going to love Quattro Pro. "But," you ask, "isn't math one of the main things you do with Quattro Pro?" Yep. Sure is. And that's why I appreciate this program so much. Any time a project involving lots of calculations rears its ugly head, I just crank up Quattro Pro. I get the answers I need in no time, without needing to tax my numerically challenged brain.

Of course, if you're the sort who gets all giddy when presented with a fresh column of numbers to add, you should like Quattro Pro even more. One of the top spreadsheet programs on the market, Quattro Pro gives you advanced mathematical features you've only dreamed about until now.

This chapter gets you started on the road to spreadsheet heaven by explaining the basics of the Quattro Pro 9 spreadsheet window and showing you how to open, close, and save your work.

So What Can I Do with This Thing?

You may be wondering exactly what a spreadsheet program can do. For starters, Quattro Pro is a whiz at figuring out the answers to any problem that involves numbers. The program is also a handy record-keeping tool. Here are just some projects you can manage with Quattro Pro:

- **Keep a household or business budget:** You can record monthly expenses by category — rent, gas, utilities, and so on. You can then have Quattro Pro calculate your total monthly expenses, quarterly expenses, year-to-date expenses, and your actual expenses versus your budget forecast.

- **Perform a profit and loss analysis:** You can determine the net return on your company's latest product, given various pricing and manufacturing scenarios. You can try out different price points, for example, to determine which pricing structure nets you the most profit, considering your production, marketing, and distribution costs.

- **Track business sales and inventories:** You can record monthly sales for each item you sell and then calculate the totals of all items in a certain category, figure out your net profit on different items, keep track of your remaining inventory, and even determine the top salesperson in your store for a particular month.

- **Create tables of information:** You can create an employee work schedule that includes names, phone numbers, departments, hours, and more. Of course, you can do the same thing in WordPerfect, but I find that Quattro Pro makes entering and formatting table data easier. And in Quattro Pro, you can easily perform related tasks, such as calculating the total number of hours worked per employee and multiplying the hours worked by the employee's hourly wage.

- **Create charts to clarify data:** After you create an income and expense spreadsheet, for example, you can create a pie chart showing expenses by category so that you can easily see where your money goes each month.

In other words, if your project involves many different pieces of data or lots of calculations, Quattro Pro can help you get the job done. Quattro Pro also gives you a painless way to turn spreadsheets into professional-looking reports.

Start It Up, Shut It Down

Starting Quattro Pro is just like starting any other program in WordPerfect Office 2000: Click the Quattro Pro DAD icon or click the Windows Start button, click Programs, click WordPerfect Office 2000, and click Quattro Pro 9. (If you need help installing the program on your computer, see the appendix in this book.)

To send Quattro Pro packing, click the program window's Close button, press Alt+F4, or choose File➪Exit. If you haven't saved your work yet, Quattro Pro prompts you to do so. (Saving is explained in the section "Open Me! Close Me! Save Me!," later in this chapter.)

Your Field Guide to Quattro Pro

Figure 10-1 shows the Quattro Pro window. Many elements in the Quattro Pro window are standard Windows program elements. (You can find more information in Chapter 2.) But Quattro Pro also comes with a few unique window accessories. The next two sections explain how these bells and whistles work.

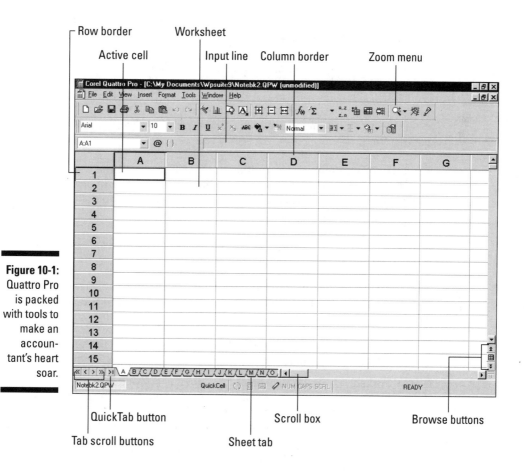

Figure 10-1: Quattro Pro is packed with tools to make an accountant's heart soar.

Anatomy of a Quattro Pro spreadsheet

In pre-computing days, business people recorded accounting data in ledgers. Ledgers held sheets of ruled (lined) paper designed for entering data in rows and columns. Quattro Pro provides you with the digital equivalent of a ledger.

But in Quattro Pro, the "ledger" is known as a *notebook.* And you can create as many notebooks as you need without ever stepping into the office supply store. To start a new notebook, you simply choose the File➪New command or use one of the other approaches that I discuss later in this chapter. Each notebook appears in its own window, just as a WordPerfect document has its own window.

Within a notebook, you find a hefty supply of *worksheets,* or simply *sheets* for short. You can think of a worksheet as one page — a really big page — in a ledger. That big, white, gridlike thing that consumes most of the Quattro Pro window is a worksheet (refer to Figure 10-1).

Previous editions of Quattro Pro limited you to 256 worksheets per notebook. Version 9 notebooks offer *18,000* worksheets! Gad! I doubt that you will ever need all 18,000 pages, but you never know. (Corel actually expanded the notebook capacity to accommodate users who wanted to import spreadsheets created in a competing spreadsheet program, Microsoft Excel, into Quattro Pro.)

A Quattro Pro notebook also contains a special page without a real-world equivalent. The *Objects sheet* is a page that holds charts and other special objects you can create but probably won't (such as custom dialog boxes). Chapter 14 explains more about the Objects sheet.

So much for the general makeup of a Quattro Pro spreadsheet. Now, some must-know, nitty-gritty details:

✔ Every worksheet has a name. By default, Quattro Pro assigns letters as names, with the first worksheet named sheet A. The worksheet names appear on the Sheet tabs, labeled in Figure 10-1. See the next section for information on how to move from sheet to sheet using these tabs, and check out "Naming Your Pages," later in this chapter, for instructions on changing the worksheet name.

✔ A worksheet, like a piece of ledger paper, is divided into *columns* and *rows.* Spreadsheet wonks call the lines that mark off the column and row boundaries *gridlines.* Columns are identified by the letters on the column border, and rows are identified by the numbers on the row border.

Version 9 worksheets contain approximately 1 million rows and 18,000 columns, a major increase from Version 8. Again, the jump accommodates high-end users who want to bring huge Microsoft Excel files into Quattro Pro. But ordinary users like you and me probably will never need all those rows and columns.

✔ The little boxes created by the intersection of columns and rows are called *cells.* Cells hold individual pieces of spreadsheet data.

✔ Each cell has a unique *cell address* (name) that includes its worksheet name followed by its column letter and row number. The cell in the upper-left corner of the notebook in Figure 10-1, for example, is cell A:A1.

✔ The black border around a cell indicates that the cell is the *active* cell — the one that will be affected by your next edit. The active cell in Figure 10-1 is cell A:A1. To make a cell active, just click it.

✔ The *input line* shows the data or mathematical formula in the active cell. You can enter and edit data and formulas either in the input line or directly in a cell. The address of the active cell appears at the left end of the input line.

How to move from here to there

Quattro Pro gives you a variety of ways to get around in your notebook:

✔ To move from one worksheet to another, click the sheet tabs, labeled in Figure 10-1. Or click the *tab scroll buttons,* also labeled in Figure 10-1. From left to right, the buttons are Go Back Several Sheets, Move Backward One Sheet, Move Forward One Sheet, and Move Forward Several Sheets.

You can display more sheet tabs by dragging the border between the last visible tab and the horizontal scroll bar. Place your cursor over the border until you see the double-headed arrow cursor. Then drag to the right to devote more screen space to the tabs.

✔ Click the *QuickTab button* to beam directly to the Objects sheet. Click the button again to return to the last active worksheet.

✔ You can move within a worksheet by using the standard Windows scroll arrows and scroll boxes (read Chapter 2 if you're unfamiliar with these tools). If you drag the scroll box on the vertical scroll bar, a little box displays row numbers as you scroll to tell you how far you're going. If you drag the horizontal scroll box, Quattro Pro displays column letters as you scroll.

✔ Like WordPerfect 9, Quattro Pro now offers a trio of Browse buttons at the bottom of the vertical scroll bar. The Browse buttons give you a convenient way to jump back and forth between different cells in your spreadsheet. You can see the three buttons in Figure 10-1.

Right-click the middle Browse button to display a QuickMenu of cell categories. The selected category determines what cells you can browse using the other two Browse buttons. Say that you want to browse all the cells that contain mathematical formulas. Choose the Formulas – Numbers option in the QuickMenu, and Quattro Pro highlights all cells that contain mathematical formulas (which Chapter 12 explains in agonizing detail). The first cell in the bunch becomes the active cell. Click the bottom Browse button to jump to the next cell and make that cell active. Click the top Browse button to jump back one cell.

If you're a spreadsheet newbie, most options on the QuickMenu will sound like Greek to you. In fact, until you start creating really advanced spreadsheets, few of the options even apply. The options that enable you to browse by formula, value, or label are the most helpful to beginners. (See Chapter 11 for an explanation of the terms *value* and *label*.)

✔ If you want to move to a specific cell in a very large spreadsheet, try out the Go To command. Press Ctrl+G or F5 (shortcuts for the Edit⇔Go To command) to display the Go To dialog box. Enter the cell address in the Reference option box and click OK. Type the cell address in this order: worksheet name, colon, column number, and row number — as in A:F238.

Using the Go To box is a bit of a bother, though. So unless you need to find a cell that's buried deep in your notebook or worksheet or is way off-screen, using the mouse and the scroll arrows is usually quicker.

✔ You can also navigate your notebook by using the keyboard shortcuts outlined in Table 10-1. Remember that the keyboard shortcuts, as well as some other Quattro Pro features, don't work if you're in edit mode (in the process of entering data in a cell). So, if you click a button or press a keyboard shortcut and nothing happens, click outside the cell and try again. Most shortcuts and features become unavailable when you're inside a dialog box, too. And some shortcuts do other things than described in Table 10-1; for example, pressing Tab inside a dialog box moves you to the next dialog box option.

If you can't remember what a particular button in the Quattro Pro window does, pause your mouse cursor on it for a few seconds. A little flag (QuickTip) appears to give you some helpful hints. See the next section for information about turning on QuickTips.

Table 10-1	Keys That Really Move You
Press This	*To Do This*
↑	Move up one cell.
↓	Move down one cell.
→ or Tab	Move right one cell.
← or Shift+Tab	Move left one cell.
Home	Go to the first cell in the active worksheet.
Ctrl+Home	Go to the first cell in the first worksheet of the notebook.
Ctrl+←	Scroll left one screen.
Ctrl+→	Scroll right one screen.

Press This	To Do This
PgDn	Scroll down one screen.
PgUp	Scroll up one screen.
End+↑	Go to the first filled cell in the current column.
End+↓	Go to the last filled cell in the current column.
End+←	Go to the first filled cell in the current row.
End+→	Go to the last filled cell in the current row.

I Don't Like What I See Here!

You can alter many aspects of the Quattro Pro display. Here's a look at just some of your options:

✔ You can zoom in or out on your work by clicking the Zoom button on the toolbar (refer to Figure 10-1) and choosing a zoom ratio from the drop-down list.

To focus on a particular area of your spreadsheet, select the area (see Chapter 13 for how-to's) and choose the Selection option from the Zoom menu. Quattro Pro enlarges or reduces the selected cells to fill the available screen space.

✔ You now have three different View modes available from the View menu:

• Choose View⇨Draft for the standard view mode. Your worksheet appears without any margin guidelines, headers and footers, or page break guidelines.

• Choose View⇨Page to see and manipulate margins and headers and footers right in the spreadsheet window, as shown in Figure 10-2. (If you work in Draft view, you must switch to the Print Preview window, covered in Chapter 15, to work with these elements.) If you place your cursor over a margin guideline, the cursor changes to a two-headed arrow, as shown in the figure. You can then drag the guideline to move the margin, just as you can in WordPerfect.

This mode also enables you to see page breaks — the places where Quattro Pro will start a new page when you print the spreadsheet. Quattro Pro displays thick lines in the spreadsheet to indicate the page breaks, which are based on your page margins and the page size you select in the Spreadsheet Page Setup dialog box. (Chapter 15 explains the dialog box.)

- Choose View⇨Page Breaks to view your spreadsheet in Draft view, but with page breaks visible. This view offers the advantage of displaying page breaks without dedicating any screen space to headers, footers, and margins.

✔ Normally, WordPerfect displays the result of a formula, rather than the formula itself, in spreadsheet cells. But if you choose View⇨Formulas, you see the formulas in the cells. Don't know what I mean by *formula?* Head for Chapter 12, which will no doubt make you sorry that you asked. And choose the Formulas command again to return to the normal, formula-less display.

✔ Choose Tools⇨Settings or press Alt+F12 to open the Settings dialog box, known as the Application dialog box in Version 8. In the Settings dialog box, you control things related to Quattro Pro in general. Click the Display tab to access options that hide or display the input line, scroll indicators (the row and column position boxes that appear as you drag the scroll box), and QuickTips (the little boxes that appear as you pause your mouse over a button or other on-screen element).

Margin move cursor   Header

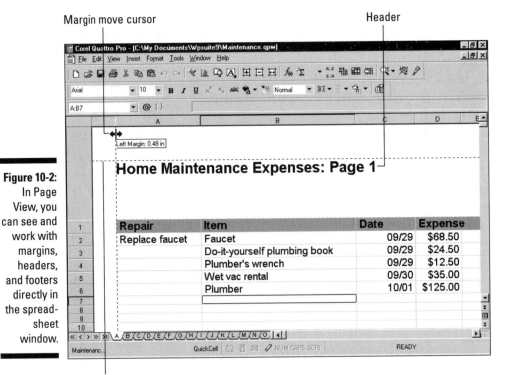

Figure 10-2:
In Page View, you can see and work with margins, headers, and footers directly in the spreadsheet window.

Margin guideline

The Display tab also contains a check box for turning the new RealTime Preview option on and off. With RealTime Preview enabled, you can preview the results of some edits, such as changing fonts, in the spreadsheet window. According to Corel, you can take advantage of this feature without worrying about straining your computer's memory or other system resources.

✔ Choose Format➪Notebook or press Shift+F12 to display the Active Notebook dialog box, which contains settings pertinent to the current notebook. The Display tab offers options for hiding the scroll bars and page tabs and also for controlling the display of objects such as charts and graphs. If you choose Show All, these objects appear in their entirety. If you choose Show Outline, you see only the outline of the object — this option can speed up screen displays if you use very complex objects. The Hide option, none too surprisingly, hides objects from view.

✔ Choose Format➪Sheet or press Ctrl+F12 to open the Active Sheet dialog box, where you establish display preferences for the current worksheet. You can get to this same dialog box by right-clicking the worksheet tab and choosing Sheet Properties from the QuickMenu.

However you get to the dialog box, click the Display tab to uncover the options shown in Figure 10-3. The Display Zeros options determine whether Quattro Pro displays a zero in a cell that has a value of zero or simply leaves the cell blank. The Border Options check boxes enable you to turn row and column borders on and off. And the Grid Lines check boxes are for hiding and displaying the horizontal and vertical gridlines that separate the cells in your worksheet. Note that the Grid Lines check boxes here only control on-screen display; to specify whether you want gridlines to print, you use the Gridlines option in the Spreadsheet Page Setup dialog box. You can find out more about printing and this option in Chapter 15.

Want to add a little color to your view? Quattro Pro enables you to assign colors to your worksheet tabs. Just click the Tab Color tab of the dialog box and deselect the Use System Color check box. Then click the drop-down list directly beneath the check box to display a palette of available colors. Click the color you want to use and then click OK.

✔ You can't open the Settings, Active Notebook, or Active Sheet dialog box while you're in the process of entering or editing data in a cell. Click another cell or press Enter to regain access to these dialog boxes.

✔ You can also display or hide the Property Bar and Application Bar. To toggle the bars on and off, choose their names from the View menu.

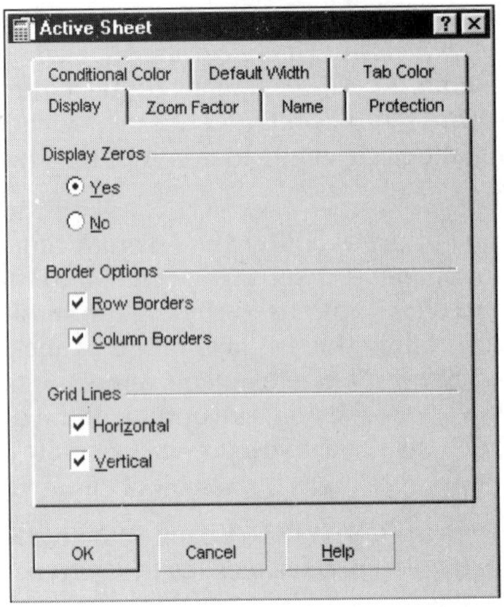

Figure 10-3:
You can
control
whether
zeros,
borders, and
gridlines
display via
this dialog
box.

✔ Like WordPerfect, Quattro Pro offers a selection of toolbars. You can select which toolbars display by choosing View⇨Toolbars to display the Toolbars dialog box. Check the boxes for the bars you want to see and then click OK.

✔ Right-click the Application Bar to display a QuickMenu that enables you to change the position and size of the bar.

Naming Your Pages

By default, Quattro Pro gives the spreadsheets in a notebook alphabetical names. The first sheet in the notebook is A, the second is B, and so on. The worksheet tabs at the bottom of the spreadsheet window reflect these names.

You can change a spreadsheet name if you want. If you put your June sales data on a worksheet, for example, you can name that sheet *June* (or something more inventive, if you're in the mood). Naming your sheets helps you remember what sort of data you're keeping on each one.

To name (or rename) a worksheet, double-click the worksheet tab, type the name, and press Enter. Or open up the Active Sheet dialog box (press Ctrl+F12 to get there quickly), click the Name tab, enter the new page name, and click OK.

Remember to use the new name in your cell addresses when entering formulas. See Chapter 12 for more information about using cell addresses in formulas.

My spreadsheet's in 3-D? Cool!

You may hear Quattro Pro and other advanced spreadsheet programs referred to as 3-D spreadsheets. But this kind of 3-D is different from the kind you get if you wear those funky 3-D glasses at the movies.

Each document you create in Quattro Pro is really thousands of individual spreadsheets — known as worksheets — stacked like pages in a notebook. On any individual worksheet, you can calculate in two dimensions — that is, you can calculate data in horizontal rows and in vertical columns. But you can also calculate in a third dimension, which in this case, happens to be up and down through the stack of worksheets.

Confused? Don't be. This 3-D business simply means that, in addition to calculating data you enter in a worksheet, you can calculate data entered in many different worksheets. Say, for example, that worksheet A contains your

monthly sales activity for January: how many units you sold of each item, the price of each item, your cost for each item, the date of the sale, and the total sales for the month. Worksheet B contains the same information for February, and worksheet C contains the data for March. With Quattro Pro, you can create a fourth worksheet that takes the data from worksheets A, B, and C and calculates all the sales information on a quarterly basis.

Before the days of 3-D spreadsheets, you could calculate only data contained in a single worksheet, which meant that spreadsheet documents could quickly become very large and cumbersome. The real benefit of a 3-D spreadsheet is that you can segment your data into more easily managed, easily updated, and easily viewed chunks. And you don't even need to wear special glasses to see your results.

Open Me! Close Me! Save Me!

Opening, closing, and saving files in Quattro Pro is handled pretty much the same way as in WordPerfect. The following sections provide a brief review of how things work; see the sections on opening and closing documents in Chapter 4 and the section on saving documents in Chapter 5 if you need more help.

Opening a new or existing notebook

To create a new blank notebook, choose File➪New, press Ctrl+N, or click the New toolbar button. If you want to create a notebook based on one of the Quattro Pro templates, choose File➪New from Project or press Ctrl+Shift+N. Quattro Pro displays the PerfectExpert dialog box, in which you can choose to create a blank notebook or to create a notebook based on a template, just as you can in WordPerfect.

Templates produce spreadsheets you can use to handle some common tasks, such as household budgets and business forms. The templates contain pre-formatted data that you can edit as necessary. To use a template, click its name in the list on the Create New tab and click Create. To create a blank notebook, select the Quattro Pro Notebook item and click Create.

 To open an existing notebook, choose File⇨Open, press Ctrl+O, or click the Open toolbar button. Quattro Pro answers your command by displaying the Open File dialog box. Chapter 4 contains details about this dialog box.

 Files that you create and save in Quattro Pro 9 end with the letters QPW. If you want to open a file that you created in an earlier version of Quattro Pro or in another spreadsheet program, select that program's file type from the File Type drop-down list. Quattro Pro can open many different types of files, including spreadsheets created in Microsoft Excel and Lotus 1-2-3, as well as database files created in Paradox and dBASE.

Closing a spreadsheet

To close a spreadsheet, click the spreadsheet window's Close button, choose File⇨Close, or press Ctrl+F4. Quattro Pro gives you a gentle reminder to save your work if you haven't done so yet. Saving, in fact, is the subject of the very next section.

Saving your work

Saving early — and saving often — is essential. If you don't, your efforts can go up in electronic smoke after you shut down Quattro Pro, if the power goes out for some reason, or if your computer crashes just to see what kind of response it can get from you.

 To save your spreadsheet for the first time, choose File⇨Save, press Ctrl+S, or click the Save toolbar button. Quattro Pro leaps to attention and shows you the Save File dialog box, which, conveniently enough, works just like the WordPerfect Save File dialog box. For all the ins and outs of this dialog box, see Chapter 5.

 Quattro Pro can save your file in a variety of file formats, including those used by other, lesser spreadsheet programs. Be aware, however, that some of these file formats can save only the current worksheet in your notebook. Quattro Pro alerts you if the file format can't save multiple-page spreadsheets.

Remember, too, that saving a document once doesn't protect you forever. If you make any changes to your spreadsheet, those changes aren't saved until you choose the Save command again. The second time you save your spreadsheet, Quattro Pro doesn't bother you with the Save File dialog box.

If you want to save your spreadsheet under a different name, to a different folder or drive, or in a different file format, choose File⇨Save As. Again, check out Chapter 5 if you need more details about this option.

To protect yourself even further, turn on Quattro Pro's automatic backup feature. Choose Tools⇨Settings or press Alt+F12 to display the Settings dialog box. Click the File Options tab, select the Timed Document Backup Every check box, and set the interval for the backup in the neighboring option box.

With automatic backup turned on, Quattro Pro stores a backup copy of your document as you work. If Quattro Pro or your system crashes, the program can open this backup copy, enabling you to recover most, if not always all, of your work.

The automatic backup doesn't mean that you don't need to save your document in the normal way (using the Save command) before you close it. The backup copy is only temporary and is saved only in the event of a program crash. When you click the Close button or choose the Close command to exit a document normally, Quattro Pro erases the backup copy.

Chapter 11

Filling in the Blanks

● ●

In This Chapter

▶ Taking the spreadsheet plunge

▶ Entering values and labels — and knowing which is which

▶ Finding out about Quattro Pro data-entry rules

▶ Letting QuickFill enter data for you

▶ Applying basic formatting

● ●

*W*hen you launch Quattro Pro, the program graciously presents you with a sparkling new notebook. What Quattro Pro doesn't do is give you any hints about what to do next. Where do you start? How do you get from rows and rows of empty cells to a spreadsheet that actually does something?

Try this: Press your forehead to your computer screen, close your eyes, and chant, "Spreadsheet, spreadsheet, spreadsheet," in a loud falsetto voice. Rumor has it that, if you do this long and hard enough, Quattro Pro divines your problem and builds your spreadsheet for you.

Didn't work? Hmm, guess that rumor was off the mark. Fortunately, this chapter tells you everything you need to know to turn that blank notebook into a working spreadsheet.

Building a Spreadsheet

Before you get into the nitty-gritty of entering data, you need a basic understanding of the process of building a spreadsheet. Take a look at Figure 11-1. It shows a spreadsheet that calculates the total sales and profits for one day — June 15, as indicated on the sheet tab. The approach I used to create this spreadsheet, sketched out in the following steps, is the same approach that you use to create any spreadsheet:

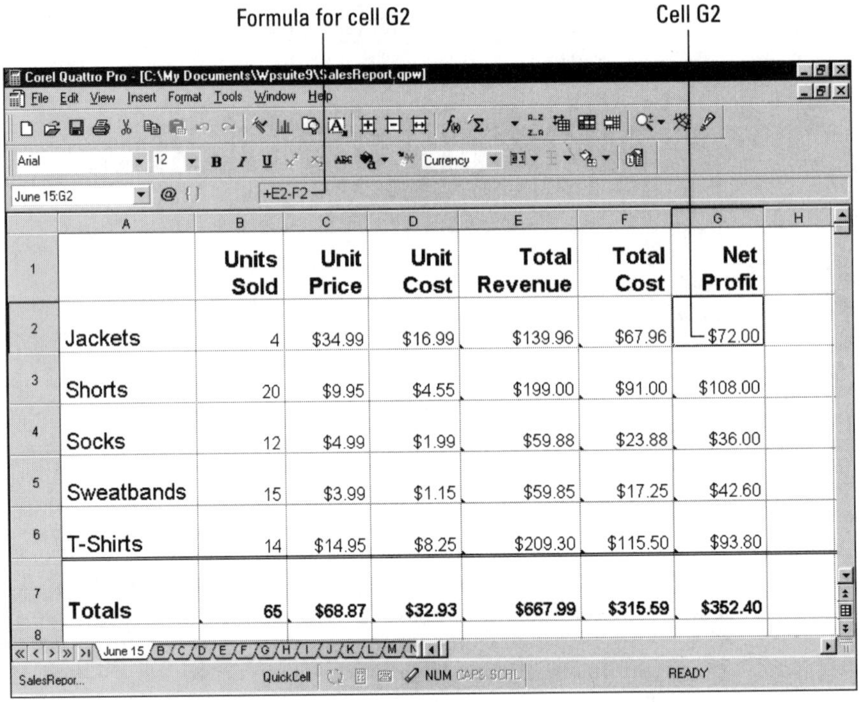

Formula for cell G2   Cell G2

	A	B	C	D	E	F	G	H
1		Units Sold	Unit Price	Unit Cost	Total Revenue	Total Cost	Net Profit	
2	Jackets	4	$34.99	$16.99	$139.96	$67.96	$72.00	
3	Shorts	20	$9.95	$4.55	$199.00	$91.00	$108.00	
4	Socks	12	$4.99	$1.99	$59.88	$23.88	$36.00	
5	Sweatbands	15	$3.99	$1.15	$59.85	$17.25	$42.60	
6	T-Shirts	14	$14.95	$8.25	$209.30	$115.50	$93.80	
7	Totals	65	$68.87	$32.93	$667.99	$315.59	$352.40	

Figure 11-1:
Quattro Pro makes calculating the day's sales totals and profits easy.

1. **Enter the column and row labels.**

   I'm referring to the category names found at the top of each column and the beginning of each row. In Figure 11-1, the column labels are *Units Sold, Unit Price*, and so on, and the row labels are *Jackets, Shorts, Socks,* and so on.

2. **Enter the known values.**

   Next, enter the known data — that is, the data that already exists and doesn't require any calculating by Quattro Pro. In Figure 11-1, for example, the known values are the units sold, the unit price, and the unit cost.

3. **Enter the formulas for the values you want Quattro Pro to find.**

   If you're reading this book in order, from front to back, you may recall that I said in Chapter 10 that you don't need to do any math to use Quattro Pro. Well, that's not completely true. You don't need to do the actual calculations — the addition, the multiplication, and so on — but you do need to enter the basic mathematical formulas that you want Quattro Pro to solve. But cheer up — if I can do it, you can, too. Really. Just ask my accountant.

In Figure 11-1, I entered three different formulas: one to calculate the total revenue received from each item (Units Sold multiplied by Unit Price); one to calculate the total cost of each item (Units Sold multiplied by Unit Cost); and one to calculate the total profit of the day's sales (Total Revenue minus Total Cost). In Figure 11-1, the input line shows the actual formula used to calculate the value in cell G2, which holds the net profit from jacket sales. (Chapter 12 explains how to write and enter formulas, by the way.)

4. **Edit and format your data.**

   After you enter your initial data, you may find things that you want to fix. Chapter 13 shows you how to edit your data.

   You find out how to do basic formatting, such as making your data boldface or italic, at the end of this chapter, in the section "Handling Basic Formatting Chores." Chapters 14 and 15 explain how to add graphs and put the finishing formatting touches on your data. Chapter 15 also shows you how to print your spreadsheet.

In reality, you don't always perform these steps in this order. You may find that formatting your data as you enter it, for example, is easier than formatting later. But the basic steps involved remain the same, whether you're creating a simple spreadsheet such as the one shown in Figure 11-1 or developing some mondo-complex thing that would turn Federal Reserve chairman Alan Greenspan even greener with envy.

Entering Data

The individual pieces of data in your spreadsheet go into cells — those little squares created by the intersection of a row and a column. Spreadsheet data falls into two categories in Quattro Pro:

   ✔ A *label* is a text entry, such as a column title. Labels can actually contain numbers as well as letters (as in the title *1st Quarter,* for example).

   ✔ A *value* is a number or a formula.

I bring up this techno-nerd issue only because Quattro Pro treats labels a little differently than values, as you discover at the end of this section.

Basic data entry

To enter data — whether a label or a value — into a cell, follow these steps:

1. **Click the cell in which you want to put the data.**

   You enter data into the active cell, which is the one surrounded by the little black box. Clicking a cell makes it active.

If you want to edit existing data, double-click the cell. Then follow the editing procedures outlined in Chapter 13. If you simply click once and begin typing, Quattro Pro overwrites the existing data with whatever you type.

2. **Type the value or label.**

After you begin typing, Quattro Pro displays an insertion marker that indicates where the next character you type will appear, as shown in Figure 11-2. The mouse cursor also changes to the I-beam cursor.

The data you type appears both in the cell and in the input line, as shown in the figure. If you make a mistake as you type, press the Backspace key to erase characters to the left of the insertion marker. Or use any of the other editing techniques presented in Chapter 13. (Chapter 12 covers the specifics of entering formulas.) To move the insertion marker, place the I-beam cursor where you want the insertion marker to be and then click.

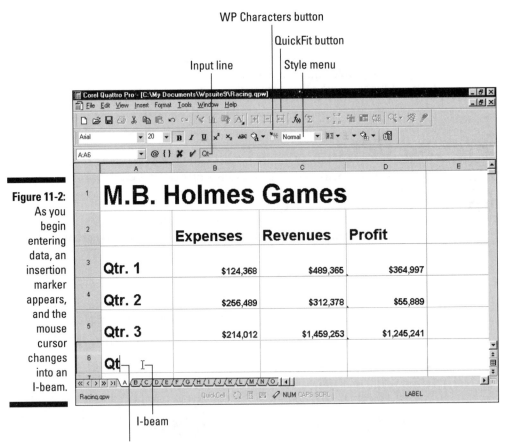

Figure 11-2: As you begin entering data, an insertion marker appears, and the mouse cursor changes into an I-beam.

3. Press Enter.

To complete your data entry, press Enter.

4. Move on to the next cell and enter the next piece of data.

By default, Quattro Pro activates the next cell down in the worksheet when you press Enter. But you can tell the program to move one cell up, one cell to the left, or one cell to the right instead. Here's how: After you press Enter to finish entering data, press Alt+F12 to open the Settings dialog box. (You can't open the dialog box while you're in the process of entering data into a cell.) Click the General tab and look for the Move Cell Selector/Enter key option. Make sure the option is turned on (a check mark is in the box) and then choose a direction option from the adjacent drop-down list. If you turn the check box off, the current cell remains active after you press Enter.

You can also move to another cell by clicking that cell or using the keyboard shortcuts listed in Table 10-1, in Chapter 10.

A handy Version 9 change makes entering special symbols such as foreign letters, copyright symbols, and the like a breeze. The Property Bar now offers a WP Characters button (refer to Figure 11-2). Click the button or press Ctrl+W to open the WordPerfect Symbols dialog box, which gives you access to the available special symbols. Chapter 8 explains how to select and insert characters from this dialog box.

Basically, that's all you do to enter data. But the following things may trip you up:

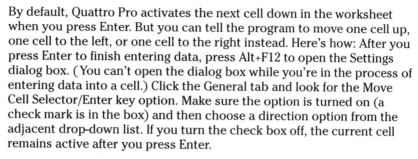

 ✔ If you see a row of asterisks or some other weird characters in the cell after you press Enter, the cell is too small to hold the value you entered. Chapter 13 explains how to precisely resize cells, columns, and rows. But for a quick fix, click the cell and then click the QuickFit button on the toolbar.

You can avoid this problem entirely for some types of entries by turning on the Fit-As-You-Go feature, found on the General tab of the Settings dialog box. (Click any cell and then press Alt+F12 to open the dialog box.) If Fit-As-You-Go is active, Quattro Pro automatically enlarges a too-small cell. This feature works only when you're entering values, and even then, it's disabled if the General, Text, or Scientific numeric format is selected. See "Handling Basic Formatting Chores," later in this chapter, for an explanation of this numeric format stuff.

 ✔ If a label is too long to fit in a cell, it spills over into the neighboring cell. But if that neighboring cell contains an entry, Quattro Pro hides the part of the label that doesn't fit. The data's still in there, but it doesn't appear or print correctly until you fix things. Again, you can use the editing approaches that I explain in Chapter 13 or just click the QuickFit button. Fit-As-You-Go has no effect on too-long labels.

✔ Quattro Pro automatically formats your cell data according to the current style, which appears on the Style menu on the Property Bar (refer to Figure 11-2). You can find out more about styles later in this chapter, in the section "Handling Basic Formatting Chores." But for now, just be aware that the style can change what you enter into the cell. If the Normal style is active and you enter *9.00,* for example, Quattro Pro automatically changes your entry to just *9,* which complies with the numeric formatting used by the Normal style. "Changing the numeric format," later in this chapter, tells you how to apply the numeric format you want.

✔ The QuickType feature, introduced in Version 8, tries to help you enter data. Say that you type the word *Blech* into a cell, press Enter, and type a capital *B* into the cell directly below the first cell. Quattro Pro thinks, "Hey, you must want to enter *Blech* again, so I'll just go ahead and put that label into the cell for you." If you don't, in fact, want to enter *Blech,* you can press Delete or just keep typing the real label. Quattro Pro gets rid of the unwanted *lech* and slinks away in embarrassment. The same thing happens if you enter a formula, except that Quattro Pro tries to intuit what formula you want to use.

On some occasions, you may find QuickType helpful, but my guess is that, more often than not, you'll just say *blech.* The check box that turns QuickType on and off is located on the General tab of the Settings dialog box (choose <u>T</u>ools➪<u>S</u>ettings or press Alt+F12). Remember that you can't open the dialog box while you're entering data in a cell. So click another cell or press Enter before you press Alt+F12.

Data entry do's and don'ts

As you enter data into a cell, Quattro Pro furrows its brow and tries to determine whether you're entering a label or a value. Quattro Pro bases its guess on whether the cell contains letters. If your entry contains any letters, Quattro Pro deems the entry a label. If the entry contains numbers only, Quattro Pro considers the entry a value. The difference is important because Quattro Pro applies different automatic formatting to labels than it does to values.

To make sure that your labels get treated as labels and values as values, be careful not to break any of the following rules:

✔ Don't use spaces or currency symbols when entering values. If you do, Quattro Pro treats the data as a label rather than a value. (The exception is the dollar sign, which you can use without problems.) If you're entering numbers that call for commas, Quattro Pro inserts the commas for you automatically. But if you forget and enter the commas yourself, you don't do any harm.

If you want a currency symbol to appear before a number — for example, the symbol for the dollar or pound — don't bother entering the symbol yourself. Instead, enter your monetary data without any symbol. Then set the currency style according to the instructions given in "Changing the numeric format," later in this chapter. Quattro Pro can automatically insert the currency symbol for the cells you select.

✔ To enter a negative number, type the minus sign (-) before the number. Don't put the number in parentheses, as some accountants do in their reports. After you enter your negative numbers, you can tell Quattro Pro to get rid of the minus signs and put parentheses around the numbers if you want. See "Changing the numeric format," later in this chapter, for details.

✔ By Quattro Pro decree, labels can't start with the following punctuation marks: a forward slash (/), the plus sign (+), minus sign (–), dollar symbol ($), left parenthesis (( ), at symbol (@), period (.), number symbol (#), or equals sign (=). If you really, really want to start a label with one of these characters, enter one of the following label-prefix characters at the start of the label: single quote ('), double quote ("), or caret (^). The apostrophe aligns the label with the left edge of the cell; the quotation mark aligns it with the right edge of the cell; and the caret centers the label in the cell. The label prefix characters don't appear in the cell after you press Enter, but they do appear in the input line.

So what if you want to start out a label entry with a quotation mark? Enter one of the label-prefix characters first, according to the alignment you want. Then type your quotation mark.

✔ If you're not a fanatic about whether your stuff lines up perfectly in your spreadsheet, you can just enter a space before your label text instead of trying to remember the quotation mark and caret stuff.

✔ If the first character in the cell is a backslash (\), Quattro Pro repeats the characters that follow over and over to fill up the cell. In other words, if you enter \Hey!, Quattro Pro fills your cell with *Hey!Hey!Hey!* I'm not sure whether you may ever find this feature helpful, but I thought you ought to know. (If you don't want the characters to repeat, enter a space before the backslash.)

QuickFilling Cells

Quattro Pro offers a neat feature called QuickFill that speeds up the entry of labels and values that fall in a sequence. Suppose that you want to fill the first 30 rows of Column A with the numbers 1 though 30 — to label the rows with the days of the month, for example. Instead of typing each number, have QuickFill enter them for you.

Figure 11-3 shows several rows and columns that I filled by using QuickFill. As you can see, you can QuickFill dates, months, and even a mixture of text and numbers. Follow these steps to try out QuickFill:

1. **Type the first label or value in the first cell that you want to fill and press Enter.**

2. **Click the cell you filled in Step 1.**

3. **Put your cursor at the lower-right border of the cell to display a plus-sign cursor.**

   Make sure that the cursor is a plus sign and not a double-headed arrow. The double-headed arrow appears if the cursor is over the bottom of the cell but not in the right end of the cell. You move cells when the double-headed arrow cursor is active.

4. **Drag over the rest of the cells that you want to fill.**

   The cells become highlighted, as shown in Figure 11-3. When you release the mouse button, Quattro Pro fills the cells. The cell you filled in Step 1 remains the active cell.

If you have trouble maneuvering the mouse so that the plus sign cursor appears, try this method instead. In Step 3, place the cursor in the center of the cell, so that the regular arrow cursor appears (again, stay away from the bottom left and center of the cell, or you get the double-headed arrow cursor). Now drag over the cells you want to fill, release the mouse button, and click the QuickFill button on the toolbar. Or right-click the selected cells and choose QuickFill from the QuickMenu.

You can create your own series, as I did in Column F in Figure 11-3, by typing all the elements of the series once. (I entered Red, Green, and Blue in the first three cells.) After typing the series once, click and drag from the first cell, using the QuickFill methods I just described. Quattro Pro repeats the series as many times as necessary to fill the selected cells. You can also create number patterns, such as 1,3,5,7,9, by entering the first numbers in the pattern (1 and 3, in this case) and then using QuickFill to fill the following cells.

Another way to quickly fill cells is to copy the contents of one cell and paste the contents into other cells. Chapter 13 dishes the dirt on this topic.

QuickFill button

```
Corel Quattro Pro - [C:\My Documents\Wpsuite9\QuickFill.qpw]
File  Edit  View  Insert  Format  Tools  Window  Help
```

Arial   12   B I U   Normal

A:G1   @ {}   1996

	B	C	D	E	F	G	H
1	January	Monday	06/01	$10	Red	1996	
2	February	Tuesday	06/02	$11	Green		
3	March	Wednesday	06/03	$12	Blue		
4	April	Thursday	06/04	$13	Red		
5	May	Friday	06/05	$14	Green		
6	June	Saturday	06/06	$15	Blue		
7	July	Sunday	06/07	$16	Red		
8	August	Monday	06/08	$17	Green		
9	September	Tuesday	06/09	$18	Blue		
10	October	Wednesday	06/10	$19	Red		
11	November	Thursday	06/11	$20	Green		
12	December	Friday	06/12	$21	Blue		
13	January	Saturday	06/13	$22	Red		
14	February	Sunday	06/14	$23	Green		

QuickFill.qpw   QuickCell   NUM CAPS SCRL   READY

Figure 11-3: QuickFill automates the entry of values and labels that fall in sequence.

Handling Basic Formatting Chores

Like WordPerfect, Quattro Pro uses *styles,* which automatically apply certain basic formatting attributes such as font, type size, and numeric format to your data. The default style is Normal, which uses 10-point Arial type and the General numeric format.

To apply a different style, first select the cells you want to format. For a single cell, just click the cell to select it. For a block of cells, drag over the block. (Chapter 13 presents additional ways to select cells, if you're curious.) Then just choose the style from the Style menu on the Property Bar, labeled back in Figure 11-2.

To change the default formatting used by the Normal style or any other style, choose Format⇨Styles to open the Styles dialog box, shown in Figure 11-4. Choose the style you want to change from the Define Style For drop-down list. Click the button (not the check box) for the formatting attribute you want to change — Font for font (duh!), type size, and style; Format for numeric format; and so on. Quattro Pro then displays the appropriate dialog box for changing the formatting you want to alter. If you want Quattro Pro to use the new default formatting for all new notebooks, select the Apply as Default for All New Notebooks (duh again) check box. After you finish setting all the default formatting attributes, click OK to make your changes official.

Figure 11-4:
In this
dialog box,
you can
alter the
formatting
attributes
applied by a
style.

Styles	? ☒
D̲efine Style For:	**OK**
Normal ▼	D̲elete Merge... **Cancel**
Included Properties	**H̲elp**
☑ 1 Alignment... ☐ 5 Shading...	
☑ 2 F̲ormat... ☑ 6 F̲ont...	
☑ 3 Protection... ☐ 7 T̲ext Color...	
☑ 4 Line Drawing...	
☐ Apply as default for all n̲ew notebooks	

Regardless of what style is selected, you can override the effects of the style by applying different formatting to selected cells. You can even apply some character formatting attributes, including type size and font, to individual characters within a cell. You can make one character in a cell bold, for example, and leave the rest plain. To apply formatting to specific characters in a cell, double-click the cell, drag across the characters you want to format, and apply the formatting.

The following sections tell you how to change the font, type size, type style, alignment, and numeric format of your data.

Changing the numeric format

Numeric format refers to how values are formatted. Numeric formatting controls such things as how many decimal places you can have and whether a dollar sign appears before the number. Several of Quattro Pro's built-in styles, including Currency and Date, apply formatting designed to accommodate specific types of values.

If one of these styles doesn't suit your fancy, click the cell you want to format (or select a range of cells) and click the Format Selection button on the Property Bar. Or press F12 or choose Fo̲rmat⇨S̲election.

Quattro Pro leaps to attention and displays the Active Cells dialog box, shown in Figure 11-5. Click the Numeric Format tab to display a variety of formatting options for numbers, dates, and times. After you click some of the formatting radio buttons, additional options appear that enable you to get even more specific. If you select the Currency option, for example, you can specify how many decimal places you want to include and select which country's currency standards you want to use. You can even format your monetary entries using the new Euro as the currency symbol (select Euro as your country of choice, not Italy or some other country in the Euro community). The little preview box in the lower-right corner of the dialog box shows you how your data looks in the chosen format.

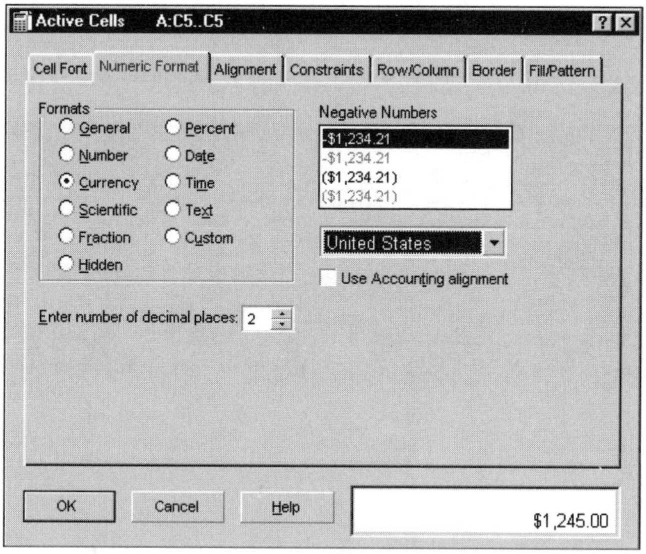

Active Cells   A:C5..C5   ? X

Cell Font | Numeric Format | Alignment | Constraints | Row/Column | Border | Fill/Pattern

Formats
○ General   ○ Percent
○ Number   ○ Date
● Currency   ○ Time
○ Scientific   ○ Text
○ Fraction   ○ Custom
○ Hidden

Negative Numbers
-$1,234.21
-$1,234.21
($1,234.21)
($1,234.21)

United States ▼

☐ Use Accounting alignment

Enter number of decimal places: 2

OK   Cancel   Help $1,245.00

Figure 11-5:
You can
specify
exactly how
you want
Quattro Pro
to format
your
numbers.

After you're satisfied with your choices, click OK or press Enter to apply the format. Or click another tab in the dialog box to make other formatting changes.

Changing the font, type size, and type style

To change the font, select the data you want to format and select a new font from the Font drop-down list on the Property Bar, shown in Figure 11-6. To change the type size of selected data, select a size from the Type Size drop-down list.

You can change the font, size, and style of just some characters in a cell if you want. To do so, double-click the cell to display the I-beam cursor, drag over the characters you want to format, and then choose your font.

As shown in Figure 11-6, the Property Bar also offers buttons for several type-style attributes, including boldface, italics, underline, superscript, subscript, and strikethrough. All these buttons act as toggles — that is, click once to apply the formatting; click again to remove it. The superscript and subscript buttons become available _only_ if you double-click a cell and go into edit mode. So, if you want to apply superscript or subscript to all the letters in a cell, double-click the cell and then drag over all the letters to select them. Then click the superscript or subscript button, depending on your preference.

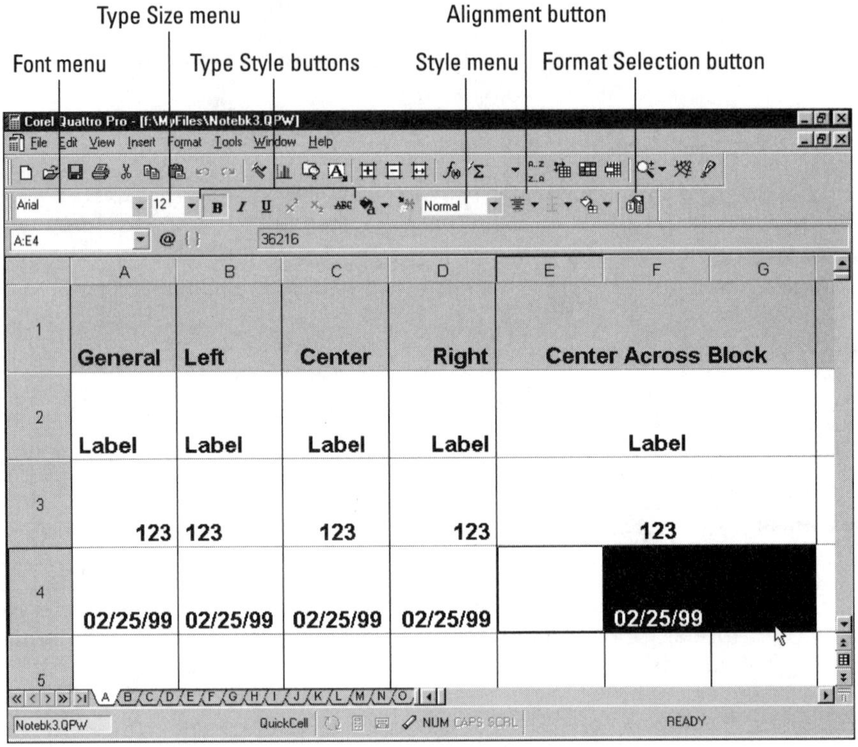

Type Size menu
Alignment button
Font menu
Type Style buttons
Style menu | Format Selection button

Figure 11-6:
You can
align data
within a cell
or center it
across a
block of
cells.

You can also access the font, type size, and type style formatting attributes on the Cell Font tab of the Active Cells dialog box, discussed in the preceding section. Press F12 or click the Format Selection button on the Property Bar to open the dialog box. If you select individual characters in a cell before you press F12 or click the Format Selection button, Quattro Pro displays a QuickMenu rather than the Active Cells dialog box. Choose the Text Properties option to access the Cell Font portion of the Active Cell dialog box. You can't access the other dialog box options in this situation.

Changing text alignment

One of the many formatting attributes applied by Quattro Pro's built-in styles is the horizontal alignment of data within the cell. The Normal style uses the General alignment option, which aligns labels with the left edge of the cell and aligns numbers, formulas, and dates to the right edge of the cell.

Click the down-pointing arrow on the Alignment button on the Property Bar to display a menu of horizontal alignment options, which include General, Left, Right, Center, Center Across Block, and Indent. Figure 11-6 shows how labels and values are aligned using the first five options. The Indent option indents the first line of your data from the left edge of the cell, just as a first-line indent does in WordPerfect.

To apply any alignment but Center Across Block, select the cell or cells you want to format and then select the option from the menu. The Center Across Block option, which centers the value or label within a specified number of cells, works a little differently. First, enter the data in the leftmost cell of the block of cells you want to center the data across. In the highlighted example in Figure 11-6, I entered the data in cell E4. Next, select the cell that contains the data, along with the rest of the block you want to center the data across. In Figure 11-6, I selected cells E4 through G4. Then select the Center Across Block option from the drop-down list.

 To uncover still more alignment options, select the cells you want to format and press F12 or click the Format Selection button to open the Active Cells dialog box. Click the Alignment tab to display the alignment options, shown in Figure 11-7.

The Alignment tab contains the same horizontal alignment options found on the Property Bar menu, plus these additional options:

✔ You have three vertical alignment options. Top aligns the data with the top of the cell; Center places the data smack-dab in the middle of the cell; and Bottom sinks the data to the bottom of the cell. The default is Bottom.

✔ If you turn on the Wrap Text option, Quattro Pro expands the cell vertically to accommodate text that exceeds the width of the cell. It then wraps the overflow text to the next line in the cell. Figure 11-8 shows an example of this option in action.

✔ The Text Orientation options determine whether your text runs horizontally or vertically in the cell. You can also place your data diagonally in the cell by selecting the Rotated radio button and entering an angle of rotation in the corresponding option box.

✔ The Join Cells option enables you to link two or more cells together and then align text within the entire block of cells as if it were contained in one cell. This option can be handy for creating titles or subtitles within your spreadsheet. You can also use it to create a "vertical" heading, as shown in Figure 11-8. To create the heading, I joined several cells in Column A, entered my text, and selected the Rotated option with a value of 90 degrees. I chose the Center option for both Horizontal and Vertical alignment and, just to make things pretty, gave the cell a dark background and made the text white. (See Chapter 15 for more tips on how to dress up your spreadsheet with backgrounds and colored text.)

To join cells and center the text horizontally within the cell block, you can simply click the Join and Center Cells button on the toolbar.

This chapter covers just the basic formatting you can do in Quattro Pro. For information on how to add even more spice to your spreadsheets, see Chapters 14 and 15.

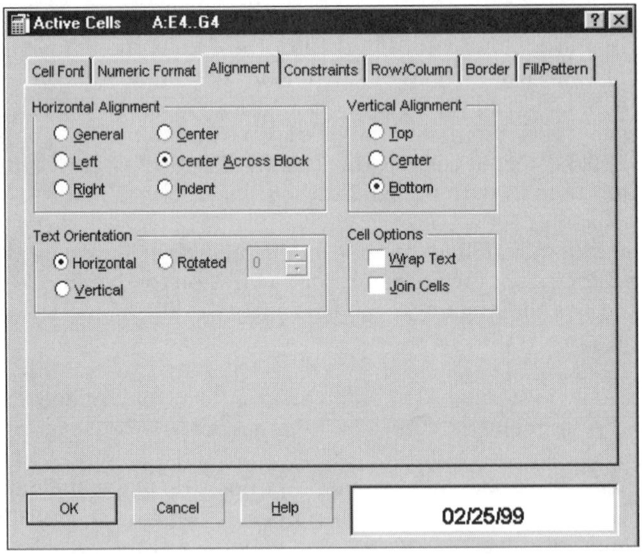

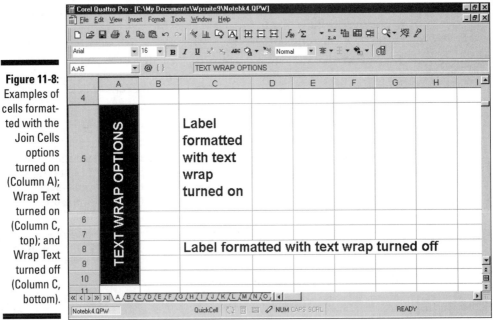

Figure 11-7: More alignment options reside in the Active Cells dialog box.

Figure 11-8: Examples of cells formatted with the Join Cells options turned on (Column A); Wrap Text turned on (Column C, top); and Wrap Text turned off (Column C, bottom).

Chapter 12

The Formula for Success

*R*emember algebra class, when you had to solve inane problems involving *x* and *y* and two trains headed for the same station at different speeds? Well, if you really got into that sort of thing, you're going to love this chapter, which shows you how to use those old algebra skills to write equations (a.k.a. *formulas*) for Quattro Pro to solve.

If, on the other hand, you spent most of your time in algebra class like I did, alternately wailing in frustration and complaining loudly that you didn't know *why* you needed to know this stuff *anyway*, you may be turned off by the fact that Quattro Pro requires you to create formulas before it does any work for you. Don't be.

First of all, most formulas you'll use are simple, involving basic addition, subtraction, multiplication, and division. Secondly, Quattro Pro offers some built-in formulas — called *functions* — that make creating more complex equations easy.

Creating a Basic Formula

Writing a formula is like being back in algebra class — only this time, you're the teacher. You give Quattro Pro a formula to solve, and it does the math for you.

You can enter formulas in two ways: You can type the formula directly into the cell, or you can use a combination type-and-click approach. The following sections give you the lowdown on both methods. But first, I want you to be aware of two new formula features in Version 9:

✔ You can now choose whether Quattro Pro displays formulas in cells or the *results* (answers) to the formulas. Choose View⇨Formulas to toggle between the two display options. If you see a check mark next to the Formulas command, formulas appear in the cells.

✔ Even if you turn off the Formulas view, you can get a quick peek at the formula for a cell by using another new feature. Any cell that contains a formula is marked with a little blue triangle in the lower-left corner of the cell. (I labeled one of these triangles in Figure 12-1.) Pause your cursor over the cell to see a QuickTip that shows you the formula (see the bottom of column E in Figure 12-1 for an example). These formula QuickTips appear whether or not you enable the QuickTips option in the Settings dialog box.

Of course, if you have the input line displayed, the formula for the active cell appears there, too. See Chapter 10 for information about enabling QuickTips and hiding and displaying the input line.

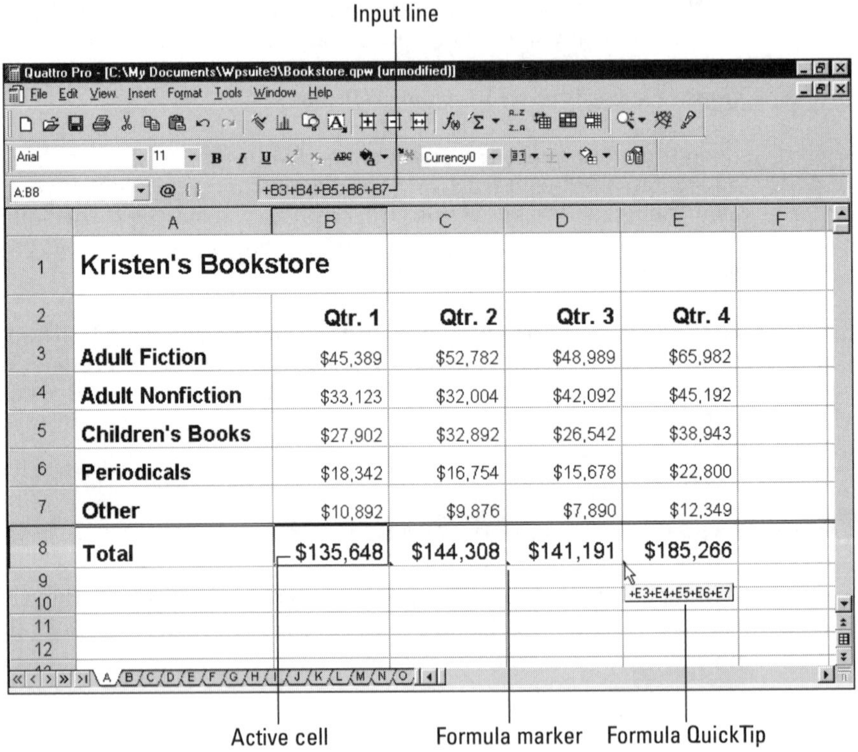

Input line

	A	B	C	D	E	F
1	**Kristen's Bookstore**					
2		**Qtr. 1**	**Qtr. 2**	**Qtr. 3**	**Qtr. 4**	
3	**Adult Fiction**	$45,389	$52,782	$48,989	$65,982	
4	**Adult Nonfiction**	$33,123	$32,004	$42,092	$45,192	
5	**Children's Books**	$27,902	$32,892	$26,542	$38,943	
6	**Periodicals**	$18,342	$16,754	$15,678	$22,800	
7	**Other**	$10,892	$9,876	$7,890	$12,349	
8	**Total**	$135,648	$144,308	$141,191	$185,266	

A:B8 @ { } +B3+B4+B5+B6+B7

+E3+E4+E5+E6+E7

Figure 12-1: The input line shows the formula used to calculate the value of the active cell (cell B8 in this example).

Active cell   Formula marker   Formula QuickTip

Typing formulas for simple calculations

You can use formulas to perform a simple calculation, such as 45 + 87. To enter this type of formula, follow these steps:

1. **Click the cell in which you want the answer to the calculation to appear.**

2. **Type a plus sign followed by your formula.**

    The plus sign tells Quattro Pro that you're entering a formula. To calculate the value of 45 + 87, for example, you enter

    ```
    +45+87
    ```

    Formulas can also start with a parenthesis, as discussed in the upcoming section "Telling Quattro Pro What to Calculate First," or with the function symbol (@), as covered in the section "Working with Built-In Functions."

    If you're used to starting formulas with an equal sign, as some other spreadsheet programs require, you can do so in Quattro Pro as well. Quattro Pro converts the equal sign to a plus sign when you complete the formula.

3. **Press Enter.**

    If you have Formulas view turned on (see the preceding section), the formula appears in the cell. Otherwise, the answer to the formula appears in the cell, and the formula itself appears in the input line.

In building formulas, you don't always use standard mathematical symbols, such as x for multiply and ⊡ for division. Instead, you use the symbols listed in Table 12-1, which are known as *operators* in spreadsheet country.

To calculate simple numbers as in the preceding steps, you really don't need to enter the plus sign at the beginning of the formula. As long as your formula contains only numbers, Quattro Pro assumes that you want it to perform a calculation. In some cases, however, Quattro Pro can get mixed up. The formula for finding the result of 8 divided by 2, for example, is 8/2. Quattro Pro may think that you're entering the date August 2 instead of a mathematical formula. For this reason, I recommend that you always start your formulas with +, @, or (, which are the three symbols that Quattro Pro has established for starting formulas. Or, if the first number in your formula is a negative number, you can enter a minus sign (–) before the number instead. Don't use parentheses to indicate a negative number, though. For more on this subject, see the section regarding data entry do's and don'ts in Chapter 11.

Table 12-1	Smooth Operators
Operator	*Function*
+	Addition
−	Subtraction
/	Division
*	Multiplication
%	Percentage
^	Exponentiation

Typing formulas using cell addresses

Although you can use Quattro Pro to perform simple calculations such as the example in the preceding section, more often than not, you want to perform calculations on values that are stored in different cells in your spreadsheet. You can have Quattro Pro add the values in one row of cells, multiply that total by the value in another cell, and so on. You can even do calculations involving cells on different worksheets in your notebook.

To enter this kind of formula, you use cell addresses instead of actual numbers to identify the values you want to calculate. Consider the spreadsheet in Figure 12-1, for example. This simple spreadsheet calculates total sales for each quarter. To find the total for Quarter 1, you can enter the following formula into cell B8, where you want the total to appear:

+B3+B4+B5+B6+B7

The formula tells Quattro Pro to add the values in cells B3, B4, B5, B6, and B7. The totals in columns C, D, and E use the same formula, except with different cell addresses — C3, C4, and so on for column C, for example.

If you don't enter the plus sign before the cell address, Quattro Pro assumes that you're entering a label, not a formula, because the entry contains a letter.

Suppose that, after finding the quarterly sales totals in Figure 12-1, you want to calculate the total sales for all four quarters and put the result in cell F8. You click cell F8 and enter the following formula:

+B8+C8+D8+E8

If you then want to find the average quarterly sales for the year, you enter this formula into another cell:

+F8/4

The formula tells Quattro Pro to divide the value in cell F8 (which contains the total sales for all four quarters) by 4.

If you want to perform a calculation on cells contained on different worksheets of your notebook, include the sheet name before the cell address in the formula. To add the value of cell B8 on worksheet A to the value of cell B8 on sheet B, for example, you enter

+A:B8+B:B8

If you named your worksheet, as I explain in Chapter 10, substitute that name in the cell address. If sheet A has the name *July* and sheet B has the name *August*, for example, write the formula

+July:B8+August:B8

Would you like that address relative or absolute?

After you create a formula, you can copy it to other cells to save yourself the trouble of entering it again and again. (Chapter 13 has the details.) Before you enter a formula that you want to copy, though, you need to decide whether you want Quattro Pro to use relative or absolute cell addressing.

If you don't do anything special to your formulas, relative addressing is in force. Here's how a relative address works: Suppose that you have four columns of numbers — Column A through Column D. Each column contains three rows of numbers, and you want to find the total of each column. You enter the formula +A1+A2+A3 in cell A4. Then you copy the formula to cells B4, C4, and D4. Quattro Pro is smart enough to realize that you don't want to calculate exactly the same thing as you did in the first column, so it adjusts the formula to match each column. In cell B4, for example, it changes the formula to

+B1+B2+B3. In other words, the formula always calculates the sum of the three cells directly above it.

What if you don't want Quattro Pro to tamper with your formulas in this way? Put a dollar sign before the column and the row name: +$A$1+$A$2+$A$3. The dollar sign tells Quattro Pro to use absolute addressing — as in "I absolutely don't want you to change this formula." The program then refers strictly to cells A1, A2, and A3 as it calculates your answer, no matter where you copy the formula.

You can mix absolute and relative cell addresses in the same formula, by the way. You can even make one part of the address absolute and the other part of the address relative, if you're so inclined. You could use the address $A1, for example, to make the column address absolute and the row address relative.

If you have the QuickType option enabled, Quattro Pro sometimes tries to "help" you by inserting the formula that it thinks you're trying to create. If Quattro Pro guesses wrong, just keep entering your formula; the inserted formula disappears. And see Chapter 11 to find out how to turn off QuickType if it becomes bothersome.

When you want to add a long row or column of numbers, as in the examples I gave in this section, you can bypass the step of entering each cell address by using Quattro Pro features called @SUM and AutoTotal. Check out "Adding things up," later in this chapter, for details.

Entering cell addresses with the mouse

If you're creating a long formula and you're weary of typing cell addresses — this computing business is such hard work! — use the mouse to enter the addresses instead. Here's how:

1. **Click the cell in which you want the answer to the formula to appear.**

2. **Type a plus sign.**

3. **Click the cell you want to reference in the formula.**

   For the formula +B4*52, for example, you click cell B4, as shown in Figure 12-2. The Application Bar displays the word Point, and the cell address appears in the input line and in the cell where you're entering the formula. In Figure 12-2, I entered the formula in cell C4.

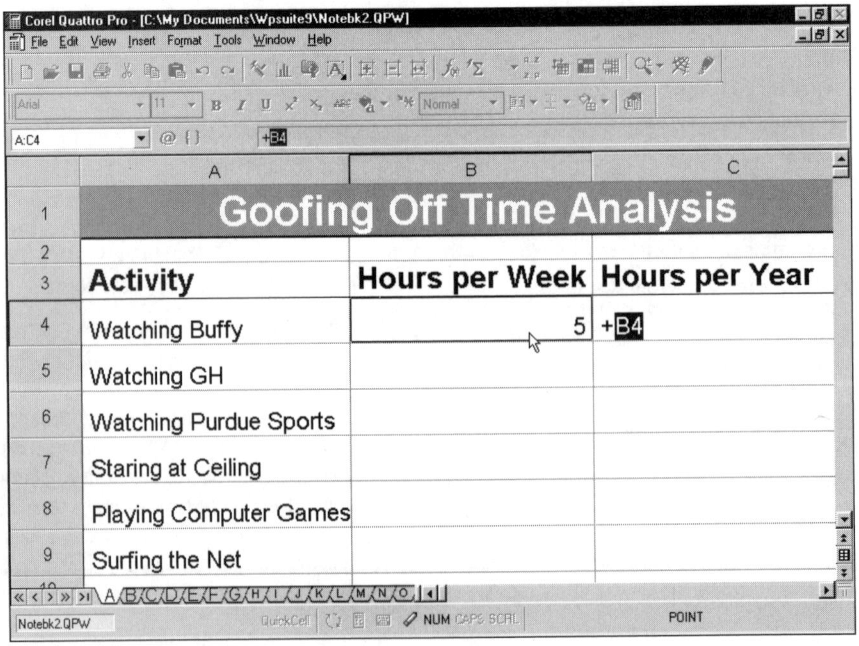

Figure 12-2: To enter a cell's address into a formula, just click that cell.

	A	B	C
1	Goofing Off Time Analysis		
2			
3	**Activity**	**Hours per Week**	**Hours per Year**
4	Watching Buffy	5	+B4
5	Watching GH		
6	Watching Purdue Sports		
7	Staring at Ceiling		
8	Playing Computer Games		
9	Surfing the Net		

Corel Quattro Pro - [C:\My Documents\Wpsuite9\Notebk2.QPW]

File Edit View Insert Format Tools Window Help

A:C4   @ {}   +B4

Notebk2.QPW   QuickCell   NUM CAPS SCRL   POINT

4. **Type the next operator in the formula.**

   To continue the formula, type the next operator. In the example formula, you type the * (multiplication operator). The cursor jumps back to the cell where you're entering the formula.

5. **Continue clicking cells and typing operators or known values until the formula is complete.**

   In this example, all you need to do to complete the formula is to type 52.

6. **Press Enter.**

Telling Quattro Pro What to Calculate First

If your formula contains more than one type of operator, you need to tell Quattro Pro the order in which you want to calculate the formula. Take a look at the following formula:

```
+B1+B2*B3
```

You may expect Quattro Pro to calculate this formula from left to right, adding B1 and B2 and then multiplying the sum by B3. But, in fact, Quattro Pro first multiplies B2 by B3 and then adds B1 to the result.

If you substitute numbers for the cell addresses, you can see that you get two different answers depending on which order you calculate the formula. Suppose that B1=4, B2=5, and B3=6. If you add 4 and 5 and then multiply the sum by 6, you get 54. If you multiply 5 times 6 and then add 4, you get 34.

So how does Quattro Pro decide which numbers to work on first? By following a set of mathematical rules called *order of precedence,* which assign a level of importance to each operator. For example, the rules say that a multiplication sign is more important than an addition sign, so the multiplying gets done first. If the formula contains several operators that are at the same level, Quattro Pro calculates the numbers separated by the leftmost operator first and then works its way to the right through the rest of the formula.

Table 12-2 shows the order of precedence for the most common operators. But the truth is, you really don't need to remember this stuff — unless you like filling your head with complex technical data, of course. You can tell Quattro Pro how to calculate your formulas by using another method you probably learned in algebra class — don't you wish you'd paid closer attention now? You can use *parenthetical expressions* to indicate which parts of your formula you want Quattro Pro to calculate first, second, third, and so on. In non-nerd lingo, that means that you put portions of your formula inside parentheses. Quattro Pro thinks about values inside parentheses first.

Table 12-2	Operator Order of Precedence
Operator	*Precedence*
^ (exponentiation)	1
* (multiplication)	2
/ (division)	2
+ (addition)	3
– (subtraction)	3

Suppose that you want to add B1 to B2 and then multiply the sum by B3. Enter the formula this way:

(B1+B2)*B3

If your formula begins with a left parenthesis, as here, you don't need to add the plus sign at the beginning as you do with other formulas. If you do, however, you don't hurt anything.

In long formulas, you may need to create several sets of parenthetical expressions, one inside the other (spreadsheet gurus call this *nesting* expressions). Here, for example, is how to structure a formula that finds the sum of B1 and B2, multiplies the sum by B3, subtracts the result from B4, performs the same calculations on cells C1, C2, C3, and C4, adds the two results together, and divides the whole shooting match by 2 (ow, that hurt!):

((B4-((B1+B2)*B3)) + (C4-((C1+C2)*C3)))/2

To dissect this formula, Quattro Pro first calculates whatever parts of the formula are the most deeply nested — that is, enclosed by the most sets of parentheses. In this case, the winners are B1+B2 and C1+C2, each enclosed by four sets of parentheses. The program then works its way outward, evaluating the expressions enclosed by three sets of parentheses and then those enclosed by two sets and then one set before moving on to divide the entire result by 2.

Now that I have your head completely spinning, let me just give you one more little nugget of information. If you type a left parenthesis, Quattro Pro initially displays it in red. After you type the corresponding right parenthesis, both parentheses turn neon green. This Christmas-tree color coding — or I guess you could consider it stoplight color coding — is Quattro Pro's way of helping you make sure that you always have a right parenthesis to match every left parenthesis.

If you leave out a parenthesis, Quattro Pro sometimes adds one at the end of your formula — which may or may not be okay, depending on the formula. Other times, you may get an error message or the formula may just sit there, doing nothing, after you press Enter. To track down the missing parenthesis, move the insertion marker through the cell. After you hit the parenthesis that doesn't have a matching open or close parenthesis, it turns red.

Well, now. I think that's just about enough of that, don't you?

Working with Built-In Functions

Quattro Pro wants to be your friend — it really does. And because it realizes that creating formulas can be a bit of a drag, your little math buddy thoughtfully provides some built-in formulas to make your life easier. These prefab formulas are formally called *functions*. (Just because Quattro Pro wants to be your friend doesn't mean that it's willing to speak to you in plain English.) Because functions are always preceded by the @ symbol in a formula, they're sometimes called *at functions*.

To take a peek at the available functions, click an empty cell and choose Insert⇨Function or click the @ symbol on the input line. Either approach displays the Functions dialog box, shown in Figure 12-3. Click a category in the Function Category list, and the functions related to that category appear in the Function list box. In keeping with a proud computing tradition, the functions have odd, meaningless names, which is why Quattro Pro displays some explanatory information at the bottom of the dialog box.

The following sections show you how to work with functions and introduce you to a few popular functions. See Chapter 22 for a look at a couple more interesting functions.

Making function arguments

Functions take some of the chore out of creating formulas. But you still need to do part of the work.

As an example, consider the @MIN function. This function looks at the values in a group of cells and tells you the smallest value in the bunch. Say that you want to find the smallest value lurking in cells B1 through B100. You enter the following as your formula:

```
@MIN(B1..B100)
```

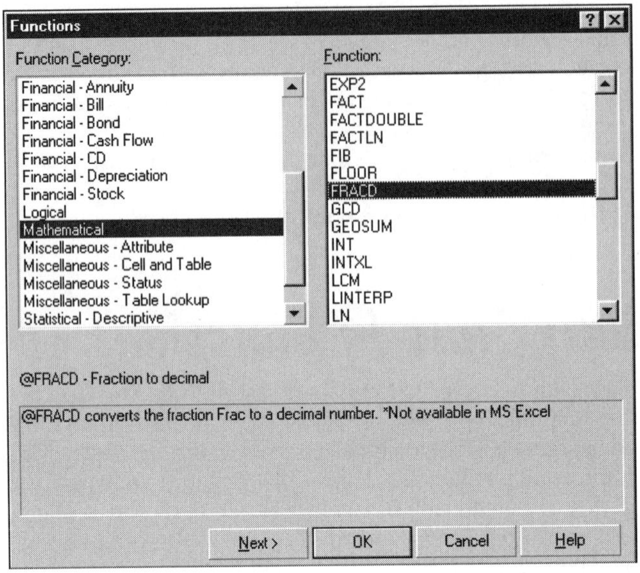

Figure 12-3:
Quattro
Pro's built-in
functions
range from
the simple
to the extra-
ordinarily
complex.

The Functions dialog box:

Functions

Function Category:

Financial - Annuity
Financial - Bill
Financial - Bond
Financial - Cash Flow
Financial - CD
Financial - Depreciation
Financial - Stock
Logical
Mathematical
Miscellaneous - Attribute
Miscellaneous - Cell and Table
Miscellaneous - Status
Miscellaneous - Table Lookup
Statistical - Descriptive

Function:

EXP2
FACT
FACTDOUBLE
FACTLN
FIB
FLOOR
FRACD
GCD
GEOSUM
INT
INTXL
LCM
LINTERP
LN

@FRACD - Fraction to decimal

@FRACD converts the fraction Frac to a decimal number. *Not available in MS Excel

Next >   OK   Cancel   Help

The @ symbol tells Quattro Pro that you're entering a function; MIN is the name of the function. The parentheses contain the *argument* — that is, the range of cells that you want the function to calculate. The two periods in the formula are Quattro Pro shorthand for *through*. So this formula tells Quattro Pro to find the minimum value of cells B1 through B100.

Functions always begin with the @ symbol. If your formula begins with a function, you don't need to put in the plus sign that you use to begin other formulas; the @ sign is enough. And Quattro Pro always displays function names in all caps. But you don't need to enter the names in all caps; lower-case letters are fine.

If you want to calculate values from cells that don't fall in a continuous block, you separate the numbers by using commas instead of periods. If you want to find the lowest value from cells B1 though B20, C2, and C6, for example, you enter

@MIN(B1..B20,C2,C6)

To have a function calculate data that's found on different worksheets, include the worksheet names in the argument. To find the minimum value from cells A1 through A3 on sheet A as well as cells A1 through A3 on sheet B, for example, enter the sheet range and then the cell range as follows:

@MIN(A..B:A1..A3)

Or, if you don't want to include the same cells on both pages — for example, if you want to find the minimum value in cells A1 through A3 on sheet A as well as the cells A4 through A6 on sheet B — enter both ranges and separate them with a comma, like this:

@MIN(A:A1..A3,B:A4..A6)

You can use functions by themselves or incorporate them into a longer formula that you create. If you want to find the minimum value from cells B1 though B20 and then divide the result by 4, you enter

@MIN(B1..B20)/4

In some functions, you must enter a specific value in addition to or instead of a cell address as the function argument. For example, a function that calculates the total cost of a real-estate loan requires you to enter the interest rate, the length of the loan, and the amount of the loan.

Figuring out how to structure the function argument can be a little confusing at times. Fortunately, Quattro Pro provides the Formula Composer, described in the next section, to help you out.

Entering functions with the Formula Composer

The Formula Composer serves as a coach to help you enter function arguments correctly. The following steps introduce you to this feature, using the @FRACD function as an example. This function converts a fractional number into an ordinary decimal number. For this example, suppose that you want to convert the fraction $5\frac{1}{8}$ to a decimal number.

1. **Click the cell where you want to enter your formula.**

2. **Choose Insert⇨Function or click the @ symbol on the input line.**

   The Functions dialog box, shown earlier in Figure 12-3, appears.

3. **Click the Mathematical category in the left list box.**

4. **Click the FRACD function in the right list box.**

5. **Click Next.**

   Quattro Pro transports you to the Formula Composer dialog box, shown in Figure 12-4. This dialog box looks intimidating, to say the least. But if you squint your eyes and focus just on the elements that I point out here, you can keep the queasiness factor low.

Syntax help

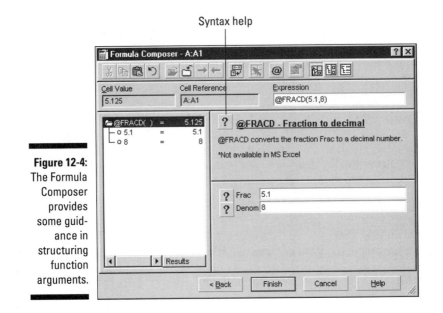

Figure 12-4:
The Formula
Composer
provides
some guid-
ance in
structuring
function
arguments.

6. **Click the question mark button that's labeled *Syntax help* in Figure 12-4.**

   Syntax just means "the way to enter the function argument." Loosely defined, anyway. When you click the question mark, Quattro Pro opens the Help system and displays a window that explains what information you need to include in the function argument and how to enter that information. (PS: Don't feel stupid if the help information seems as though it's written for mathematical geniuses — unfortunately, the explanations sometimes aren't all that clear.) After you work your way through the Help window, you can close it.

7. **Enter the requested argument information.**

   In the bottom half of the Formula Composer, Quattro Pro provides data-entry boxes for each value that you need to enter to complete the function argument. In some cases, you enter the range of cells that you want to calculate; see the preceding section for information on how to do so. For this example, you must provide specific numeric values, which Quattro Pro calls Frac and Denom. My, that's user-friendly, isn't it?

   If you paid attention when reviewing the Help window displayed in Step 6, you know that the Frac value should be the whole number in the original value (5, in this case), followed by the numerator of the fraction. For those who can't remember their childhood math classes, the numerator is the top number in the fraction (1, in the example). The syntax information in the Help window instructs you to separate the two values with a decimal point (period), so enter the value in the Frac box like this: **5.1**. (Don't put the second period in — that's my period to end the sentence.)

Now enter the second requested value, named Denom. This value is the denominator of the fraction (the bottom number), so you enter **8** in this example.

Note that if your numerator is a one-digit number and the denominator has two or more digits, you need to enter a zero before the numerator. For example, to find the decimal equivalent of $1\frac{1}{100}$, you would enter 1.01 in the Frac option box and 100 in the Denom box. See the Help system for more about this quirkiness.

If you want to skip going to the main Help window or just need a refresher about how to enter a value, click the question mark button next to the value. Quattro Pro displays a small help screen related to the value.

8. **Click Finish.**

If you want to return to the Formula Composer dialog box to edit the argument for a function, click the cell containing the function and then click the Formula Composer button on the toolbar.

I used the FRACD function as an example because it's an easy one to wrap your brain around. But here's a secret: You don't need to bother with the function to convert fractional numbers to decimal numbers — and, in fact, because of that stuff about sometimes having to enter a zero before the numerator and sometimes not, I don't really recommend the function for casual users. Instead, when you want to convert a fractional number to a decimal number, simply change the Numeric format in the Active Cells dialog box. Select the cells you want to convert, press F12 or choose Format⇨Selection to open the Active Cells dialog box, click the Numeric Format tab, and click the Number radio button. Set the number of decimal places by using the Enter Number of Decimal Places option (finally, a sensibly named option). Conversely, you can convert decimal numbers to fractions by clicking the Fraction radio button. See Chapter 11 for more information about numeric formats.

Working without a net

If you're using simple functions or if you're an experienced spreadsheet guru, you can probably get along fine without the Formula Composer's help. You can enter functions and the related arguments using these quicker alternatives:

- ✔ Type the function and argument directly into the cell. Enter the @ symbol and the function name, followed by the argument, and press Enter.

- ✔ If you can't remember the function name, choose Insert⇨Function and choose the function from the Functions dialog box, shown back in Figure 12-3. Click OK, and Quattro Pro inserts the function name into the cell and waits for you to input the function argument.

Need some help remembering how to input that function argument? Click the left mouse button once to display the argument syntax on the Application Bar. As you enter each part of the argument, Quattro Pro displays a QuickTip to serve as a further guide. If you need further help, click the Formula Composer button to open the Formula Composer dialog box (see the preceding section for more information).

✔ For the quickest route to a few common functions, check out the new QuickFunctions menu on the toolbar. The next section explains how to insert functions from the menu.

Inserting functions from the QuickFunctions menu

In previous editions of Quattro Pro, the Property Bar contained a QuickSum button that enabled you to insert the @SUM function, which finds the total of a block of cells, with a single click. Version 9 improves on that feature by providing a QuickFunctions menu on the toolbar (see Figure 12-5). The menu puts the @SUM function along with a selection of other popular functions a click away.

To insert a function from the menu, click the cell where you want to put the function. Then click the arrow on the QuickFunctions menu button and select a function. After you choose a function, its icon appears on the QuickFunctions menu button face. You can just click the button face again to insert the same function.

If you put the function into a cell that's below or to the right of cells containing values, Quattro Pro calculates the result of the function based on the values in the row or column.

Take a look at Figure 12-5 for an example of what I mean. Say that you click in cell B11 (the empty cell at the end of the January column of sales numbers). If you then choose the @SUM function from the menu, Quattro Pro automatically totals all values in the column and puts the total in cell B11. If you enter the function from the Functions dialog box (using Insert⇨Function), Quattro Pro enters the @SUM portion of the formula and then waits for you to enter the range of cells you want to sum — which, in this case, you enter as (B6..B10).

If Quattro Pro can't figure out what cells you want to calculate, it enters the function name and waits for you to provide the argument, just as when you input the function using the Functions dialog box.

Formula Composer

QuickFunctions menu

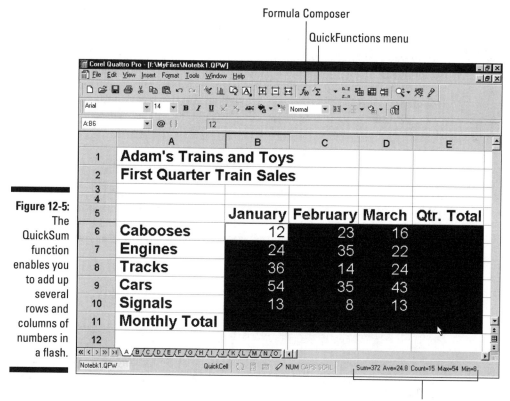

Calc-As-You-Go values

Figure 12-5:
The
QuickSum
function
enables you
to add up
several
rows and
columns of
numbers in
a flash.

Here's a quick way to tell Quattro Pro what cells to include in the equation: After Quattro Pro inserts the function name, just use your mouse to select the cells you want to include. (See Chapter 13 for information on how to select cells.) Then press Enter.

Alternatively, if you're working with cells in a single column or row, select the cells plus an empty cell at the end of the column or row *before* you choose the function from the QuickFunctions menu. Quattro Pro puts the formula in that empty cell.

To apply the same function to several columns and/or rows at a time, select the cells in those rows and/or columns, plus enough empty cells to hold the sums. In Figure 12-5, for example, you could use this technique to simultaneously find the quarterly and monthly totals for each train item by selecting the block of cells highlighted in the figure. The first three empty cells in Row 11 will hold the monthly sales totals for January, February, and March. The first five empty cells in Column E will hold the quarter sales totals for each category of goods. The empty cell at the lower-right corner of the block of cells (cell E11) will hold the total sales for the entire quarter.

Notice the Application Bar at the bottom of Figure 12-5. Thanks to a feature called Calc-As-You-Go, the Application Bar displays five values after you select a row or column of cells. From left to right, you can see the sum of all the selected cells, the average of all values, the total number of cells containing values, and the maximum and minimum value in all the cells. If you don't see the values on your Application Bar, press Alt+F12 to open the Settings dialog box, click the General tab, and select the Calc-As-You-Go check box. (You can't open the dialog box while entering data in a cell.)

Trying out some popular functions

To be honest, if your spreadsheets tend to be simple, like mine, you may not have much need for functions. Many of the Quattro Pro functions are designed for users who work with really complex equations. But a few, like the ones in the next three sections, come in handy in everyday spreadsheets.

Adding things up

If you want to add a bunch of cells — say, cells A1 through A10 — you could do things the long way, writing the following formula:

+A1+A2+A3+A4+A5+A6+A7+A8+A9+A10

But if you were really sharp — and I can tell just by looking that you are — you'd use Quattro Pro's @SUM function. Then you could simply write the formula as follows:

@SUM(A1..A10)

Actually, you don't even need to go to the trouble of typing the formula. Instead, select the @SUM function from the QuickFunctions menu. In some scenarios, Quattro Pro even automatically enters the function argument for you. (If you need help understanding the QuickFunctions menu or how to structure function arguments, see "Making function arguments" and "Inserting functions from the QuickFunctions menu," earlier in this chapter.)

To add one more summing possibility — pun intended, but not very good — Quattro Pro 9 offers a feature called AutoTotal. This feature works when you have a column of labels to the left of a column or columns of numbers, as in Figure 12-5. If you enter the word *Total* in the labels column, Quattro Pro adds up the values in each of the adjacent columns and places the results in the Total row, using the @SUM function to get the job done. In Figure 12-5, if you were to enter the Total label in cell A11, the totals of the values in columns B, C, and D would appear in cells B11 through D11.

Note that you have to enter just the word *Total* — entering *Monthly Total,* as I did in the figure, doesn't work. Also, you must enter the *Total* label *after* you enter the values you want to sum.

Finding the average and median values

Suppose that you run a flower shop and want to find your average daily sales for the month of May. The daily sales totals are stored in cells A1 through A30. To find the average daily sales, use the @AVG function by entering the following formula:

@AVG(A1..A30)

You can also select the @AVG function from the QuickFunctions menu. Trek back to "Inserting functions from the QuickFunctions menu" for details about this quick and convenient option.

Now suppose that you're an eighth-grade teacher (you just do that flower-shop thing on the side) and you've stored all the scores for your final exams in cells A1 through A26. You can use the @MEDIAN function to find the median score. The median score is the score that's smack-dab in the middle of all the scores. Write the formula this way:

@MEDIAN(A1..A26)

Displaying the date

If you want a certain cell to always display the current date, you can enter the @TODAY function into the cell. Quattro Pro initially displays the date as a serial number (trust me, you don't even want to hear why). To display the date as a real date, you need to change the numeric format to Date, which you can find out how to do in Chapter 11.

Fighting the ERR Message and Other Snafus

Writing formulas and function arguments can be pretty tricky stuff, especially if you're doing complex calculations. If things go awry, the following troubleshooting tips may help:

- ✔ Sometimes Quattro Pro displays the letters ERR or NA in a cell after you enter a formula and press Enter. This message is Quattro Pro's not-so-subtle way of telling you that you goofed. Something is wrong with your formula. Perhaps you entered a cell address incorrectly or made some other mistake that prevents Quattro Pro from performing the calculation. Double-click the cell to find and fix the mistake. (See Chapter 13 for specifics on how to edit your data.)

✔ If Quattro Pro displays a message about a syntax error or unknown function, you've left out a parenthesis, an argument, or some other vital portion of the formula. If you're entering a function, check the Help system for information about the function and make sure that you structured the function argument correctly. Also review the rules presented throughout this chapter for help on writing formulas correctly.

✔ Alternatively, click the Formula Composer button to open the Formula Composer dialog box. Discussed earlier in this chapter, the Formula Composer offers assistance with structuring each part of your function argument.

✔ On occasion, a Cell Reference Checker dialog box may pop up to alert you to some potential disaster. Typically, you encounter the dialog box when you're copying formulas that reference other cells. To get some help sorting things out, click the Details button in the dialog box to see the original formula along with a recommended fix. If you want Quattro Pro to make the change, click the Fix It button. Like the results? Click Close to put the dialog box away. If not, click Undo Fix to put things back to the way they were before. You can then close the dialog box and attempt to straighten things out on your own.

✔ If all else fails, beg your local Quattro Pro guru for assistance. Offering some sort of little math-related bribe is helpful — a slide rule or one of those tiny calculator keychains is always good.

Chapter 13

Editing Your Spreadsheet

· ·

In This Chapter

▶ Undoing mistakes

▶ Editing and deleting cell contents

▶ Selecting stuff before you edit

▶ Inserting, deleting, and adjusting columns and rows

▶ Copying stuff from one cell to another

▶ Moving data around

▶ Pasting data in a special way

▶ Transposing data

· ·

*D*on't you wish people would react to your mistakes the way they do whenever those celebrities on TV blooper shows muff their lines? Oh sure, it's funny if somebody *famous* goofs up, but if *you* make a mistake, nobody laughs hysterically and shouts, "That's a great one for the blooper reel!" Well, I'm sorry to say that the stuffy network brass who control our nation's TV viewing aren't likely to realize the appeal of *World's Funniest Quattro Pro Bloopers and Blunders* any time soon. So you may as well go ahead and fix those typos, faulty formulas, and other laughers that find their way into your spreadsheet.

This chapter shows you how to undo mistakes, edit data, and otherwise wipe all traces of comedy out of your spreadsheets. It also explains how to make other sorts of changes, such as inserting rows and columns and turning your spreadsheet on its ear.

Selecting Stuff

Before you can do much at all to your spreadsheet — whether you want to format or edit the data — you must select one or more cells. Selecting tells Quattro Pro exactly where to apply your next command or change.

If you select a single cell, Quattro Pro displays a black border around the cell. If you select only part of the data in a cell or select several cells, the selection appears highlighted on-screen, as shown in Figure 13-1. Notice that the active cell — the first (or sometimes the last) cell in a range of selected cells — does not appear highlighted, but is still part of the selection.

Here's a list of the most popular selection techniques known to man and Quattro Pro:

- ✔ To select a single cell, click it.

- ✔ To select part of the data in a cell, first get into edit mode by double-clicking the cell, or clicking the cell and pressing F2, or clicking the cell and then the input line. Then drag across the data you want to select.

- ✔ If you double-click a cell that contains a formula, a blue border appears around the cells referenced by that formula. (If the cell contains the formula +A1+A2, for example, the border appears around cells A1 and A2.)

- ✔ To select a *block* (range) of cells, click the first cell in the range and drag to highlight the rest of the range.

- ✔ If you don't like dragging, click the first cell you want to select, press Shift, and use the arrow keys to add adjacent cells to the selection.

- ✔ Here's an even quicker way to select a large block of cells: Click the cell in one corner of the block you want to select. Then hold down the Shift key as you click the cell in the opposite corner of the block.

- ✔ To select all cells in the current worksheet, choose Edit⇨Select All. Or click the Select All button (see Figure 13-1).

- ✔ To select an entire row of cells, click the row border. (Your cursor changes into a right-pointing arrow as you move it onto the border.) To select several rows at once, drag across them in the row border.

- ✔ To select an entire column, click the column border. To select several columns, drag across them in the column border.

- ✔ To select two or more noncontiguous cells — that is, cells that aren't touching — click the first cell you want to select. Then hold down the Ctrl key as you click the other cells you want to select. You can use this same technique to select noncontiguous blocks of cells.

- ✔ To "unselect" stuff, just click again.

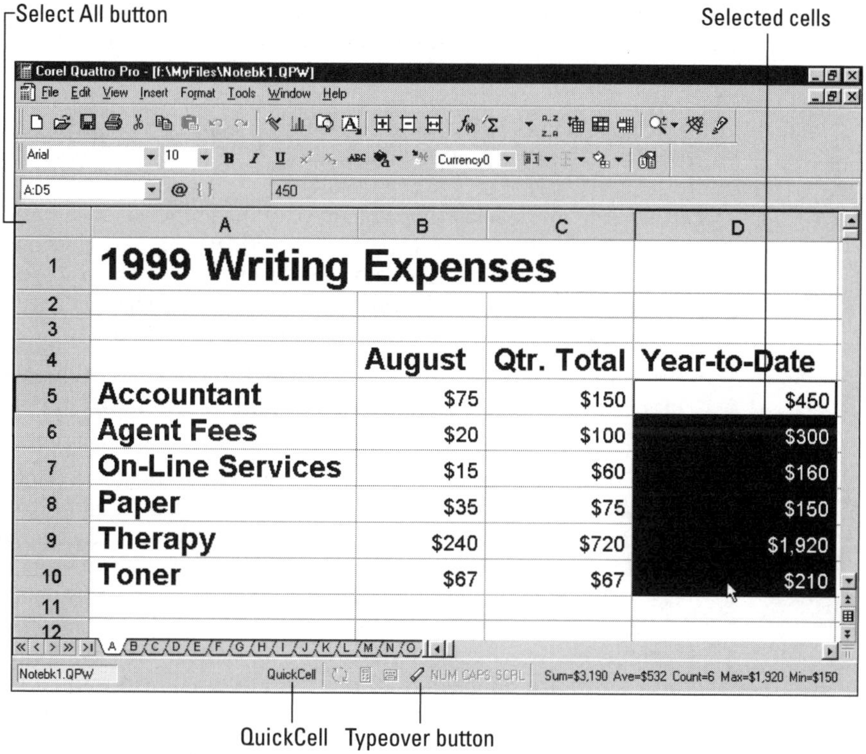

Select All button · Selected cells

Figure 13-1:
Selected
text appears
highlighted
— except
for the first
cell in the
selection,
which looks
like an ordi-
nary active
cell.

QuickCell · Typeover button

Getting Rid of Bloopers

If the data you want to change is short, the fastest method for fixing mistakes is to simply retype the data. Click the cell, type the data again, and press Enter. Quattro Pro replaces the existing cell contents with the new data.

If you want to make a minor change to a long piece of data (such as a formula), editing the data is probably easier than retyping it. You can make your edits in the cell or in the input line. But you first must shift Quattro Pro into edit mode, which you can do in the following ways:

✔ Click the cell and press F2.

✔ Double-click the cell.

✔ Click the cell and click the input line.

Whichever method you choose, the I-beam cursor and insertion marker appear, and the contents of the cell appear in the input line, just as they do when you enter data for the first time. If you use method number three — that is, you click the cell and then click the input line — the insertion marker and I-beam hop to the input line rather than appearing in the cell. You then do your editing in the input line, not in the cell.

Editing data in Quattro Pro is pretty much the same as editing text in WordPerfect. Here's a recap of the basics:

✔ The insertion marker and I-beam play the same roles as they do when you enter text into a cell initially. The insertion marker shows where the next thing you type will appear. Click with the I-beam or press the left- and right-arrow keys to position the insertion marker. For a review of these and other data-entry techniques, see Chapter 11.

✔ Press Delete to erase the character just to the right of the insertion marker; press Backspace to wipe out the character to the left of the insertion marker.

✔ If you want to keep an eye on how your edits affect the contents of a particular cell, click that cell and then click the QuickCell button on the Application Bar (refer to Figure 13-1). For example, say that you want to track the status of cell B30, which contains the formula +A1+A2. Click cell B30 and click the QuickCell button. Now, whenever you make a change to the value in cell A1 or A2, you can see the new result of the formula on the QuickCell button. (This feature was available in Version 8, but you use different methods to activate it in Version 9.)

✔ Normally, Quattro Pro operates in insert mode. Any character you insert shoves the characters that follow to the right. If you press the Insert button on your keyboard (sometimes labeled Ins) or click the Typeover button (labeled in Figure 13-1) on the Application Bar, you switch to typeover mode. Now any new characters you type take the place of existing characters. Click the button or press Insert again to return to Insert mode. (Quattro Pro also returns you to Insert mode when you press Enter.)

✔ If you centered data across a block of cells, select the leftmost cell in the block to edit the data. Although the data may appear to be contained in another cell, it's really stored in the leftmost cell. The same holds true for labels that are too long to fit inside a single cell and spill over into adjoining cells. See Chapter 11 for details on all these formatting issues.

✔ After you fix up the cell contents, press Enter or click another cell to make your changes official. Or, if you want to put things back the way they were before you began editing, press Esc.

Deleting versus Clearing Cell Contents

To get rid of the contents of a cell, click the cell and press Delete. Simple enough, right?

Ah, but Quattro Pro throws in a little curve. The Delete key does wipe out the data in a cell, but any formatting you applied to the cell — such as numeric style, type size, and so on — remains intact. So the next data you enter into the cell uses that formatting, too.

To wipe out the formatting along with the cell contents, click the cell and choose Edit⇨Clear⇨Cells. Or right-click the cell and choose Clear from the QuickMenu. Quattro Pro zaps the data and returns all the formatting to the default settings.

To clear just the formatting from a cell, choose Edit⇨Clear⇨Formats. Edit⇨ Clear⇨Values clears values and leaves formatting intact — the same as pressing Delete.

To delete an entire row or column of cells, follow the steps in the section, "Inserting and Deleting Columns and Rows," a little later in this chapter. (Don't you just love these imaginative titles?)

Undoing Bad Moves

Like WordPerfect, Quattro Pro has an Undo command that can take you back in time to the moment before you made that awful decision that you now regret. Unfortunately, Quattro Pro's Undo command can reverse only your last action — you can't undo several actions, as you can in WordPerfect.

To undo your last action, choose Edit⇨Undo, press Ctrl+Z, or click the Undo button on the toolbar. If you change your mind about the undo, choose the Edit⇨Redo command, press Ctrl+Shift+Z, or click the Redo button to undo your undo.

If Undo doesn't seem to be working, the feature may be turned off. You can undo some actions with Undo disabled, but not all. To turn Undo on, press Alt+F12 to open the Settings dialog box, click the General tab, select the Enable Undo check box, and press Enter.

Inserting and Deleting Columns and Rows

You can add an empty row or column of cells any time, any place, with just a few mouse clicks and drags. You can delete rows or columns from your spreadsheet just as easily.

Inserting an empty row or column

If you insert a row or column, Quattro Pro adjusts formulas in other cells as needed. If your spreadsheet contains the formula +A1+A2, for example, and you insert a row before row A1, Quattro Pro changes the formula to +A2+A3 to accommodate the new arrangement of the cells. This automatic adjustment is the result of Quattro Pro's relative addressing feature, which you can explore in Chapter 12.

Here's how to insert a row or column of empty cells:

- ✔ To insert a row, click the row border of the row immediately *below* where you want the new row to appear. Then click the Insert button on the toolbar.

- ✔ To insert several rows at once, select however many rows you want to insert in the row border. To insert three rows, for example, select three rows in the row border. Then click the Insert button. Quattro Pro inserts the new rows immediately above the top row in your selection.

- ✔ To insert a column, click the column border of the column immediately right of where you want the new column to appear. Then click the Insert button. To insert several columns, select the number of columns you want to insert and then click the Insert button. Your new columns appear just to the left of the leftmost column in your selection.

- ✔ Here's another quick option for adding rows and columns: Right-click the column or row border and choose Insert from the QuickMenu.

- ✔ You can also insert rows and columns by using the Insert⇨Column or Insert⇨Row command. But really, using the Insert button or the QuickMenu is a heck of a lot easier.

Deleting rows and columns

Whenever you delete rows or columns, make sure that you aren't deleting cells that are referenced in formulas found elsewhere in your spreadsheet. If you do, you wind up with formulas that Quattro Pro either can't calculate or calculates incorrectly.

Insert button

Delete button   Column/Row Select cursor

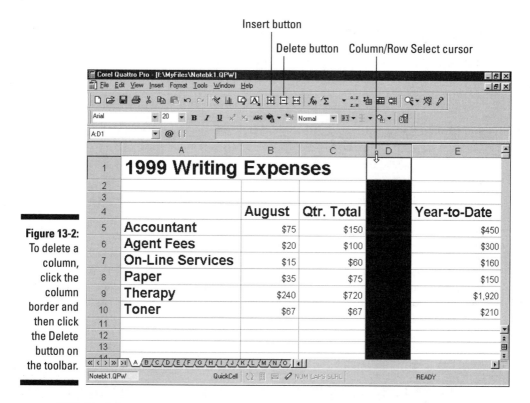

Figure 13-2:
To delete a
column,
click the
column
border and
then click
the Delete
button on
the toolbar.

 To delete a row or column, click the row or column border, as shown in Figure 13-2, and click the Delete button on the toolbar or choose Edit⇨Delete. Or right-click the border and choose Delete from the QuickMenu. Whichever approach you take, Quattro Pro tosses the column or row into the electronic wastebasket and shifts the remaining rows or columns over to fill up the empty space. To delete several rows or columns at once, select them in the row or column border and then click the Delete button (or use the other deleting methods).

REMEMBER

The Delete button on the toolbar doesn't do the same thing as the Delete key on your keyboard. The Delete button deletes the entire column or row, while the Delete key just deletes the contents of the cells in the column or row.

Adding a Worksheet

If you need to insert a worksheet between two worksheets in your notebook, right-click the sheet tab for the second worksheet and choose Insert Sheet from the QuickMenu.

To delete a worksheet, right-click its sheet tab and choose Delete Sheet from the QuickMenu.

Resizing Columns and Rows

You can shrink or enlarge the columns to fit your data if needed. You can also change the height of any row in your spreadsheet.

✔ The easiest way to change the column width is to place your cursor in the column border, directly over the line that separates the column you want to resize from its neighbor to the right. After you see the cursor change to a two-headed arrow, as shown in Figure 13-3, drag right or left to resize the column.

✔ You can change row height by dragging up or down on the line that separates the row you want to resize from the row directly beneath it.

✔ To resize several rows or columns at once, select them in the row or column border and then drag the bottom or right border of any of the selected rows or columns.

✔ To have Quattro Pro automatically fit the column width to fit the longest entry in the column, click the column border and then click the QuickFit button on the toolbar. Or, even quicker, double-click the column border.

Resize cursor

QuickFit button

Corel Quattro Pro - [f:\MyFiles\Notebk1.QPW]

File Edit View Insert Format Tools Window Help

Arial 10 B I U Normal

A:E4

	A	B	C	D	E
1	**1999 Writing Expenses**				
2					
3					
4		**August**	**Qtr. Total**	**Year-to-Date**	
5	**Accountant**	$75	$150	$450	
6	**Agent Fees**	$20	$100	$300	
7	**On-Line Services**	$15	$60	$160	
8	**Paper**	$35	$75	$150	
9	**Therapy**	$240	$720	$1,920	
10	**Toner**	$67	$67	$210	
11					
12					
13					

A/B/C/D/E/F/G/H/I/J/K/L/M/N/O

Notebk1.QPW   QuickCell   NUM CAPS SCRL   READY

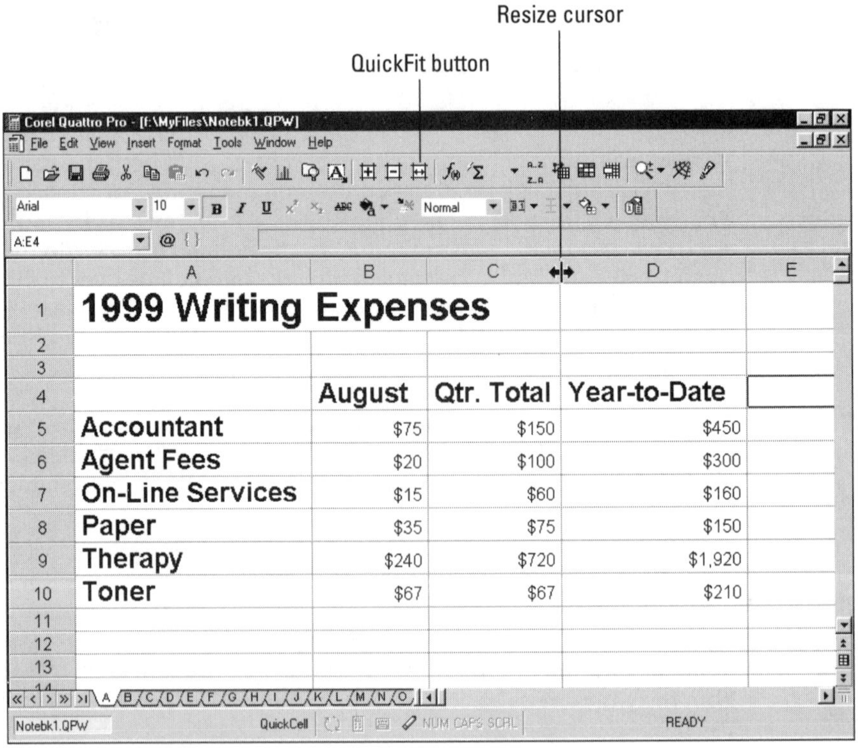

Figure 13-3: Drag the border between a column to resize the column.

✔ If you want Quattro Pro to enlarge cells automatically as you type, turn on the Fit-As-You-Go feature, found on the General tab of the Settings dialog box (which you access by pressing Alt+F12). This feature doesn't work for labels or for values when the General, Text, or Scientific numeric format is selected. See Chapter 11 for an explanation of numeric formats.

If you want more precision over your column and row sizes — for example, if you want each column to be exactly 1½ inches wide — click the column or row you want to adjust. Then choose Format➪Selection, press F12, or click the Format Selection button to open the Active Cells dialog box, shown in Figure 13-4. Click the Row/Column tab.

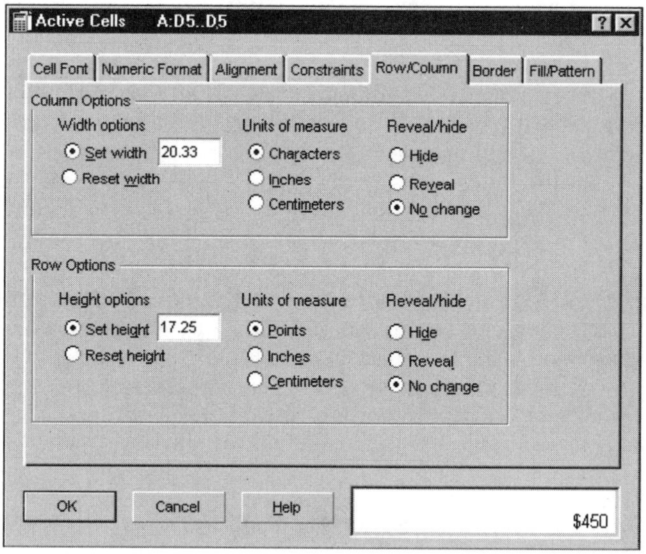

Figure 13-4: To make your columns or rows a precise size, press F12 to open this dialog box and then adjust the width and height values.

You can change row/column sizes as follows:

✔ To set the column width, enter a value in the Set Width option box. Click the Reset Width radio button to return the column to its original default size.

✔ You can choose from three measurement units for your columns: Characters, Inches, and Centimeters. I recommend that you avoid the Characters option because it's pretty vague. The number of characters you can fit in the cell depends on the type size you use, the font, and the type style (bold or italic). In other words, you may set the column width at 15 characters, but you may be able to fit only 13 characters in the cell if those characters are in boldface.

✔ To set the row height, enter a new value in the Set Height option box and click one of the Units of Measure radio buttons to establish the unit of measurement. You can set your row height in terms of points (a point is a publishing unit of measure equal to $\frac{1}{72}$ inch), inches, or centimeters. The Reset Height button returns your row to its default size.

✔ The other options on the Row/Column tab are used to temporarily hide rows and columns. If you're itching to know more, see Chapter 15.

Copying Data from Here to There

If you have a label or formula that you need to use more than once, don't keep entering it again and again — save yourself some time and effort and copy it.

Quattro Pro offers several methods for copying data, as outlined in the following sections. But before you begin your grand copying adventure, you need to be aware of an important piece of business: If you copy a formula, Quattro Pro automatically adjusts the formula relative to its new location *unless* you used absolute addressing when you entered the formula. (See Chapter 12 for information on relative versus absolute addressing.)

By default, Quattro Pro copies both the cell data and the formatting (font, type size, alignment, and so on). But you can copy just certain aspects of the cell by using the new Paste Special command, explained later in this chapter. And Chapter 21 presents some additional copying techniques, including ways to copy data from Quattro Pro to other programs.

Dragging and dropping a copy

For simple copy jobs, the quickest method is to drag and drop the copy, as follows:

1. **Select the data you want to copy.**

   You can copy a single cell or a block of cells. (The section "Selecting Stuff," earlier in this chapter, outlines selection techniques.)

2. **Place your cursor along the border of the selected cell (or block of cells) until the four-headed arrow cursor appears.**

   You can put the cursor over any area of the cell boundaries except the lower-right corner (if you're copying a block of cells, the lower-right corner of the lower-right cell). If you put the cursor in that position, you see a plus sign cursor, which you use when filling cells with the QuickFill feature. (Check out Chapter 11 for more information on that feature.)

3. Press and hold the Ctrl key as you drag the cell or block to its new location.

Your cursor should change to a little page with a plus sign next to it, as shown in Figure 13-5. Be sure that you see a little plus sign — otherwise, you're moving the selected cells instead of copying them.

If you drag-and-drop data to cells that already contain data, Quattro Pro displays a dialog box to warn you that you're about to overwrite the existing data. If that's what you want to do, click Yes; otherwise, click No to cancel the copy.

To copy cells to another open notebook, Ctrl+drag them to the Application Bar button for the second notebook. After that document appears on-screen, drag the cells to the spot where you want to place them and release the mouse button.

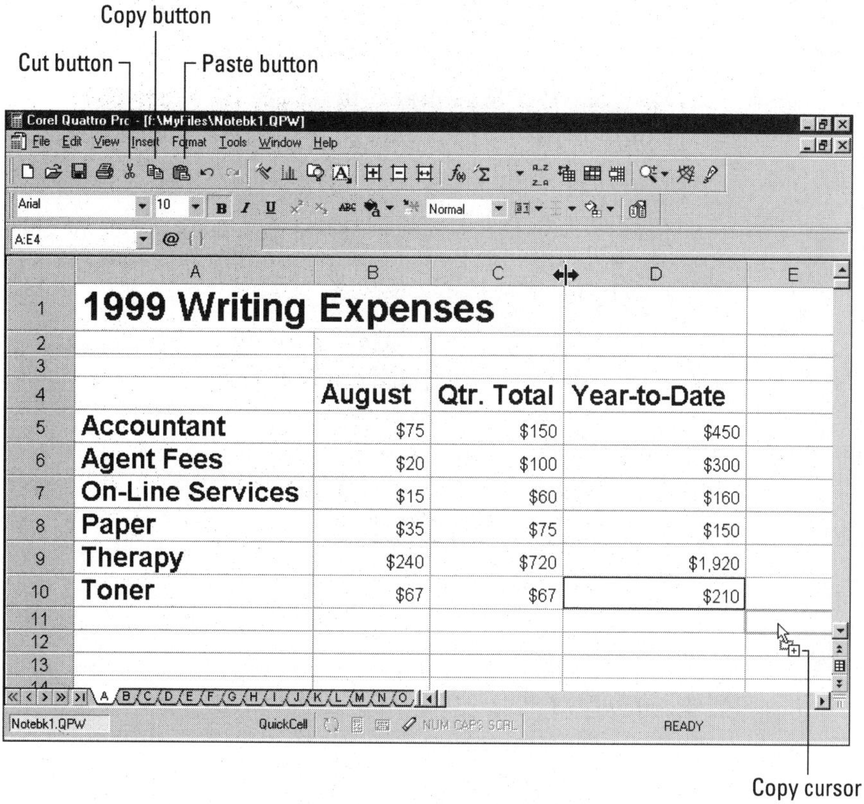

Cut button ⌐   ┌ Paste button

Copy button

	A	B	C	D	E
1	**1999 Writing Expenses**				
2					
3					
4		**August**	**Qtr. Total**	**Year-to-Date**	
5	**Accountant**	$75	$150	$450	
6	**Agent Fees**	$20	$100	$300	
7	**On-Line Services**	$15	$60	$160	
8	**Paper**	$35	$75	$150	
9	**Therapy**	$240	$720	$1,920	
10	**Toner**	$67	$67	$210	
11					
12					
13					

Corel Quattro Pro - [f:\MyFiles\Notebk1.QPW]

File   Edit   View   Insert   Format   Tools   Window   Help

Arial   10   **B** *I* U   Normal

A:E4

Notebk1.QPW   QuickCell   NUM CAPS SCRL   READY

Figure 13-5: To copy data to another cell, just Ctrl+drag it.

Copy cursor

Using Copy and Paste to copy data

Another way to copy data is to use the Copy and Paste commands, as described in the following steps:

1. **Select the cell or block of cells you want to copy.**

2. **Press Ctrl+C or click the Copy button on the toolbar.**

   Alternatively, you can choose the Edit⇨Copy command or right-click and choose Copy from the QuickMenu. Quattro Pro sends the data to the Windows Clipboard, where the copy stays until the next time you use the Copy or Cut command.

3. **Click the cell where you want to place the copy.**

   If you're copying a block of cells, click the upper-left cell of the block where you want to put the copy.

   Make sure that you don't copy the data to cells that already contain data. If you do, Quattro Pro replaces the existing data with the data you're copying — and doesn't warn you first.

4. **Press Ctrl+V or click the Paste toolbar button.**

   Or choose Edit⇨Paste or right-click and choose Paste from the QuickMenu. Quattro Pro pops your copy into its new home.

If you want to copy the data to yet another cell, just click the cell and use any of the methods described in Step 4 to paste the data again. You can paste the data as many times as you want.

You can paste the contents of a single cell into a whole block of cells at the same time. To do so, select the block of cells right before you choose the Edit⇨Paste command. Quattro Pro duplicates the data in every cell selected.

Moving Data Around

If you *move* cells that contain formulas, Quattro Pro *does not* adjust the cell addresses as it does when you *copy* cells that contain formulas. If you move the formula +A1/A2 from cell A3 to cell B3, the formula doesn't change to +B1/B2, for example, as it does when you copy it. The formula continues to refer to the same cells it did before you moved it.

If you move a cell that's referenced in a formula, however, Quattro Pro adjusts the formula so that it continues to reference that same cell. If, for example, you enter the formula +A1+A2 and then move cell A2 to cell A3, Quattro Pro adjusts the formula to read +A1+A3.

If you're moving cells just a short distance, using the drag-and-drop method is usually easiest. Use the same procedure outlined in the section "Dragging and dropping a copy," earlier in this chapter, but don't press the Ctrl key as you drag.

To move data from one open notebook to another, drag the selected cells to the Application Bar button for the second notebook. Don't let up on the mouse button when you reach the Application Bar. When the second notebook appears on-screen, drag the cells to the spot where you want to place them and release the mouse button.

Alternatively, you can use the Cut and Paste commands to move data. To use Cut and Paste, follow the steps outlined in the section "Using Copy and Paste to copy data," earlier in this chapter — but choose the Cut command or click the Cut button in Step 2.

If you use Cut/Paste to move data, Quattro Pro doesn't warn you that you're about to move data into cells that already contain data. It simply overwrites the existing data with the moved data.

Pasting with Special Glue

When you paste data using the standard Paste command, Quattro Pro pastes the cell contents along with the cell formatting. But by using the new Paste Special command, you can paste some aspects of the data and not others.

If you're upgrading from an earlier version of Quattro Pro, you may know that the Edit⇨Copy Cells command, which is still available, provides a similar function. But Copy Cells works only for data that you copy using the Copy command. Paste Special not only works in conjunction with both the Copy command and the Cut command, but also offers some options not available when you use Copy Cells. In other words, if you're in the habit of using Copy Cells, investigate Paste Special — you may like it better.

The following steps show you how to use Paste Special to get specific with your Quattro Pro glue:

1. **Cut or copy the original data to the Clipboard.**

   Select the data and then choose the Copy or Cut command, depending on whether you want to duplicate or move the original data. If you need help, see the earlier sections "Using Copy and Paste to copy data" and "Moving Data Around."

2. **Select the cells where you want to paste the copied or cut data.**

   If you're planning on pasting a block of cells, you can just click the top left cell in the block where you want to put the data.

Keep in mind that Quattro Pro will overwrite the existing data when you paste your copied or cut data — and without giving you any advance notice.

3. Choose Edit⇨Paste Special.

Or right-click and choose Paste Special from the QuickMenu. Either way, the dialog box shown in Figure 13-6 appears. Here, you find a variety of options that enable you to specify what aspects of your copied or cut data get pasted into your destination cells. Select the check boxes for the options that you want to include. You can paste just cells containing formulas and leave behind cells that contain labels, for example (select the Formula Cells check box and deselect the Label Cells check box). To paste data without any formatting attributes, deselect the Properties check box.

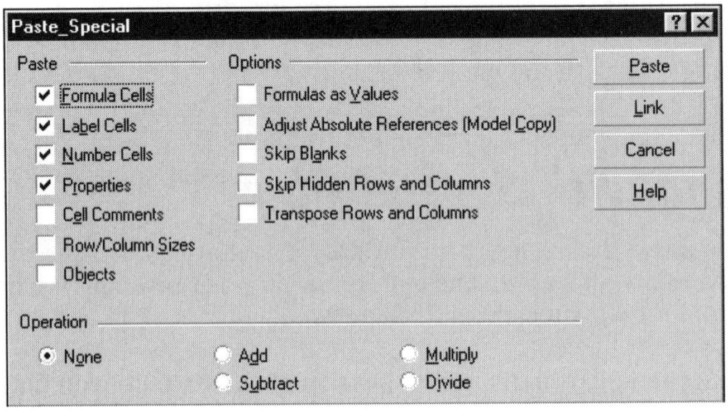

Figure 13-6:
The Paste
Special
command
enables you
to paste just
certain
aspects of a
copied or
cut cell.

Paste_Special

Paste
- ☑ Formula Cells
- ☑ Label Cells
- ☑ Number Cells
- ☑ Properties
- ☐ Cell Comments
- ☐ Row/Column Sizes
- ☐ Objects

Options
- ☐ Formulas as Values
- ☐ Adjust Absolute References (Model Copy)
- ☐ Skip Blanks
- ☐ Skip Hidden Rows and Columns
- ☐ Transpose Rows and Columns

Paste
Link
Cancel
Help

Operation
- ⦿ None
- ○ Add
- ○ Subtract
- ○ Multiply
- ○ Divide

Use caution when selecting the Transpose Rows and Columns option. This option turns your row data into column data and vice versa, a move that can be problematic if your cells contain formulas. See the next section for more insights.

The Operation options at the bottom of the Paste Special dialog box enable you to perform simple mathematical calculations on the value you're pasting and the value in the current cell. For example, say that you copy cell A1, which contains the value 6, and paste the copied data into cell B1, which contains the value 10. If you select the Add button in the Paste Special dialog box, Quattro Pro adds the 6 to the 10, changing the value in cell B1 to 16.

4. Click the Paste or Link button.

If you click Paste, Quattro Pro pastes the data using the parameters you selected in the dialog box. End of story.

If you click Link, the pasted data is linked to the cells that contained the original data you copied or cut to the Clipboard. And any time you change the values in those original cells, Quattro Pro automatically updates the values in the pasted cells, too. To let you know that a pasted cell is linked to another cell, Quattro Pro displays a little triangle in the lower-left corner of the pasted cell. Pause your mouse cursor over the triangle to display a QuickTip that reveals the address of the original cell.

Linking pasted cells to the original cells can come in handy when you need to put the same data in several places in your notebook. If you want to update that data, you can just make the changes in the original cells rather than editing the original cells and the pasted cells. Unfortunately, this option is unavailable if you select the mathematical Operation buttons discussed in Step 3.

To break the link between a pasted cell and the original, simply enter a new value in the pasted cell. Deleting the contents of the pasted cell also eradicates the link.

The magic of linking occurs thanks to something known as Object Linking and Embedding, or *OLE* for short. You can take advantage of linking when pasting data between programs as well as when pasting cells in Quattro Pro. Check out Chapter 21 for more information.

Transposing Cells

You're halfway through creating your spreadsheet, and you realize that you'd be better off if you oriented your data in a different way. You want to change your spreadsheet so that your columns become rows and vice versa — as I did with the data in Figure 13-7.

No problem; Quattro Pro is happy to transpose your data for you. Just select the block you want to flip and then choose Tools⇨Numeric Tools⇨Transpose. The Transpose Cells dialog box appears. In the To text box, enter the address of the upper-left cell of the block where you want to put the transposed data and then click OK. Or click the arrow at the end of the To box, click the cell, press Enter, and then click OK (the Transpose Cells dialog box minimizes itself while you click the cell). Quattro Pro obediently turns your data on its ear.

Avoid transposing blocks that contain formulas. Quattro Pro's brain usually isn't up to the task, and your formulas can get completely messed up. And if you tell Quattro Pro to put the transposed data into cells that already contain data, it overwrites the existing data without warning you. So be very careful whenever you set the upper-left corner of the block that's to hold the transposed data.

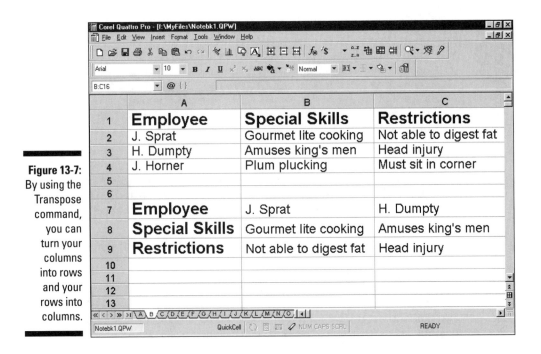

Figure 13-7:
By using the Transpose command, you can turn your columns into rows and your rows into columns.

Did anyone else notice that the hot keys for opening the Transpose Cells dialog box are TNT? Just thought I'd ask.

Chapter 14

Charting Your Course

· ·

In This Chapter

▶ Turning a boring block of numbers into a dazzling chart

▶ Uncovering the Chart command and chart tools

▶ Choosing a chart type and layout

▶ Editing chart data and design

▶ Getting acquainted with the Objects sheet

▶ Naming your charts

▶ Printing charts by their lonesomes

· ·

*B*y using Quattro Pro's graphics capabilities, you can quickly turn a batch of boring numbers into an eye-catching chart that would make Ross Perot's heart pound. Charts not only add some flash to your spreadsheet, but they also help people make sense of your numbers.

This chapter gives you a lightning-fast tour of Quattro Pro's charting capabilities so that you, too, can captivate audiences by using pie charts, bar charts, and just about any other type of chart you can dream up.

Creating a New Chart

Consider the chart shown in Figure 14-1. The chart presents the data in the table of numbers to the left in a way that's easily understandable. You can tell at a glance which types of shows are more popular.

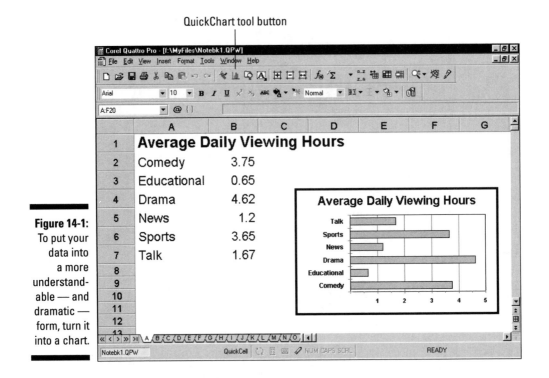

QuickChart tool button

Figure 14-1:
To put your
data into
a more
understand-
able — and
dramatic —
form, turn it
into a chart.

Quattro Pro gives you two ways to create a chart:

- ✓ **Use the Chart Expert.** The Expert walks you through the steps of selecting a chart type, adding labels, picking colors, and making other decisions
  regarding your chart. Using this method, you can put your chart on a
  worksheet or in a special chart-editing window, cleverly titled the Chart
  window. The chart then exists separately from the spreadsheet.

- ✓ **Use the QuickChart tool.** When you use this tool, labeled in Figure 14-1,
  Quattro Pro makes the chart formatting decisions for you and creates
  the chart on the active worksheet. You can change the formatting later if
  you want.

The following two sections explain each of these options in more detail.

Using the Chart Expert

The Chart Expert is supposed to be self-explanatory, but if you ask me, it's
not. So the following steps guide you through the process:

1. **Select the data that you want to turn into a chart.**

   Select the column and row labels if you want them included in the chart — but don't select any titles or subtitles you may have given your spreadsheet. You add those to your chart later.

2. **Choose Insert⇨Chart.**

   The Chart Expert dialog box appears, as shown in Figure 14-2. A preview shows you the chart layout that Quattro Pro suggests; you get the chance to change the layout later. The two check boxes in the dialog box enable you to rearrange the order of the data in the graph. For more information about these two options, see the section "Exchanging Rows, Columns, and Series," later in this chapter. You can also rearrange data after you create your chart.

Figure 14-2:
The Chart
Expert
walks you
through
the steps of
creating a
chart.

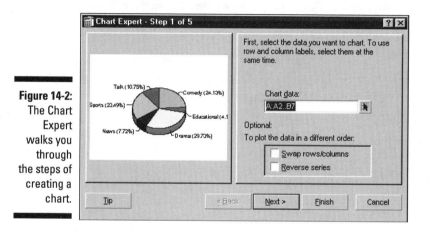

3. **Click the Next button to advance through the remaining panels of the Chart Expert.**

   You advance first to a panel that asks you to select a general chart type. Click Next again, and you get to refine your chart type a little more. Subsequent panels enable you to add a title, subtitle and axis labels, and also to select a color scheme for your chart.

   In the panel for adding a chart title and subtitle (panel 4), pay special attention to the two Destination radio buttons near the bottom of the dialog box. Click the Current Sheet radio button if you want to insert your chart right in the active worksheet. Click Chart Window if you want to create the chart in a separate window.

   As you make selections, the preview provides updates to show how your chart is going to look. At any point, you can return to the previous panel and change a setting by clicking the Back button.

4. **Click Finish.**

What happens now depends on the Destination radio button you selected earlier. If you chose Current Sheet, Quattro Pro returns you to the active worksheet, and your cursor looks like a little chart. Place the cursor at the spot where you want to put the upper-left corner of the chart and drag to the opposite corner, as shown in Figure 14-3. After you release the mouse button, Quattro Pro draws your chart.

If you selected the Chart Window option, Quattro Pro creates your chart and displays it in the Chart window, as shown in Figure 14-4. To return to the active worksheet in your notebook, click the notebook's button on the Application Bar or choose its name from the Window menu.

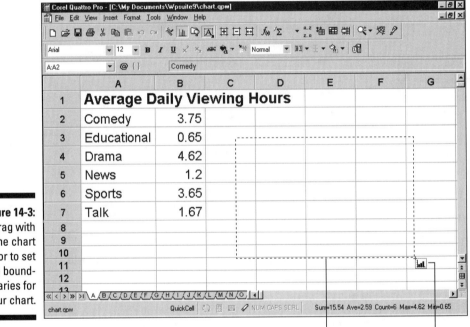

Figure 14-3:
Drag with the chart cursor to set the boundaries for your chart.

Chart boundary   Chart cursor

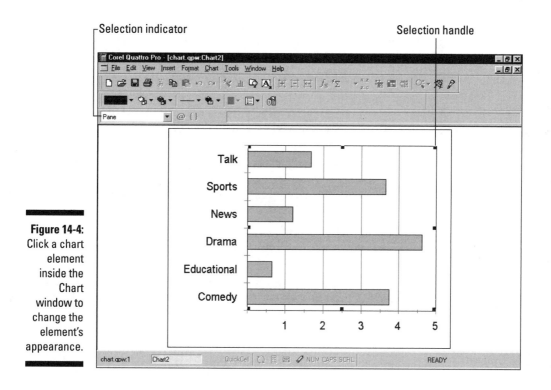

Figure 14-4:
Click a chart
element
inside the
Chart
window to
change the
element's
appearance.

Creating charts with the QuickChart tool

 To use the QuickChart tool, select the data you want to chart, click the QuickChart button on the toolbar, and drag with the chart cursor to set the boundaries for the chart (refer to Figure 14-3). After you release the mouse button, Quattro Pro draws the chart using the design that it believes is most appropriate for your data. You can change the chart layout, titles, colors, and other features, as I explain in the following section.

Editing a Chart

To change the data in a chart, change the original spreadsheet data you used to create the chart. Any changes to the spreadsheet are automatically reflected in your chart.

To change design-related aspects of your chart, such as the chart type, label font, titles, and so on, you edit the chart itself. The following list provides a brief overview of your chart-editing options. Later sections provide more detail on specific editing tasks.

✔ To edit a chart that you created in a Chart window, select the chart's name from the Window menu or click its name in the Application Bar. Your chart appears in living color inside the Chart window, as shown in Figure 14-4.

Click the chart element that you want to change. Little boxes called *selection handles* appear around the element, and the Property Bar changes to offer tools related to the item you clicked. You can also access chart-editing options from the Chart menu.

On the left end of the input line, the selection indicator (labeled in Figure 14-4) displays the name of the chart element that's selected. In Figure 14-4, the background pane of the chart is selected.

Another editing avenue is to right-click the element you want to change and then select the Properties item from the bottom of the QuickMenu that appears. A dialog box related to the item you right-clicked swaggers into view.

To switch from the chart window back to your notebook, click the note-book name in the Application Bar or choose the name from the Window menu.

✔ You can also edit charts that live on worksheets in the Chart window if you prefer. You can do your editing right on the worksheet (the next bullet point explains how), but I prefer the Chart window for extensive editing because it offers a better view of the chart. If your chart lives on a worksheet, right-click the chart and choose Open from the QuickMenu. Or double-click the chart border and then click the Edit Chart button to display a dialog box listing all your charts. Choose the chart you want to edit and click OK.

To return to your notebook, click the notebook name in the Application Bar or choose the name from the Window menu. All changes you made to your chart are automatically made in your worksheet as well.

After you edit a chart in the Chart window, simply click the chart on the worksheet to reopen the chart in the Chart window.

✔ If you want to change the overall look of a chart that's housed on a work-sheet without going to the Chart window, click the chart border. Selection handles appear around the perimeter of the chart, and the Property Bar changes to provide you with several chart-editing buttons.

To edit the fine details of the chart, such as the font of a particular label, click inside the chart boundary. The chart becomes surrounded by a dashed line, and a Chart menu appears on the main menu bar. Click the element you want to edit, and use the Property Bar buttons and Chart menu commands to make your changes. Or right-click the element you want to change and select the Properties item from the bottom of the resulting QuickMenu.

✔ You can also edit a chart by choosing <u>V</u>iew➪<u>O</u>bjects or clicking the QuickTab button to go to the Objects sheet. (See Figure 14-5, where the QuickTab button is labeled.) The Objects sheet contains a little icon representing each chart in your spreadsheet, as shown in Figure 14-5. Double-click the icon for the chart you want to edit. Quattro Pro opens the chart in the Chart window.

Unfortunately, the little icons on the Objects sheet don't look anything like the charts they represent, and Quattro Pro gives your charts vague names such as Chart 1, Chart 2, and so on. You can give a chart a more meaningful name by right-clicking its icon on the Objects sheet, choosing Icon Properties from the QuickMenu, and entering the name in the Name dialog box that appears, as shown in Figure 14-5. Quattro Pro limits you to a 15-character name.

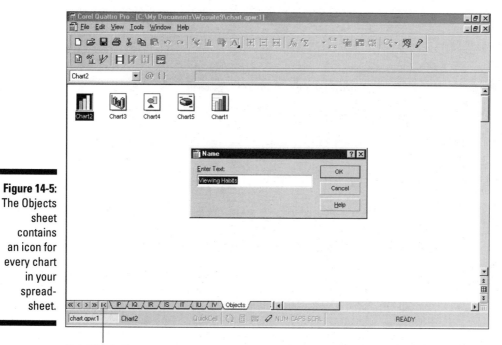

Figure 14-5: The Objects sheet contains an icon for every chart in your spreadsheet.

QuickTab button

To return to the Objects sheet in your notebook, click the notebook name in the Application Bar or choose the name from the Window menu. Then click the QuickTab button to return to the active worksheet in your notebook.

✔ To get a really good look at your chart, click the View Chart button or choose Chart⇨View Chart. To get access to the button when you're working in a worksheet, you must click the chart border. The menu appears if you click the interior of the chart. In the Chart window, click the chart background to display the View Chart button if you don't see it on the Property Bar. Quattro Pro fills the entire screen with your chart. Click to exit the full-screen view.

Changing the chart type and color scheme

If you want to change the color scheme, chart type, or layout of your chart, click the Chart Gallery button on the Property Bar or choose Chart⇨Gallery to display the Chart Gallery dialog box, as shown in Figure 14-6. (If you're editing your chart in the spreadsheet window, click the chart border to display the Chart Gallery button on the Property Bar. Or click inside the border to display the Chart menu.)

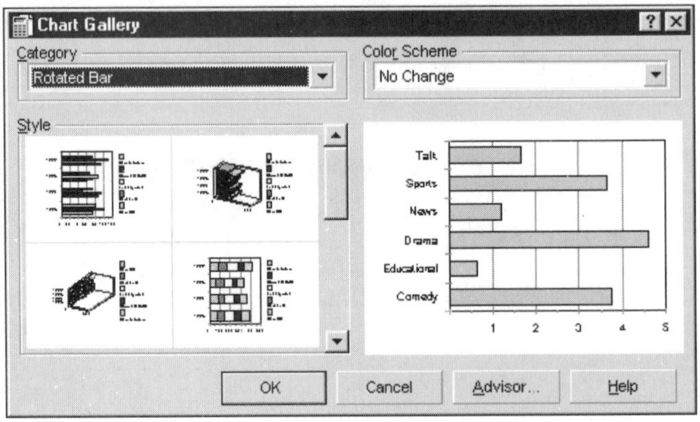

Figure 14-6:
Inside the
Chart
Gallery
dialog box,
you can
change the
chart type,
layout, and
color
scheme.

Select the color arrangement you want to use from the Color Scheme drop-down list. You can also change the chart type and layout in this dialog box. Select a chart type from the Category drop-down list and click a chart style in the scrolling Style list. The preview box shows how your chart looks with the selected changes. Click OK to apply your changes.

If all you want to do is change the chart type, you can click the Chart Type button on the Property Bar and choose a new type from the drop-down menu. (In the Chart window, click the chart background to display the button on the Property Bar.)

Giving your chart a title and a border

To add a title, subtitle, or axis title to your chart, click the Chart Title button on the Property Bar or choose Chart⇔Titles. (If you're editing on a worksheet, click the chart boundary to display the button; click inside the boundary to display the Chart menu. In the Chart window, click the chart background to display the button.) Alternatively, right-click the chart and choose Titles from the QuickMenu. Quattro Pro opens a dialog box that enables you to enter a main title, a subtitle, and labels for the *X* and *Y* axes, if your chart has them. (The *X axis* is the horizontal one; the *Y axis* is the vertical one.) Click OK to apply your titles.

The process for changing the chart border depends on whether you're working in the Chart window or the spreadsheet window:

✔ In the Chart window, choose Chart⇔Background. Or click the chart background and then press F12 or click the Format Selection button. Whichever method you choose, the Background dialog box appears. On the Box Settings tab, you can select a color and line style for your border. If you don't want a border at all, choose the first line-style button — the one with the X through it.

Borders that you create in the Chart window are *not* applied to your chart in the spreadsheet window. The specialized borders available in the Chart window can be created, displayed, and printed inside the Chart window only.

✔ In the spreadsheet window, right-click the chart and choose Chart Properties from the QuickMenu. Or, if you prefer, click the border and choose Format⇔Selection, click the Format Selection button, or press F12. Any way you go about things, the Chart dialog box appears, with the border options available on the Box Type and Border Color tabs. Your options are more limited than they were in editing the border in the Chart window.

Alternatively, you can click the chart border and choose a new border style and color from the drop-down lists that appear on the Property Bar. Borders that you apply in the spreadsheet window affect the chart when it is printed with the spreadsheet.

Editing individual chart elements

In addition to playing with your chart style and border, you can alter the look of individual chart elements. For example, you can change the font used for the titles or the color used for a bar in a bar chart.

Whether you're working in the Chart window or directly in a worksheet, click the element you want to change. Then use the Property Bar buttons and drop-down lists to change the element's color and other formatting attributes. (Pause your cursor over each button to discover your options.) To display all your formatting controls in one dialog box, click the Format Selection button, press F12, or choose Format⇨Selection.

Exchanging Rows, Columns, and Series

Take a gander at Figure 14-7. Obviously, this layout is not the best way to present this particular data; the arrangement shown in Figure 14-8 makes comparing how each gender reacts to the various life irritants much easier.

Figure 14-7:
This chart makes absorbing the meaning of the data difficult.

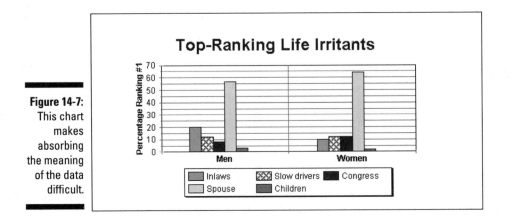

To change the arrangement of the data in your chart, you can go back and re-enter the data in the spreadsheet, changing your rows into columns and vice versa. Or you can take the easy way out: Right-click the chart and choose Series from the QuickMenu. Or click the chart background and then click the Chart Data button on the Property Bar.

Either way, the Series dialog box appears. Ignore the top half of the dialog box; the option you want is the Row/Column Swap check box at the bottom of the dialog box. Click the check box and click OK to make the swap official. In some cases, Quattro Pro may select another design for the chart if the original one isn't suitable for the new arrangement of data.

The other check box in the Series dialog box, Reverse Series, changes the order of the data series in your chart. If I applied the option to the chart in Figure 14-8, the bars representing the female point of view would move to the left of the bars representing the male perspective.

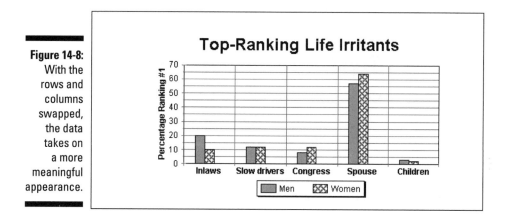

Figure 14-8: With the rows and columns swapped, the data takes on a more meaningful appearance.

Moving, Resizing, and Deleting Charts

Want to move that chart from one place in your spreadsheet to another? Place your cursor over the chart border until you see the four-headed arrow cursor. Then drag your chart to its new home. If you want to duplicate the chart and move the copy, press Ctrl as you drag. You can also move and copy charts by using the Cut, Copy, and Paste commands, just as you do in using Cut, Copy, and Paste to move and copy cells. (See Chapter 13 for details.)

To copy a chart from the Chart window into a spreadsheet, choose Edit⇨ Select All and then choose Edit⇨Copy or press Ctrl+C. Or right-click the chart icon on the Objects sheet and choose Copy from the QuickMenu. Then return to your spreadsheet page, click the spot where you want to place the chart, and choose the Paste command (Ctrl+V).

To resize a chart in the spreadsheet window, click its border to display the chart selection handles. Drag a top or bottom handle to change the height of the chart only; drag a side handle to change the width only; drag a corner handle to change both the width and height. You can't resize a chart in a chart window, but you can reduce or enlarge it for printing by using the print-scaling options that I describe in Chapter 15.

Finally, to delete a chart from your spreadsheet, click the chart border and press Delete. Quattro Pro deletes the chart from your spreadsheet and from the Objects sheet. To delete a chart in the Chart window, choose Chart⇨ Delete Chart. A dialog box appears, listing all your existing charts. Select the chart you want to delete and click OK. You can also click a chart's icon on the Objects sheet and press Delete.

Printing a Chart without Its Spreadsheet

Chapter 15 spells out the steps for printing a spreadsheet. If you created your chart on your spreadsheet page and want to print both the spreadsheet data and chart, follow the instructions in that chapter. If you want to print your chart without the spreadsheet data, however, click through the following steps. These steps work whether you're printing a chart from the spreadsheet window or Chart window.

1. **Click the chart border to select the chart.**

   If you created the chart in its own window, you can skip this step.

2. **Choose File⇨Print, click the Print button, or press Ctrl+P.**

   The Chart Print dialog box appears, with the Selected Chart radio button selected, which is exactly what you want.

3. **Adjust other print settings as needed.**

   The options in the Chart Print dialog box are the same as their cousins in the regular Spreadsheet Print dialog box. You can find out about these options in Chapter 15.

4. **Click Print or press Enter.**

If you want to print several charts at once, click the first chart and Shift+click the others. Then choose the Print command.

You can also print charts from the Objects sheet. Click the QuickTab button to go to the Objects sheet. (The QuickTab button is labeled back in Figure 14-5.) Then click and Shift+click the icons of the charts you want to print and choose the Print command.

Chapter 15

The Finishing Touches

● ●

In This Chapter

▶ Formatting in a flash with SpeedFormat

▶ Adding lines, borders, and colors

▶ Adding headers and footers

▶ Adjusting margins by dragging guidelines

▶ Hiding columns or rows temporarily

▶ Inserting a page break

▶ Printing your spreadsheet

● ●

*P*ackaging is everything. Think about it: Would you rather open a present that's encased in shiny, colorful wrapping paper or one that's stuffed in a dirty, wrinkled bag that smells suspiciously like last night's Chinese carry-out? Why, given the right presentation, even a cheap gift can convey the impression that somebody really cares about you.

The same is true with spreadsheets. You make a much better impression on the folks who see your spreadsheet if you fancy up the page with borders, headers, and the like. In fact, a nicely formatted spreadsheet can help divert everyone's attention from the actual information you're presenting, which can be really helpful on occasion.

Of course, you don't always want to dress up your spreadsheets in their Sunday best. For everyday number-crunching, you just want to enter your formulas, run your calculations, and print the results. For those times, skip to the end of this chapter, which tells you how to print your spreadsheet.

But if you want your spreadsheets to really wow your audience — whatever your motives — play around with the advanced formatting options discussed in the rest of this chapter. With a little effort on your part, you can make even the most horrible spreadsheet data look as delightful as a gift-wrapped box from Tiffany's.

Using SpeedFormat

Don't want to spend much time formatting your spreadsheet? Afraid of making some awful formatting faux pas? Let SpeedFormat take care of everything for you. The SpeedFormat command enables you to apply a predesigned set of formatting attributes to your data — font, shading, alignment, and more — with a wave of your hand (or rather with a few clicks of the old mouse).

 To use this handy feature, select the cells you want to format and click the SpeedFormat button, press Ctrl+Shift+F, or choose Format➪SpeedFormat. The SpeedFormat dialog box appears, as shown in Figure 15-1.

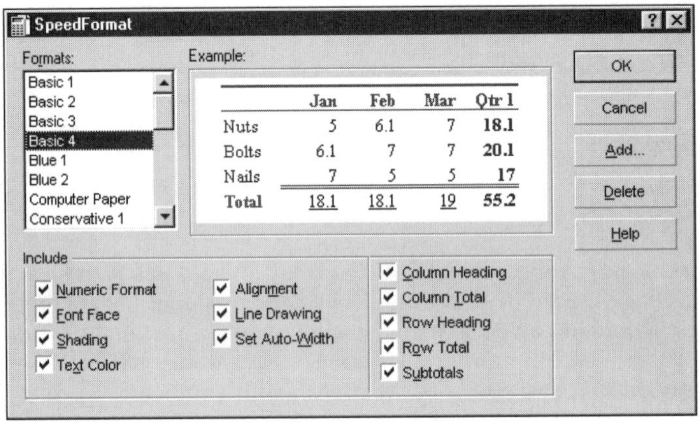

Figure 15-1:
To quickly turn your spreadsheet from dull to dazzling, use one of the SpeedFormat design templates.

SpeedFormat					
Formats:	**Example:**				

Formats list: Basic 1, Basic 2, Basic 3, Basic 4, Blue 1, Blue 2, Computer Paper, Conservative 1

	Jan	Feb	Mar	Qtr 1
Nuts	5	6.1	7	18.1
Bolts	6.1	7	7	20.1
Nails	7	5	5	17
Total	18.1	18.1	19	55.2

Buttons: OK, Cancel, Add..., Delete, Help

Include:
- ✔ Numeric Format
- ✔ Font Face
- ✔ Shading
- ✔ Text Color
- ✔ Alignment
- ✔ Line Drawing
- ✔ Set Auto-Width
- ✔ Column Heading
- ✔ Column Total
- ✔ Row Heading
- ✔ Row Total
- ✔ Subtotals

You can select from a variety of different spreadsheet designs, which are listed in the Formats list box. Click a design name to display a preview of that format in the Example box.

At the bottom of the dialog box are check boxes that enable you to select which parts of the design you want to incorporate into your spreadsheet. If you don't want to use the font that the design applies, for example, deselect the Font Face check box.

After you're satisfied with your selections, click OK or press Enter. Don't like what you see? Choose Edit➪Undo or press Ctrl+Z.

 If you insert rows or columns within the block of cells that you formatted with SpeedFormat, Quattro Pro automatically applies the same SpeedFormat design to the inserted cells.

You can add your own design to the SpeedFormat dialog box. First, format and select a block of cells. Then open the SpeedFormat dialog box, click the Add button, and give your design a name. Any time you want to use that design again, you can apply it from the SpeedFormat dialog box.

Adding Lines, Borders, and Colors

Quattro Pro enables you to draw lines around cells, surround blocks with borders, and even paint your spreadsheet with color. To whet your artistic appetite, the spreadsheet in Figure 15-2 shows an example that incorporates all these options.

Notice anything different about the spreadsheet in Figure 15-2? The cell gridlines that normally appear on-screen are missing. When you're adding lines, borders, and color to your spreadsheet, turn the gridlines off so that you can get a better idea of how your printed spreadsheet is going to look. (Gridlines normally don't print; see "Choosing print options," later in this chapter, for more details.)

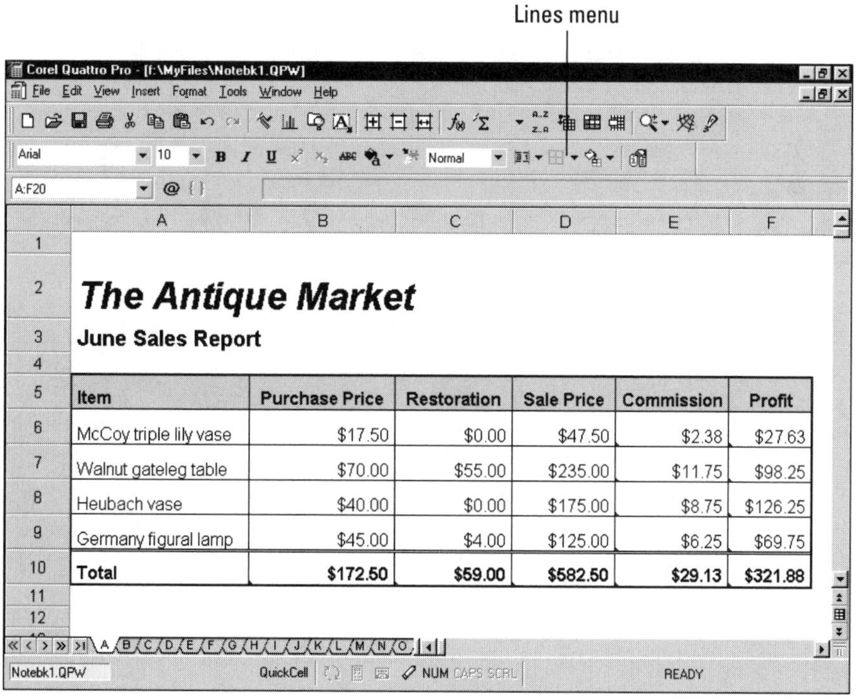

Lines menu
Corel Quattro Pro - [f:\MyFiles\Notebk1.QPW]
File Edit View Insert Format Tools Window Help
Arial
10
Normal
A:F20
The Antique Market
June Sales Report
Item
Purchase Price
Restoration
Sale Price
Commission
Profit
McCoy triple lily vase
$17.50
$0.00
$47.50
$2.38
$27.63
Walnut gateleg table
$70.00
$55.00
$235.00
$11.75
$98.25
Heubach vase
$40.00
$0.00
$175.00
$8.75
$126.25
Germany figural lamp
$45.00
$4.00
$125.00
$6.25
$69.75
Total
$172.50
$59.00
$582.50
$29.13
$321.88
Notebk1.QPW
QuickCell
NUM CAPS SCRL
READY

Figure 15-2: Exercise your creativity by using the Quattro Pro formatting options.

To turn off gridlines, press Ctrl+F12 or choose Format➪Sheet to display the Active Sheet dialog box. Then deselect the Gridlines check boxes on the Display tab and press Enter.

Drawing lines and borders around cells

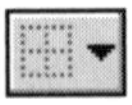

For a quick line-drawing approach, select the cells that you want to format and click the arrow on the Lines menu button on the Property Bar (refer to Figure 15-2). A menu of line options appears; click the one you want to use. The selected line style then appears on the face of the Lines menu button. If you want to apply that same line style to other selected cells, click the button face itself instead of the arrow. To remove all lines from around a cell, choose the first option in the menu.

 If none of the options on the Lines menu suits you, head for the Active Cells dialog box. Select the cells you want to format, press F12, choose Format➪Selection, or click the Format Selection button to open the dialog box. Then click the Border tab, as shown in Figure 15-3.

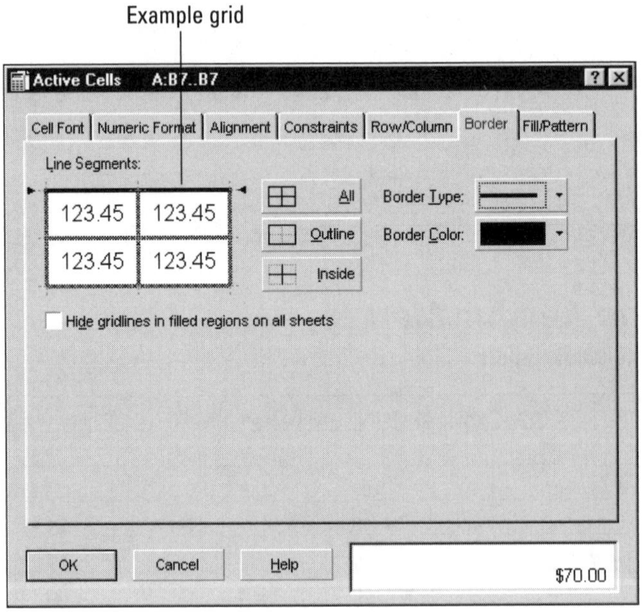

Example grid

Figure 15-3:
The process
of drawing
borders
around cells
isn't really
as compli-
cated as the
Active Cells
dialog box
makes it
seem.

In Version 8, this tab was labeled the Border/Fill tab and contained an option for coloring the interior of a cell. You can now find the fill options on their own tab, the Fill/Pattern tab. What hasn't changed is the way you use the line-drawing options, which can be baffling, to say the least. Here's the drill:

- If you click the All button, you get lines around each and every selected cell. If you click the Outline button, Quattro Pro draws a line around the perimeter of the selected block of cells. And if you click the Inside button, you get lines between the cells but not around the perimeter of the block.

- You aren't limited to the All, Outline, or Inside options, however. You can select whatever lines you want by clicking in the example grid on the left side of the dialog box. If you click at the intersection of two lines — on a corner, for example — both intersecting lines are selected. To select a line by itself, click anywhere on the line except at the point where it intersects with another line.

  The little black arrows in the example grid indicate which lines are selected. In Figure 15-3, the arrows indicate that the line at the top of the block is selected.

- With normal clicking, you can activate only one line on the grid at a time. If you click to put a line at the top of the grid, for example, and then click on the bottom of the grid, Quattro Pro deletes the line at the top of the grid and adds the line at the bottom of the grid. But if you press Shift as you click, you can place multiple lines on the grid. You can also Shift+click a line to erase it from the grid.

- Click the Border Type button to display a menu of line styles. Click the style you want to use. If you want to remove a previously drawn line, select the No Line option, which is the one with an X through it. If you want to cancel your changes to the line, click the empty spot at the top of the menu, which represents the No Change option.

- The default line color is black. If you want to select another color, click the Border Color button and click the color that tickles your fancy.

- You can specify as many different types of lines in the dialog box as you want. You can add a thick line to the top and bottom of the block, for example, and put a thin line on the right and left sides of the block. For each line type, just select the lines you want to format in the example grid and then select a line type and color.

- Just underneath the Example grid, you see a check box named Hide Gridlines In Filled Regions on All Sheets. This option really belongs on the Fill/Pattern tab because it has nothing to do with the lines you draw using the border options. Rather, it hides the normal spreadsheet grid-lines in and around any cells that you fill with a color or pattern.

If you already have the gridline display turned off for the entire work-sheet, this option has no effect on the on-screen appearance of your spreadsheet. But it *does* affect whether gridlines print. Even if you select the Gridlines option in the Page Setup dialog box (which tells Quattro Pro to print the gridlines), the gridlines don't print for cells filled with a color or pattern. For more on this bizarre setup, see "Choosing print options," later in this chapter.

✔ After you finish applying your lines, press Enter or click OK to see the results. If you don't like what you see, go back to the Border tab to make some changes or just press Ctrl+Z to get rid of all the lines you just applied.

Applying color to text and backgrounds

If you have a color printer or if you're creating an on-screen presentation, you may want to add some color to your spreadsheet. Even if you plan to print your spreadsheet on a black-and-white printer, you can get some nice effects by coloring the background of some cells with shades of gray or by reversing your text (putting white text on a dark background).

 To change the color of spreadsheet text, select the text you want to format and click the arrow on the Text Color button on the Property Bar. A palette of standard color swatches appears. To see even more colors, click the More button. Click the color you want to use.

Alternatively, you can apply a new color via the Active Cells dialog box. (Press F12, click the Format Selection button on the Property Bar, or choose Format⇨Selection to access the dialog box.) The Color drop-down list appears on the Cell Font tab of the dialog box. I see no reason to go this route unless you already have the dialog box open to apply other formatting options.

 If you select the cell(s) and then choose a color, the color is painted onto all text in the cell(s). But you don't need to apply the same color to all text in a cell; you can select individual characters and apply color to those characters only. For details on how to select text, see Chapter 13.

To change the background color of a cell, click the cell and select a color from the Cell Color menu on the Property Bar. This menu works like the Text Color button.

The Cell Color menu enables you to apply a solid color to your cells. But if you want to get more creative, press F12 or click the Format Selection button to open the Active Cells dialog box. Click the Fill/Pattern tab to uncover the myriad options shown in Figure 15-4.

Here, you can fill your selected cells with a pattern of color. Click the icon representing the pattern you want to use, and then select your two colors from the Pattern Color and Background Color menus. To switch back to a solid color, click the first pattern icon (the solid block of color) and then choose the color you want to use from the Pattern Color menu. Or just make a selection from the Cell Color menu on the Property Bar.

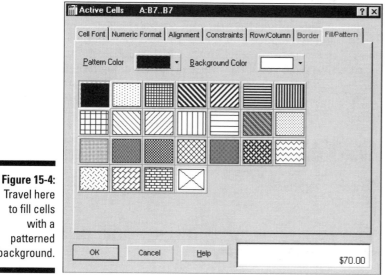

Figure 15-4:
Travel here
to fill cells
with a
patterned
background.

To remove the pattern or color from a cell, select the cell and then choose the No Fill option from the Cell Color menu. Or, inside the Active Cell dialog box, choose the last pattern icon on the Fill/Pattern tab (the icon has a big X through it).

Inserting Page Breaks

As you enter spreadsheet data, Quattro Pro automatically inserts a page break at the bottom of the page. You can see the page breaks by switching to Page view (View⇨Page) or the new Page Breaks view (View⇨Page Breaks) and then zooming out on your spreadsheet. Quattro Pro indicates page breaks with a thick line (blue, by default).

If you want to insert a page break at some other spot, do the following:

- ✔ To insert a horizontal page break, select the leftmost cell in the row where you want the break to occur. Then choose Insert⇨Page Break⇨Create.

- ✔ To insert a vertical page break, click the topmost cell in the column where you want the break to occur. Then choose Insert⇨Page Break⇨Create.

- ✔ To insert both a vertical and horizontal page break, click the cell where you want the break to occur. Choose Insert⇨Page Break⇨Create and then select Intersection from the lone drop-down menu in the resulting dialog box. Click OK to close the dialog box.

Quattro Pro inserts a line (or lines) across your spreadsheet to indicate the page break(s). To remove the page break, click the cell that contains the break. For a horizontal page break, click the cell just underneath the page break line. For a vertical page break, click the cell just to the right of the page break line. For an intersection page break, click the cell that's bordered on the left and top by the page break line. After you select the cell, choose Insert⇨Page Break⇨Delete.

Quattro Pro determines where to insert its automatic page breaks by looking at the paper size that is selected in the Spreadsheet Page Setup dialog box (more about that in the next section). If you change the page size, your page breaks are likely to change as well.

Changing the Page Setup

If you want to change the paper size, change the page orientation, set new margins, or add a header or footer to your spreadsheet, choose File⇨ Page Setup to open the Spreadsheet Page Setup dialog box, shown in Figure 15-5. You can also access this dialog box by clicking the Page Setup button inside the Print dialog box or in the Print Preview window (both discussed later in this chapter, in "Going from Screen to Printer").

This dialog box contains six tabs, two of which — Options and Print Scaling — are related specifically to printing and are covered in the section "Choosing print options," later in this chapter. The page setup options on the remaining tabs are discussed in the following two sections.

Figure 15-5:
Choose your
paper size,
orientation,
and other
layout
options
inside the
Spreadsheet
Page Setup
dialog box.

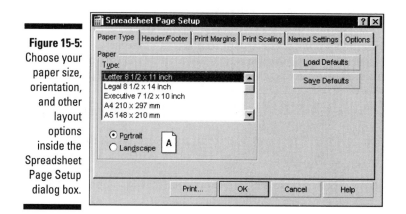

 Any settings you make in the dialog box are stored with your spreadsheet and remain in effect until you change them again. If you want to return all the settings to their default values, click the Load Defaults button on any tab of the dialog box. To save your current page setup values as the new default values, click the Save Defaults button.

 The Named Settings tab enables you to save all your page setup settings under a specific name so that you can easily reuse those same settings when you print another spreadsheet. To save your settings, enter a name in the New Set option box and click the Add button. To reuse a setting, select it from the settings list box and click the Use button.

Changing margins, paper size, and page orientation

The options on the Paper Type tab and Print Margins tab control . . . uh, I think you're clever enough to figure out the end of that sentence. But here are a few details that may not be so obvious:

- Select your paper size from the Type list box on the Paper Type tab.

- Select the paper orientation by clicking either the Portrait or Landscape radio button. In Portrait orientation, the rows of your spreadsheet run parallel to the short edge of the paper. In Landscape orientation, things print out sideways, so that the rows print parallel to the long edge of the paper.

- Set your page margins on the Print Margins tab. Alternatively, you can drag the margin guidelines that appear after you choose View➪Page (see Figure 15-6 for a look at the guidelines). Place your cursor over a guideline until you see the double-headed arrow and then drag the guideline to the spot where you want to place the margin, just as you do in WordPerfect. You can also drag the margin guides in the Print Preview window, as explained in the section "Previewing before you print," later in this chapter.

✔ The Break Pages check box on the Print Margins tab determines whether your pages print with or without any automatic page breaks that Quattro Pro inserted. (You may want to turn the option off to print on continuous-feed printer paper.) If the check box is turned off, the spreadsheet prints without the page breaks. Any page breaks that you inserted on your own do print, however. (For more information on page breaks, see "Inserting Page Breaks," earlier in this chapter.)

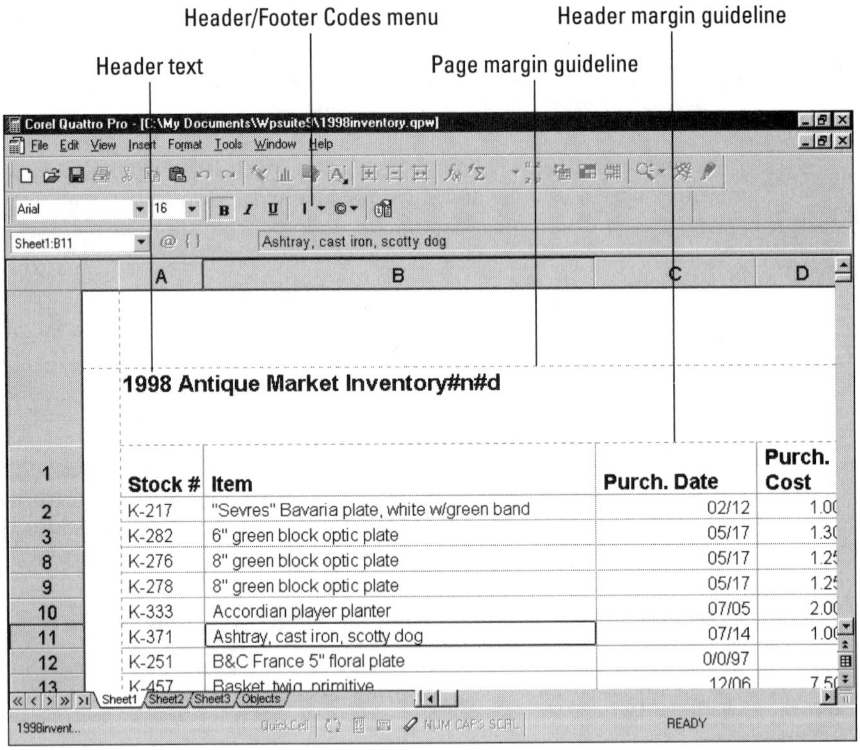

Figure 15-6:
You can edit headers and footers on the spreadsheet page by switching to Page view.

Adding headers and footers

The Header/Footer tab of the Spreadsheet Page Setup dialog box enables you to add a header (text that appears at the top of every page) and a footer (text that appears at the bottom of every page). You may, for example, want your name to appear on the bottom of every printed page.

✔ To create a header or footer, click the Create check box and then type your text into the adjacent text box. Click the Font button to pick a font, size, and style for your text. The Height value sets the amount of distance between the header or footer and the data in your spreadsheet.

✔ In Page view, you can see your header and footer on-screen along with the rest of your spreadsheet, as shown in Figure 15-6. And you can edit the header or footer text by double-clicking the header or footer area. Drag the margin guideline between the header and the spreadsheet cells to adjust the distance between header and data. Click in the main worksheet area to exit the header/footer zone and resume work on your spreadsheet.

✔ Quattro Pro uses special codes for inserting line breaks, setting text alignment, and inserting dates, page numbers, and other stuff into headers and footers. To see a list of the available codes, choose the Headers or Footers item in the Help index. (See Chapter 3 for more about using Help.)

Or, if you're editing a header or footer in Page view, click the Header/Footer Codes button to display a menu of some popular header/footer codes. In Figure 15-6, the #n code inserts a line break, and #d inserts the current date. (Quattro Pro inserts the pound sign before the code automatically; you don't see the sign on the menu.) After you exit the header/footer editing area, Quattro Pro formats your text according to the codes.

✔ To remove a header or footer, switch to Page view, right-click the header or footer, and choose Remove Header or Remove Footer from the QuickMenu. Or go back to the Header/Footer tab of the Spreadsheet Page Setup dialog box and deselect the Create check box for the offending header or footer.

Hiding a Row or Column

Suppose that you create a bang-up spreadsheet that lists each of your employees' names, titles, phone numbers, years at the company, and salaries. Someone asks you for an employee information list, and the spreadsheet immediately pops into your head. It would be a quick way to deliver the information, but the person who needs the information isn't supposed to know how much money everybody makes.

Here's the solution: You can temporarily hide the salary information for printing or on-screen viewing. Just right-click the border of the row or column you want to hide and choose Hide from the QuickMenu. Or select the border and press F12 or choose Format⇨Selection to display the Active Cells dialog box. Then click the Row/Column tab, select the Hide radio button in the Column Options or Row Options section (depending on what you want to hide), and click OK or press Enter.

If you hide a row or column, the following rows or columns shift over to fill the empty space. But the row numbers and column letters don't change — which gives you one easy way to see that you hid some data.

To redisplay a hidden row or column, select the rows or columns on both sides of the hidden row or column. Then right-click and choose Reveal from the QuickMenu. Or press F12 to open the Active Cells dialog box and follow the same procedure outlined for hiding data, but this time select the Reveal radio button.

You can also use the mouse to hide and reveal rows and columns, as follows:

- To hide a column, drag its border to the left until you reach the right border of the preceding column. To reveal a hidden column, put your cursor slightly to the right of the border of the column that lies to the right of the hidden column and then drag. If you hide Column A, for example, place your cursor just to the right of the left border of Column B. (Try it; this stuff all makes more sense if you see it on-screen.)

- To hide a row, drag up on the bottom row border until you reach the bottom border of the preceding row. To redisplay the hidden row, put your cursor slightly below the top border of the row that falls after the hidden row. To redisplay the hidden Row 1, for example, place your cursor slightly below the top border of Row 2 and drag.

Going from Screen to Printer

Ready to make the leap from digital spreadsheet to printed page? The following steps give you the basic how-to:

1. **Choose File⇨Print, press Ctrl+P, or click the Print button.**

   The Spreadsheet Print dialog box appears from out of nowhere, as shown in Figure 15-7.

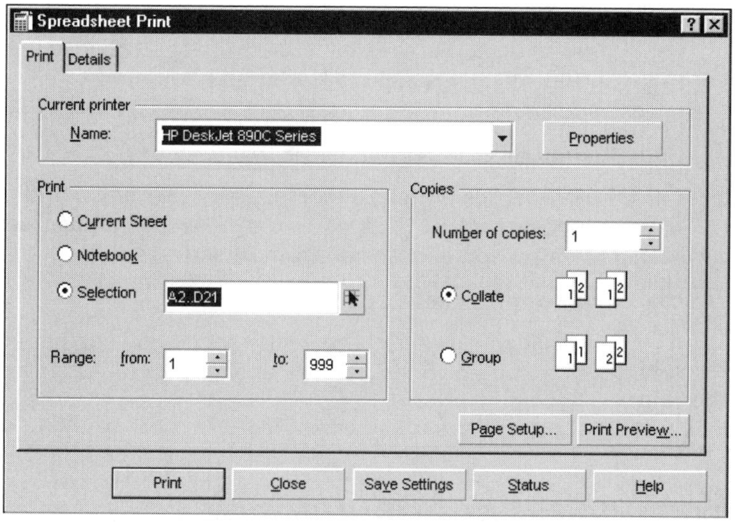

Figure 15-7:
Use the
Spreadsheet
Print dialog
box to shove
your work
out of the
computer
and onto
paper.

2. **Choose a printer from the Name drop-down list.**

   If you're hooked into a network and have access to several printers, you may need to select a printer. Otherwise, you can probably skip this step.

3. **Tell Quattro Pro what you want to print.**

   Select the Current Sheet radio button to print just the current worksheet. Select Notebook to print all worksheets in the notebook that contain data.

   If you want to print just a portion of a worksheet or notebook, specify the range of pages to print in the From and To options boxes. (Leave the options set at the default settings, 1 and 999, to print all pages in the worksheet or notebook.)

   You can also print specific cells or a chart by selecting them before you choose the Print command and then selecting the Selection radio button. (For more about printing charts, see the last section in Chapter 14.)

   If you forget to select the area you want to print before you open the dialog box, click the Selection button and then click the arrow at the end of the adjacent option box. The Spreadsheet Print dialog box minimizes itself temporarily. Select the cells you want to print and press Enter to redisplay the dialog box.

4. **Enter the number of copies you want to print in the Number of Copies option box.**

If you're printing more than one copy, you can have Quattro Pro collate your pages by selecting the Collate button. If you choose the Group radio button, all copies of page 1 print first, followed by all copies of page 2, and so on.

5. **Choose your specific printer settings (optional).**

   Click the Properties button to enter a dialog box full of options related to your specific printer. Click OK to return to the Spreadsheet Print dialog box after you choose your printer settings.

6. **Click Print or press Enter.**

   Assuming that your printer is correctly set up and configured to work with your computer, your spreadsheet should come sliding out of your printer any minute now.

Previewing before you print

Before you print, you may want to take a look at what the printed piece is going to look like. You may decide that you want to shrink or enlarge the margins, adjust the type size or font, or make other formatting changes before you actually transfer your spreadsheet to paper.

To preview your spreadsheet, choose File➪Print Preview to open the Preview window, as shown in Figure 15-8. Or click the Print Preview button in the Spreadsheet Print dialog box. The figure shows the preview of a budget spreadsheet I created to track everyday expenses. I've zoomed way out on the page so that no one can see how much I spend per week on sugar-free Fudgsicles and *Soap Opera Digest*.

The Preview window offers a number of helpful tools and options:

✔ After you first open the preview window, it shows you a full-page view of the first page in your notebook. Click the page to zoom in; right-click to zoom out. Keep clicking or right-clicking until you reach the magnification you want to use. Alternatively, you can zoom in and out by clicking the Zoom buttons.

✔ To see a different page of your notebook, enter the page number in the Page option box or click the Previous Page or Next Page button.

✔ Use the Black-and-White Preview and Color Preview buttons to switch between a preview that shows your spreadsheet in stark black and white and one that reveals glorious living color.

✔ To display or hide margin guidelines (see Figure 15-8), click the Margins button. You can drag the guidelines to change the page margins (see "Changing margins, paper size, and page orientation," earlier in this chapter).

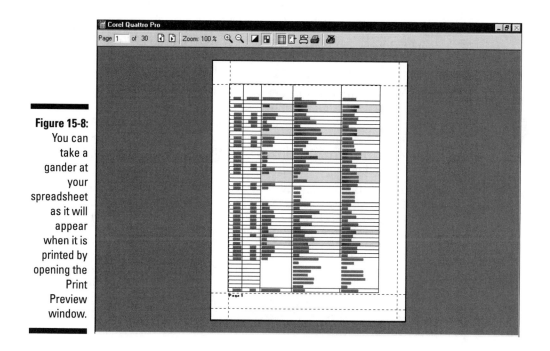

Figure 15-8:
You can take a gander at your spreadsheet as it will appear when it is printed by opening the Print Preview window.

✔ Click the Page Setup button to open the Spreadsheet Page Setup dialog box with the Header/Footer tab at the forefront. I describe this dialog box in witty and insightful detail in "Changing the Page Setup" and "Choosing print options," elsewhere in this chapter.

✔ Click the Print Options button to display the Options tab of the Spreadsheet Page Setup dialog box, where you can make still more adjustments to the way your spreadsheet prints. For more information, see the following section.

✔ To go ahead and print your spreadsheet, click the Print button. To close the Preview window, click the Close Preview button or press Esc.

Choosing print options

As if you hadn't already had your fill of printing options, still more adventures in printing await you on the Print Scaling and Options tabs of the Spreadsheet Page Setup dialog box. To get to the dialog box, choose File➪Page Setup or click the Page Setup button in the Print Preview window or the Print dialog box. Look at the control you can wield on these two tabs:

✔ You can *scale* — that is, reduce or enlarge — your spreadsheet by a certain percentage by clicking the first radio button on the Print Scaling tab and entering a percentage value. A value of exactly 100% prints the spreadsheet at its actual size; a value lower than 100% reduces the spreadsheet; and a value higher than 100% enlarges the spreadsheet.

If you want Quattro Pro to scale your spreadsheet so that it fits on a certain number of pages, click the second radio button and specify how many pages wide and how many pages tall you want your spreadsheet to be.

✔ If you have a long spreadsheet that can't print entirely on a single page, you may want to print the top row and/or left column of the spreadsheet on every page. Why? Because the top row and left column usually contain the titles of the rows and columns of data in your spreadsheet, and without those titles, you can easily forget what type of information each row and column holds.

To print the column and row titles, click the Options tab, shown in Figure 15-9. Enter the name of the row (or rows) you want to appear in the Top Heading option box; enter the name of the column (or columns) you want to print on each page in the Left Heading option box.

✔ Normally, Quattro Pro prints the answers to formulas and not the formulas themselves. But if you want to print the formulas rather than the answers, select the Cell Formulas check box on the Options tab. This option can come in handy when you're having trouble making your spreadsheet work and you want to have a Quattro Pro guru review the formulas you're using.

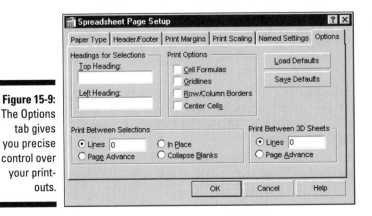

Figure 15-9: The Options tab gives you precise control over your printouts.

✔ By default, the gridlines marking the boundaries of each cell on-screen don't print. If you want these gridlines to print, select the Gridlines check box. But be forewarned that including the gridlines increases the amount of printer memory you need to print your spreadsheet.

If your printer memory isn't sufficient to handle gridlines, you can create "fake" gridlines by drawing them as explained in the section "Drawing lines and borders around cells," earlier in this chapter. Select the part of your spreadsheet that needs gridlines and then choose the All line segments button and the thin Border Type option on the Border tab of the Active Cells dialog box.

✔ If you want to print row and column borders, check the Row/Column Borders option box. You may want to do so if you want to know the exact cell address of each cell in the printed spreadsheet so that you can go back and edit specific cells easily.

✔ To center the spreadsheet on the page, check the Center Cells check box. Otherwise, the spreadsheet aligns to the left margin.

✔ If you chose the Selection printing option and are printing more than one block of selected cells, select the Page Advance radio button in the Print Between Selections area of the dialog box to print each block on a separate page. If you select the Lines option, the different blocks are printed on the same sheet of paper but are separated by the number of lines you enter in the Lines option box. (To find out how to select multiple blocks to print, see Chapter 13.)

✔ If you want each worksheet of your notebook to start on a new sheet of paper, select the Page Advance radio button in the Print Between 3D Sheets area of the dialog box. If you just want to separate the different worksheets with a few lines of space, select the Lines radio button and enter the number of line spaces you want in the option box.

✔ To reset the print options to Quattro Pro's defaults, click Load Defaults. To make your settings the new default settings, click Save Defaults.

You now know more than you ever wanted about printing spreadsheets in Quattro Pro. That headache you have is a sure sign that your brain is growing by leaps and bounds.

Part IV
Those Other Programs

The 5th Wave — By Rich Tennant

"THE FUNNY THING IS, I NEVER KNEW THEY HAD DESKTOP PUBLISHING SOFTWARE FOR PAPER SHREDDERS."

In this part . . .

This part of the book is a heaping smorgasbord of information about the programs not covered in Parts I, II, and III. In this part, I dish up tasty servings of techniques and tips for using Corel Presentations, CorelCentral, Dragon NaturallySpeaking, and Corel Print Office. For dessert, I offer valuable insights on how to use all the programs in the WordPerfect Office 2000 suite together to save yourself some time and effort.

Dig in, and bring a hearty appetite. As they say, there's something here to satisfy every taste. And at this buffet, you can fill your plate as many times as you want without winding up with that uncomfortable bloated feeling or adding any extra pounds.

Chapter 16

Let's All Get Together and Put on a Show!

▶ Using Corel Presentations to create multimedia slide shows

▶ Choosing slide backgrounds and layouts

▶ Viewing your slides

▶ Adding text to slides

▶ Working with bulleted lists, data charts, and organizational charts

▶ Creating cool text

*H*oo, boy. You really stepped in it this time, didn't you? When they asked if you'd give a presentation to the big brass at the annual company meeting, you didn't even hesitate before saying yes. Okay, maybe you hesitated just a little, but you didn't want to look uncooperative, so you acted as though the idea was a good one. Or maybe you out and out refused, but they said that if you didn't agree to their evil plan, you'd be looking for another employer.

Well, however you got yourself into this predicament, Presentations 9 can help you create a show that not only entertains and informs your audience, but also draws attention away from the fact that you spilled salad dressing on your shirt during lunch. With this program, you can create a multimedia slide show that you can play back on any computer running Microsoft Windows — even one that doesn't have Presentations installed. You can also create regular 35mm slides and printed drawings.

This chapter gets you started by introducing you to the basics of creating a slide show, from choosing a show design to putting text on your slides. Chapter 17 provides the second half of your Presentations mini-course. There, you find out how to create simple drawings, add animation and sound effects to your show, and then package up your presentation for distribution to your breathless audience. (That's breathless with anticipation, not breathless because they've expired from boredom, by the way.)

Starting and Stopping

To start Presentations, click the Presentations DAD icon. Or click the Start button on the Windows taskbar and then choose Programs⇨ WordPerfect Office 2000⇨Corel Presentations 9. Presentations pops to life and presents you with the PerfectExpert dialog box, which works just like the one in WordPerfect and Quattro Pro.

✔ Click the Create New tab to create a new slide show or drawing. Like WordPerfect and Quattro Pro, Presentations offers a variety of templates that can serve as the basis for your creation. Click the template you want to use and click Create. See Chapter 3 for more information about templates. Chapter 3 also explains the PerfectExpert help window that appears when you work with templates.

✔ If you prefer not to use a template, choose the Presentations Drawing or Presentations Slide Show item. The Slide Show option enables you to create a multimedia presentation; the Drawing option enables you to create standalone artwork, such as a banner or advertisement. If you choose the Presentations Slide Show item, Presentations takes you to the Startup Master Gallery dialog box, which I explain in "Building a Really Big Shew," later in this chapter. If you're creating a new drawing, a shiny new drawing page appears. See Chapter 17 for information on how to access your artistic tools.

✔ The Work On tab lists the documents you've edited most recently. If you want to work on one of these documents, select it from the list and click Open.

After you open one document, you can open additional documents as follows:

✔ To work on an existing document, press Ctrl+O, click the Open button on the toolbar, or choose File⇨Open to display the Open File dialog box. See Chapter 4 for information on this dialog box.

✔ Want to use one of the Presentations templates? Press Ctrl+Shift+N or choose File⇨New from Project to open the PerfectExpert dialog box, which gives you access to the templates. Or, if you have DAD enabled (see Chapter 2), click the Corel New Project DAD icon on the Windows taskbar to open the dialog box. (Be sure to click the icon on the taskbar, not the one on the Presentations toolbar, which opens the PerfectExpert help window.)

✔ Click the New button, press Ctrl+N, or choose File⇨New to get a new blank drawing page or presentation without mucking around with the PerfectExpert dialog box. The type of document you get depends on the type that you last selected in the dialog box — if you selected a presentation on your last trip to the dialog box, you get another presentation.

Hey! Where'd my favorite buttons go?

Users upgrading from Version 8 may notice one major screen change in Version 9. Some buttons that were formerly on the toolbar or Property Bar have been relocated to a vertical toolbar on the left side of the Presentations window. Corel refers to this toolbar as the Tool Palette.

If having the toolbar on the side of the window bothers you — a little uncomfortable with change, are we? — put your cursor over the edge of the Tool Palette until you see the four-headed arrow cursor. Then drag the palette to another location. If you drag up to the standard toolbar area, you dock the palette, and it behaves like a normal toolbar. Otherwise, it becomes a free-floating palette. You can drag

the palette around by its title bar and put it away altogether by clicking the close button (that little X button in the upper-right corner).

To reopen the palette, choose View➪Toolbars and then select the Tool Palette check box in the dialog box that appears. You can also display or hide the standard toolbar and Property Bar via this dialog box. And, if you really like to have things your way, you can drag the Property Bar and standard toolbar around on-screen just as you can the Tool Palette.

Be sure to check out Chapter 2 for more information on toolbars, the Property Bar, and other basic window elements.

To close a drawing or presentation, choose File➪Close, press Ctrl+F4, or click the document window Close button. To shut down Presentations, choose File➪Exit, press Alt+F4, or click the program window Close button.

Building a Really Big Shew

Although you can use Presentations to create drawings and do some basic photo editing, the program's primary purpose is to create multimedia presentations — jazzed up, digital equivalents of the old-fashioned slide show.

A presentation consists of a series of "slides" that display in sequence when you play the show on a computer. In Presentations, each slide has these three layers:

- ✔ The *Background layer* contains a picture or design that appears behind the text and graphics on your slides.

- ✔ The *Layout layer* is a template that contains preformatted areas to hold your slide text. You select a layout for each type of slide you create — such as title slide, bullet chart, and so on.

- ✔ The *Slide layer* holds the actual text and graphics that you put on the slide.

The following sections show you how to combine these three layers to create your slides. Later sections in this chapter and in Chapter 17 explain how to edit your slides and save, print, and play your show.

Choosing a Master

After you tell Presentations that you want to create a slide show, it presents you with the Startup Master Gallery dialog box, shown in Figure 16-1. The *Master* determines the overall look of your show. The Master includes the background for your slides, plus layouts to hold different types of slide text. Although the purpose of the Master is to give your show a consistent design, you can override the background and layout for any slide.

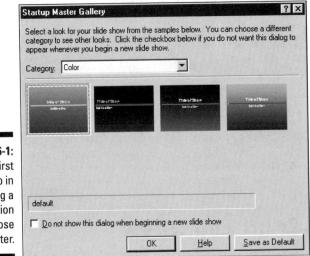

Figure 16-1: The first step in creating a presentation is to choose a Master.

The available Masters are organized into seven different categories; display a different category by choosing it from the Category drop-down list. You can use any category that tickles your fancy, but keep these tips in mind:

- ✔ Most business people today play presentations on a computer. But, if you want, you can print each slide in your presentation as a standard 35mm slide and then show the slides in a slide projector. (See the end of Chapter 17 for details on this process.) If you plan to go this route, select a Master from the 35mm category.

- ✔ Another output alternative is to print your show as black-and-white transparencies. You can also print black-and-white copies of your slides to use as handouts. Masters in the Printout category are especially designed for both purposes. Again, check out Chapter 17 for printing information.

After selecting a category, click the picture of the Master you want to use and press Enter or click OK. Presentations displays the first slide in the program window, as shown in the upcoming Figure 16-2.

Although Presentations prompts you to choose a Master as the first step in creating a show, you can actually apply the Master at any time. So, if you don't want to be bothered with the Startup Master Gallery dialog box when you start a new slide show, select the Do Not Show This Dialog check box at the bottom of the dialog box and press Enter.

If you choose to bypass the Startup Master Gallery, you can select the Master for your show – or change the existing Master — by clicking the Master Gallery button on the toolbar or choosing Format➪Master Gallery. Presentations opens the Master Gallery dialog box, which is different from the one shown in Figure 16-1 in name only.

Viewing and selecting slides

If you're working your way through this chapter in order, you have only one slide in your presentation so far. But, eventually, your presentation will contain multiple slides, so you need to know how to move from slide to slide and take advantage of the different slide-viewing options available to you.

Presentations gives you three ways to ponder your slides. You can choose from Slide Editor view, Slide Outliner view, and Slide Sorter view; simply click the corresponding tab along the right side of the Presentations window to switch views.

- Slide Editor view is the standard, default view. In this view, you can edit your slides and see them as they will appear in your presentation. The screen in Figure 16-2 shows you this view.

- Slide Outliner lists your slides in outline format, much as though you had made a list of all your slides on a piece of notebook paper. You can't see graphics in this mode, but you can view and edit slide text, add slides, delete slides, and rearrange slides.

- In Slide Sorter view, you see thumbnail views of your slides, along with information about the transition and advance modes selected for each slide. (You can read more about transition and advance modes in Chapter 17.) In this view, you can see several slides on-screen at once, and you can rearrange slides by dragging them.

Regardless of what view option you select, you can select a slide in your show by clicking its slide tab or selecting the slide from the slide list (see Figure 16-2).

Layout button

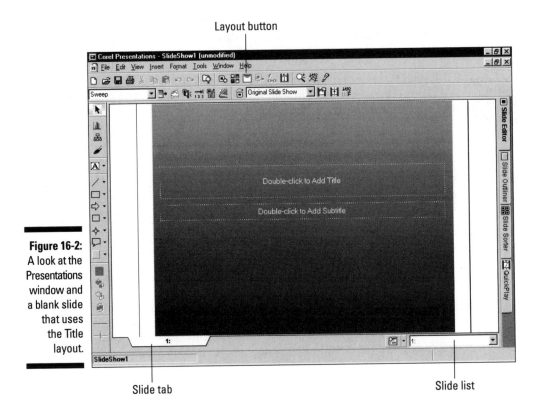

Figure 16-2:
A look at the
Presentations
window and
a blank slide
that uses
the Title
layout.

Slide tab

Slide list

 In Slide Editor view, you can zoom in and out on your work by clicking the Zoom button on the toolbar and choosing a view size from the drop-down list.

While you're working in Slide Sorter view, the toolbar Zoom button becomes unavailable. But you can magnify and reduce the display of your slides by clicking the Zoom In and Zoom Out buttons at the bottom of the Presentations window (the buttons are next to the slide list in this view).

Choosing a slide layout

Although Masters control the overall appearance of your slides, *layouts* aid you in placing text on slides. The layouts position and format your text in a way that meshes with the Master you selected. You can choose from the following layouts:

> ✔ **Title:** The background from the Master Gallery, plus text boxes formatted to hold a title and subtitle

- ✔ **Bulleted List:** The background and formatted text boxes to hold a title, subtitle, and bulleted list of information

- ✔ **Text:** The background, plus areas formatted for a title, subtitle, and paragraph text

- ✔ **Org Chart:** The background and areas formatted to hold a title, subtitle, and organizational chart

- ✔ **Data Chart:** The background, plus areas formatted for a title, subtitle, and data chart (such as a bar chart or pie chart)

- ✔ **Combination:** The background and formatted areas for a title, subtitle, paragraph text, and data chart

- ✔ **None:** The background and nothing else

After you start a new show and select a Master, Presentations displays the first slide. Presentations assumes that you want your first slide to contain the title and subtitle of your show, so it selects the Title layout for you. To change to a different layout, click the Layout button (labeled in Figure 16-2) and choose the layout you want from the drop-down list. The icon on the Layout button changes to reflect the selected layout for the current slide.

To change the layout for several slides in your show, choose Format⇨ Slide Properties⇨Appearance to display the Appearance tab of the Slide Properties dialog box, shown in Figure 16-3. (You can also right-click the slide background and choose Appearance from the QuickMenu to display the dialog box.)

The seven layout options are presented as icons at the top of the dialog box. By using the arrows and the drop-down list at the bottom of the dialog box, you can move from slide to slide and change the layout for each slide. Click OK to apply the new templates in one grand, sweeping gesture.

Another option for changing layouts is to switch to Slide Sorter view, click the first slide you want to change, and Ctrl+click the others. Then choose a new layout via the Slide Properties dialog box or the Layout button on the toolbar. Presentations applies the layout to all selected slides. Click the Slide Editor tab to return to the standard slide view.

Don't fret too much about this layout business. The layouts just give you some guidance in placing stuff on your slides. But you can rearrange, delete, and add text boxes at whim, regardless of which layout you use.

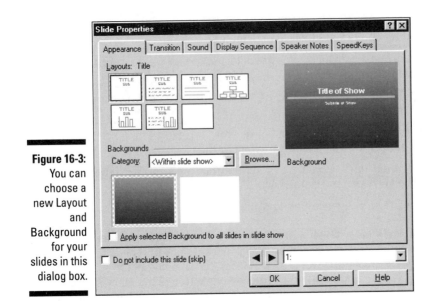

Figure 16-3:
You can
choose a
new Layout
and
Background
for your
slides in this
dialog box.

Playing with backgrounds

The curious (or very bored) in the crowd may have noticed that the Appearance tab of the Slide Properties dialog box shown in Figure 16-3 also has options related to the slide background. You can get to this tab by choosing Format⇨Slide Properties⇨Appearance or right-clicking the slide background and choosing Appearance from the QuickMenu.

To change the background for a slide, first select that slide by using the arrows or the drop-down list near the lower-right corner of the dialog box. The dialog box contains previews of the backgrounds currently available — by default, you get the background that comes with the slide show Master and a blank white background. But you can choose from a mess of other backgrounds by selecting an option from the Category drop-down list.

When you stumble across a background that sets your heart racing, click it. To apply the background to the selected slide only, press Enter. To apply the new background to all slides, select the oddly named Apply Selected Background to All Slides in Slide Show check box. (The Do Not Include This Slide check box, although visible while you're working on the Appearance tab, is related to playing slide shows and has no effect on applying backgrounds and layouts.)

REMEMBER

Don't forget your safety net!

As you build a drawing or slide show, don't forget that you can reverse most actions you take by clicking the Undo button (↶), pressing Ctrl+Z, or choosing Edit⇨Undo. And if you think better of your undo, click the Redo button (↷), press Ctrl+Shift+R, or choose Edit⇨Redo to put things back the way they were.

Unfortunately, you can undo only the last action, not a whole series of blunders as you can in WordPerfect. Be sure to choose Undo or Redo immediately after you make a mistake, or you lose your chance to change your mind.

Adding and deleting slides

To add a slide to your show, click the tab of the slide that falls immediately before the spot where you want to insert the new slide. For example, if you want to insert a slide between Slide 1 and Slide 2, click the tab for Slide 1. Then click the arrow on the Add Slide button, which lives next to the slide list at the bottom of the Presentations window (see the upcoming Figure 16-4). A menu appears, listing the seven layout choices available for your slide (Title, Bulleted List, and so on). Click the layout you want to use, and Presentations inserts the new slide after the current slide.

You can add several slides at once by clicking the New Slide toolbar button or choosing Insert⇨New Slide to open the New Slide dialog box. Click the icon for the layout you want to use and then enter the number of slides you want to insert in the Number to Add box. Press Enter or click OK to insert the slides after the current slide. Keep in mind that you can always change the layout later, so the New Slide dialog box is a good choice for adding multiple slides even if you don't want to use the same layout on all of them. Pick one layout and then change the layout for selected slides as described earlier in this chapter.

To chuck a slide from your show, click its tab and choose Edit⇨Delete Slides. Presentations asks for reassurance that you really want to lose the slide. Click Yes or No, depending on your feelings.

For an easy way to delete several slides at once, switch to Slide Sorter view, click the first slide you want to delete, and Ctrl+click the others. If you select a slide by mistake, Ctrl+click it again. After you select all the slides you want to delete, choose the Delete Slides command.

Adding Tantalizing Text and Dynamic Data

Whew, here we are already several pages into this chapter, and all you've discovered so far is how to establish the look of your slides and add and delete slides. You're no doubt squirming with impatience, wondering when I'm going to tell you how to actually put some information on your slides. Or . . . is something else causing that pained look on your face? No, that's okay — really, I don't want to know.

Regardless, the time to add text to your slides has arrived. Text goes into text boxes, such as the one shown in Figure 16-4. You can use the text boxes provided by the slide layout or draw your own.

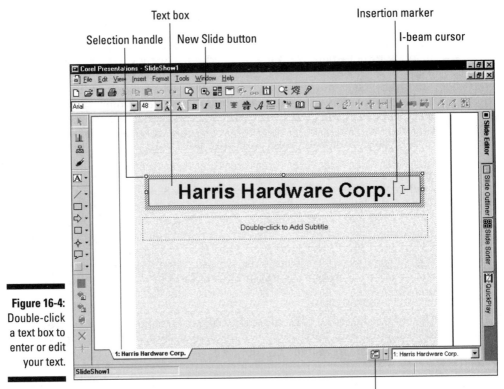

Figure 16-4:
Double-click a text box to enter or edit your text.

Working with existing text boxes

To enter your pithy quotes into an existing text box, move your mouse cursor over the text box. Then take a look at your mouse cursor. If it looks like an arrow, double-click the text box. But if you see any other cursor, first click the Selection tool button in the Tool Palette — the button is the arrow-shaped button at the top of the palette. Now double-click the text box.

After you double-click, the text box border changes, and selection handles appear to show that the box is selected, as in Figure 16-4. You also see the standard blinking insertion marker and I-beam cursor used for entering text in WordPerfect, Quattro Pro, and almost every other Windows program.

After you activate the text box, type your text, keeping these rules in mind:

- ✔ The insertion marker indicates where the next character you type will appear. To reposition the insertion marker, click at the spot where you want it to appear. Or use the arrow keys to move the insertion marker.

- ✔ As soon as a text box is selected, the Property Bar and Tool Palette display tools and drop-down menus for formatting text, including controls that change the font, text color, alignment, and so on. Pause your cursor over the buttons and menus to see QuickTips that describe the function of each gadget. (If the QuickTips don't appear, choose Tools⇨Settings, click the Display icon, select the QuickTips check box in the Display dialog box, click OK, and then click Close.) The later section "Playing with colors, fonts, and other fun stuff" tells you how to use these controls to dress up your text.

- ✔ If the characters you type fill up the text box, the box enlarges and text wraps to the next line. You can also press Enter to start a new line of text.

- ✔ After entering your text, click outside the text box to deselect it or press Esc to deselect the text but leave the text box selected.

- ✔ Entering and editing text in data charts, bulleted lists, and organization charts involves some special tricks, as I explain in upcoming sections in this chapter.

- ✔ Text boxes in which you don't enter text don't appear on your finished slide.

To edit your text, just double-click the text box to make the insertion marker and I-beam reappear. You can then use most of the standard text-editing techniques you use to edit text in WordPerfect (see Chapter 6).

Creating your own text boxes

You're not limited to using the text boxes that Presentations provides. You can add your own text boxes wherever you like. Here's how:

1. **Click the arrow on the Text Object Tools flyout menu.**

   The flyout menu, labeled in Figure 16-5, is now located on the Tool Palette. For more about this insidious design change, see the sidebar "Hey! Where'd my favorite buttons go?" earlier in this chapter. Clicking the arrow displays a flyout menu of four text tools, as shown in the figure.

2. **Choose a text tool from the flyout menu.**

   As shown in Figure 16-5, your menu options are: the Text Area tool, which creates a regular text box; the Text Line tool, which creates a text box for a single line of text; the Bulleted List tool, which creates a text box formatted to hold a bulleted list; and the Text Art tool, which opens up the Text Art dialog box, where you can apply special effects to your text. (See Chapter 22 for more information on this last option.)

   Click the button for the tool you want to use. After you choose a text tool, your cursor changes to a little hand, as shown in Figure 16-5. (Note that the Text Objects Tools flyout menu closes after you choose a tool; I kept it open in Figure 16-5 through a little digital-imaging trickery.)

3. **Drag or click to create your text box.**

   If you're working with the Text Area or Bulleted List tool, drag to create your text box. Just click if you're using the Text Line tool. Presentations automatically selects the new text box and waits for you to enter your text. If you click outside the text box or otherwise deselect it before entering text, the text box disappears.

After you select a Text Object tool, that tool appears on the Text Object Tools flyout button face. To use the same tool again, click the button instead of the arrow.

If you select a text tool and then change your mind about creating a text box, click the Selection tool (see Figure 16-5) to return to the regular arrow cursor.

Creating and editing data charts

Certain slide layouts contain text boxes formatted for charts. Presentations offers two types of charts: organizational charts and regular data charts. You work with both types of chart text boxes a little differently than you do with ordinary text boxes.

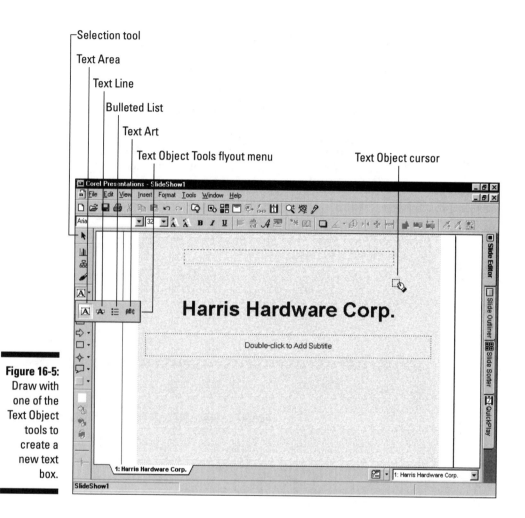

Selection tool

Text Area

Text Line

Bulleted List

Text Art

Text Object Tools flyout menu

Text Object cursor

Harris Hardware Corp.

Double-click to Add Subtitle

Figure 16-5:
Draw with
one of the
Text Object
tools to
create a
new text
box.

To create a data chart, walk your chart-minded self this way:

1. **Open a data chart box.**

   To enter data into an existing data chart box, double-click the box.
   (Make sure that the Selection tool is active before you double-click. The
   Selection tool is located at the top of the Tool Palette; refer to Figure
   16-5.) Or, to create a new data chart box, click the Data Chart button and
   then drag to draw the boundaries of the box.

   After you double-click the text box or release the mouse button, the
   Data Chart Gallery dialog box appears.

2. Select a chart design.

Click a chart type option from the list on the left side of the dialog box. Presentations then displays icons that show you the available designs for that chart type. Click the icon for the design you like best.

Now take a gander at that Use Sample Data check box in the lower-left corner of the dialog box. If you select that option, Presentations creates a template chart that's filled with sample data. You then have to select and replace the sample data with your own data. In my humble opinion — IMHO, as they say on the Internet — this option means extra work for you. So deselect the check box and save yourself some time.

3. Click OK.

A Datasheet window appears, as shown in Figure 16-6. The Datasheet window resembles a Quattro Pro worksheet. You enter your chart data into the cells in the Datasheet.

You can drag a corner of the Datasheet window to enlarge the window if needed. And drag the title bar to relocate the window.

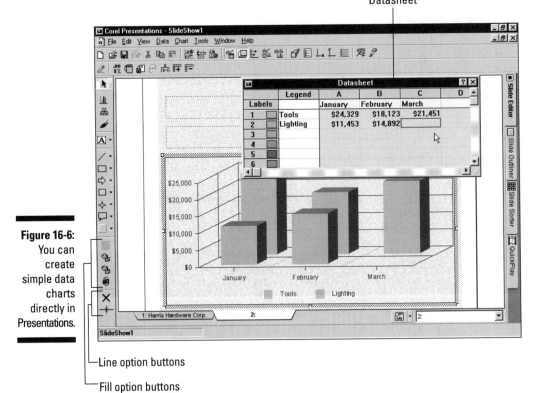

Figure 16-6:
You can create simple data charts directly in Presentations.

Line option buttons

Fill option buttons

4. Enter your chart data.

Just click a cell to put your text or numbers into the cell. To close the cell, press Enter or click another cell. As you enter your data, Presentations begins building your chart in the slide window. (If Presentations doesn't draw your chart, the Auto Redraw option in the View menu may be turned off. Click the option to toggle it on and off.) Don't worry about the program's color choices at this point; you can change the colors later.

If you want to reopen a cell to edit its data, double-click the cell. The Edit Current Cell dialog box appears. Enter the revised data into the Data box and click OK.

5. Click the Datasheet window Close button after you enter all your data.

(The Close button is the little X in the upper-right corner of the window.) Your chart remains selected in the slide window.

6. Refine the chart design if needed.

The Chart menu, which appears whenever a chart is selected, offers all kinds of options for playing with your design. If you choose the Legend command, for example, you get a dialog box where you can change the font, color, and position of your chart legends.

To make quick, simple changes such as the font used in chart labels or the color of a chart element, click the element — this time using the left mouse button — to display selection handles (little boxes) around the element. Then use the fill and line option buttons on the Tool Palette and the various buttons on the Property Bar to play with your design.

7. Click outside the chart to deselect it.

To change some data in an existing chart, double-click the chart and choose View⇨Datasheet. (You can also double-click the chart and then right-click the chart and choose Display Datasheet from the QuickMenu.) The Datasheet window reappears, and you can change your data as needed.

To alter the chart design, double-click the chart and use the options on the Chart menu. Or double-click the chart, click the element you want to change, and use the Tool Palette and Property Bar options to do the job. If you simply want to resize the chart, drag one of the corner selection handles that appears when you double-click the chart. (The selection handles are those boxes around the perimeter of the chart boundary.)

The chart-making capabilities in Presentations are best suited to drawing simple charts from simple data. For complicated charts, you're better off entering your data and creating your chart in Quattro Pro and then pasting the chart into Presentations. For information about bringing items created in one program into another program, see Chapter 21.

Creating and editing organizational charts

The Org Chart layout provides a text box for creating an organizational chart. This chart provides you with the classic organizational chart design — you know, the kind that shows who's the top banana in the department and who's merely an underling plotting to take the top banana's job.

To enter data into the chart, first double-click the Org Chart text box. (Be sure that the Selection tool is active before you double-click. The Selection tool is the first tool in the Tool Palette — the one that looks like an arrow.) Then double-click a name box in the chart to enter a person's name and title into the box. Click outside the name box to deselect it. Click outside the chart boundary after you're through promoting and demoting people.

If you don't like the default chart style, create a custom chart design instead of relying on the Org Chart layout. Choose Insert➪Organization Chart or click the Organization Chart button and then drag to create your chart. Presentations displays the Layout dialog box, in which you can choose from many different chart styles.

To edit the contents of a name box, double-click the chart and then double-click the box. And, if you want to play around with your chart design — changing the color of the lines that connect the name boxes and so on — double-click the chart and then single-click the element you want to change. The Property Bar, toolbar, Tool Palette, and Format menu then offer buttons and commands related to the chart design. The Format menu also provides commands for altering the structure of the chart — for example, adding a new branch to the chart.

Shooting out bulleted lists

Bulleted lists are easy to create in Presentations. Shoot a list onto your page as follows:

✔ If you created your slide using the Bulleted List layout, the main text box is formatted for your list. To enter text into a bulleted list text box, double-click the text box, first making sure that the Selection tool is active (the arrow-shaped tool at the top of the Tool Palette). A bullet appears for the first item in your list. Type the item and then press Enter to create a bullet for the second item in the list.

✔ To create a bulleted list text box from scratch, click the Bulleted List button on the Text Object Tools flyout menu (refer to Figure 16-5) or choose Insert➪Bulleted List. Then drag to create the text box. The text box becomes selected, and the first bullet appears. Enter your text as just described.

✔ If you want your second bullet item to appear as a second-level bullet underneath the first item, press Tab at the beginning of the line for that second item. Presentations indents the line and displays a different bullet style for the item. You can create as many levels of items as you want; just keep pressing Tab to increase the indent.

✔ Similarly, to enter a new item at a higher level than the preceding one, press Shift+Tab at the beginning of the line for the new item. Press Shift+Tab as many times as necessary to get to the level you want.

✔ To change the level of an existing item, click at the beginning of the line and press Shift+Tab or Tab, depending on whether you want to promote or demote the item. Keep pressing Shift+Tab or Tab until the item is at the right level.

✔ Click outside the text box when you finish entering your bulleted text. To edit the text, double-click the box. Then use the basic editing techniques you use in any word processor to correct your text.

✔ Now for the fun part: You can change the color, bullet style, and other design aspects of your bulleted chart. Select the text box (click it) and then click the Bulleted List Properties button on the Property Bar. The Bulleted List Properties dialog box opens, to no one's surprise. The box contains a slew of options for designing your list; play around until you get a look you like or get bored with the whole process, whichever comes first.

✔ For even more ways to format your list, see the next section and Chapter 17.

Playing with colors, fonts, and other fun stuff

You can use various formatting commands to add artistic touches to your text, as shown in Figure 16-7. You can use these same techniques to format text in a Presentations drawing.

Before you can format text, you must select it. To apply the formatting to the entire text box, first choose the Selection tool (the top, arrow-shaped tool in the Tool Palette). Then click the box once to display the square selection handles. To apply the formatting only to certain characters, double-click the text box and then drag across those characters. (These selection techniques vary slightly if you're working on text in an organization or data chart; an extra double-click or click may be needed. See the sections related to these two types of charts earlier in this chapter for more help.)

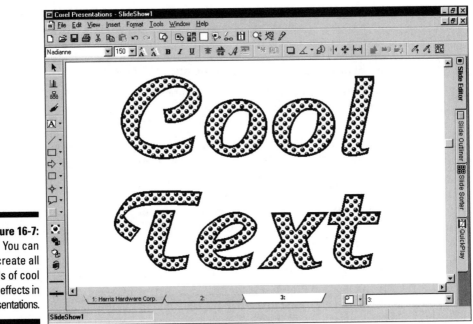

Figure 16-7:
You can
create all
kinds of cool
text effects in
Presentations.

Here are just some of the different ways to make your text stand out:

✔ If text is selected, the Property Bar and Tool Palette display all kinds of menus and buttons for jazzing up your text. At the left end of the Property Bar, you find menus for changing the font and type size, just as in WordPerfect. Buttons for changing the text color, fill, and outline live at the bottom of the Tool Palette.

✔ Like WordPerfect and Quattro Pro, Presentations now offers a RealTime Preview feature that enables you to preview the results of some formatting that you apply via the Property Bar and Tool Palette. As you pause your cursor over a font name in the Font menu, for example, Presentations displays your selected text in that font. Note that you can't turn RealTime Preview on and off as you can in Quattro Pro and WordPerfect; the feature is always turned on by default.

✔ You can also access formatting controls through the Font Properties dialog box. To open the dialog box, click the Font Properties button on the toolbar, press F9, or choose Format⇨Font.

✔ Some effects, such as a drop shadow, can be applied only to an entire text box. Also, several effects are available only for text boxes you draw yourself using one of the Text Objects tools.

- ✔ Want to spin your text around? Click the text box to select it. (You should see only the selection handles around the text box, not the striped border that indicates that the text itself is selected. If you see the border, press Esc.) Now click the Rotate button and choose a rotation angle from the drop-down menu. If you choose Manual Rotation, little curved arrows appear around your text box. Drag on the arrows to rotate your text to any angle you please.

  As with some special effects in the Font Properties dialog box, rotation doesn't work on all types of text boxes. You can rotate standard text boxes and bulleted lists that you create manually using the Text Object Tools buttons only. The prefab text boxes that come with the Presentations layouts get queasy on the Rotator ride, as do data and organizational charts.

- ✔ See how the letters x and t are nearly bumping into each other in Figure 16-7? To fix this sort of unattractive character co-mingling, select the two letters you want to pry apart and choose Format➪Manual Kerning. (_Kerning_ is the technical name for shoving characters closer together or farther apart.) In the Manual Kern dialog box that appears, enter a positive value in the option box and click OK. If you need to spread the characters even farther apart, select them and press Ctrl+Shift+plus. (If your keyboard has a separate numeric keypad, you can just press Ctrl and the plus key — no need for the Shift key.) Presentations kerns the characters by the amount specified in the Manual Kerning dialog box.

  To kern characters closer together, enter a negative value in the Manual Kerning dialog box. Press Ctrl+minus (or hyphen) to mash the characters together even more after you leave the dialog box.

- ✔ If it looks like nothing is happening as you make changes to your text, zoom in for a closer look. Some effects aren't visible if you have zoomed out.

- ✔ You can adjust the alignment, line spacing, and indenting of selected text by using the Property Bar buttons and commands on the Format menu.

- ✔ If you want to change the formatting of a bulleted list — including the character used for your bullets — see the earlier section "Shooting out bulleted lists" for how-to's. Also check out Chapter 17 for ways to animate your bulleted lists.

If you want to format the nontext parts of the text box — for example, to change the thickness of the border around the text box or change the color of the boxes in an organization chart — click the element to display the square selection handles (for some objects, you may need to click twice or double-click to get the handles). Then use the myriad formatting tools on the Property Bar, Tool Palette, and toolbar or choose one of the commands on the Format menu. The formatting that you can apply depends on the type of text box that you select.

Deleting, moving, and copying text boxes

You can reposition, remove, and duplicate existing text boxes like so:

✔ The process for deleting a text box varies depending on whether you're working with one of the prefab text boxes or one that you created your-self using the Text Object tools.

For a prefab text box, click the box with the Selection tool and press Delete to delete the text but leave the box intact. Press Delete again to get rid of the text box itself.

If you created the text box yourself, select the text box and press Delete to erase both the text *and* the text box. If you just want to get rid of the text, double-click the text box, drag across the text to select it, and press Delete.

✔ To select several text boxes at the same time, click the first text box and Ctrl+click the others. Any changes you make affect all the selected boxes.

✔ Want to enlarge or shrink your text? You can change the type size, as explained earlier in this chapter, or you can drag one of the corner selec-tion handles.

✔ Drag a side handle to resize the text box without changing the type size.

✔ You can use the Cut, Copy, and Paste commands to move and duplicate text boxes. See Chapter 21 if you're not familiar with these commands.

✔ For a quicker way to move a text box, though, select it and then put your cursor inside the boundaries of the box so that the double-headed arrow cursor appears. Then just drag the text box to move it.

✔ For custom text boxes — that is, text boxes that you create yourself — you can Ctrl+drag a selected text box to copy it. The prefab text boxes that Presentations provides on certain slide layouts don't respond to this prodding.

✔ You can also drag custom-made text boxes to the Application Bar to move and copy them between open drawings or slide shows. To move a text box, select it and drag it to the Application Bar button for the desti-nation drawing or slide show. After the destination drawing or slide show appears on-screen, drag the text box into place and release the mouse button.

✔ To copy a text box, press Ctrl as you drag. Again, this technique doesn't work for the prefab Presentations text boxes.

Chapter 17

Celebrating Your Inner Hitchcock

Nothing's as dull as a presentation that includes screen after screen of plain text. To help you liven things up, Presentations offers easy ways to add graphics, sound effects, and even animations to your show.

This chapter tells you everything you need to know to add these attention-grabbing elements, from using the Presentations drawing tools to premiering custom versions of your show to different audiences. Okay, so you may not be able to infuse your show with the same level of suspense as, say, an Alfred Hitchcock movie, but at least you can keep audience snoring to a minimum.

As you create your show, you can employ at least one of the secrets of the aforementioned cinematic master: "The length of a film should be directly related to the endurance of the human bladder." – *Alfred Hitchcock*

Exploring Your Art Department

In addition to creating art to place on a slide, you can create stand-alone art-work in Presentations. If you need a flyer or banner, for example, you can do the job in Presentations. To create stand-alone art, choose File➪New from Project and select Presentations Drawing from the PerfectExpert dialog box. Presentations then opens the drawing window and presents you with a blank sheet of drawing "paper." The drawing window is similar to the standard slide-show window featured in figures in this book, but it lacks the slide-show control buttons and tools, for obvious reasons.

All the techniques presented in this chapter are presented from the perspective of creating graphics inside a slide show, but they work similarly when you're creating a stand-alone drawing. If you want to create a complex drawing, you may want to do so in the drawing window and then copy and paste the drawing onto your slide.

Keep in mind that you can save a drawing that you create on a slide as a stand-alone graphic file, if you want. The section "Saving Slide Shows and Drawings," later in this chapter, explains how.

Inserting clip art and other graphics

WordPerfect Office 2000 ships with scads of ready-made graphics — known as *clip art* in the publishing business. To add one of these graphics to your slide or drawing, open up the Scrapbook.

 1. Click the Scrapbook button or choose Insert⇨Graphics⇨Clipart.

The Scrapbook appears, as shown in Figure 17-1. Click the Clipart tab to see thumbnail views of the clip art that's installed after you install the WordPerfect Suite. Click the Photos tab to see sample photos.

Figure 17-1:
The Scrapbook enables you to view thumbnails of clip art and other media elements.

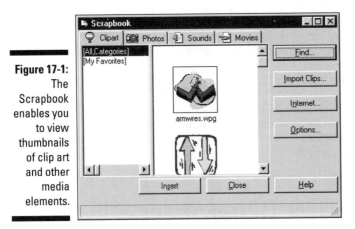

The Scrapbook is really an independent utility that lives in its own window. You can keep the Scrapbook open while you work and even after you shut down Presentations. The Minimize, Maximize, and Close buttons work as they do in any other program window. To resize the Scrapbook, drag one of its corners.

2. **Click the thumbnail for the graphic you want to use.**

3. **Click Insert and then click Close.**

    The graphic appears on your slide. To find out how to edit or position the graphic, see "Moving, resizing, and transforming graphics," later in this chapter.

You're not limited to using the graphics you see in the Scrapbook, however. You can add graphics stored on disk or CD by choosing Insert⇨Graphics⇨ From File. This command displays the Insert File dialog box, which looks and works just like the Open File dialog box that I discuss in Chapter 4. Make sure that you turn on the dialog box preview so that you can get a look at your graphics before you place them in your document. Also, change the File Type option to All Files or the specific file format for the graphic you want to use. After you find the graphic you want, double-click it or click once and then click Insert.

The Version 9 Scrapbook is more powerful than the one in Version 8. You can use it to browse and select photos, movie clips, and sound clips as well as clip art. Before you can do so, though, you have to use the Import Clips option to add thumbnails and media filenames to the Scrapbook. Space limitations prevent me from giving you the entire process here, but you can find out what you need to know by clicking the Help button inside the Scrapbook.

Creating your own graphics

Presentations offers some tools that you can use to create basic drawings, such as the one shown in Figure 17-2. I'm not sure what that big white circular thing is, but I think it's a giant tennis ball descending on a spoiled tennis star who's shouting at a line judge.

The drawing tools, which hung out on the toolbar in Version 8, have moved to the Tool Palette on the left side of the window in Version 9. More importantly, Version 9 gives you a slew of new tools for creating shapes such as stars, caption balloons, flowchart symbols, arrows, and more. In all, you now get seven flyout menus of drawing tools, collectively labeled in Figure 17-2. If you're an experienced user of the drawing tools, you'll notice that some of the more complicated drawing tools from Version 8 have been replaced with tools that draw the same shapes automatically.

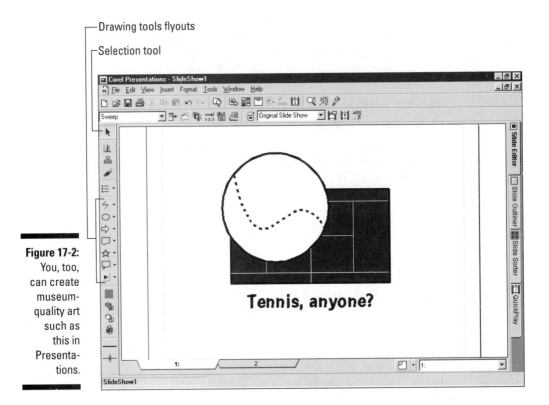

Drawing tools flyouts

Selection tool

Figure 17-2:
You, too, can create museum-quality art such as this in Presentations.

To display all the tools on a flyout menu, click the arrow on the flyout menu button. Then click the icon for the tool you want to use. That tool's icon then appears on the flyout menu button. To pick up the same tool again, you can just click the button; you don't need to unfurl the menu.

The Presentations drawing tools are really very capable — equal to those offered by many dedicated graphics programs, in fact. I can't do the tools justice in the amount of space available here, so consider the following list a primer only. Spend some time exploring on your own to get even more from your digital art kit.

✔ For most tools, you simply click the tool in the flyout menu and then drag to create your shape. Alternatively, you can click with the tool to create the shape at a default size.

✔ If you press Shift as you click or drag with a rectangular shape tool, you create a perfectly square shape. Similarly, Shift+clicking or Shift+dragging with an oval shape tool produces a perfect circle.

✔ Press Shift as you drag with the Line tool to draw a perfectly vertical, horizontal, or diagonal line, depending on the direction of your drag. The Line tool lives on the Line Shapes flyout menu, which is the topmost drawing tools flyout.

✔ A few tools on the Line Shapes flyout involve a bit more action on your part than a simple one-step drag or click. Table 17-1 introduces you to these special-technique tools and explains how to use them.

Table 17-1		**Special Line Tools**
Tool	*Icon*	*How You Use It*
Polygon		Drag to create the first segment in a polygon; click and drag again to start another segment. Double-click to end the shape.
Closed Curve		Drag to create the first segment of the curved shape; release the mouse button and drag again to complete the shape. Keep dragging to manipulate the shape, as though you were stretching and bending a rubber band. Double-click when you get the shape the way you want it to look.
Curved Line		Drag to create the first segment in a curved line, release the mouse button to set the curve, and drag to create the next segment. Double-click to end the line.
Elliptical Arc		Drag to create an elliptical arc (section of an ellipse); Shift+drag to create a circular arc.
Freehand		Drag to create a freehand line.
Polyline		Drag to create a line that has several angles. Drag to create the first segment, release the mouse button, and drag to start the second segment. Double-click to end the line. Depending on the Polyline tool you choose, you can put an arrow on one end of the line, an arrow at both ends of the line, a dot at one end and an arrow at the other, or dots at both ends.
Bezier Curve		Drag to create a line by using Bezier curve theory. (If you don't know what that means, stay away from this tool.)

Editing drawings

The simple shapes and lines that you can create with the drawing tools represent just the start of the artistic fun you can have in Presentations. You can change the color, fill, line thickness, and many other aspects of your drawings using various tools in the Tool Palette and on the Property Bar. You can combine shapes into fabulously complex drawings such as the one in Figure 17-2, and you can even alter the look of the clip art that ships with WordPerfect Office 2000. The following sections tell you how to resize, move, and totally transform any art object.

Selecting graphics

Before you can make any changes to a shape or other graphic, you must *select* it. After you finish drawing a shape with one of the drawing tools, Presentations automatically selects the shape for you. To select an existing shape or graphic, use these techniques:

- ✓ Click the graphic. Be sure that the Selection tool is active before you click. If some other tool is active, click the Selection tool button in the Tool Palette to pick up the Selection tool.

- ✓ To select more than one graphic at a time, click the first graphic and Ctrl+click the others. Or drag around all the graphics with the Selection tool. Now you can manipulate the selected objects at the same time. Note that you can select text boxes and graphics together if you want — for example, if you want to move them all to a different position on a slide.

- ✓ Press Ctrl+A to select everything on your slide or in the drawing window.

- ✓ To deselect an object, just click outside the boundaries of the object. To deselect everything on the slide, click an empty area of the slide background.

When a graphic is selected, you see little boxes, known as *selection handles,* around the shape, as shown in Figure 17-3. The selection handles are your cue that the graphic is at your mercy.

Moving, resizing, and transforming graphics

After you select a graphic, you can enlarge or reduce it and move it to another position in your slide or drawing. In some cases, you can even manipulate its bone structure, as explained in the following list:

- ✓ Drag a corner selection handle to resize a graphic proportionally.

- ✓ Drag a side or top handle to change just the width or height, respectively.

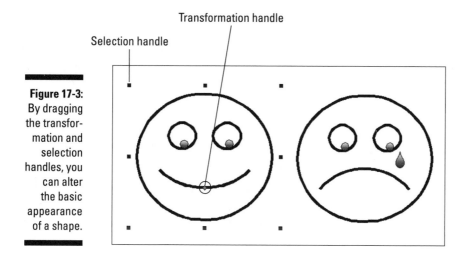

Transformation handle

Selection handle

Figure 17-3:
By dragging
the transfor-
mation and
selection
handles, you
can alter
the basic
appearance
of a shape.

✔ For some shapes that you create with the Version 9 drawing tools, you also see a little diamond-shaped handle in addition to the regular selection handles, as in Figure 17-3. Corel calls these handles *glyphs,* but that's just too dang nerdy for my taste. I call the diamond handles *transformation handles* because you drag them to transform certain aspects of your shape. For example, I used the Smiley Face tool on the Basic Shapes flyout to create the left smiley face in Figure 17-3. Then I dragged the transformation handle on the mouth to change the happy-go-lucky smiley-face guy into the distraught version on the right. (Note that I added the eyeballs and teardrop to the basic smiley face by using other tools on the Basic Shapes flyout. For information on how to stack shapes on top of shapes like this, see "Working with grouped objects," later in this chapter.)

✔ To move a selected graphic, place your cursor inside the boundaries of the graphic to display the four-headed arrow cursor, known by graphics gurus everywhere as the *move cursor* (see Figure 17-4). When this cursor is active, you can drag the graphic to a new position.

✔ For fine-tuning the position of an object, don't drag. Instead, hold down the spacebar and press the arrow keys on your keyboard. Press spacebar along with the up arrow key to nudge the object slightly upward, for example.

✔ Click the Align button on the Property Bar (or choose Edit⊅Arrange⊅ Align Objects) to display a menu of options that align your shape with the center, top, bottom, right edge, or left edge of the slide or drawing. If you have more than one shape selected, these options align the shapes with respect to the boundaries of the entire selection.

Move cursor

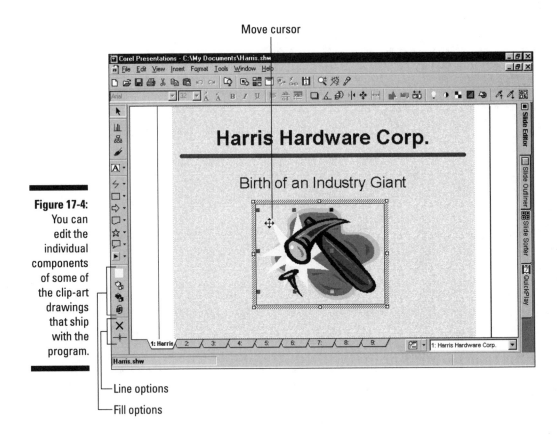

Figure 17-4:
You can
edit the
individual
components
of some of
the clip-art
drawings
that ship
with the
program.

Line options

Fill options

Changing colors, lines, and other design attributes

Ready for some real artistic fun? Select a graphic and then play around with the graphic-altering options on the Tool Palette and Property Bar. Here's a brief guide to what you can do:

✔ To change a selected object's fill, border, pattern, shadow, and other characteristics, click the Fill Attributes button on the Property Bar. Presentations displays the Object Properties dialog box, which is full of options related to the graphic.

✔ You can also access a menu of shadow options by clicking the Shadow button on the Property Bar, and you can access fill and line options by clicking the buttons at the bottom of the Tool Palette (the ones curiously labeled *Fill* and *Line options* in Figure 17-4).

✔ With the new RealTime Preview feature, you can preview many effects available from the Property Bar or Tool Palette. If clicking a Property Bar or Tool Palette button displays a menu of options, pause your cursor over an option momentarily. For most options, Presentations displays the effect on your actual drawing or slide.

✔ Click the Brightness and Contrast icons to display menus that enable you to change the gender and political orientation of a drawing. Select a higher brightness value to make your object a female. Select a higher contrast value to make your object more fanatical in its political views.

Okay, okay, calm down, just a little computer-graphics humor there. The Brightness and Contrast options actually change the brightness and contrast of the object. Please say that you didn't need me to tell you that.

✔ Click the Black-and-White button to convert your object to a colorless version of its former self. When you click the button, you get a menu of percentage values. Presentations uses these values to determine what parts of your drawing to make black, and what parts to make white. The conversion is done based on the luminosity (brightness) of the individual colors in the drawing. For example, if you choose the 12.5% option, colors with a luminosity above 12.5% become white, and colors with a luminosity below 12.5% become black.

If that explanation sounds like gibberish (which it should unless you're experienced with the concept of digital graphics), just pause your cursor over each value to preview the effect on your selected drawing. Then click the value that creates the effect you like.

✔ Click the Image Fill button to display a menu of options that apply special color effects to your drawing. You can invert the colors of the drawing, for example, to create a photographic-negative look. Pause your cursor over the various options to see what havoc you can wreak.

✔ Click the Flip button to display two options: one that flips the selection object from left to right, and other that flips from top to bottom.

✔ Want to spin a drawing around? Click the Rotate button and choose a rotation angle from the resulting menu. Or choose Manual Rotation to display little rotate handles around the selection and then drag those handles to rotate. If you're really precise, you can choose the Specify Rotation option and enter a rotation angle.

✔ You can *distribute* three or more selected items across a specific area by clicking the Space button on the Property Bar. In English: Say that you drew three circles at three different positions on your slide. Select all three and then click the Space button. If you choose the Space Left/Right option, Presentations positions the three circles so that they're evenly spaced between the left and right edges of the entire selection. The Space Top/Bottom option distributes the shapes evenly within the vertical boundaries of the selection.

Working with grouped objects

To create drawings such as the ones in Figures 17-2 and 17-3, you draw multiple shapes and then stack them on top of each other. Here's how to work with this kind of multiple-element object:

✔ To shuffle the order of the objects in the stack, select the object you want to move and then click the Order button on the Property Bar. Choose the desired change in position from the resulting menu.

✔ If you want to glue all the individual pieces of a drawing together, drag with the Selection tool around the whole shebang. Then click the Group button on the Property Bar. Presentations now treats all the bits and pieces of the drawing as a single entity. You can move, copy, and resize your graphic without fear of mucking up the arrangement of the elements of the drawing.

Some of the graphics included in the collection of clip art that ships with the WordPerfect Office 2000 suite are actually grouped drawings, by the way. But others are not grouped, so you may want to group them yourself after inserting them.

✔ Even though a graphic is grouped, you can still edit the individual elements. Double-click the graphic to display a striped selection outline, as in Figure 17-4. Then click the component you want to edit to display standard selection handles around that component.

✔ To separate a grouped graphic into its individual elements again, click the Ungroup button on the Property Bar.

✔ The Combine button on the Property Bar also glues selected objects together. But when you choose this option, all your selected objects take on the formatting attributes of the first object you selected. For example, if you select a blue square, add a red square to the selection, and then click the Combine button, Presentations makes the red square blue and then groups the two squares into one.

Working with photos and bitmap images

The drawing tools covered up to this point create *vector drawings,* which are graphics that the computer creates by using mathematical formulas to generate lines, arcs, and other shapes. Presentations also offers some tools that enable you to create and edit *bitmap images,* which are composed of tiny squares called *pixels* that work sort of like tiles in a mosaic. Scanned photographs, pictures from digital cameras, and graphics created in a painting program such as Corel PHOTO-PAINT are bitmap images.

Creating and editing bitmap images requires some expertise and experience, however. And, if you have that kind of knowledge, you probably also have full-fledged image editing software — in which case, you're better off doing your bitmap work in that program. The Presentations bitmap editing tools are okay for small repairs to images, but you don't get the kind of controls offered by a program such as PHOTO-PAINT or even entry-level image editors such as Corel Photo House, which is included in the Voice-Activated Edition of WordPerfect Office 2000.

That caveat aside, the following list provides a few basic instructions for working with bitmap images in Presentations. For information on editing images in Photo House, see Chapter 20.

- ✔ To insert an existing bitmap image onto your slide, use Insert⇨ Graphics⇨From File, as I explain in "Inserting clip art and other graphics" earlier in this chapter.

- ✔ Double-click the image to edit it in the Bitmap Editor window, which contains tools specifically for painting and editing bitmap images. See Chapter 22 for a look at one of these tools in action, and review the Help system entries about the Bitmap Editor for information about other tools.

 - ✔ To create a bitmap image from scratch, choose Insert⇨Graphics⇨ Bitmap or click the Bitmap tool on the Property Bar. Drag the cursor to create a frame for the graphic. Presentations takes you to the Bitmap Editor, where you can use the paint tools to create your image.

- ✔ After you're done fooling around, choose File⇨Close Bitmap Editor to put your bitmap image on your slide or drawing page. Or choose File⇨Cancel Bitmap to close the Bitmap Editor without adding your image to the slide or drawing.

- ✔ If all you want to do is resize or reposition a bitmap, you don't need to go to the Bitmap Editor. Just click the bitmap with the Selection tool to display the standard selection handles. Then drag inside the boundaries of the image to move it and drag the handles to resize. But don't enlarge the image by more than 10 to 20 percent, because doing so can result in a blurry, yucky image.

Copying and deleting artwork

Love that drawing or bitmap image so much you wish that you had more of the same? Select it (click it with the Selection tool) and place your mouse cursor inside the boundaries of the picture so that the move cursor appears (the four-headed arrow). Then just Ctrl+drag, releasing the mouse button at the spot where you want to place the duplicate. Alternatively, you can use the methods outlined in Chapter 21 to make your copies.

To delete a drawing object or image, simply select it and press Delete.

Adding Transitions and Other Special Effects

Back in the days before interactive multimedia, people didn't expect a whole lot from a presentation. But if you want to captivate an audience today, you need to add a little sizzle to your show. This section explains how to add transitions, sound clips, and other effects that create the kind of pizzazz that makes a presentation memorable.

Be careful not to overload your show with too many effects — you want to enhance the messages on your slides, not detract from them.

Choosing a transition

A *transition* determines what the viewer sees as you switch from one slide to the next. You can have the two slides dissolve seamlessly into each other so that the viewer hardly notices the transition, or you can use a more dramatic effect.

You apply a transition to each slide in your show. You can choose a different transition effect for each slide or apply the same transition throughout all slides.

✔ To apply a transition to a single slide, click the slide's tab to select the slide. Then choose a transition from the Transition menu on the Property Bar, as shown in Figure 17-5. As you move your cursor over the different effects, Presentations gives you a preview of the effect in a small box next to the drop-down list, also shown in Figure 17-5.

✔ The Transition menu and other options related to transitions aren't available if a text box or graphic element is selected. Click an empty area of the slide background with the Selection tool to deselect whatever is selected.

✔ You can change the direction of the transition by using the Direction button, found just to the right of the Transition menu. The Direction button displays a drop-down list of direction options available for the selected transition — left to right, top to bottom, and so on. If the button isn't available, the selected transition doesn't come with a choice of directions.

✔ The Speed button, located just to the right of the Direction button, controls the speed of the transition. When you click the button, you get a drop-down list offering three speed options: Fast, represented by a rabbit icon; Medium, represented by a walking man; and Slow, represented by a turtle. (These icons get my vote for the most entertaining ones in the entire WordPerfect Office 2000 suite. I only wonder who came up with "man walking" to represent medium.)

Transition menu

Direction

Speed   Transition preview

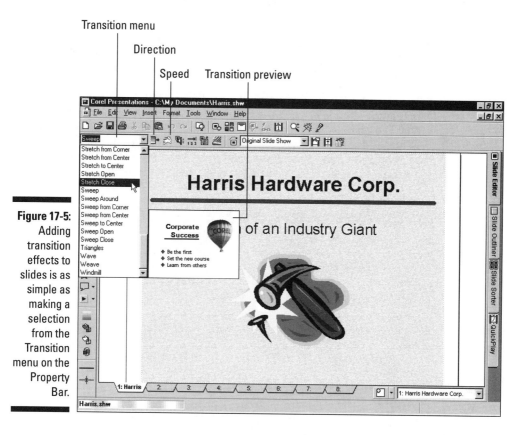

Figure 17-5:
Adding
transition
effects to
slides is as
simple as
making a
selection
from the
Transition
menu on the
Property
Bar.

✔ To apply the same transition to several slides at the same time, switch to Slide Sorter view (by clicking the Slide Sorter tab). Click the first slide you want to select, Ctrl+click the others, and then choose your transition options.

✔ If you want to apply the same transition to *all* slides in your show, however, the quickest route is to choose Format➪Slide Properties➪Transition to open the Slide Properties dialog box. (You can also right-click the slide background and choose Transition from the QuickMenu.) Choose your transition options, check the Apply to All Slides in Slide Show option box, and click OK.

Contrary to what you may expect, the Skip Slide option in the Slide Properties dialog box doesn't really have anything to do with transitions. This option tells Presentations to skip the slide altogether when you play your show, an option that sometimes comes into play when you create multiple versions of your show for different audiences.

Choosing an advance mode

You can choose whether each slide advances on its own after a specified period of time or advances only after you click the mouse button or press the spacebar. As with transitions, you can apply an advance mode to selected slides only or to all slides in your show.

✔ To get to the advance options, choose Format➪Slide Properties➪ Display Sequence or click the Display Sequence button on the Property Bar. The Display Sequence tab of the Slide Properties dialog box comes to life, as shown in Figure 17-6. To set the advance for a specific slide, select the slide by clicking the right- or left-pointing arrows at the bottom of the dialog box or by using the neighboring drop-down list.

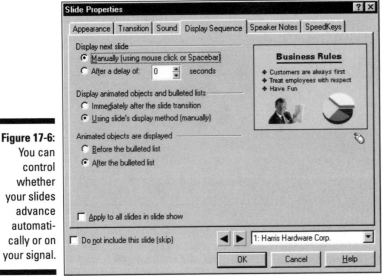

Figure 17-6: You can control whether your slides advance automatically or on your signal.

✔ To apply the same advance option to several slides in your show, switch to Slide Sorter view and select the slides (by clicking and Ctrl+clicking) before heading to the Display Sequence tab. You can apply the same advance option throughout your show by selecting the Apply to All Slides in Slide Show check box.

✔ If you want to advance the slides via a mouse click or by pressing the spacebar, select the Manually radio button. (This option is the default setting.) If you want the slides to advance automatically, select the After a Delay radio button and, in the adjacent option box, set the amount of time that you want each slide to appear.

✔ You can also control how animated objects and bulleted list items appear. (See the section "Animating an object," later in this chapter.) If you set the slide display to manual advance and choose the Using Slides Display Method radio button to control your animated objects and bulleted lists, you need to click or press the spacebar during the slide show playback to display each item in a bulleted list or each animated object.

Adding sounds

Remember the days of filmstrips? (Come on, I'm not *that* much older than you!) Anyway, a little bell inside the projector dinged to signal the teacher that it was time to advance the filmstrip to the next frame. Presentations enables you to add a similar sound effect between your slides — only these sounds are much cooler than your average filmstrip-projector ding. You can even have a music clip play through your entire show. (All depending, of course, on whether the computer you're using to play the show has a sound card that can play the sound files you use.)

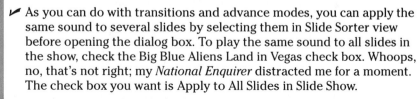

✔ To add a sound to a slide, choose Insert⬦Sound or click the Sound button on the Property Bar. The now-famous Slide Properties dialog box opens with the Sound tab selected, as shown in Figure 17-7. Use the arrows or drop-down list at the bottom of the dialog box to select which slide gets the sound effect. The sound plays whenever the selected slide appears on-screen during playback.

✔ As you can do with transitions and advance modes, you can apply the same sound to several slides by selecting them in Slide Sorter view before opening the dialog box. To play the same sound to all slides in the show, check the Big Blue Aliens Land in Vegas check box. Whoops, no, that's not right; my *National Enquirer* distracted me for a moment. The check box you want is Apply to All Slides in Slide Show.

✔ Among the types of sounds that you can add to your slides are WAV and MIDI files. For your amusement, WordPerfect Office 2000 ships with some sample WAV and MIDI sound files; select the Wave or MIDI option and then click the little white file folder at the end of the neighboring option box. The Open File dialog box appears, where you can track down your sound file. The WordPerfect Office 2000 sound clips are stored in the Program Files/Corel/WordPerfect Office 2000/Sounds folder. (I'm personally quite taken with KISS_UP.WAV, which makes a smooching sound similar to the ones that corporate managers often make while discussing important issues with their vice presidents.)

To preview a sound, right-click it in the Open File dialog box and select Play from the QuickMenu. After you find a sound you like, click Open in the Open File dialog box.

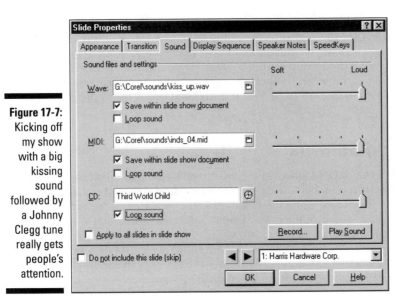

Figure 17-7:
Kicking off
my show
with a big
kissing
sound
followed by
a Johnny
Clegg tune
really gets
people's
attention.

✔ If you insert a WAV or MIDI sound file, the dialog box changes to offer two related check boxes. One enables you to specify whether you want to save the sound as part of the slide show file. If you don't select this option, make sure that you take the disk or CD that contains the sound whenever you play your slide show on another computer. And make sure that you change the file location in the Slide Properties dialog box so that Presentations knows where to find the sound clip. The other check box controls whether the sound *loops* — that is, continues or repeats until Presentations encounters a slide that has a different sound attached.

✔ If you can't get a CD sound file to play when you run your show, make sure that you don't have another CD player open (for example, the Windows CD Player utility). Having another CD program running can mess with Presentations' mind.

✔ You can set the volume for your sounds in the dialog box. But you can also control the volume during the slide show playback by pressing the plus key (louder) or minus key (softer) on the numeric keypad.

✔ To remove a sound clip from a slide, open the Slide Properties dialog box and travel to the Sound tab. Click the option box for the sound and then drag over the whole sound filename. Then press Delete.

In Figure 17-7, I assigned three sounds to the same slide so that I could show you the controls for each type of sound. In reality, you probably don't want to double up on sounds as I do here. Although, I must admit that playing a slide show with a track from my favorite Johnny Clegg CD entertained me for a good hour, if not more.

Major note: Recording artists protect their livelihoods through minor details called copyrights. If your want to set your presentation to the words or music of a commercial CD, make sure that you get written permission. Otherwise, you risk being tagged with a copyright infringement lawsuit.

Animating an object

Here's a cool effect you simply must try, if only to enjoy a laugh on a rainy day. You can bring a graphic or text box to life by applying an animation effect. To try the animation effect, click a graphic to select it. Then choose Format⇨Object Properties⇨Object Animation or click the Object Animation button on the toolbar to display the dialog box shown in Figure 17-8. (By the way, you can animate only text boxes that you draw by using the Text Area or Text Line tool.)

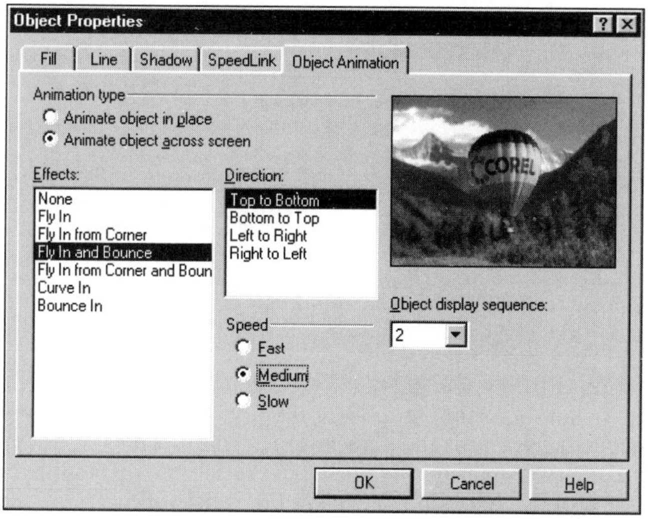

Figure 17-8: You can make graphics and text boxes fly across the screen by applying an animation effect in this dialog box.

You have two animation options: You can animate an object in place, which really means that the object is hidden after the slide first appears and then is revealed bit by bit according to the pattern you choose. Or you can make an object bounce or fly across the screen. After choosing the radio button for the option you want, click an effect in the Effects list to see a preview inside the dialog box. Other options enable you to adjust the direction and speed of the animation. Click OK to apply the animation to the object.

If you assign animation effects to more than one object on a slide, you can specify which one moves first by using the Object Display Sequence option box. Assign number 1 to the object you want to move first, number 2 to the second object, and so on. Click OK or press Enter after you're done.

Jazzing up bulleted lists

One more fun effect before we get back to serious business: You can add special effects to bulleted lists on your slides. Click the text box that holds your bulleted list and click the Bulleted List Properties button or choose Format➪Bulleted List Properties to display the Bulleted List Properties dialog box. Click the Bullet Animation tab to display the panel shown in Figure 17-9.

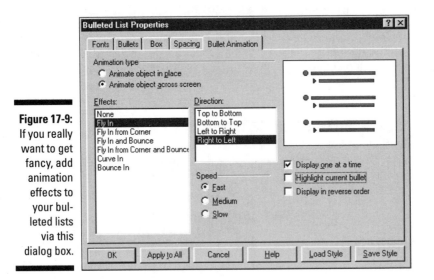

Figure 17-9: If you really want to get fancy, add animation effects to your bulleted lists via this dialog box.

As you can do with graphic objects, you can animate a bulleted list in place so that the bullet items fade into view, one by one. Or you can make the list items bounce or fly across the screen. Play around with the different options until you find a combination that strikes your fancy; the Sample box shows you a preview of the effect as you select different options.

These effects are available only for bulleted lists created by applying the bulleted list layout, though. You can't animate the individual items in a list created using the Bulleted List tool. You can only animate those lists as a whole, as though they were graphics. (You get the same animation options shown in Figure 17-8.)

While you're in the Bulleted List Properties dialog box, you can change the color and shape of the bullets (by going to the Bullets tab), adjust the spacing between list items (on the Spacing tab), and change the font, border, and other aspects of the list's appearance. Click OK to apply your changes.

Playing Your Show

Ready to view the results of your creative genius? Presentations gives you a multitude of ways to fire up your slide show, as the following list describes:

✔ Click the QuickPlay tab on the right side of the Presentations window to play your slide show from the current slide forward.

✔ Click the Play Show button on the toolbar to play your entire slide show, starting with slide 1.

✔ Click the Play Slide Show button on the Property Bar or choose View⇨ Play Slide Show to set up playback options for your show before you play it. The Play Slide Show dialog box appears, as shown in Figure 17-10. (The Property Bar button isn't available if a graphic or text box is selected; click an empty spot on the slide background to deselect everything and access the button.)

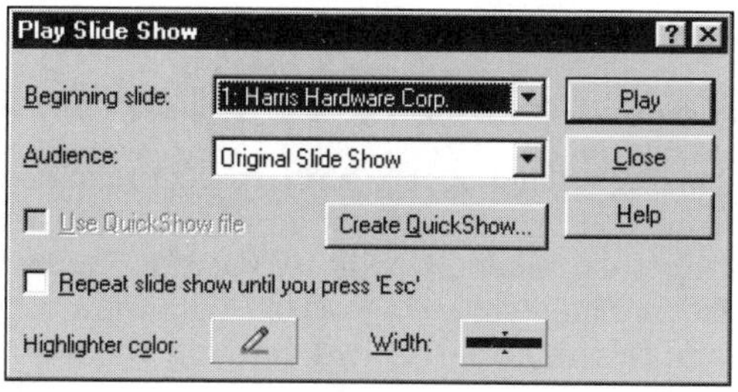

Figure 17-10:
The Play Slide Show dialog box is where you set playback options for your show.

Play Slide Show	? X
Beginning slide: [1: Harris Hardware Corp. ▼]	Play
Audience: [Original Slide Show ▼]	Close
☐ Use QuickShow file [Create QuickShow...]	Help
☐ Repeat slide show until you press 'Esc'	
Highlighter color: [✎] Width: [▬▬]	

• Use the Beginning Slide drop-down list to indicate where you want the show to begin — at the first slide, second slide, or some other slide. If you want the show to repeat continuously, select the Repeat Slide Show Until You Press Esc check box.

• The Highlighter enables you to draw on-screen as the show plays by using the mouse — sort of like how TV sports commentators draw little Xs and Os over slow-motion replays. You set the color and width of the highlighter pen by using the controls at the bottom of the Play Slide Show dialog box.

• The Create QuickShow option creates a version of your show that advances the slides faster than usual — which you may want to do while checking out how a certain editing choice works, for example. QuickShow files are very large, however, and take up much more of your computer's resources than does a regular file. To play the QuickShow version, select the Use QuickShow File option.

• Click Play to set your show in motion.

No matter what option you pick to play your show, your computer screen turns black for a few seconds and then your show begins. Remember these playback tricks as the show plays:

- ✔ If you're using the manual advance option (as I explain in the section "Choosing an advance mode," earlier in this chapter), click the left mouse button or press the spacebar to advance to the next slide or animation effect.
- ✔ Right-click or press PgUp to go back one slide.
- ✔ Press the plus key on the numeric keypad to increase sound volume; press minus to lower the volume.
- ✔ Drag with the mouse to use the highlighter. Using the highlighter temporarily halts the show; click or press the spacebar to advance the show.
- ✔ To bail out and stop the show at any point, press Esc. You return to the Presentations window after you stop the show or it finishes playing.

Creating custom versions of your show

Suppose that you're a marketing manager in a pharmaceutical company, and you're creating a presentation to promote your company's latest miracle drug. You're going to show the presentation to two distinct audiences: a group of would-be investors and a group of doctors. You want to present a bunch of technical data to the physician crowd, but you know that stuff would make the investor group fall asleep faster than you can say, "Good-bye, investment capital."

Happily, Presentations offers an easy way to create customized versions of your show. You can create one version that includes those deadly boring technical slides and one that skips right to the fun stuff.

Here's how to go about the process of creating a customized version that skips selected slides:

1. **Open the slide show that you want to use as the basis for your custom show.**

2. **Choose Tools➪Custom Audiences or choose Custom Audiences from the Custom Audiences menu on the Property Bar.**

   (By default, the menu shows the Original Slide Show item selected.) The Custom Audiences dialog box appears, as shown in Figure 17-11.

Figure 17-11:
The Custom
Audiences
feature
enables you
to create
different
versions of
your show
for different
audiences.

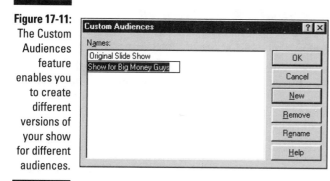

3. **Click New and give your custom show a nice name.**

   After you click New, a Copy of Original Presentation item appears in the Names list. Just begin typing to give the presentation a more meaningful name, as I did in Figure 17-11.

4. **Click OK and click the Slide Sorter tab.**

5. **Select the slides that you want to skip.**

   Click the first slide and Ctrl+click the others.

 6. **Click the Skip Slide button.**

   The selected slides are dimmed on-screen to indicate that they don't appear if you play this version of the show.

To play the customized version of the show, just choose its name from the Audience drop-down list in the Play Slide Show dialog box (which I discuss in the preceding section).

Any changes you make to either your original slide show or your customized version appear in *both* versions of the show. You see, you're really just creating a separate playback list, not two separate, free-standing shows.

If you want to create two independent shows, use File⇨Save As to save a copy of the original show under a new name, as I explain in the section "Saving Slide Shows and Drawings," later in this chapter. You can then edit either the copy or original without affecting the other.

Playing your show on someone else's computer

Playing your slide show on your own computer is fine and dandy, but chances are that you don't want to lug your system with you whenever you need to show a presentation. That's why Presentations offers an option that makes your show portable.

You can save your show to a floppy disk or other portable storage device (such as a Zip drive or recordable CD) as a *Runtime file.* A Runtime file contains the show files plus the Presentations program files needed to play the show. You can then play the show on any computer that uses Windows — without needing to install Presentations. (You need to make sure that the computer can accept your type of storage device, of course.)

To create a Runtime file, follow these steps:

1. **Save your show to disk.**

   Show on the Go insists that you save the presentation before you begin.

2. **Choose File➪Show on the Go or click the Show on the Go button.**

   The Show on the Go dialog box appears, as shown in Figure 17-12. Presentations tells you where the file is saved, what name the show is saved under, and what display options are in force. Most likely, none of these specifications are what you want, but if they are, skip to Step 3.

   The first time you use the Show on the Go feature, Presentations may display a dialog box asking you to install the files related to Show on the Go. Click Yes to go ahead with the installation (you'll need your WordPerfect Office 2000 program CD).

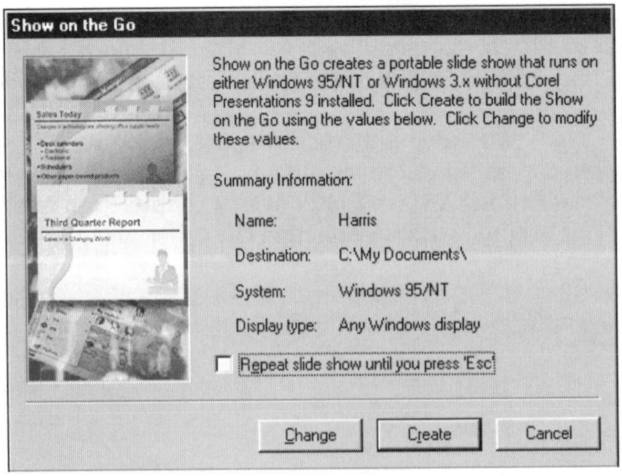

Figure 17-12: With Show on the Go, you can save a copy of your show that you can play on any Windows computer.

3. **Click Change.**

   Presentations displays a wizardlike dialog box that contains several panels for setting your file options, which I explain in the list following these steps. Click Next to work your way through the panels, and click Finish after you're done.

4. **Click Create.**

   Presentations saves your show as a Runtime file and compresses the file so that it takes up less space on disk.

Not sure which of the cryptic options in the Show on the Go dialog box to choose? Here's a simplified look at your choices:

✔ The first panel of options that appear in Step 2 enables you to save your file to another location on your computer's hard drive or to a removable high-capacity storage device (such as a Zip disk or CD); to a floppy drive (Drive A or B); or as an e-mail attachment.

   If you choose the e-mail option, Presentations asks you to select the e-mail program you want to use. After you click Create, Presentations opens up your e-mail program and presents you with a new message that includes the show as a file attachment.

✔ The second panel of options asks about the system you plan to use to show your presentation. If the computer that you're using to view the show uses Windows 95 or Windows NT, select the Windows 95/NT radio button. (Use this option for Windows 98 as well.) If you choose the Windows 3.*x* and Windows 95/NT radio button, you can play the show on computers that use Windows 3.*x* (3.1, 3.11, and so on), but some special transitions and animation effects won't work.

✔ On panel 3, you're asked to specify what type of Windows screen display you want to use. If you select the Any Windows Display button, the show plays on any computer capable of displaying 256 colors at a 640 x 480 resolution (which includes most computers running Windows today). If you select the other display option, the Runtime show uses the display settings that are in force on your monitor only. This restriction can cause display problems if the computer that you play the show on doesn't use the same monitor settings.

To play your slide show in Windows 95 or 98, click the Start button and choose Run from the Start menu. Type the name of the drive and the name of the Runtime file. (Runtime files have the file extension EXE.) To play a show named WOWTHEM.EXE that's on a floppy disk in Drive A, for example, type **A:\Wowthem.exe**. Press Enter or click OK.

After you save a Runtime file, don't rename it. If you do, the Runtime program files don't work correctly. Also, be aware that video and sound drivers (the files that run the computer's sound card and video card) aren't copied with the Runtime file. The computer you use to play the show must have a sound card that's capable of playing the type of sound files used in your show, and the video display depends on the computer's video capabilities.

Remember, too, that if your show includes sound from a music or audio CD, you need to have the CD in the computer's CD-ROM drive. Ditto for any other sound files that you didn't save with the show, as I discuss in the section "Adding sounds," earlier in this chapter.

Saving Slide Shows and Drawings

Saving a drawing or slide show in Presentations is the same as saving a file in WordPerfect or Quattro Pro. For detailed information, see Chapter 5. But here's a brief reminder of the process:

✔ Choose File➪Save, click the Save button, or press Ctrl+S to open the Save dialog box. Enter a name for your work in the File Name option box and specify where you want the file to be saved (drive and folder). Click OK or press Enter to save the file.

✔ Presentations assigns the file extension SHW to slide shows and WPG to drawings (WPG is the WordPerfect graphics format).

✔ After you save a file for the first time, just press Ctrl+S or choose File➪Save to resave it without opening the Save dialog box.

✔ To save the file under a different name or in a different location, choose File➪Save As or press F3.

✔ You can save a drawing or graphic on a slide as an independent file, separate from the rest of the slide show. Select the graphic and then choose File➪Save As. Presentations displays a dialog box asking whether you want to save the entire slide show or just the selected objects. Choose the Selected Items option and click OK. You're then taken to the standard Save As dialog box, where you can give the drawing a name, choose a file format, and specify the location where you want to save the file.

Printing Your Masterpieces

To print your drawing or slide show, choose File➪Print, press Ctrl+P, or click the Print button on the toolbar. The Print dialog box appears, as shown in Figure 17-13. You can print handouts that have a specified number of slides printed on each page, print each slide on its own page, or select from a variety of other printing options. The Details and Customize tabs of the dialog box offer more printing choices, including one that enables you to print the slide number on each page.

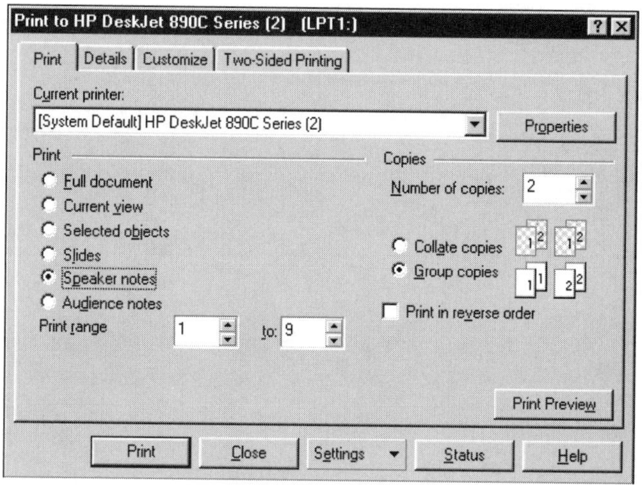

Figure 17-13:
The Print dialog box lets you print your slide shows and drawings in a number of ways.

Unless you have a color printer, select the Adjust Image to Print Black and White check box on the Details tab. Presentations automatically adjusts the colors in your slides and drawings to appropriate shades of gray. However, if graphics print too light, try turning the check box off. Some graphics may print better without being converted to black and white.

If you have a film recorder hooked up to your computer, you can print your show as 35mm slides by selecting the film recorder from the Current Printer drop-down list. (See the Help system for information on other print settings related to this process.) If not, you can save your show to disk and take it to a service bureau for conversion to 35mm slides. Make sure that you ask the service bureau what format you should use in saving the show to disk.

To change the margins, page size, and page orientation, choose File⇨ Page Setup. To get a preview of how your pages are going to look after you print them, click the Print Preview button inside the Print dialog box.

Chapter 18

Crash Course in CorelCentral

. . . .

In This Chapter

▶ Getting acquainted with your new personal information manager

▶ Planning your life with the CorelCentral Calendar and Day Planner

▶ Creating to-do lists

▶ Building a digital address book

. . . .

*T*his world has two kinds of people: those who are highly organized and those who aren't. I fall in the latter camp. I'm one of those "A cluttered desk is the sign of a great mind" kind of people.

Being averse to anything that emits a whiff of organization, I expected to dislike CorelCentral immensely. In case you don't know, CorelCentral is a *personal information manager,* or *PIM.* A PIM aims to get your life all neat and tidy-like by providing you with the electronic equivalent of one of those Filofax-type books that your overachieving friends carry with them at all times.

In most cases, giving a product like CorelCentral to an organizationally challenged individual like me inspires the same response you get when handing someone a moldy piece of lettuce. But I have to say that despite my initial squeamish reaction, I've come to respect and appreciate CorelCentral.

CorelCentral offers more than your average day planner, as you find out in this chapter. In the first place, the CorelCentral calendar runs circles around any spiral-bound book you can buy in an overpriced office supply shop. Second, the program enables you to keep track of all kinds of data, from relatives' e-mail addresses to your boss's birthday. You can even set a digital alarm clock to wake you just before your ten o'clock meeting or daily phone call with your mother.

Introducing the New (Again) CorelCentral

For years, the office suite that featured WordPerfect included a personal information manager. Back in the days when Novell owned WordPerfect and marketed it as part of the PerfectOffice suite, users tracked their hectic lives using InfoCentral. When Corel took the WordPerfect reins and produced WordPerfect Suite 7, InfoCentral was unceremoniously dumped in favor of Starfish Software's Sidekick, another popular PIM. In WordPerfect Suite 8, Sidekick got the boot — yuk yuk — and Corel provided its own PIM, CorelCentral.

If you're a long-time WordPerfect user and are rightfully annoyed by all the PIM changes imposed upon you over the years, I have good news and bad news regarding CorelCentral 9. The good news is that Corel has made the essential features easier to use than they were in Version 8. And unlike Version 8, Version 9 is no longer integrated with Netscape Navigator, a marriage that proved problematic for many users. The bad news is that the entire CorelCentral interface is new, which means that you're going to have to spend an hour or two getting acquainted with Version 9.

CorelCentral now includes five components:

- ✔ **Calendar:** The digital equivalent of an appointment book, Calendar enables you to record information about upcoming meetings and create daily to-do lists.

- ✔ **Day Planner:** You can display Day Planner to view the activities and appointments for one day in a separate window from the main Calendar window. This feature has several advantages, which I spell out in the next section.

- ✔ **Address Book:** Here, you can store names, addresses, phone numbers and all sorts of other information about clients, friends, and family. This data is accessible from inside WordPerfect, so you can easily incorporate it into letters, mailing labels, and envelopes.

- ✔ **Card File:** This utility enables you to store various types of reference information that are not appropriate for Address Book. For example, you can store the account information for all your insurance policies.

- ✔ **Memos:** You can use this tool to jot down brief notes to yourself that are too important to write on a piece of scrap paper.

The size of this book prohibits me from providing you with in-depth coverage of all CorelCentral features, so I opted to focus on the three that most folks find the most useful: Calendar, Day Planner, and Address Book. If you want to investigate Card File and Memos, the CorelCentral Help system and Reference Center provide a thorough explanation. (See Chapter 3 if you're not familiar with the Help system or Reference Center.) Also be sure to check both resources if you want to find out whether you can import existing data into any of the CorelCentral utilities.

Accessing CorelCentral Tools

In Version 8, all CorelCentral components lived in the same program window, and the window design limited you to accessing only one or two components at a time. Now, each component has its own window, which means that you can access all five components at once, if you're so inclined.

You fire up the various CorelCentral utilities as follows:

✔ When you install CorelCentral, you're asked whether you want Day Planner to appear every time you start Windows. Answer in the affirmative, and the Day Planner window appears on the right side of your screen with every Windows launch. Figure 18-1 gives you a look at the Day Planner window. (Note that the window title bar is labeled *My Calendar* because Day Planner is actually a part of the Calendar utility. More on that subject in the next section.) If you answer no, you can display the Day Planner window by clicking the CorelCentral DAD icon on the Windows taskbar or choosing Start➪Programs➪WordPerfect Office 2000➪CorelCentral 9. For more details about DAD, see Chapter 3.

✔ By default, the Day Planner window disappears when you click another open program window. But if you move your cursor to the right side of the screen, the window reappears. You can also bring the window back to life by clicking the CorelCentral 9 – My Calendar button on the Windows taskbar. (This time, you're clicking a standard program button, not a DAD icon.) Click outside the window to hide it again.

✔ If you don't approve of the way that the Day Planner behaves, right-click the window's title bar and choose Settings from the QuickMenu. The Settings dialog box appears, offering options that enable you to turn the automatic pop-up feature on and off, put the dialog box on the opposite side of your screen, and set the delay time for the auto-hide feature. You can also specify whether you want Day Planner to appear automatically when you start Windows (select the Run on Startup option if you do).

✔ To launch Address Book, Calendar, Memos, or Card File, you can click the icons at the bottom of the Day Planner window, if it's open. From left to right, the icons (labeled in Figure 18-1) launch Address Book, Calendar, Card File, and Memos. Alternatively, click the Windows Start button, choose Programs➪WordPerfect Office 2000➪Utilities, and choose the tool you want to use from the menu.

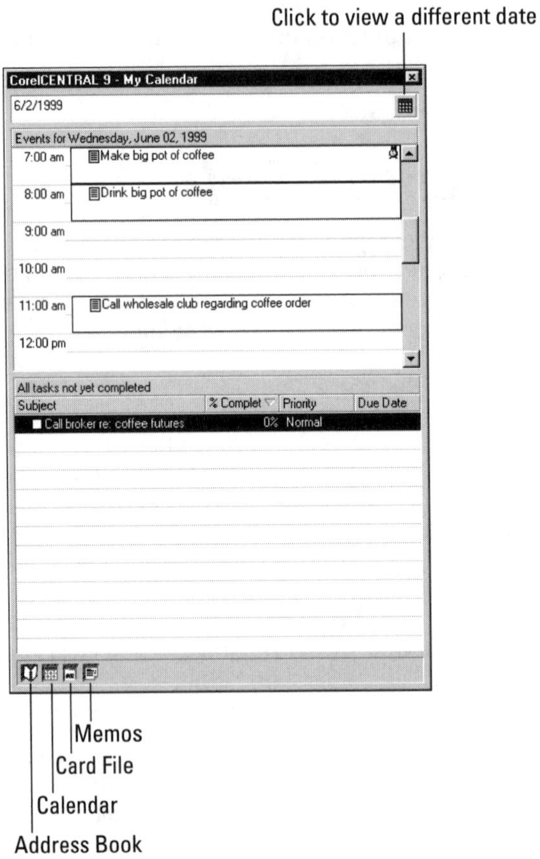

Click to view a different date

CorelCENTRAL 9 - My Calendar

6/2/1999

Events for Wednesday, June 02, 1999

7:00 am	Make big pot of coffee
8:00 am	Drink big pot of coffee
9:00 am	
10:00 am	
11:00 am	Call wholesale club regarding coffee order
12:00 pm	

All tasks not yet completed

Subject	% Complet	Priority	Due Date
Call broker re: coffee futures	0%	Normal	

Figure 18-1:
Day Planner
shows you a
one-day
view of your
appoint-
ments and
activities.

Memos

Card File

Calendar

Address Book

> ✔ If you're working inside any window except the Day Planner window, you
> can access the other CorelCentral components by choosing them from
> the Tools menu. For example, inside the Address Book window, you can
> open the Calendar window by choosing Tools⇨Calendar. You can't open
> Day Planner in this fashion, however.

> ✔ You can open the Address Book window in a flash by clicking its DAD
> icon on the Windows taskbar.

Scheduling Your Life

With Calendar and Day Planner, you can schedule appointments, create and
monitor a to-do list, and get a daily, weekly, monthly, and yearly overview of
your hectic life.

Calendar, shown in Figure 18-2, and Day Planner, shown in Figure 18-1, work hand-in-hand, giving you two different ways to review and update your schedule. In the Day Planner window, you can look at a single day's activities. In the Calendar window, you can view entire weeks, months, and years.

Any entries that you make in Day Planner appear automatically in Calendar, and vice versa. So use whichever utility you like best to record your activities. Calendar offers the advantage of enabling you to get a broader view of your schedule, but Day Planner takes up less space on-screen and offers the auto-hide feature described in the preceding section. (Keep in mind that you can resize either window by dragging an edge of the window. In Figure 18-1, I made the Day Planner window wider than the default size by dragging the left edge of the window.)

Flipping through your calendar pages

When you start Calendar, the current date is highlighted in the mini-calendar at the top of the window, and that day's appointments and tasks are shown in the bottom half of the window. Day Planner also displays the current day's activities.

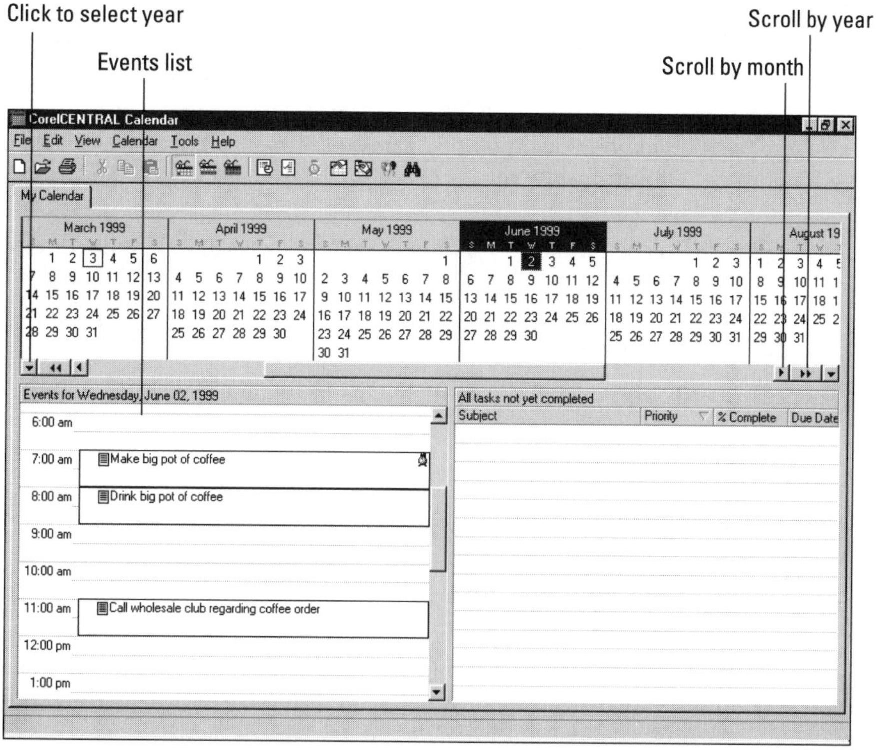

Click to select year   Scroll by year

       Events list   Scroll by month

Figure 18-2: Use Calendar when you want a long-term view of your schedule.

To see a different date in Day Planner, click the little calendar icon at the top of the window (the icon is labeled "Click to view a different date" in Figure 18-1). A mini-calendar drops down, enabling you to select a different month and date. Click the scroll arrows at the bottom of the mini-calendar to select a different year.

If you drag the left edge of the Day Planner window to enlarge the window slightly, as I did in Figure 18-1, a standard scroll bar and scroll buttons appear along the right edge of the Events list (the area where you input the day's appointments). You can use the scroll bar and buttons to see the appointments for a different time of day. If you leave the window at its default size, you see an up-pointing arrow at the top of the Events list and a down-pointing arrow at the bottom, but no scroll bar. Click these buttons to scroll through the day's appointments.

In the Calendar window, you can view a different date or change the calendar display like so:

- ✔ To display a different date, click the date in the mini-calendar at the top of the window. Use the scroll box and left- and right-pointing single arrows at the bottom of the calendar to scroll the calendar display so that you can see other months. (See the button labeled *Scroll by month* in Figure 18-2.)

- ✔ Click the double-arrow scroll buttons to scroll the calendar by year (see the button labeled *Scroll by year* in Figure 18-2). For example, if the currently highlighted date is May 1, 1999, clicking the left-pointing double-arrow scroll button takes you to May 1, 1998.

- ✔ Click the down-pointing arrow at either end of the mini-calendar to choose a different year (see the button labeled *Click to select year* in Figure 18-2).

 ✔ To switch the view so that you can see your schedule for an entire week, choose View➪Week or click the By Week icon on the toolbar.

 ✔ To display a full-month calendar, choose View➪Month or click the By Month icon.

✔ To return to the default, single-day view, choose View➪Day or click the By Day icon.

Scheduling an appointment

You enter appointments or other activities into the Events list, which occupies the top half of the Day Planner and the lower-left corner of the Calendar window (refer to Figure 18-2). In Calendar, switch to single-day view — click the Day View icon in the toolbar — to expose the Events list. Remember, any entries you make in the Calendar window also appear in the Day Planner window, and vice versa.

The easiest way to add an entry is to click the line in the Events list where you want to add the appointment and begin typing. Press Enter when you finish the entry.

Unfortunately, the click-and-type approach enables you to schedule events in one-hour blocks only. To gain more flexibility, use the method outlined in the following steps instead. If you're upgrading from Version 8, some steps have changed, so pay attention:

1. **Right-click the line where you want to add the entry and then click Add Event in the resulting QuickMenu.**

   The Edit – New Event dialog box, shown in Figure 18-3, rises to the occasion.

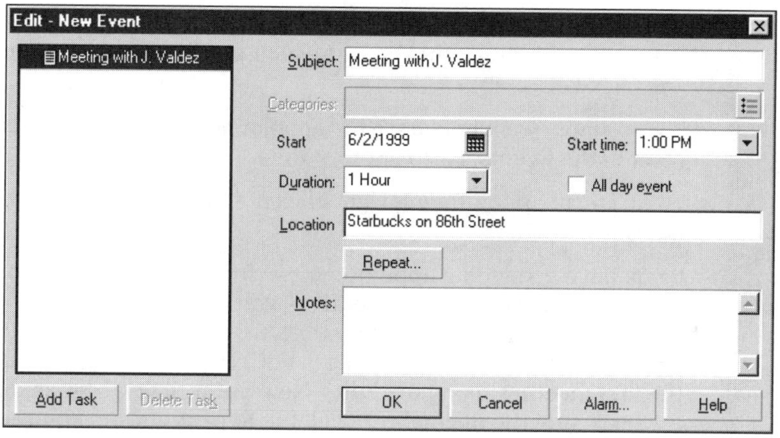

Figure 18-3: Schedule and edit appointments using this dialog box.

2. **Enter the name of the appointment or event in the Subject box.**

   When you open the dialog box, the Subject box is highlighted, so you can just begin typing. The text in the Subject box is the text that will appear in the Events list. You also see the text in the list on the left side of the dialog box.

3. **Enter the start time and duration for the appointment.**

   Enter the appointment time in the Start Time option box. Enter the expected length of the appointment in the Duration option box.

   For the Start Time and Duration options, you can either choose a time from the drop-down list or click inside the box and enter a specific time. Be sure to include "a.m." or "p.m." if you enter a custom start time and include "hours" or "minutes" in the Duration option box.

4. **Note the meeting place in the <u>L</u>ocation box.**

5. **Add any notes about the appointment in the <u>N</u>otes box.**

6. **Click OK.**

The text you typed in the Subject option box appears in the Events list.

If you want to review information about an entry, just pause your cursor over the appointment in the Events list. A QuickTip-like box appears showing your appointment data. You can also double-click the appointment in the Events list to redisplay the Edit – New Event dialog box. (This time, the dialog box title bar shows the name of the event you're editing, but the contents of the dialog box are the same.)

Here are a few more tidbits to keep in mind about scheduling appointments:

✔ To change an appointment listing, double-click the appointment in the Events list to reopen the dialog box, change the necessary information, and click OK.

✔ If you simply want to change the appointment time, just drag the appointment in the Events list to another time.

✔ To delete an appointment, right-click it and choose Delete Event from the QuickMenu.

✔ If you have a standing appointment — for example, you have a meeting the first Saturday of every month — you don't have to re-enter the same appointment information every time. Instead, have CorelCentral copy the information to the pertinent dates. First, enter the date and time for the first meeting, using the Edit – New Event dialog box, as discussed earlier. Inside the dialog box, click the Repeat button. You see the Repeat Event dialog box, where you can specify how often the appointment occurs. To discontinue a recurring appointment, click the Off button in the Repeat Event dialog box.

Sounding the alarm

Want CorelCentral to sound an alarm to remind you of an upcoming appointment? When you're entering the appointment in the Edit – New Event dialog box, click the Alarm button to display the Alarm dialog box. Use the dialog box options to specify how far in advance the alarm should sound and what sound file you want to hear as your alarm. An alarm clock icon appears alongside the appointment information in the Events list. When the alarm "goes off," CorelCentral plays the sound file and also displays a pop-up alert box. Click OK to hide the alert.

To apply the same alarm settings to another appointment, just right-click the appointment in the Events list and choose Alarm from the QuickMenu. (A check mark indicates that the alarm is turned on.) Double-click the alarm clock icon for the event to open the Alarm dialog box and change the alarm settings. To remove an alarm, right-click the appointment and choose Alarm from the QuickMenu.

If you have DAD enabled (see Chapter 3), an Alarm icon appears in the Windows taskbar. (If you don't see the alarm icon, choose Programs⇨ WordPerfect Office 2000⇨Utilities⇨CorelCentral Alarms.) This icon launches the CorelCentral Alarms utility, which enables you to set an alarm on the fly — that is, you don't need to enter an appointment or event. Click the icon to display the Quick Alarm dialog box. Give the alarm a name — for example, Nap Time — and specify how long you want CorelCentral to wait before sounding the alarm (enter the value in the Alarm After option box). Click OK to set the alarm.

If you click the Advanced button in the dialog box, you can set a specific alarm time and date as well as choose the alarm sound and set a "snooze" interval. To turn off the alarm utility, right-click the alarm icon and select Exit CorelCentral Alarms. (The utility will be turned on again automatically if you set an alarm for an appointment in CorelCentral.)

Creating task lists

Located in the lower-right corner of the Calendar and the bottom half of the Day Planner, the Task list is designed for recording your daily chores. You can list all the jobs that have been dumped on you and then enjoy the satisfaction of checking them off your list after you complete them or — better yet — find someone else to do them for you.

As with appointments, the process for entering tasks is slightly different in Version 9 than it was in Version 8. Here's the drill for basic chore-recording:

1. **Click an empty line in the Task list.**

   CorelCentral highlights the line and adds an entry named New Task, as shown in Figure 18-4.

2. **Type the task name.**

   Whatever you type replaces the New Task label.

3. **Press Enter.**

These steps are fine for jotting down simple reminders about projects you need to complete in one day, but for more complex jobs, use the following approach. You can then assign a due date and priority to your project and also keep track of how much of the job is already done.

Filter Task List button

Column button

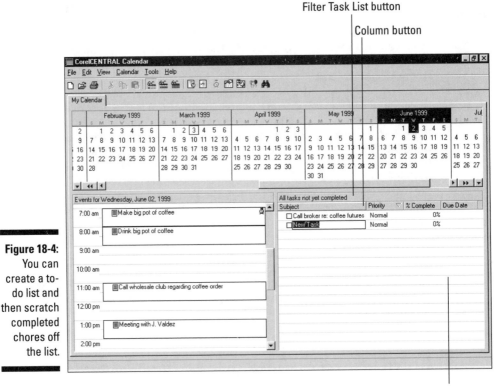

Task list

Figure 18-4:
You can create a to-do list and then scratch completed chores off the list.

1. **Right click an empty line and click Add Task in the resulting QuickMenu.**

   The Edit – New Task dialog box appears. This dialog box looks much like the Edit – New Event dialog box shown in Figure 18-3, so I won't waste the page space to show it again here.

2. **Enter the necessary information about the task.**

   Type a brief description of the item in the Subject box; this text will appear in the Task list.

   You can also assign a starting date and ending date for the project by entering the dates in the Start and Due Date boxes, assign a priority level to the task using the Priority drop-down list, and indicate how far along you are with the project by entering a value in the % Complete option box. If you want, you can click in the message area and type some notes about the task.

As an added organizational trick, click the button at the end of the Categories option box. The Categories dialog box appears, listing two categories, Business and Personal. Check the box that applies. Or, to create a new category, type the name in the option box at the bottom of the dialog box and click Add. Click OK to return to the Edit – New Task dialog box.

What's the point of assigning a category? Well, in the Task list, you can display just those tasks in a particular category, as explained a bit later in this section.

3. Click OK.

As if all that weren't exciting enough, the following list contains still more fun things you can do with the Task list. Most of these features are new to Version 9 or at least activated differently than in Version 8, by the way.

✔ When you finish a chore, click the box to the left of the task name. A check mark appears in the box, indicating that your slavish duty is done. There, now, doesn't that feel good?

✔ By default, the Task list shows four columns of information: the subject (the task name you assigned); Priority; % Complete; and the Due Date. The column buttons at the top of the Task list (refer to Figure 18-4) reflect these categories of information. If you right-click any column button, a dialog box appears that enables you to select what columns you want CorelCentral to display. Aside from the default options, you can display the start date of the task.

✔ Click the various column buttons to sort your tasks according to the button you click. For example, to list tasks in alphabetical order by name, click the Subject button. After you click a column button, a little up- or down-pointing arrow appears on the button. The arrow indicates the order in which tasks are sorted within the category. For example, when the Subject arrow points down, tasks are listed in ascending alphabetical order. If you click the Subject title again, the arrow points up and tasks are listed in descending alphabetical order.

✔ To edit the information you entered for a task, double-click the task to redisplay the Edit – New Task dialog box. (The dialog box now shows the name of the task in the title bar.) After changing the information, click the OK button.

✔ Pause your cursor over a task entry to display a QuickTip-style box that shows you all the pertinent task information.

✔ Click the Filter Task List button, labeled in Figure 18-4, to specify which of your tasks you want to see in the Task list. When you click the button, the Filter Task List dialog box, shown in Figure 18-5, appears.

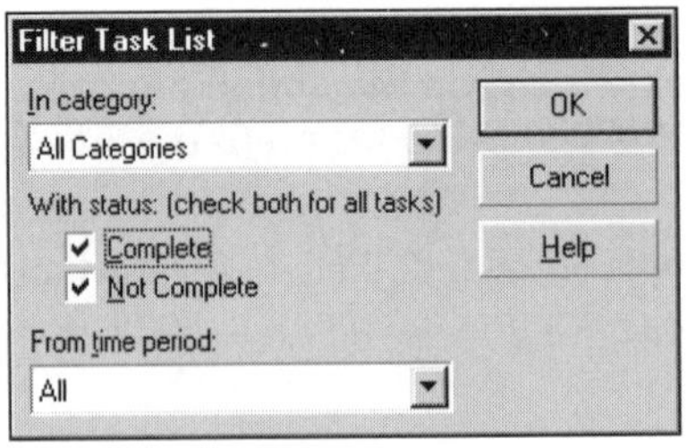

Figure 18-5:
Use the
Filter Task
List dialog
box to
specify what
categories
of tasks you
want to
view.

If you entered category information for your chores, you can display just the items in a specific category by selecting it from the In Category drop-down list. Check the Complete check box if you want tasks that you've marked as completed to appear in the Task list. Check the Not Complete check box to display tasks that you haven't found time to do yet. Finally, select a time from the From Time Period drop-down list to display or hide tasks depending on their due date or start date. Click OK to see your task list as you specified in the dialog box.

✔ To eliminate an entry from your list, right-click it and choose Delete Task from the QuickMenu.

Building Your Digital Address Book

With CorelCentral Address Book, you can compile your own phone book and mailing list, all rolled up into one handy electronic package. You can then insert addresses into letters and other documents, print mailing labels and envelopes, or just enjoy the convenience of having everybody's vital data a mouse click away.

The following sections explain how to input your contact information into Address Book. For information on using Address Book data in WordPerfect documents, see Chapter 9. And for details on generating hard-copy printouts of Address Book data, see "Creating Hard Copies (Printing Stuff)," later in this chapter.

Exploring the new Address Book

In WordPerfect Suite 8, users could choose from two different address books. CorelCentral had an address book, and WordPerfect had an address book. The two worked differently and offered different tools, causing plenty of confusion.

This dual-address book silliness has been rectified in WordPerfect Office 2000. Now, CorelCentral Address Book is the one and only address utility. When you choose the Address Book command inside WordPerfect, you open CorelCentral Address Book, not a dedicated WordPerfect utility. (See Chapter 9 for information on accessing Address Book inside WordPerfect.)

To display Address Book, click the Address Book DAD icon on the Windows taskbar or at the bottom of the Day Planner window, if that's open. Alternatively, choose <u>P</u>rograms⇨WordPerfect Office 2000⇨Utilities⇨ CorelCentral Address Book from the Windows Start menu. The Address Book window, shown in Figure 18-6, appears.

Summary view

Tree view   Field button

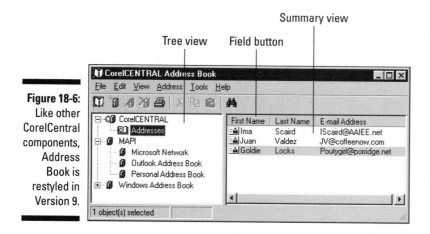

Figure 18-6: Like other CorelCentral components, Address Book is restyled in Version 9.

Featuring a design similar to Windows Explorer, the Address Book window is divided into two panes. On the left, you see what geeks refer to as the *tree view*. The tree view shows your address book directories, which are sort of like the directories on your computer's hard drive. If you click the plus sign next to one of the directories, you display all the individual address book files in that directory — the "branches" of the tree, if you will. Click the minus sign next to a directory to hide the branches from view.

On the right side of the window, the *summary view* appears. This view simply shows you all the address entries in the selected address book. To select an address book, click it in the tree view area.

You can customize the appearance of the Address Book in several ways, including the following:

✔ Drag the gray border between the two panes to change the amount of space devoted to each pane.

✔ At the top of the summary view pane, you see several *field* buttons — the visible buttons in Figure 18-6 are First Name, Last Name, and E-mail Address. The field buttons represent the categories of information — called *fields* by techno-people — that you can enter for each contact. If a button is visible, the corresponding information appears in the summary view.

To display or hide fields, choose View⇨Columns or right-click a field button to display the Columns dialog box. The dialog box contains a long list of fields; fields marked with a check mark appear in the window. Click the box next to a field name to toggle the field on and off. Click OK when you're done selecting fields.

✔ Drag the borders between the field buttons to change the amount of space devoted to each column of information. You can also drag the buttons themselves to change the button order. For example, to make the Last Name field shown in Figure 18-6 the first field in the display, drag the button to the left of the First Name button.

✔ You can change the order in which your addresses appear by clicking the field buttons. If you want the addresses sorted by first names, for example, click the First Name button.

After you click a field button, a little arrow appears on the button to indicate the order in which entries are sorted within the category. For example, if you sort entries by Last Name, a downward-pointing arrow shows that the entries appear in ascending alphabetical order. Click the button again to change the direction of the arrow and reverse the sort order of the listings.

If you previously created address books that store information using the MAPI standard (Messaging Application Programming Interface), you should be able to access them via CorelCentral Address Book. For example, if you created an address book in Microsoft Outlook, you can manage it through CorelCentral. The program searches your system and lists any MAPI-compliant address books it finds in the tree view.

If you need more information about importing old address books or you want to export a CorelCentral address book to another program, you can find out what you need to know in the CorelCentral Help system. See Chapter 3 for advice on how to take advantage of the Help system.

Also check the Help system for information on synchronizing CorelCentral with your 3Com PalmPilot, if you happen to own one of those space-age gadgets.

Creating new address books

By default, CorelCentral presents you with one address book, called Addresses, stored in the CorelCentral directory. You can store all your addresses here, or you can create additional address books if you like. You may want to keep all your business addresses in one book, for example, and personal addresses in another.

The following steps explain how to create a new address book. Note that these steps assume that you want to create an address book inside the CorelCentral directory. If you want to create an address book for company-wide use via a network directory or create a MAPI-compliant address book for use in another program, check the CorelCentral Help system for details.

1. **Click the New Address Book icon or choose File➪New.**

   CorelCentral asks you to select an address book type.

2. **Click CorelCentral and click OK.**

   The New Address Book Properties dialog box appears.

3. **Enter a name for the address book in the Name option box.**

4. **Click OK or press Enter.**

   Your new address book appears in the tree view pane.

Adding addresses

Adding an address to an address book is an easy process — one that, like other aspects of CorelCentral 9, is quite different than in Version 8. The new procedure is as follows:

1. **Select an address book in the tree view pane.**

   Just click the address book where you want to add an address.

2. **Click the Add Entry button or choose Address➪New Entry.**

   The New Entry dialog box appears, asking you what type of address you want to create. You have four choices:

   - **Person:** For storing personal and business information about a contact

   - **Organization:** For storing information about a business or organization

- **Resource:** For storing data about a resource, such as a library, meeting room, or conference facility

- **Group:** For recording the names of the members of a group

3. **Click an entry type and click OK.**

   CorelCentral presents you with a dialog box into which you can type all the pertinent information about your contact, group, resource, or organization. The dialog box that appears when you select the Person option in Step 2 is featured in Figure 18-7.

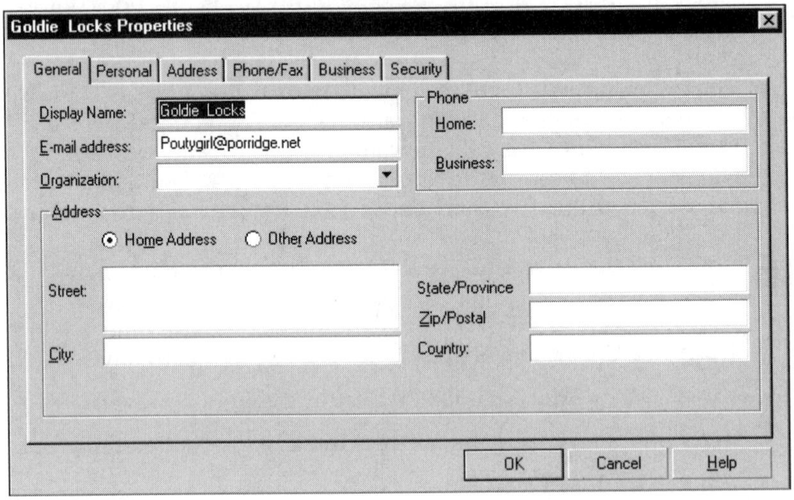

Figure 18-7: Enter information about a personal contact in this dialog box.

4. **Enter your address information and click OK.**

   The data appears in the summary view pane, according to the field display options you enabled. (See the bulleted list in the earlier section "Building Your Digital Address Book" for information on that intriguing topic.)

   Note that these steps apply to entering data into a CorelCentral address book. If you're entering contact information into a MAPI-compliant address book or directory server address book, you may encounter different dialog boxes and options along the way. As always, the CorelCentral Help system offers guidance if you don't understand what to do.

Editing, deleting, and moving addresses

To update an address, double-click it to redisplay the Properties dialog box for the address. Then just enter the new information in the dialog box and click OK.

If you have a falling-out with some folks and want to wipe their addresses out of your system, Ctrl+click their addresses in the summary view pane and press Delete. That'll teach 'em. To delete a single address, just click it and press Delete.

You can drag and drop an address to a different address book, just as you drag and drop files to different folders in Windows Explorer. To copy an address from one address book to another, press Ctrl as you drag.

Creating Hard Copies (Printing Stuff)

Although having all the details of your life in electronic form is handy, you may at some point decide to break away from your computer and do some real-life interacting with the world. And during those times when you unchain yourself from the computer, you may find it helpful to have a hard copy of the information you store in CorelCentral.

Printing pages of data from CorelCentral is a cinch. Just display the window that contains the information you want to print and choose File⇔Print or press Ctrl+P to display the Print dialog box. The dialog box contains options appropriate to the window that's active. For example, if you're working in Address Book, the dialog box offers you options for printing the current card, all selected cards, or all cards in the current group.

Depending on what CorelCentral tool you're using, you may find a Page Setup button in the Print dialog box or a Page Setup command in the File menu. By clicking the button or choosing the command, you can access options that enable you to format the data — for example, to choose the font and type size you want to use. Click OK to return to the Print dialog box and then click Print to send that data to the printer.

Chapter 19

Computer, Do What I Say!

• •

In This Chapter

▶ Using Dragon NaturallySpeaking for the first time

▶ Dictating documents in WordPerfect 9

▶ Formatting and editing text by voice command

▶ Improving your dictation results

• •

*M*ost of us have been talking to our computers since we first put the big glowing boxes on our desks (or laps, if you're a mobile warrior). But not too much of what we've said was fit for repeating in the presence of children or polite adults. And even the strongest language, the most heartfelt pleas couldn't induce our stubborn machines to respond.

The advent of voice-recognition programs changed all that. Now, you can control your computer by voice command in addition to using a keyboard and mouse. You can dictate a letter, for example, and watch as the words you say appear on-screen, without a press of a key from you. You can even format and edit your text simply by speaking the appropriate words.

WordPerfect Office 2000 includes a special version of a leading voice-recognition program, Dragon NaturallySpeaking from Dragon Systems, which has been integrated with WordPerfect. This chapter introduces you to the basics of Dragon NaturallySpeaking, focusing on using the program to create your letters, reports, and other documents inside WordPerfect.

Getting Started

Before you can dictate text using Dragon NaturallySpeaking, you must do a little setup work to calibrate your microphone, sound card, and voice. During this setup process, Dragon NaturallySpeaking also creates speech files that help it adapt to your vocal characteristics — accent, rate of speech, and so on.

If you're upgrading from a previous version of the program, you don't need to go through this process if you specified that you wanted to retain your existing speech files during program installation.

To begin the setup process, click the Windows Start button and then choose Programs➪Dragon NaturallySpeaking Personal for WordPerfect➪Naturally Speaking Personal for WordPerfect. The New User Wizard dialog box appears.

The wizard consists of three phases:

✓ In the first stage, Run Audio Setup, you take care of system stuff, such as specifying what kind of sound card you have.

✓ In the second stage, you begin *training* — teaching Dragon NaturallySpeaking to understand your voice. You do this by reading aloud some sample documents that the setup wizard displays on-screen.

✓ In the third stage, you run Vocabulary Builder, which acquaints Dragon NaturallySpeaking with specialized terms that you use on a regular basis as well as how you commonly use different words together in your documents. To perform this step, you need to point the program to some documents that are typical of the kind you'll be dictating. You can postpone this stage of the setup if you like, but I recommend that you go ahead and do it now because you'll get better results when you begin using the program in earnest.

Because the wizard instructions in the first two stages are very simple to follow, I won't bore you by repeating them here — just follow the on-screen prompts and do as you're told. Plan on spending about 30 minutes to an hour completing the process.

The Vocabulary Builder phase is less intuitive. If you need help, see the section "Expanding your vocabulary," later in this chapter.

Speaking Your Mind

You can dictate inside WordPerfect or the Dragon NaturallySpeaking program window, which appears if you start Dragon NaturallySpeaking by itself (Start➪Programs➪Dragon NaturallySpeaking Personal for WordPerfect➪ NaturallySpeaking Personal for WordPerfect). If you dictate inside the Dragon NaturallySpeaking window, you don't have access to all the word processing tools available in WordPerfect. Also, you can save documents only in the plain-text format (TXT) or rich-text format (RTF). RTF preserves document formatting, but the plain-text format does not.

This chapter focuses on dictating inside WordPerfect. If you want to work inside the Dragon NaturallySpeaking window, you use similar techniques, although the specific voice commands you use may be slightly different.

Consult the program's Help system or Reference Center manuals for a list of all the available commands.

After you install Dragon NaturallySpeaking, a program button appears on the WordPerfect toolbar, and a Dragon NaturallySpeaking menu appears on the menu bar. Follow these steps to start telling your computer what to do:

1. **Click the Dragon NaturallySpeaking button or choose Dragon NaturallySpeaking⇨Use NaturalWord.**

   WordPerfect activates Dragon NaturallySpeaking and asks you to select your user name. This is the name you assigned yourself when completing the setup wizard discussed in the preceding section.

2. **Click your user name and click Open.**

   The toolbar changes to provide you with a total of four buttons that access different program tools, as shown in Figure 19-1. (Later sections explain what each of these buttons do.) One button, which controls your microphone, appears on the Windows taskbar as well as on the WordPerfect toolbar.

Dragon NaturallySpeaking buttons

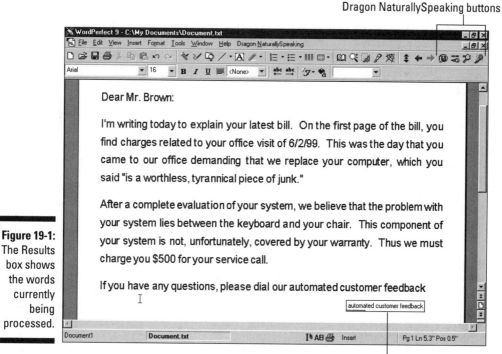

Figure 19-1:
The Results box shows the words currently being processed.

Results box

3. Click the Microphone button on the toolbar or Windows taskbar to turn on your microphone.

You're now ready to begin dictating. Speak your mind, using the techniques outline in the next few sections.

To shut the microphone off, click the Microphone button again. Or, to pause dictating and shut the mike off temporarily, say **"go to sleep."** When you want to resume dictating, say **"wake up"** or click the Microphone button twice. Your first click turns the mike off; the second click turns it back on.

You can control several aspects of how Dragon NaturallySpeaking behaves by choosing Dragon NaturallySpeaking⇨Tools⇨Options. The resulting dialog box includes settings that let you specify such things as whether you want one or two spaces inserted at the end of sentences and whether you want the program to emphasize speed over accuracy or vice versa.

Dictating text

To enter text, you simply speak the words you want to enter, as if you were dictating to a secretary. But your digital secretary isn't quite as clever as a human secretary, so you also must say any punctuation marks you want to include — commas, periods, and so on. And you must indicate when you want to start a new line, new paragraph, or new text formatting. In other words, you must give a voice command for anything that you normally would do with your mouse or keyboard.

For example, to enter the letter salutation shown in Figure 19-1, you say **Dear Mr. Brown colon new paragraph**. You don't need to say the period after *mister* because Dragon NaturallySpeaking is smart enough to add that automatically. The program also knows to capitalize proper names and the word at the beginning of a sentence.

As you speak, the Results box (labeled in Figure 19-1) shows you what words Dragon NaturallySpeaking is processing. After the words are processed, they appear on-screen. The Results box appears in the upper-left corner of the program window by default, but you can drag it to another location on-screen if you want, as I did in Figure 19-1.

When you dictate text, the insertion marker and mouse cursor work just as they do when you're entering text from the keyboard. The insertion marker indicates where the next thing you say will be entered. You can position the insertion marker with the mouse — just click where you want to put the marker — or by using voice commands.

Table 19-1 provides you with a list of some commands related to entering text and positioning the insertion marker. The following two sections explain what to do if Dragon NaturallySpeaking misunderstands you and how to edit and format your text.

Table 19-1	Basic Text Entry Commands
To Do This	*Say This*
Start a new line	New line
Start a new paragraph	New paragraph
Tab to the next tab stop	Tab key
Move insertion marker to beginning of document	Move to top
Move insertion marker to end of document	Move to bottom
Move insertion marker to beginning of line	Move to start of line
Move insertion marker to end of line	Move to end of line
Move insertion marker left/right one character	Move back/forward one character
Move insertion marker up/down one line	Move up/down one line
Move insertion marker up/down one paragraph	Move up/down one paragraph
Move insertion marker before a specific word	Insert before (*say word*)
Move insertion marker after a specific word	Insert after (*say word*)

Correcting dictation errors

Sometimes, Dragon NaturallySpeaking works wonderfully, accurately turning your spoken words into typed text. Other times, the program behaves as though it doesn't understand a word you say.

If the text that appears on-screen isn't what you said, you can simply say **"scratch that"** or **"undo that"** to erase the last thing you said. Then say the word or phrase again. If Dragon NaturallySpeaking still doesn't respond correctly, do the following:

1. **Say** "correct that" **to open the Correction dialog box, shown in Figure 19-2.**

   Dragon NaturallySpeaking selects the last word or phrase you spoke and highlights it in the top text box in the Correction dialog box. If the text isn't what you wanted to correct, click the Cancel button or say **"click**

Cancel" to close the dialog box. Select the phrase you need to correct using the mouse or the selection techniques outlined in the next section and then say **"correct that"** again to reopen the Correction dialog box.

You can also say **"correct"** followed by the words you want to change to select the words and open the Correction dialog box.

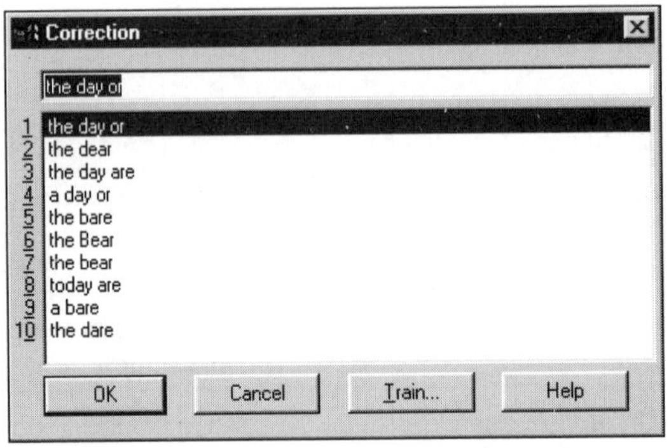

Figure 19-2:
If Dragon
Naturally
Speaking
misunder-
stands you,
say "correct
that" to
open the
Correction
dialog box.

⊞ Correction	✕
the day or	

1	the day or
2	the dear
3	the day are
4	a day or
5	the bare
6	the Bear
7	the bear
8	today are
9	a bare
10	the dare

OK	Cancel	Train...	Help

Dragon NaturallySpeaking responds better if you select both the mistaken word or words and some surrounding text, because it looks at how words are used in context when figuring out what you say.

2. **Select or enter the correct text.**

   Beneath the mistaken word or phrase, you see a list of possible corrections. If one of them is correct, say **"choose"** followed by the number of the correct item. For example, to substitute *today are* for the mistaken phrase *the day or* in Figure 19-2, you say **"choose eight."**

   You can also spell the word or phrase, letter by letter. But many times, simply typing the correct word or phrase in the top text box is the quickest option.

   If you use the **"choose"** command to make your correction, the dialog box closes, and your text is corrected. If you use another method, you must click OK or say **"click OK."**

If you have to make the same correction several times, use the Train Words command to give Dragon NaturallySpeaking additional guidance in recognizing how you say the word or phrase. The upcoming section "Training Dragon NaturallySpeaking" explains how to do this. You can click the Train button inside the Correction dialog box to do this training if you prefer.

Use the Correction dialog box to fix mistakes that occur when Dragon NaturallySpeaking misinterprets your words. *Don't* use this dialog box to correct mistakes that you make when dictating or to otherwise edit your text. The next section explains how to clean up these personal flubs.

Editing text

To edit text, you use the same approach as you do when working with a keyboard and mouse. The only difference is that you can use your voice to do the job.

Keep in mind that you don't have to rely solely on word of mouth — the mouse and keyboard are always available to you, too. (If you need a refresher on editing techniques in WordPerfect, see the chapters in Part II.) At present, you can't choose most menu commands or dialog box options using voice commands in WordPerfect, unfortunately, so you'll need to do that the old-fashioned way.

To fix a mistake that you just made, you can use these two on-the-fly commands:

- ✔ Say **"scratch that"** or **"undo that"** to erase the last phrase you spoke or to undo your last voice command. You can undo multiple actions, just as when choosing the Undo command from the Edit menu.

- ✔ Say **"resume with"** followed by the last correct word in the text. Dragon NaturallySpeaking erases everything following the word you specified and waits for you to begin dictating again.

For other edits, you need to select the text you want to change. Again, you can use ordinary mouse-and-keyboard selection techniques, or you can use voice commands. The following list explains a few commands for selecting individual words; Table 19-2 provides additional selection commands. Table 19-3 introduces you to a few useful editing and formatting commands.

- ✔ Say **"select"** followed by the words you want to select.

- ✔ By default, Dragon NaturallySpeaking searches for the words you want it to select starting from the insertion marker backwards through the document. But you can change that behavior by choosing Dragon NaturallySpeaking⇨Tools⇨Options to open the Options dialog box. Click the Miscellaneous tab and deselect the Select Searches Backwards check box. Now, the program searches forward from the insertion marker.

- ✔ Say **"select next word"** to select the word following the insertion marker. Say **"select previous word"** to select the word before the insertion marker.

✔ Say **"select next 10 words"** to select ten words following the insertion marker. Say **"select previous 10 words"** to select ten words before the insertion marker. You can use this technique to select up to 20 words; just specify the number of words you want to select.

✔ After you select a word or phrase in one spot in your document, you can select that same text elsewhere by saying **"select again."**

✔ To select a range of words, say **"select"** followed by the first word in the range and then **"through"** followed by the last word in the range. For example, to select the first seven words in the phrase *Peter Piper picked a peck of pickled peppers,* you say **"select Peter through pickled."**

After you select text, it appears highlighted on-screen. The next text you dictate replaces the selected text. If you give a formatting command, the selected text is affected.

To cancel a selection, move the insertion marker to another spot in the text, using the commands presented earlier in this chapter, in Table 19-1.

Table 19-2	Selecting Characters, Lines, and More
To Do This	*Say This*
Select the character before/after the insertion marker	Select previous/next character
Select from 1 to 20 characters before/after the insertion marker	Select previous/next (*specify number*) characters
Select the current paragraph	Select paragraph
Select the paragraph before/after the current paragraph	Select previous/next paragraph
Select the current line	Select line
Select the entire document	Select all

Table 19-3	Editing and Formatting Commands
To Do This	*Say This (Replace Italicized Words with the Desired Setting)*
Delete selected text	Delete that
Undo your last action	Undo that
Copy selected text to Clipboard	Copy that

To Do This	Say This (Replace Italicized Words with the Desired Setting)
Cut selected text to Clipboard	Cut that
Paste Clipboard text	Paste that
Change the font	Set font *font name* (example: "Set font Arial")
Change the type size	Set size *size point* (example: "Set size 12 point")
Change font and size	Format that *font name, size* (example: "Format that Arial 12")
Boldface selected text	Bold that
Italicize selected text	Italicize that
Underline selected text	Underline that
Center a selected paragraph	Center that
Left-align/Right-align a selected paragraph	Left-align that, Right-align that
Capitalize the first letter in a selected word	Cap that
Capitalize all letters in a selected word	All caps that
Turn all caps on/off	All caps on, All caps off

Improving Dictation Accuracy

If Dragon NaturallySpeaking gets more words wrong than it gets right, don't give up. You can do several things to improve the program's accuracy:

- ✔ Speak clearly, but don't over-enunciate or pause between each word. Dragon NaturallySpeaking actually works better if you speak in complete phrases at a normal speech rate.

- ✔ Turn off any background noisemakers, such as a radio or TV set.

- ✔ Make sure that your sound card, microphone, and computer system meet the requirements for good performance that Dragon Naturally Speaking has established. You can find this information in the Dragon NaturallySpeaking reference manual in the Reference Center (see Chapter 3 for details about accessing Reference Center manuals). The

Reference Center manual includes many other tips for improving performance, too. You may also want to visit the Dragon Systems Web site at www.dragonsys.com for the latest technical support information.

✔ Take the time to do additional vocal training and run the Vocabulary Builder, as outlined in the next sections. The more training you do, the better Dragon NaturallySpeaking gets at responding correctly to your voice.

✔ If more than one person will be using the program on the same computer, each person must complete the training process discussed in the first section of this chapter. To add a new user and start the training, choose Dragon NaturallySpeaking⇨Users⇨New inside WordPerfect.

Expanding your vocabulary

To figure out what you're saying, Dragon NaturallySpeaking consults the *active vocabulary,* which is a list of common words along with data that tell the program what each word sounds like when spoken. In addition, the program consults something called a *language model,* which contains statistics about how words are used in context with other words.

The program offers two tools that enable you to personalize both the active vocabulary and the language model. Using these tools, known as Vocabulary Builder and Vocabulary Editor, you increase the program's capability to respond to you correctly.

Vocabulary Builder analyzes documents that you supply and then adapts its language model and, if you specify, its active vocabulary to better reflect the kind of documents you create. To use this tool, prepare one or two documents that contain the lingo you use frequently. Ideally, the documents should contain a total of about 17,000 words. (In WordPerfect, you can check how many words are in a document by choosing File⇨Properties and clicking the Information tab of the resulting dialog box.)

Vocabulary Builder can work with documents stored in the WordPerfect native format (WPD) from Version 8 or higher, as well as plain-text files (TXT), rich-text files (RTF), Microsoft Word files, Version 6 or higher (DOC), and HTML files (HTM and HTML).

Be sure to spell-check the documents before you begin. Then do the following in the WordPerfect window:

1. **Choose Dragon NaturallySpeaking⇨Tools⇨Vocabulary Builder.**

   The Vocabulary Builder dialog box shown in Figure 19-3 appears.

2. **Click the Add Document button and select the documents you want to use.**

3. **Click Begin.**

Dragon NaturallySpeaking presents you with a second dialog box that lists all the unknown words in the sample documents. Beside each unknown word is a check box. You have two options for handling the list:

- If you click Build without checking any words, Dragon Naturally Speaking tunes your language model but doesn't add any words to the active vocabulary. If most words on the list are common words or words that you use very infrequently, choose this option.

- If some words on the list are very specialized terms that you will use frequently, check them and click Train and Build to tune the language model and also add the selected words to your active vocabulary. The program asks you whether you really want to add words to the vocabulary; click Yes. You then see the Train Words dialog box. Click the Record button and speak each of the new words as you are prompted to do so. Then click Done.

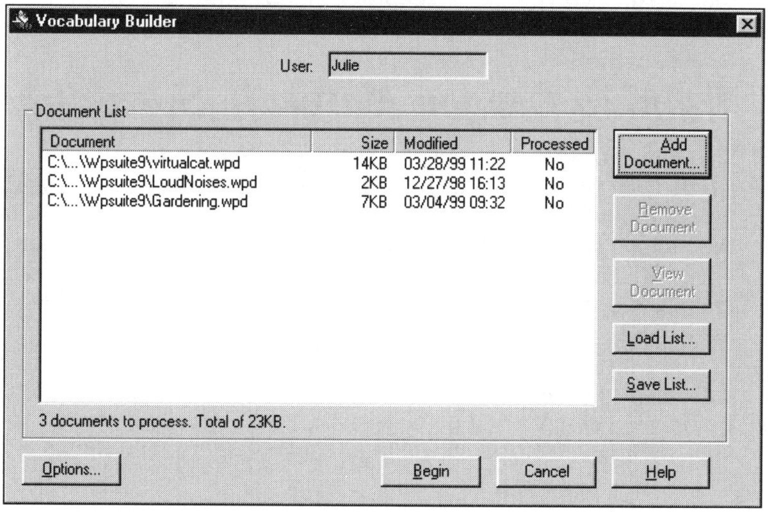

Figure 19-3:
Use
Vocabulary
Builder to
personalize
the active
vocabulary
and
language
model.

Vocabulary Builder				
User: Julie				

Document List

Document	Size	Modified	Processed	
C:\...\Wpsuite9\virtualcat.wpd	14KB	03/28/99 11:22	No	Add Document...
C:\...\Wpsuite9\LoudNoises.wpd	2KB	12/27/98 16:13	No	Remove Document
C:\...\Wpsuite9\Gardening.wpd	7KB	03/04/99 09:32	No	View Document
				Load List...
				Save List...

3 documents to process. Total of 23KB.

Options... | Begin | Cancel | Help

Be selective about words that you add to the active vocabulary, as the number of words it can contain is limited. If you add too many words, other words in the active vocabulary are dumped.

After you run Vocabulary Builder as part of the initial Dragon NaturallySpeaking setup wizard, you can run it again any time. But unless you're taking on a new project that will involve a whole new set of unfamiliar terms, don't do so. Each time you run Vocabulary Builder, the program erases the previous language model information and replaces it with data gleaned from the new set of documents you ask it to analyze.

You can add an individual word to the active vocabulary by choosing Dragon NaturallySpeaking➪Tools➪Vocabulary Editor to open the Vocabulary Editor dialog box. Type the word you want to enter in the Written Form text box. Then click Train, click the Record button, and speak the word. Click Done and then click Close.

 Alternatively, you can click the Find New Words button on the toolbar or choose Dragon NaturallySpeaking➪Tools➪Find New Words. The program searches for any unknown words in the current open document and lists them for you. To add a word to the vocabulary, click the check box beside the word and click Train. Click the Record button, speak the word, and then click Done and click Close.

To remove a word from the active vocabulary, select the word in the Vocabulary Editor dialog box and click Delete. You may want to remove a word that you never use if Dragon NaturallySpeaking keeps mistakenly typing that word when you dictate another, similar-sounding word.

Training Dragon NaturallySpeaking

Sometimes Dragon NaturallySpeaking has a hard time interpreting your words even when those words are in the active vocabulary. You can teach the program how you say a particular word by clicking the Training button on the toolbar or choosing Dragon NaturallySpeaking➪Tools➪Train Words to open the Train Words dialog box. Type the word you want to teach the program in the sole option box and click OK. The Train Words dialog box opens. Click the Record button, speak the word, and click Done.

 You can also improve accuracy by reading aloud more of the sample voice-training documents that come with Dragon NaturallySpeaking. To do so, choose Dragon NaturallySpeaking➪Tools➪General Training.

Saving Your Speech Files

When you close a document that you dictated using Dragon Naturally Speaking, you're asked whether you want to save your speech files. Be sure to answer in the affirmative so that any information the program collected about how you say certain words isn't lost. You should also click the Save Speech Files button on the toolbar periodically to save your speech files while you're working in a document.

Chapter 20

Becoming a Desktop Publishing Magnate

In This Chapter

▶ Creating brochures, newsletters, and more with Corel Print Office

▶ Using ready-made templates to get the job done fast

▶ Adding your own text and graphics

▶ Editing photos with Corel Photo House

*B*y using the WordPerfect formatting features covered in Chapters 7 and 8, you can create some fairly sophisticated documents. And with the Presentations drawing tools, explained in Chapters 16 and 17, you can create impressive graphics, such as logos and banners.

If you purchased the Voice-Activated Edition of WordPerfect Office 2000, you have two additional publishing and graphics tools at your disposal: Corel Print Office, which makes easy work of creating brochures, newsletters, and other print materials; and Corel Photo House, which you use to edit scanned photographs, pictures from digital cameras, and other bitmap images.

This chapter provides you with an introduction to both programs, explaining not only how to use ready-made templates to produce professional-looking print materials in a flash, but also how to strike out on your own and create custom-designed publications from scratch.

Shaking Hands with Print Office

Use Print Office when you want to create printed materials such as signs, newsletters, advertisements, and so on. If you just want to edit and print digital photos, skip to "Phun with Photo House," later in this chapter. You don't need Print Office to edit photos, although you can access the Photo House image-editing tools from inside Print Office if you choose (running both programs consumes more of your computer's resources, however).

Starting up

To launch Print Office, click the Windows Start button and then choose the program from the Programs submenu in the normal fashion. The Print Office program window appears, and a welcome screen instructs you to click one of the buttons on the Guides panel of the Notebook, which occupies the left third of the window.

- ✔ Click From Sample to create a project based on a Print Office template. The templates provide basic layouts and text and graphic elements that you can replace with your own text and graphics. You must have the Print Office CD in your CD-ROM drive to use the templates.

- ✔ Click From Scratch to design a custom project without using the templates.

- ✔ Click Open Existing to open a project that you previously created and saved to disk.

- ✔ Click Open Last to open the last project you did in Print Office. (This option doesn't become available until you create and save one project.)

After you click a button, the Notebook provides instructions that walk you through the next steps in starting your project. For example, if you click the From Sample button, you're asked to select the category of template you want to use and then make a few design decisions. After you complete each step, click the Next icon at the bottom of the Notebook. (If you need help, see "Flipping through the Notebook," later in this chapter.)

When you reach the final step, the Next icon changes into the Done icon. Click the icon to start your project in earnest. Your project page appears in the workspace, the Notebook offers the options shown in Figure 20-1, and more tools and menus become available to you.

The Notebook page shown in Figure 20-1 serves as the launching point for all the project-editing options available in Print Office. You can return to this page, which I refer to hereafter as the main Guides page, by clicking the Guide tool at the top of the Tool Palette, labeled in Figure 20-1.

In addition to the standard program window components — menu bar, toolbar, and so on — Print Office offers these on-screen tools:

- ✔ The Property Bar, beneath the toolbar, offers drop-down lists and buttons that provide quick access to options related to whatever you're doing at the moment. Until you select certain tools or elements in your project, the Property Bar is empty, as in Figure 20-1.

- ✔ The Color Palette provides a fast way to apply colors to text and graphics. "Editing text and graphics," later in this chapter, offers details.

- ✔ The Tool Palette holds the drawing and editing tools. Click a tool's icon to activate the tool.

Notebook · Tool Palette

Toolbar · Guide tool · Property Bar · Workspace · Color Palette

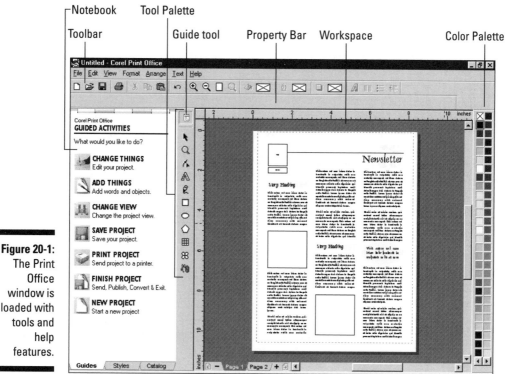

Figure 20-1:
The Print
Office
window is
loaded with
tools and
help
features.

Shutting down

You can have only one project open at a time. To close the current project
and start another, do any of the following:

✔ Click the Guide tool to return to the main Guides page and then click
Start New Project.

✔ Choose File➪New, press Ctrl+N, or click the New button to create a new
project from scratch that has the same layout as the current project.

✔ Choose File➪New Project to return to the same Guides page that you
saw when you first started Print Office. Then click one of the options to
start your new project.

✔ Choose File➪Open, press Ctrl+O, or click the Open button to open an
existing project.

Print Office asks whether you want to save the current project before opening the new one. Click Yes if you want to save the project; click No if you
don't.

To shut down Print Office, click the program Close button, press Alt+F4, or choose File➪Exit. You're prompted to save the current project if you haven't done so.

Flipping through the Notebook

The Notebook, labeled in Figure 20-1, has three panels. Click the tabs at the bottom of the Notebook to switch between the different panels.

- ✔ The Guides panel gives you access to the Print Office wizards, to tips on using various program tools, and to certain program options.
- ✔ The Styles panel provides options that enable you to do stuff like changing the color and thickness of a line and applying a shadow to an object.
- ✔ The Catalog panel provides access to all the clip art, photographs, and other design elements provided on the Print Office CD.

Depending on what you're trying to do with your project, you may see various and sundry icons in the Notebook. Your field guide to the most common icons follows:

- ✔ **Next:** Click to move to the next step in the process.
- ✔ **Back:** Click to go back one step.
- ✔ **Done:** Click to complete the current task.
- ✔ **Preview:** Click to preview the selected option in the workspace.
- ✔ **Wizard:** Click to display step-by-step instructions.
- ✔ **Presets:** Click to display ready-made effects, such as line styles and colors.
- ✔ **Custom:** Click to display options for designing your own effects.
- ✔ **Reset:** Click to reset the options on the current page to their default values.
- ✔ **Keep:** Click to save an effect that you create from scratch so that you can use it again. The effect then becomes available when you click the Presets icon.
- ✔ **Search:** Click to search the Print Office CD for a specific design element.
- ✔ **Options:** Click to specify the letter of your CD drive, so that Print Office can locate the available Print Office templates and art elements.
- ✔ **Cancel:** Click to exit the current Notebook page and return to the main Guides page.
- ✔ **Help:** Click to get more assistance with an option or task.

You can hide the Notebook to increase the size of the workspace. To toggle the Notebook on and off, choose View➪Notebook. If you hide the Notebook, it reappears when you choose some commands or click certain toolbar buttons. For example, when you choose commands on the Format menu, the Styles panel appears, displaying options related to the commands.

Perusing your project

Use the following tools to change the view of your work:

- ✔ Click the Zoom In button on the toolbar to magnify the display.

- ✔ Click the Zoom Out button to reduce the magnification.

- ✔ Click the Zoom to Page button to see your entire project page.

- ✔ Click the Zoom to Selected button to magnify selected objects so that they fill the available screen space. See "Selecting stuff," later in this chapter, to find out how to select graphics and text.

- ✔ Click the Zoom tool in the Tool Palette and then drag around the area you want to inspect. Print Office magnifies the area to fill the screen.

- ✔ Use the horizontal and vertical scroll bars and buttons to scroll the page display, just as you do in WordPerfect or any other program.

- ✔ If you're working on a multiple-page project, you see page tabs at the left end of the horizontal scroll bar, as shown in Figure 20-2. Click the tab for the page you want to see. When no more tabs can fit in the display area, little scroll arrows appear on either side of the tabs. Click the arrows to scroll through all your page tabs. Or, to display more tabs on-screen at once, drag the border between the horizontal scroll bar and the tab area.

Turning on layout aids

Print Office provides several features to assist you in positioning elements on the page, as shown in Figure 20-2.

- ✔ Rulers appear along the top and left edge of the workspace. The default unit of measurement is inches, but you can change it to millimeters if you prefer. Choose Edit➪Options, click the General tab, and select the Mm radio button. Choose View➪Rulers to toggle the rulers on and off.

- ✔ The dashed lines around the edges of the project page indicate the printable area of your page. You can turn them on and off by choosing View➪Printable Region.

The lines appear *only* if the project page size matches the default paper size selected for your printer. If you select some other page size, be sure to check your printer manual to find out how close to the edge of the paper you can position text and graphics.

✔ Choose <u>V</u>iew➪Gr<u>i</u>d to display a grid of evenly spaced dots across your page, as shown in Figure 20-2. Use the grid to position and draw elements more precisely. If you choose, you can make the grid dots act like magnets so that any element you add to the page snaps into alignment with the closest dot.

Choose <u>V</u>iew➪Snap to Gr<u>i</u>d or press Ctrl+Y to toggle the magnetic field on and off. Choose <u>V</u>iew➪Grid Sett<u>i</u>ngs to display a Notebook page where you can change the spacing of the grid dots and specify the grid offset (the distance between the edge of the page and the first grid dot).

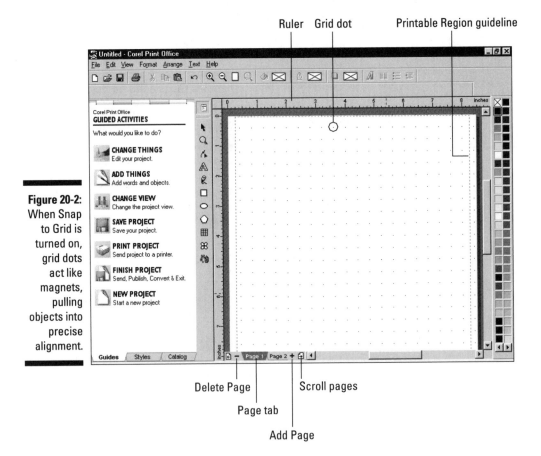

Figure 20-2:
When Snap
to Grid is
turned on,
grid dots
act like
magnets,
pulling
objects into
precise
alignment.

Building a Project

After choosing a template or creating a blank page, you're ready to begin assembling your project. The following sections provide you with the basics of setting up your pages and adding graphics and text.

Setting the basic page design

Before you get to the fun stuff of adding pictures and words, you need to understand how you control the foundation of your project, the project page. Here's the scoop:

✔ If you chose a multipage design when creating your project, you see several page buttons next to the page tabs at the bottom of the workspace, as shown in Figure 20-2. Click the Add Page button to add a page to your project. Click the Delete Page button to delete the current page. You can also choose Edit⇨Insert Page After to insert a page after the current page; choose Edit⇨Remove Page to delete the current page; and choose Edit⇨Insert Page Before to insert a page before the current page.

✔ Every project consists of two layers, known as the *foreground* and *background*. Normally, you work in the foreground. After you get an element just the way you want it, you can send it to the background to protect it from being changed accidentally when you make other edits to the foreground. Anything on the background layer can't be altered in any way when you're working in the foreground layer, and vice versa.

  • To send an item to the background layer, use the techniques outlined in the next section to select it. Then choose Arrange⇨To Background or press Ctrl+End.

  • To edit items on the background layer, choose View⇨Edit Background or press Ctrl+E. Any items in the foreground are hidden from view.

  • To send an item back to the foreground layer, select it and choose Arrange⇨To Foreground or press Ctrl+Home. Choose View⇨Edit Foreground or press Ctrl+E again to return to the foreground layer.

✔ Click the Catalog tab of the Notebook and then click the Backdrops button to access prefab backdrops that you can place on the background. You must have the Print Office CD in your CD-ROM drive. When you find a backdrop you like, click it and then click the Done icon at the bottom of the Notebook. Or just drag the backdrop onto your project page. Print Office automatically adds the backdrop to the background, regardless of which layer you're working on at the time.

To change the backdrop, check the Replace Existing check box in the Notebook and drag a different backdrop onto your page. If you uncheck the box, you add the new backdrop on top of the first one.

✔ At any time, you can change your mind about the basic project design and choose a different template or page size by choosing File➪Convert Project. After you choose the command, you're asked whether you want to save the project as it currently exists. Click Yes and give your project a name if you do want to save the project; click No if you don't want to save. The Guides panel then walks you through the steps of selecting a different design. Print Office shuffles any text or graphics in your project to match the new design.

Selecting stuff

If you want to replace, edit, move, or delete an item on a page, you must *select* it first. You can select stuff as follows:

✔ Select the Pick tool from the Tool Palette. Then click the item you want to select. Small boxes, known as *selection handles,* appear around the perimeter of the item to show that it's selected.

✔ To select individual characters in a block of text, double-click the text with the Pick tool. Your cursor changes to a standard I-beam text cursor. Drag over the characters you want to select.

✔ To select several items at once, click the first object with the Pick tool and Shift+click the others. Or drag around all the objects with the Pick tool.

✔ Choose Edit➪Select All or press Ctrl+A to select everything on the page.

✔ You can't select objects on the background layer when you're working in the foreground layer, and vice versa. For more on this issue, see the preceding section.

Adding graphics

To decorate your pages, you can choose from zillions of ready-made graphics or create your own custom graphics. Here's an overview of your options:

✔ Click the Catalog tab of the Notebook to access clip art, backdrops, borders, photos, and objects that ship with WordPerfect Office 2000. When you find a piece of art that you like, drag it to the project page. You must have the Print Office CD in your CD-ROM drive to access the Print Office graphics collection from the Catalog page.

✔ Press Alt as you drag to replace an item that's currently on the page with the new graphic. As you drag over the page, a blue outline appears to indicate what element will be replaced when you release the mouse button, as shown in Figure 20-3.

✔ To add a graphic from another source, choose File➪Import, select the graphic file from the Import dialog box, and click Import.

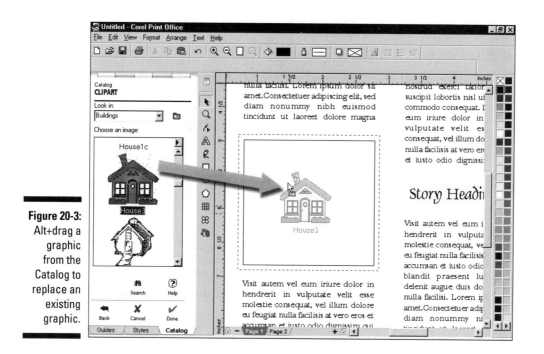

Figure 20-3:
Alt+drag a
graphic
from the
Catalog to
replace an
existing
graphic.

✔ To add an image directly from a scanner or digital camera, choose
File⇨Acquire Image⇨Select Source and select the scanner or camera
name. Then choose File⇨Acquire Image⇨Acquire to begin the image
transfer process.

✔ Feeling artistic? You can draw your own graphics using the Print Office
drawing tools. To get acquainted with these tools, click the Guide tool to
display the main Guides page of the Notebook. Click the Add Things
button and then click the Draw Something button. Choose the drawing
tool you want to explore and follow the Notebook instructions. After you
get comfortable using the tools, you don't have to work your way
through the Notebook process; simply click the tool you want to use in
the Tool Palette and begin drawing.

Adding text

Along with a huge collection of graphics, the Print Office CD provides some
text designed to be used in greeting cards. To explore these prefab phrases,
click the Catalog tab and then click the Phrases button. You can drag a
phrase onto the page just as you can a graphic. Alt+drag to replace an existing phrase with the phrase you drag in.

Frankly, though, you don't save yourself much time by using the preformatted
phrases because creating your own custom text is just as easy. You can either
type your text right in Print Office or import existing text from WordPerfect.

You have two text options in Print Office:

✔ Create *artistic text* when you want to add a single line of text or create small bits of text to which you can apply a wide variety of graphic effects. For example, if you want to wrap a line of text around a logo, you want artistic text.

✔ Create *paragraph text* for longer blocks of text, such as an article in a newsletter. With this type of text, you can use paragraph formatting features, such as columns, bulleted lists, tabs, and indents. You can also flow text between several text boxes, as explained in the next section.

So much for Text 101. Now for the advanced course, which explains how to actually put words on the page:

✔ To create artistic text, click with the Text tool and begin typing. Press Enter to create a line break and click another tool when you finish the text. You can use standard editing techniques to fix mistakes as you go.

✔ If, on the other hand, you want to create paragraph text, drag with the Text tool to create a *text frame,* which is simply a container for your text. You can resize and move the frame at any time, so don't worry about drawing it perfectly the first time. After you release the mouse button, the text cursor appears, and you can begin typing.

To resize a paragraph text frame, click it with the Pick tool to display selection handles around the frame, as shown in Figure 20-4. Drag a handle to enlarge or reduce the frame size. If the frame is too small to hold all your text, you see a black arrow in the tab at the bottom of the frame, as in Figure 20-4. You can either enlarge the text box, cut some text, or flow the extra text into another text frame, as explained in the next section.

✔ To import text that you created in WordPerfect or some other word processor, choose File⇨Import, select the text file in the Import dialog box, and click Import. Print Office creates a paragraph text frame in the center of the page to hold your text. Alternatively, if you select a text frame before choosing the Import command, Print Office puts the text in that frame. (To select a text frame, click it with the Pick tool.)

When the Text tool is active, the Property Bar and toolbar offer buttons and drop-down lists that enable you to change the font, type size, and other text characteristics easily. The available options vary depending on whether you're creating artistic or paragraph text. If you need help with text formatting chores, consult the Guides panel of the Notebook. Also check out "Editing text and graphics," later in this chapter.

You can change the size of artistic text quickly by clicking it with the Pick tool and then dragging the selection handles that appear around the text. (With paragraph text, dragging the handles simply changes the frame size, not the text inside.)

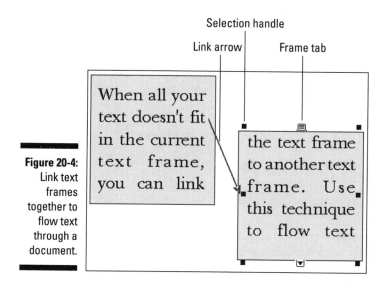

Selection handle

Link arrow | Frame tab

When all your text doesn't fit in the current text frame, you can link

the text frame to another text frame. Use this technique to flow text

Figure 20-4: Link text frames together to flow text through a document.

Print Office provides a Spell Checker that functions like the WordPerfect Spell Checker, explained in Chapter 9. Choose Text⇨Spelling or press Ctrl+Q to use the Spell Checker. If you misspell a word, a red squiggly line appears underneath the word whenever the Text tool is active. You can't turn this feature off as you can in WordPerfect, unfortunately.

Linking paragraph text frames

One advantage of creating paragraph text is that you can link frames together so that text flows from one spot on a page to another, around graphics and other design elements. If you change the text or page design, Print Office automatically reflows the text — you don't have to wipe out all the text and start over.

To flow text contained in one paragraph frame into an empty frame, do the following:

1. **Click the first frame with the Pick tool.**

   You see selection handles around the frame as well as tabs at the top and bottom of the frame.

2. **Click the bottom frame tab.**

   Your cursor changes into a little page icon. If you move the cursor near another text frame, the cursor changes into a big, fat arrow that points to the frame.

3. **Click the empty text frame.**

   Any overflow text from the first frame flows into the second frame, and
   an arrow appears to indicate that the two frames are linked, as shown in
   Figure 20-4. The tiny lines in the tab at the top of the second frame also
   indicate a linked frame. If you select the first frame, you see this linked
   frame tab at the bottom of the frame.

As you work with linked text frames, keep the following pointers in mind:

- If you resize one frame, the text automatically reflows into the other
  linked frames.

- Likewise, if you delete a frame, the text reflows into the other linked
  frames.

- The black arrow in the bottom tab of a text frame (refer to Figure 20-4)
  indicates that you still have some hidden text in the frame. Resize
  the current frame to fit or link the frame to another, empty frame.

- Want to flow text "backwards"? That is, shove the beginning text in a
  frame into another frame, rather than the ending text? Click the top tab
  instead of the bottom tab in Step 2 of the preceding steps. In Figure 20-4,
  this technique would put the text that's in the lower text frame into the
  top frame, and vice versa.

- To remove a frame from a chain of linked frames, click the frame with
  the Pick tool and choose Text⇨Separate. Or right-click the frame with
  the Pick tool and choose Separate from the QuickMenu. The text reflows
  into the remaining linked frames.

Editing text and graphics

When you select a graphic, text frame, or piece of artistic text, the Property
Bar changes to provide you with drop-down menus and buttons for altering
the selected object. Additional formatting buttons also become available on
the toolbar. Pause your cursor over each button or menu to display a
QuickTip label that identifies the option.

If you want some guidance in your editing, click the Guides tab of the
Notebook and then click the button for the thing you want to change. Then
just follow the instructions given in the Notebook.

Because the Notebook does such a good job of explaining editing basics, I
won't bore you with repeating everything here. But I do want to point out a
few special tricks and reminders:

- With artistic text, dragging the selection handles changes the size of the
  text. With paragraph text, only the frame size changes; the text size
  remains the same.

✔ Click a selected object again with the Pick tool to display rotate and skew handles, as shown in Figure 20-5. Drag the side or top handles to skew (slant) the object; drag the corner handles to rotate the object. The center circle represents the center of the rotation; drag the circle to move it. Click to return to the normal selection handles.

✔ If all you want to do is change the outline color of the selected object, right-click a color swatch in the Color Palette. Left-click a swatch to change the interior color. Click the arrows at the bottom of the Color Palette to display more swatches.

✔ Don't like any of the colors in the Color Palette? Click the Coloring button on the Style bar (labeled in Figure 20-5) to display the Styles Notebook page in which you can mix a custom color. Click the Solid radio button and then click the More button to display the dialog box shown in Figure 20-6. (If you don't see the Solid and More options, click the Custom icon at the bottom of the Notebook to display them.) Drag the Hue selector to set the basic color; drag the Saturation/Brightness selector to set the intensity and brightness. Click OK after you finish playing around.

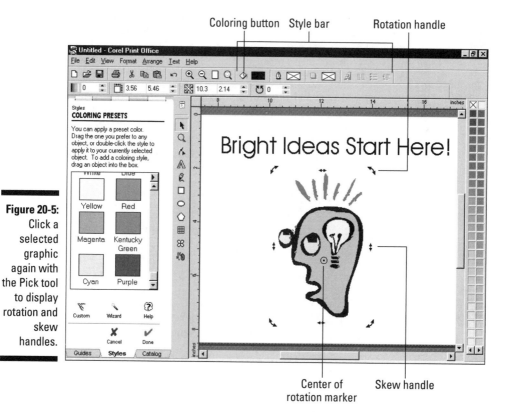

Figure 20-5: Click a selected graphic again with the Pick tool to display rotation and skew handles.

Hue selector

Saturation/Brightness selector

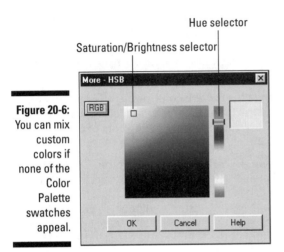

Figure 20-6:
You can mix
custom
colors if
none of the
Color
Palette
swatches
appeal.

If you want to add your custom color to the Presets color collection in the Notebook, click the Keep icon on the Styles tab. When the Coloring Presets page shown in Figure 20-5 appears, your new color appears in the scrolling list of colors, with a name like Color #58. If you want to give the color another name, type the name and press Enter. Now you can access your custom color any time by clicking the Coloring button on the Style bar and then clicking the Presets icon on the Styles tab.

✔ To edit a photo or other bitmap image in Photo House, double-click the picture. Photo House gets itself out of bed, and your picture appears in an image window, ready for editing. When you finish editing, choose Update in Print Office from the Photo House File menu. Then choose File⎟Save to save the image. (For more about photo editing, see the upcoming section, "Phun with Photo House.")

✔ To move a selected object, just drag it.

✔ Choose Edit⇨Duplicate or press Ctrl+D to make a copy of the selected item. Print Office offsets the copy slightly from the original.

✔ Press Delete to get rid of a selected object.

✔ As in other programs, you can press Ctrl+Z or choose Edit⇨Undo to reverse your last editing action. Press Ctrl+Shift+Z or choose Edit⇨Redo if you change your mind about that Undo. By default, you can undo your last ten options. To change that number, choose Edit⇨Options and change the Undo levels value on the General tab. (Remember that when you raise the value, you put additional strain on your computer's memory and other resources.)

Ordering and grouping

If you stack several objects on top of each other to create a drawing or other design element, use the first four commands on the Arrange menu to change the placement of a selected object in the stack.

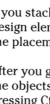

After you get a multiple-object composition just so, you may want to paste the objects together by selecting them and choosing Arrange⇨Group or pressing Ctrl+G. Now you can manipulate all the objects as one. To split the grouped object into its individual pieces again, choose Arrange⇨Ungroup or press Ctrl+G again.

Many of the graphics supplied with Print Office are grouped graphics. You can ungroup them if you want to edit just one portion of the graphic.

Phun with Photo House

Photo House enables you to edit *bitmap images,* which is a nerdy way of referring to images made up of tiny squares of color known as *pixels.* Bitmap images include scanned photos, images from digital cameras, pictures on photo CDs, and pictures that you create using bitmap painting tools.

The graphics that you draw in Print Office, on the other hand, are known as *vector* graphics because they're made up of lines, arcs, and curves that your computer translates into mathematical formulas. The computer sends the formulas to the printer, which follows the formulas to reproduce your drawing.

You can start Photo House from within Print Office by double-clicking a photo in your Print Office project or by choosing File⇨Start Corel Photo House. If you want to run Photo House on its own — which you should if you're not going to need any of the Print Office tools — choose the program from the Windows Start menu.

The Photo House window shares many features with the Print Office window, including the Notebook, Tool Palette, and Color Palette. You can read more about these components in earlier sections of this chapter.

If you're upgrading from a previous edition of Photo House, you may notice that the Notebook has been revamped to resemble the one in Print Office. However, in Photo House, the Notebook has an Effects tab rather than a Styles tab. The Effects tab provides access to all the special photographic effects.

To open a photograph and begin editing, choose one of the options on the Notebook page that appears when you first start the program. In Photo House, you can have more than one photo open at a time. Each picture appears in its own window. The photo with the blue title bar is the active photo. To make another photo active, click its window.

Although many Photo House tools work similarly to those in Print Office, you use a different approach when editing photos than when you edit graphics and text in Print Office. The following sections explain some basic techniques. If you want more guidance, refer to the Guides page of the Notebook. As in Print Office, the Guides page offers instructions, wizards, and additional Help information to guide you through every editing task.

Selecting what you want to edit

Any edits you make in Photo House affect the entire picture unless you select a portion of the image first. Photo House provides you with two selection tools:

 ✔ To select a rectangular area, click the Rectangular tool in the Tool Palette and then drag to enclose the area you want to edit in a dotted outline known as a *selection marquee*. Now any edits affect the area inside the marquee only.

 ✔ To select an irregular area, click the Freehand tool and drag around the part of the picture you want to edit. Again, a selection marquee appears to show what you selected.

To edit another part of the image, you must first get rid of your existing selection outline. You can do this in several ways:

 ✔ Click anywhere in the image with the Rectangular or Freehand tool.

 ✔ Draw a new selection outline with either tool.

 ✔ Press Ctrl+M or choose Edit⇨Merge Selection with Background.

 ✔ Right-click the image and choose Merge Selection from the QuickMenu.

Basic editing maneuvers

Want to put your head on someone else's body? Crop an ex-boss out of a favorite photo? Thanks to the miracle of modern photo editing, almost anything is possible. Here's a sampling of ways you can alter photographic reality:

 ✔ **Crop out unwanted elements:** Select the area that you want to *keep.* Then choose Image⇨Crop to Selection.

 ✔ **Apply touch-up and special effects filters:** Click the Effects tab of the Notebook to explore the available filters. You can also choose the effect you want from the Effects menu.

As you play with the filter options in the Notebook, Photo House previews the effect in the image window. If you like what you see, click Done. Or click Apply to apply the current filter settings and keep the Notebook page active so that you can reapply the filter using different settings. You must either click Done or Cancel to move on to make other edits to your image.

You can toggle the image display between the original and the preview by checking and unchecking the Show Original check box. Click the Reset icon to return to the default filter settings.

✔ **Copy a selection to another location or image:** Press Ctrl+C (Edit⇨Copy). Then do one of the following:

- Open the image where you want to place the copy. Then press Ctrl+V or choose Edit⇨Paste⇨As New Selection. Photo House pastes the copied selection and keeps the selection outline active. That means that you can drag the pasted selection around the image without harming the underlying image. To set the selection in place, click outside the selection.

- To create a new document and paste the selection into it, choose Edit⇨Paste⇨As New Document.

- Stay away from the Into Current Selection on the Paste submenu. This option pastes the copied area into an existing selection outline. The problem is that Photo House enlarges or shrinks the copied area to fit the selection outline, which can result in a blurry mess.

✔ **Move a selection:** Select the Pick tool to display selection handles around the selection. Then drag the selection to move it. Print House fills the area left behind with the Paper color, as shown in Figure 20-7. (See "Choosing paint and paper colors," later in this chapter, for more about the Paper color and how to change it.)

Figure 20-7: I selected the bus and moved it to the right, leaving a bus-shaped hole in the image.

- **Resize a selection:** Select the Pick tool to display the selection handles and then drag a corner handle to resize the selection proportionately. Drag a top or side handle to stretch the image vertically or horizontally only. Don't enlarge a selection too much, though, or you'll destroy the image quality.

- **Rotate or skew a selection:** Select the Pick tool and then click the selection to display rotate and skew handles instead of the standard selection handles. (See Figure 20-5 to see how these handles look.) Drag a corner handle to rotate the selection; drag a top or side handle to skew the selection.

- **Rotate an entire image:** Make sure that nothing is selected and then choose one of the Rotate commands from the Image menu. You may need this command if your image opens up lying on its side, for example.

- **Undo mistakes:** Goof up? Press Ctrl+Z to undo your last editing move. You can undo up to three edits; just keep pressing Ctrl+Z. Or, if you want to go back to square one, choose File⇨Revert to Last Saved. Any changes made since the last time you saved the image are wiped out.

Blending words and images

To add a caption or other text to your image, use the following tricks:

- Click the Text tool icon and then click the Custom icon in the Notebook. Choose your font, type size, and other formatting attributes in the Notebook and then begin typing. Press Enter to start a new line. If you make a mistake, press delete to erase characters to the right of the insertion marker; press Backspace to erase characters to the left.

- After you type the caption, click the Pick tool icon in the toolbox. Your text becomes surrounded by square selection handles. To reposition the text, drag it. To enlarge the text, drag the handles. Drag a corner handle to retain the characters' original proportions.

  If you click a second time with the Pick tool, the selection handles are replaced by arrows. Drag the corner arrows to rotate your text. Drag the side, top, or bottom handles to skew (slant) the text.

- While the selection handles are active, you can switch back into text-editing mode by clicking the Text tool again. The insertion marker reappears, and you can edit the text as needed. You can also change the formatting attributes, if necessary. Drag over the characters you want to reformat and then click the Custom icon in the Notebook to access the formatting options.

- The Text tool creates text in the current Paint color. See the next section for information on choosing colors.

✔ When you have your text the way you want it, switch to any tool but the Text or Pick tool. Your text then becomes forever merged with your image. If you change your mind, press Ctrl+Z immediately to get rid of the text.

You can't go back and edit your text after you merge it with the image. So always make a backup copy of your image before you apply text. That way, if the text needs to change, you can simply create the new text on the backup copy.

Choosing paint and paper colors

Like Print Office, Photo House now offers a Color Palette along the right side of the program window. But in Photo House, you have access to two colors at any one time: the Paint color and the Paper color. (Other photo-editing programs refer to these two colors as the foreground color and background color, respectively.) Some tools apply the Paint color; others apply the Paper color.

The Paint and Paper swatches at the bottom of the Color Palette indicate the currently selected colors. To choose different colors, use the following techniques:

✔ To select the paint color, click a color swatch in the Color Palette. Click the arrows at the bottom of the palette to display additional colors.

✔ To set the paper color, right-click a swatch in the Color Palette.

✔ If you don't like any color in the Color Palette, double-click the Paint or Paper swatch, labeled in Figure 20-8. You then see the color mixing page of the Notebook, as shown in the figure. This same page appears if you click the Color icon that appears on the Notebook page when you select certain tools.

You can work in two color modes. HSB mixes colors by using three values: hue, saturation (intensity), and brightness. RGB creates colors by mixing red, green, and blue light. Click the radio button for the model you want to use.

Because color monitors and most color inkjets work in the RGB color space (a fancy name for color mode), you may get better color matching by choosing colors in that mode. Drag the red, green, and blue color selectors, labeled in Figure 20-8, to adjust the amount of red, green, and blue light in the color. Keep in mind that full intensity red, green, and blue makes white, just as if you shined red, blue, and green flashlights at the same spot on a wall. If the RGB color grid is too difficult — the one in Photo House isn't terribly easy to use — just stick with the HSB color mode. You then set colors as described in the section "Editing text and graphics," earlier in this chapter.

 ✔ Click the Eyedropper tool and then click a color in your picture to "lift" that color and use it as the Paint color. Right-click to set the Paper color.

Green selector

Red selector Blue selector

Figure 20-8:
Double-click
the Paint or
Paper
swatch to
mix a
custom
color.

Paper swatch

Paint swatch

Plying the paint tools

Photo House provides several tools that enable you to paint your image with color:

✔ Drag with the Brush tool to apply the Paint color as if you were painting with a traditional paintbrush.

✔ Drag with the Spray tool to create a stroke that resembles what you would create with a can of spray paint.

✔ Drag with the Eraser tool to paint in the Paper color.

✔ When you work with the Brush, Spray, and Eraser tool, you can adjust the tool nib (tip) to vary the shape, size, and softness of your stroke. Click the Presets icon in the Notebook to choose from a variety of ready-made nibs; click Custom to design your own.

✔ Ctrl+drag with the Brush, Spray, or Eraser tool to paint a perfectly horizontal or vertical line.

✔ Click with the Flood Fill tool to fill an area of contiguous color with the Paint color. For example, if you clicked the cow's nose in Figure 20-8, the nose would be filled, but the area outside the nose would not. Click the Custom icon in the Notebook to control the range of colors affected by the tool.

Painting one image onto another

Two tools, the Clone tool and the Image Sprayer tool, enable you to "paint" a portion of one image onto another image. Here's how they work:

✔ With the Clone tool, you can copy a portion of one image and paint it onto another area of the same image or a different image. Select the Clone tool and then click the spot you want to copy. A cross-hair cursor appears to show you the area you clicked. Then drag to reproduce the area under the cross-hair cursor. As with the regular painting tools, you can click the Custom icon in the Notebook to create a custom Clone tool nib or click the Presets icon to choose a ready-made nib.

The Clone tool is most useful for covering up blemishes in the image. For example, if your lovely picture of the sunset is flawed by an ugly TV tower in the background, you can clone some sky pixels over the tower to hide it.

✔ Use the Image Sprayer to paint images found on the Print Office CD onto your photo. If you click with the tool, you spray a single image; if you drag, you spray multiple copies of the image.

Select the Image Sprayer tool and then click the Custom icon in the Notebook (you must have the Print Office CD in your CD drive). Select the image you want to replicate from the drop-down list and then use the other options to adjust the transparency and spacing of the images.

Setting the image size and properties

One of the most important things you can do to ensure the quality of your Photo House images is to understand the Image Properties options. These options, shown in Figure 20-9, appear in the Notebook when you choose Image➪Image Properties or create a new image from scratch. You use the options to control the size, resolution, and color mode of your image. The next few sections guide you through these dicey decisions.

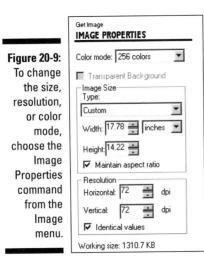

Figure 20-9:
To change
the size,
resolution,
or color
mode,
choose the
Image
Properties
command
from the
Image
menu.

Color mode and transparency

Choose a color mode to set the total number of colors that your image can contain. For true photographic color, you want 16 million colors. If you choose fewer colors, you reduce the image quality because you have fewer distinct shades available to recreate the image. However, the more colors, the larger the size of the image file, which is why most people preparing images for use on the Internet strip their images back to 256 colors, at most. If you're printing your image using a professional, four-color printing process, select the CMYK mode unless the printer's rep tells you otherwise.

The Transparent Background check box becomes available when you send an image to Photo House from inside Print Office (by double-clicking the image in Photo House). If you check the option, any areas that are colored with the Paint color appear transparent in Print Office. In other words, any unfilled background areas or areas that you erase with the Eraser tool become invisible so that any underlying objects show through the image. To see the results in Print Office, choose File⇨Update in Corel Print Office.

Image size

Adjust the Width and Height values to change the physical dimensions of your image. Check the Maintain Aspect Ratio check box to retain the image's original proportions.

The preset size options in the Type drop-down list are designed to mesh with printed materials you create with Corel Print Office. Don't worry about these options; choose the Custom option and set your own image dimensions.

You can select your unit of measure from the drop-down list next to the Width option box. If you are preparing an image for print, select inches or millimeters. For screen images, select pixels. (Pixels, remember, are those tiny squares of color that make up bitmap images.) Monitors display images using pixels, too, devoting one screen pixel to each image pixel. So you simply set the image size according to how much of your screen you want the image to consume. For example, if your monitor is set up to display 640 pixels by 480 pixels, a 640 x 480-pixel image fills the entire screen. You can check the current monitor setting in Windows by right-clicking the Windows desktop, choosing Properties from the resulting menu, and then clicking the Settings tab in the Display Properties dialog box.

When you enlarge an existing image, Photo House adds pixels — those tiny blocks of color that make up bitmap images — to fill in the increased image area. This process, called *upsampling,* usually results in a loss of image detail. So for best results, don't enlarge your image by more than about 25 percent. If you reduce the image size, Photo House *downsamples* the image — throws away pixels. Downsampling usually isn't as destructive as upsampling, but you may notice some image degradation if you downsample by a large degree. If you're setting the image size for a new image that you're creating from scratch, don't worry about this issue.

Resolution

Resolution refers to the number of pixels in the image. Typically, resolution is measured in pixels per linear inch, or *ppi.* The more pixels you have, the better your image quality. But more pixels also means bigger file sizes, so you sometimes need to make a tradeoff between file size and resolution.

For images that you want to print on a color inkjet or laser printer, a resolution in the 200 to 300 ppi range is usually best, but check your printer manual just to be sure. For Web images or images that you will display on-screen as part of a multimedia presentation, a resolution in the 72 to 96 ppi is appropriate. (If you size your image using pixels, as outlined in the preceding section, however, you don't need to pay attention to the resolution at all.)

To change the resolution of an image, use the Horizontal and Vertical resolution option boxes. Be sure to check the Identical Values box — you definitely want to use the same value for both the Horizontal and Vertical resolution. Remember that the lower the resolution, the lower the image quality.

By the same token, you can't raise the resolution of an existing image without lowering image quality. Photo House adds pixels to create your desired resolution, but the results are far from satisfactory. Try it for yourself to see what happens: Open an image, raise the resolution, and watch the image blur before your very eyes. Press Ctrl+Z to undo the change.

More powerful image-editing programs enable you to safely raise resolution by reducing the Width and Height values. Photo House doesn't. When you reduce the Width and Height values, Photo House simply throws away pixels as needed to maintain the current resolution. If you really need a higher resolution for your image, make nice with a pal who uses a more sophisticated image editor.

Saving and Printing

After you create a Print Office or Photo House masterpiece, you can print or save it as follows:

- ✔ Choose File➪Print, press Ctrl+P, or click the Print toolbar button to send your work to the printer. In Photo House, you get the standard Print dialog box. In Print Office, printing options appear in the Notebook. Click the Help icon in the Notebook if you don't understand the available options.

- ✔ Choose File➪Save, press Ctrl+S, or click the Save toolbar button to save your work. In Print Office, this command saves your work in the default Print Office file format, which has the file extension CPO. In Photo House, you can select from a variety of file formats from the Save as Type menu.

- ✔ To save another copy of the image, using a different name, location, or file type, choose File➪Save As. In Print Office, this command enables you to save your work in file formats other than the native format.

- ✔ For images or graphics that you want to use on the Web or e-mail, select the JPEG Bitmap or CompuServe Bitmat format (the latter is available only for images that have 256 colors or fewer). If you want to import your image into another program, the TIFF Bitmap option is a good choice. For more about the saving options associated with these and other file formats, check the Print Office and Photo House Help systems.

Chapter 21

Using Everything Together

In This Chapter

▶ Getting your programs to pass the ball

▶ Using different programs to create one document

▶ Making copies that update automatically when the original data changes

▶ Editing copied data when you don't have access to the original file

▶ Making friends with OLE

▶ Dragging and dropping stuff from one program to another

▶ Copying and moving data between programs with the Cut, Copy, and Paste commands

*I*magine coaching a team of basketball players who refused to play if they weren't the one with the ball. The minute one player got the ball, all the other players stomped off the court and sat on the bench.

Well, in the old days of computing, programs worked just like that. If one program was active, all the others rushed to the sidelines. But today, programs know how to play together as a team. And unlike some NBA superstars who shall remain nameless, the players in the WordPerfect Office 2000 suite don't charge into the stands to beat up fans, cover themselves with tattoos, or otherwise behave like unruly children.

This team-computing philosophy means that you can call on the collective strengths of all the programs in WordPerfect Office 2000 to create a single document. Suppose that you want to create a report that contains text and a data chart. You open a WordPerfect document and create your text. You then tell WordPerfect that you want to create a chart, and it passes the digital basketball to Quattro Pro, which is, after all, the team member best equipped for creating charts. After you build your chart, Quattro Pro passes the ball — and your chart — back to WordPerfect.

Although you can get good results by working with each member of the WordPerfect team individually, you can accomplish a whole lot more in less time if you learn the art of tag-team document creation. At the risk of carrying the sports analogy one step too far, this chapter gives you the game plan for doing just that.

Saving Time and Effort with OLE

The key to getting your programs to work together is Object Linking and Embedding, which is called OLE (pronounced *olé*). OLE isn't a command or a tool; it's a background technology built into many Windows programs. OLE enables you to do several things:

- ✔ Create data in one document, put a copy of that data into another document, and then link the copy to the original so that the copy is automatically updated any time you make changes to the original. For example, you can create a chart in Quattro Pro and then copy it into a WordPerfect document. When you update the chart in Quattro Pro, it's automatically updated in the WordPerfect document. The upcoming sections "Making Linked Copies That Update Automatically" and "Linking Copies without Automatic Updating" tell all.

- ✔ After copying data from one program into another program, you can double-click the data to edit it using the tools from the original program. This magical editing process is discussed in the section "Editing without Leaving Home," later in this chapter.

- ✔ You can use different programs to create the different elements of your document without leaving the confines of your primary program. Suppose that you're working in WordPerfect and decide that you want to create a simple drawing to illustrate your point. You can launch Presentations, create your drawing, and place it into WordPerfect — all without ever venturing outside WordPerfect. For the inside scoop, see the section "Embedding Objects on the Fly," later in this chapter.

OLE can be a great tool for sharing data between programs. But not all programs support OLE or all the OLE features discussed in this chapter. If a particular feature or command doesn't seem to be working — or even available in the program you're using — chances are that the program doesn't offer OLE support. Even without OLE, however, you can usually copy data between documents using the Cut, Copy, and Paste commands, as I discuss near the end of this chapter in the section "Sharing Data without OLE."

Deciding Whether to Link, Embed, or Copy and Paste

You can create two kinds of objects with OLE: *linked* or *embedded.* When you create a linked object, Windows establishes a link between the *source* program (the program you use to create the object) and the *destination* program (the program where you place the object). Chipheads sometimes refer to the source and destination programs as the *OLE server* and *OLE client,* respectively.

What's all this talk about OLE objects?

The term *OLE object* refers to any data — whether it's text or a graphic — that you copy or create in one program and place into another using OLE. The computer people found it tiring to keep using the phrase "text or graphics that you copy or create in one program and place into another using OLE," so they came up with a new term. Either that, or they just wanted to make you feel bad because they knew a word that you didn't.

With linking, the object is automatically updated in the destination document any time you make changes to it in the source document. Linking can be a great way to make sure that all your documents contain the same version of some text or graphic that changes frequently. If you decide that you don't want the object to be updated automatically, you can change the link settings so that you can update the object manually or sever the link altogether.

The drawback to linking is that if you want to share your document with other people, you need to give them a copy of the source documents for any linked objects along with the destination document. Plus, if the object was created in a program that they don't have installed on their computers, they may not be able to view or edit the object.

With embedding, all the information you need to display and edit the object is placed — embedded — in the destination document. If you embed a Quattro Pro chart in a WordPerfect document, for example, you can edit the Quattro Pro chart from within WordPerfect even if you no longer have access to the original Quattro Pro file. It's way cool, but embedding also increases the size of the document file. And when you edit the original object in the source program, the changes aren't automatically made to the object in the destination program as they are with linking.

If all you want to do is copy or move some data from one document to another and you don't want or need to take advantage of the OLE features I just described, you can simply use the Cut, Copy, and Paste commands, explained in the section "Sharing Data without OLE." Cutting, copying, and pasting between documents is the same as cutting, copying, and pasting within the same document.

Making Linked Copies That Update Automatically

You create a chart in Quattro Pro to illustrate your company's annual sales figures. You copy the chart into a WordPerfect document, where you're writing an executive summary to justify the dismal sales performance to the board of directors. You also copy the chart into a second WordPerfect document, in which you're creating the company's annual report, and then into a third document, in which you're creating a letter to convince stockholders that things aren't as bad as they appear.

Just when you get the chart copied into all three documents, your boss says that management wants to make a few minor changes to the sales figures. You could leap up, grab the boss by the collar, and snarl, "Not in this lifetime, pal!" Or you could smile enthusiastically and say, "Sure, no problem at all," secure in the knowledge that you can easily update all the copies at the same time through the wonder of OLE linking.

Of course, if you want to find yourself in this happy place, you have to create your copies using OLE linking in the first place. The following steps show you how to use OLE linking to copy a Quattro Pro chart into a WordPerfect document and have that chart update automatically when you make changes to the data in Quattro Pro. The process is the same no matter what programs you're using, as long as those programs support OLE — some programs don't.

You can't link a Presentations slide show file or a graphic or chart in a slide show file to another program. But you can link a Presentations drawing file as well as organizational charts and data charts that you create in a drawing file.

The *source* document contains the data you want to copy. The *destination* document is the one that receives the copy.

1. **Make sure that the source document has been saved to disk.**

   You can't link existing data from a document that hasn't been saved to disk.

2. **Select the data you want to copy and choose Edit⇨Copy.**

   If you don't know how to select stuff, look in this book's index for information related to the specific program that contains the data you're copying.

3. **Switch to the document where you want to place the copy.**

4. **Click the spot where you want to put the copy.**

5. **Choose Edit⇨Paste Special.**

   The dialog box shown in Figure 21-1 appears.

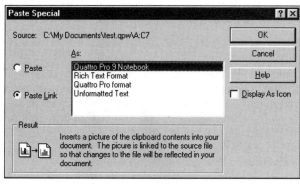

Figure 21-1:
If you want
the copy to
be updated
every time
you make
changes to
the original,
select the
Paste Link
option.

6. Select the Paste Link radio button.

If the button is dimmed, either the source or destination program doesn't support linking, or you may have forgotten to save the source document as I begged you to do in Step 1. You can click the Paste button to create an embedded object, as explained in "Creating an Embedded Copy," later in this chapter, or perform a simple copy and paste, as explained in "Sharing Data without OLE," near the end of this chapter.

Sometimes, you get several file format choices in the As list box. The computer automatically selects the best format for you, so you don't need to fool with this option unless you experience problems.

7. Click OK.

The copy appears in your destination document.

Congratulations — you just created a linked OLE object. If you have both the source and destination document open and you edit the OLE object in the source document, the destination document is updated automatically *after you resave the source document.* If the destination document isn't open when you edit and save the source document, you're alerted that the OLE object has changed the next time you open the destination document. You then have the option of updating the OLE object or leaving it as is.

In Quattro Pro, the Paste Special command works differently than described here when you copy and paste data from one Quattro Pro document into another. For details, see Chapter 13.

Linking Copies without Automatic Updating

If you don't want your linked copies to be updated automatically when you change the original, you can change the link so that you can update the copy manually when needed. Here's how to do it in WordPerfect, Presentations, and Quattro Pro. (In other programs, you may use slightly different procedures; check the program's Help file for details.)

1. **Open the document that contains the copy.**

   Make sure that no text or graphics are selected.

2. **Choose Edit⇨Links in Presentations and WordPerfect; choose Edit⇨OLE Links in Quattro Pro.**

   The Links dialog box shown in Figure 21-2 appears. Each linked object in the document is listed in the dialog box.

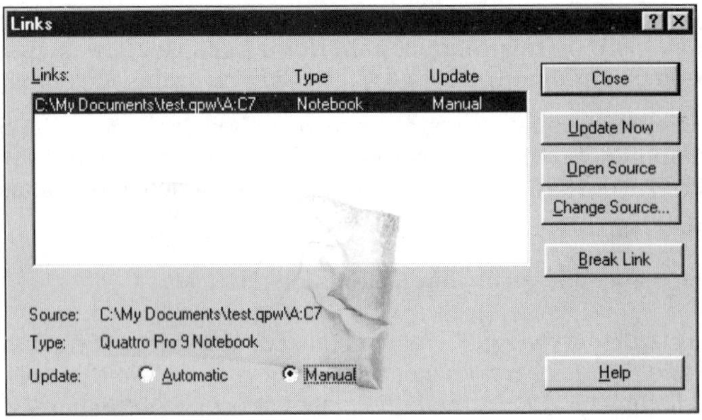

Figure 21-2:
The Links dialog box lets you automatically or manually update linked copies.

Links:	Type	Update	
C:\My Documents\test.qpw\A:C7	Notebook	Manual	

Close
Update Now
Open Source
Change Source...
Break Link

Source: C:\My Documents\test.qpw\A:C7
Type: Quattro Pro 9 Notebook
Update: ○ Automatic ● Manual

Help

3. **In the dialog box, click the linked object whose link you want to change.**

4. **Click the Manual radio button.**

5. **Click the Close button or press Enter.**

If you later change the original and decide that you want to update the copy to reflect the changes, first save the document that contains the original. Then, in the document that contains the copy, open the Links dialog box and click the Update Now button. (If the copy doesn't update, try closing and then reopening the document that contains the copy. Then try updating the link.)

The Links dialog box also offers some other options you may find useful:

✔ Click the Open Source button to open the source document. You may want to do this to check out the source data to see what changes were made since you last updated the copy.

✔ Click Change Source to link the copy to a different source document.

✔ Break Link severs any and all ties between the copy and the source document.

Creating an Embedded Copy

When you *embed* an object through OLE, you copy all the data the computer needs to display and edit the object into the destination document. Say that you create a drawing in Presentations and embed it into a WordPerfect document on your desktop computer. You then save the document to a floppy disk so that you can work on it on your laptop computer during your business trip to Tasmania. (Hey, as long as you're traveling, you may as well travel somewhere exotic.)

Anyway, assume that you forget to bring along a copy of the original Presentations file. As long as you have Presentations installed on your laptop, you can still edit that chart on the road. You double-click the graphic, and all the Presentations commands and tools appear inside the WordPerfect window.

With that ridiculous build-up, you probably expect embedding to be a very mysterious and complicated process. Sorry to disappoint you. To embed an object, just follow Steps 2 through 7 in the section "Making Linked Copies That Update Automatically," but select the Paste radio button rather than Paste Link in Step 6.

If you embed a spreadsheet from Quattro Pro, be sure to select the Quattro Pro Notebook item in the As list box inside the Paste Special dialog box. For some reason, the default setting is to paste the spreadsheet in the Rich Text Format, which doesn't keep your formulas and Quattro Pro formatting intact.

With embedding, the copy doesn't get updated if you change the original. Also, files that contain lots of embedded objects can take up lots of disk space.

Embedding Objects on the Fly

The preceding section explains how to embed an existing object into your document. But you can also create embedded objects as you work on a document. You can open up a second program, create the object, and embed it without leaving the comfy confines of your first document window. The following steps show you how to create an embedded Presentations object when you're working in WordPerfect. The steps are similar for other programs.

1. **Make sure that nothing is selected in your document.**

2. **Choose Insert⇨Object.**

   The dialog box shown in Figure 21-3 appears.

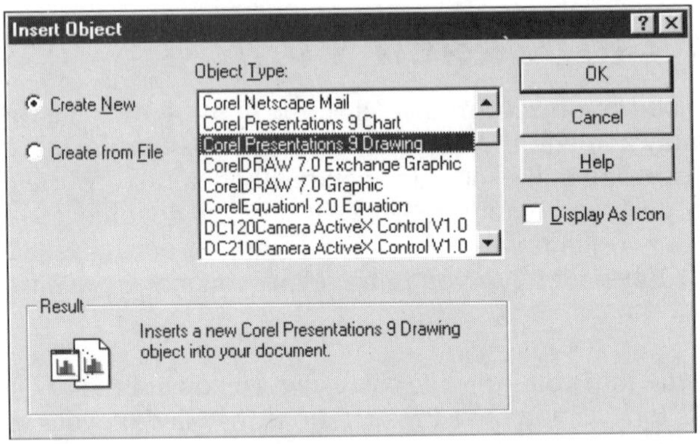

Figure 21-3:
You can create an embedded object without leaving the destination document.

3. **Select the Create New button.**

4. **Select the type of object you want to create from the Object Type list box.**

   To create a Presentations drawing, for example, click Corel Presentations 9 Drawing.

5. **Click OK or press Enter.**

   After some grinding noises from your computer, the WordPerfect menu and tools are transformed into the Presentations menu and tools, and a drawing window appears right on your WordPerfect page, as shown in Figure 21-4.

6. **Create your object.**

7. **Click outside the object boundaries.**

   Or, in some programs, you can click a Return to Document button on the toolbar, labeled in Figure 21-4. Your drawing is embedded in WordPerfect and appears selected in the WordPerfect window. Now, anytime you want to edit the graphic, just double-click it to redisplay the Presentations drawing tools.

Return to document

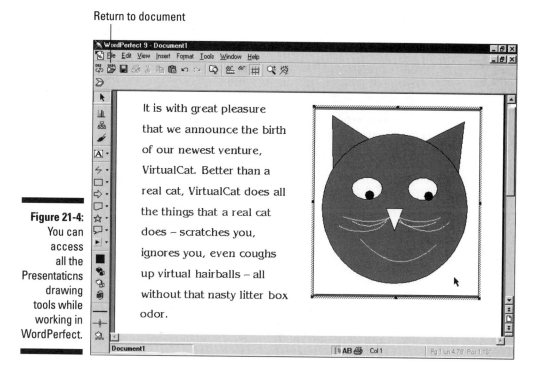

WordPerfect offers some special commands that give you another way to create an embedded Presentations drawing or data chart. To create a drawing in Presentations, choose Insert⇨Graphics⇨Draw Picture. If you want to create an embedded Presentations data chart, choose Insert⇨Chart. Choosing these commands lets you bypass the Insert Object dialog box. Everything else works the same as in the preceding steps.

Dragging and Dropping to Embed

Many programs enable you to drag and drop data from one program to another. You can use drag and drop to create an embedded copy or to move data from one document and embed it in another. Here's the 1-2-3:

1. **Open both the source document and the destination document.**

2. **Select the data you want to copy or move.**

3. **Drag or Ctrl+drag the data from the source document to the destination document's button on the Windows taskbar.**

Dragging deletes the data from the source document and embeds it in the destination document. Press Ctrl as you drag to copy the data and embed it in the destination document.

When you drag the object to the taskbar, don't release the mouse button — just pause for a second until the destination program window appears.

If you're dragging and dropping a selection in Quattro Pro, place your cursor on the border of your selection. When you see the four-headed arrow, press the mouse button and drag.

4. **Drag the object from the taskbar into place inside the destination program window and release the mouse button.**

If you have your screen arranged so that both program windows are visible, you can simply drag and drop from one window to the other instead of working via the Windows taskbar.

Embedding or Linking a Document

If you want to embed or link an entire file into your document, first make sure that nothing is selected in the document. Then select the Object command from the Insert menu to display the Insert Object dialog box and select the Create from File option. Enter the name of the file you want to copy in the File option box. (You must specify the entire pathname — that is, the location of the file on disk as well as the filename.)

If you want to copy the file as a linked object, select the Link option box. If you want to copy the file as an embedded object, deselect the Link button. Click OK to make the copy.

Editing without Leaving Home

One of the advantages of OLE linking and embedding is that you can edit an OLE object by simply double-clicking it. The process varies depending on whether you double-click an embedded or linked object:

✔ If you double-click a linked object, the source document launches, and your object appears in its own window, ready for editing. Make your changes and then save them in the source program. Then choose File⇨Exit to close the source program and return to the destination document or just click outside the source document window to return to the destination document and keep the source program open.

✔ If you double-click an embedded object, the menus and tools of the source program become available in the current window. Make your changes and then click outside the object boundaries.

Sharing Data without OLE

You don't *have* to use OLE to share data between programs. You can also copy and move data using the Cut, Copy, and Paste commands. If you go this route, you lose some of the advantages of OLE: The copy doesn't get updated when the original changes, and, depending upon the programs you're using, you may not be able to double-click the copy to edit it in the source program. Then again, you don't have to tax your brain with all that OLE linking and embedding rigmarole, either.

At any rate, the following steps show you how to copy data between any two programs or documents.

1. **Open the document that contains the data you want to copy.**

2. **Select the data you want to copy.**

3. **Press Ctrl+C or click the Copy button on the toolbar.**

    If you're a menu-lover, choose Edit⇨Copy instead.

4. **Open the document where you want to place the copy.**

5. **Click the spot where you want to insert the copy.**

6. **Press Ctrl+V or click the Paste toolbar button.**

    Or choose Edit⇨Paste instead.

You can paste the same copy repeatedly if you want. Just keep choosing the Paste command. The copy is available to be pasted until the next time you choose the Copy or Cut command.

You can use these same steps to move data between programs. Just choose Edit⇨Cut, press Ctrl+X, or click the Cut button on the toolbar in Step 3 instead of using the Copy command.

You can copy and move data *between documents in the same program* by dragging the data from the source document to the Application Bar button for the destination document. Don't let up on the mouse button when you reach the Application Bar — wait until the destination document appears on-screen and then drag the data into place and release the mouse button. Drag to move the data; Ctrl+drag to copy it.

Part V
The Part of Tens

In this part . . .

Welcome to the short-attention-span part of the book. The next three chapters contain tidbits of information that you can digest in minutes — seconds, really, in some cases. You discover ten cool tricks to amaze and astound your friends, ten shortcuts you can use to get things done with less effort, and ten tips to trim some time off your workday. If you need a quick fix of information or inspiration, look here first.

Chapter 22

Ten Cool Tricks to Try on a Slow Day

It's 4:00 on a Friday afternoon, the boss is gone, and you're sitting around trying to kill time until you can shut the door on another long work week. You could fire up one of those games that comes with Windows, but frankly, you're a little tired of losing to a machine.

That's the time to check out the ten features described in this chapter. Tucked inside the menus and toolbars of various programs in the WordPerfect Office 2000 Suite are some pretty nifty tools that I haven't covered elsewhere because they're not the sort of features most people need on a regular basis. They are, however, lots of fun to play with — heck, they may even prove useful now and again.

So that everyone can join in this chapter's reindeer games, I limited coverage to features available in the Standard Edition of the WordPerfect Office 2000 suite.

Start Off with a Drop Cap

Many magazines, newsletters, and other publications begin articles with a *drop cap.* A drop cap is a letter that's enlarged and dropped down into surrounding lines of text, as shown in Figure 22-1.

WordPerfect makes creating a drop cap easy. Just click anywhere inside the paragraph you want to start with a drop cap and choose Format⇨Paragraph⇨ Drop Cap or press Ctrl+Shift+C. WordPerfect turns the first letter in the paragraph into a drop cap. Click to the left of the drop cap to display Property Bar buttons that enable you to change the drop cap's style, font, and position, as shown in the figure. Click the first three buttons to display drop-down menus of formatting options; the second three buttons open formatting dialog boxes.

Thanks to the new RealTime Preview feature, you can pause your cursor over options located on the drop-down menus to preview the effect on your drop cap in the document window. See Chapter 4 for more information about RealTime Preview.

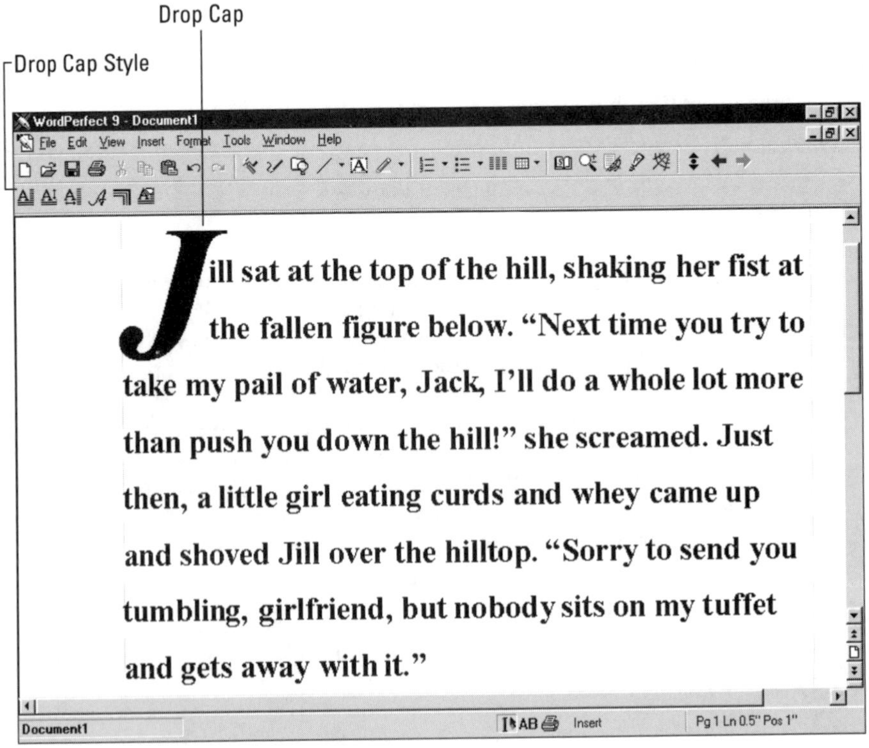

Drop Cap

┌Drop Cap Style

Figure 22-1:
A drop cap
is a great
device to
call
attention to
the start of
an article.

> **WordPerfect 9 - Document1**
> File Edit View Insert Format Tools Window Help
>
> **J**ill sat at the top of the hill, shaking her fist at the fallen figure below. "Next time you try to take my pail of water, Jack, I'll do a whole lot more than push you down the hill!" she screamed. Just then, a little girl eating curds and whey came up and shoved Jill over the hilltop. "Sorry to send you tumbling, girlfriend, but nobody sits on my tuffet and gets away with it."
>
> Document1   AB   Insert   Pg 1 Ln 0.5" Pos 1"

You may need to adjust the spacing between the drop cap and the surrounding text in some cases. For best results, click between the drop cap and the next letter and then choose Format⇔Typesetting⇔Manual Kerning. In the resulting dialog box, adjust the Add/Remove Space value as necessary.

To remove the drop cap formatting, click to the left of the drop cap, click the Drop Cap Style button, labeled in Figure 22-1, and select the No Cap option from the drop-down list (the one with the X through the drop cap icon).

Twist and Stretch Your Words

TextArt lets you turn ordinary words into graphic masterpieces, as shown in Figure 22-2. You can access TextArt from inside WordPerfect, Quattro Pro, or Presentations. Try it out:

1. **Click the spot where you want to add a TextArt object.**

   Or select the word that you want to manipulate.

2. **Choose Insert⇔Graphics⇔TextArt.**

   A TextArt window appears, as shown in Figure 22-2. The word you selected appears in a TextArt box, or, if you didn't select a word, the word *Text* appears in the box. The TextArt dialog box also opens.

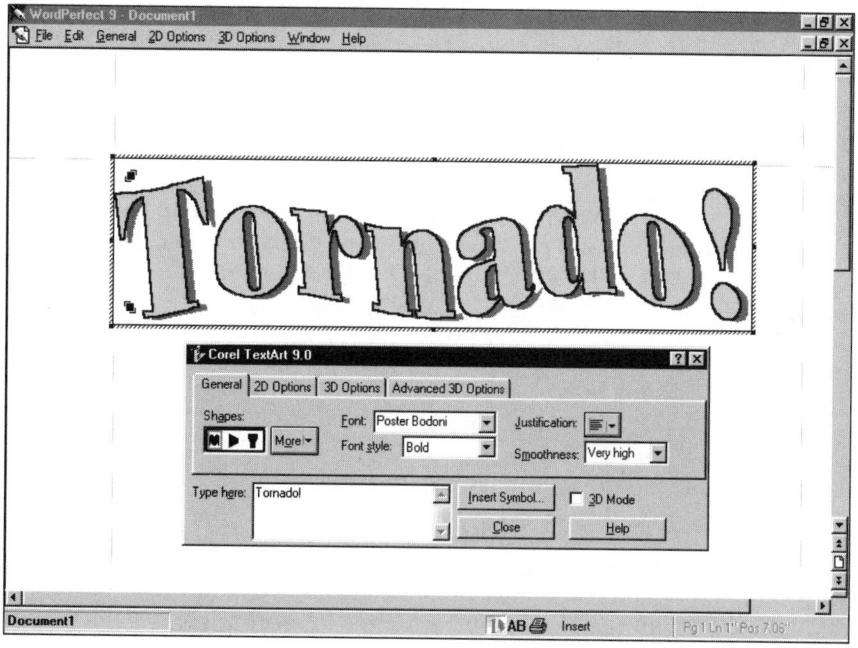

Figure 22-2:
You can turn plain text into a masterpiece by using TextArt.

3. **Play with your text.**

The panels in the TextArt dialog box are full of options that let you stretch, shape, color, outline, and add other cool effects to your text. Most of the effects are self-explanatory, but a few require some instrution:

- If you want to edit your text, do so in the Type Here box.

- To change the shape of your text, click one of the icons in the Shapes option box. Click the More button to display more shapes.

- Unless you're trying to create text with jagged edges, select the Very High setting from the Smoothness drop-down list.

- Click the Rotation button on the 2D Options tab to display four little handles around your text. Drag a handle to rotate the text. Or double-click the Rotation button and enter a specific angle of rotation in the resulting dialog box.

- You can create 3-D text art effects by selecting the 3D Mode check box at the bottom of the TextArt dialog box. The options on the 3D Options and Advanced 3D Options panels then become available to you. Be aware, though, that your 3D text object increases the size of your document file.

4. **Click the Close button in the TextArt dialog box.**

Your TextArt object is inserted into your document. To edit it, double-click the image. You can move, copy, and resize the TextArt object as you can any graphic (see Chapters 8 and 17 for some tips). Click the object and press Delete to wipe it off your page.

Make Your Letters Sing

If your computer is equipped with a sound card and microphone, you can record your voice as a sound clip and insert the clip into your WordPerfect documents. Anyone viewing the document on a computer that has a sound card can click the clip to hear it. Here's how to record your favorite song and insert it into a WordPerfect document:

1. **In your document, choose Insert⇨Sound to display the Sound Clips dialog box.**

2. **Click Record.**

The Windows Sound Recorder launches.

3. **Record your song.**

The Sound Recorder controls work pretty much like those on a regular tape recorder; click the red Record button to start your recording and click the black Stop button to stop recording. Use the Rewind and Play buttons to preview your clip.

4. Choose File➪Save in the Sound Recorder and save the clip to disk.

Give your sound a name and click Save. Then close the Sound Recorder window.

5. Click the Insert button in the Sound Clips dialog box.

The dialog box shown in Figure 22-3 appears.

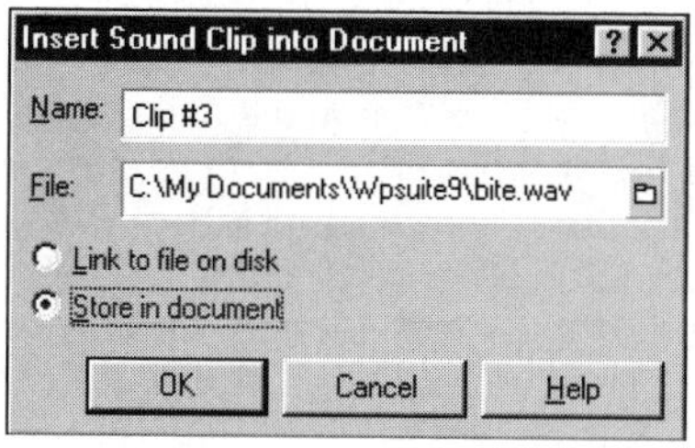

Figure 22-3:
You put
sound in
your letters
through this
dialog box.

> **Insert Sound Clip into Document**
>
> Name: Clip #3
>
> File: C:\My Documents\Wpsuite9\bite.wav
>
> ○ Link to file on disk
> ● Store in document
>
> OK   Cancel   Help

6. Select the sound file you want to insert.

Click the file icon at the end of the File option box to display the Select Sound dialog box, which operates just like a standard Open File dialog box (see Chapter 4 if you need help). Select the file you want to use and click Select.

Alternatively, you can just enter the name of the sound clip in the File option box. But you have to enter the complete pathname (directory and complete file location information).

7. Choose a storage option.

Select the Store in Document radio button if you're going to send the document to someone else. If you choose the Link to File on Disk option, the clip can be played on your computer only (or to another computer that contains the same sound file, in the same location as your computer).

8. Click OK.

The dialog box closes and your sound is inserted into your document.

To play the sound clip, just click the speaker icon in the left margin of the document. Or choose Insert➪Sound and click the Play button in the Sound Clips dialog box.

If you insert two sound clips right next to each other, you see a little balloon with quotation marks in the margin instead of a speaker icon. Click the balloon to display the speaker icons for each sound clip and then click the one you want to play.

In addition to sending your friends and coworkers a clip of yourself singing *Don't Cry for Me, Argentina,* you can insert digital (WAV) and MIDI sound files into your document. Follow the preceding steps, but skip Steps 2 through 4.

Save by Refinancing a Loan

Trying to decide whether you should refinance that mortgage? Don't tax your brain; tax Quattro Pro instead. Choose Tools⇨Numeric Tools⇨Analysis to open the Analysis Experts dialog box. Choose the Mortgage Refinancing item from the Analysis Tool list box and click Next. In the Output Cells option box, enter the cell address of the upper-left corner of the block of cells where you want the results to appear in your spreadsheet. Enter your current remaining mortgage term, balance, and rate. Then enter the proposed new rate and any financing fees and click the Finish button. Quattro Pro creates a spreadsheet that spells out your potential savings or loss if you refinance the loan.

Figure Out How Many Days Until . . .

Counting the days till your next day off? Instead of using your calendar — which could look a little obvious to anyone walking by — use Quattro Pro to make the calculation for you. To figure out the number of days between the current date and another day, enter this formula into a cell in a Quattro Pro spreadsheet:

@CDAYS(@TODAY,@DATE(*year,month,day*),1)

When you enter the formula, replace *year, month,* and *day* with the date that you're looking forward to. For example, to find out how many shopping days until Christmas 1999, enter 99,12,25.

The 1 at the end of the formula, in case you care, tells Quattro Pro to count days using the actual number of days in a year rather than using some other arbitrary calendar in its databank. For more about this intriguing distinction, look in the Quattro Pro Help system index under the topic of calendar conventions.

Play with Photo Effects in Presentations

Chapter 17 briefly touches on the subject of adding scanned photos and other digital images to your Presentations slides and drawings. Although you shouldn't mistake Presentations for a full-fledged image editor, you can do some basic image editing and even apply a few special effects.

After inserting an image into your drawing or slide show, double-click the image to open the Bitmap Editor. Choose Tools⇨Special Effects to display the Special Effects dialog box, shown in Figure 22-4. The preview in the upper-right corner of the dialog box shows the entire image. The previews at the bottom of the dialog box give you before and after views of the portion of the image that's surrounded by the selection box in the full image preview. Drag the box to move the preview.

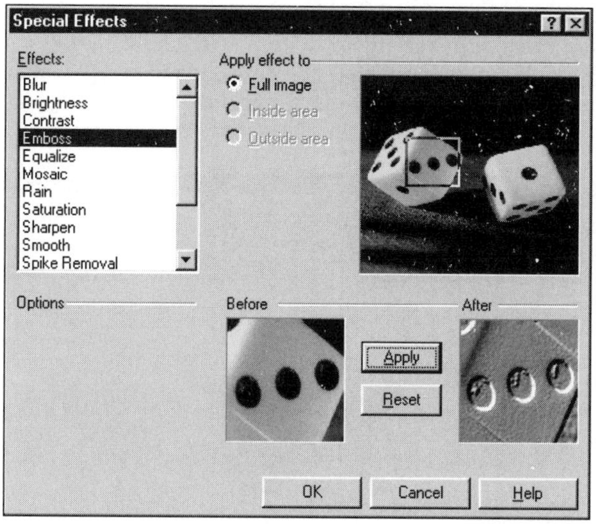

Figure 22-4:
Presentations offers a few photographic special effects.

To see what an effect looks like, click it in the Effects list box. Then click the Apply button. If you like the result, click OK to apply the effect to the image and return to the Bitmap Editor. To undo the effect, click Reset. When you finish applying effects, click OK to return to the Bitmap Window. Then choose File⇨Close Bitmap Editor to save your edits and return to your drawing.

A few more effects are possible via the Tools⇨Image Tools command, which you choose in the regular Presentations window rather than in the Bitmap Editor. Click your photo once to display selection handles around the image and then experiment with the different effects on the Image Tools submenu. Invert Colors, which creates a negative of your image, is especially entertaining.

Of course, if you have the Voice-Powered Edition of WordPerfect Office 2000, Corel Photo House offers a slew of other special photographic effects to investigate. Check out the Effects menu to see what havoc you can wreak on your pictures (and see Chapter 20 for more information on Photo House).

Send an Object into the Third Dimension

The Presentations Quick3-D command adds instant 3-D depth to a drawing or text object. Select any object in Presentations and then choose Tools⇨ Quick3-D. Up pops the Quick3-D dialog box, where you can add depth to an object, change the perspective, and rotate the object around the X, Y, and Z axes. Figure 22-5 shows a star before (top) and after (lower-left) I applied 3-D effects.

I created the lower-right image by applying the Tools⇨QuickWarp command to the original star. Like the Quick3-D command, the QuickWarp command gives you some interesting ways to distort and reshape an object.

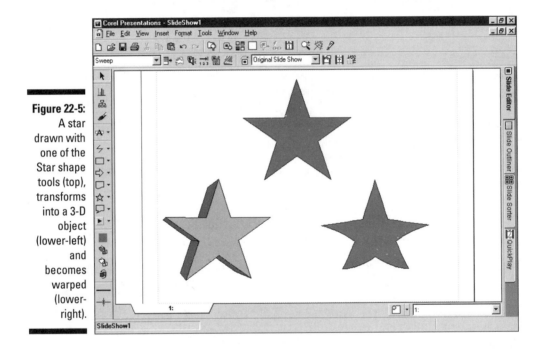

Figure 22-5: A star drawn with one of the Star shape tools (top), transforms into a 3-D object (lower-left) and becomes warped (lower-right).

Wrap Text around a Circle

With the Contour Text command in Presentations, you can adhere text to a circle, curved line, or any other simple shape. In graphics circles, this process is known as *fitting text to a path*. Here's how it's done:

1. **Create shape and text.**

You must create the text with the Text Line or Text Area tool. You can't perform this trick with text in a prefab text box. As for the shape, plain old circles, ovals, and rectangles work best.

2. **Click the shape to select it.**

3. **Shift+click the text block to select the text, too.**

4. **Choose Tools⇨Contour Text.**

   The Contour Text dialog box appears. Here you can choose the position of the text relative to the shape. You can also specify whether you want to see the shape itself after you contour the text. Turn on the Display Text Only check box to hide the shape. Deselect the check box to see both shape and text.

5. **Click OK.**

   Presentations welds the text to the shape. If you don't like the results, press Ctrl+Z, choose the Contour Text command again, and try different settings.

To separate the shape and the text, right-click the shape and choose Separate Objects from the QuickMenu.

If the text clings too closely to the shape, press Ctrl+Z to undo the contouring or right-click the graphic and separate the text and shape. Then give the shape a thick border in the color of your background, as explained in Chapter 17. The result is an invisible border that serves as a separator between the shape and the text. If you really want your circle to have a visible border, draw a second circle, slightly smaller than the first, and drag it on top of the first circle. Then apply the border to the top circle.

You can't choose the Contour Text command when a piece of clip art or bitmap image is selected. The option is also not available for some of the special shapes drawn by the shape drawing tools. But you can make it _look_ as though the text is fit to these restricted graphics: Use the Freehand tool to draw a line around the portion of the graphic where you want the text to appear. Select the line, select the text, and apply Contour Text, making sure that the Display Text Only check box is selected. Check out Chapter 17 for details about using the Freehand tool.

Add a Watermark to Your Pages

Companies with tons of money pay to have watermarks imprinted on their stationery. A _watermark_ is an image that appears behind the printed text on your page. You can create a simulated watermark in WordPerfect, thereby reserving your ton of money for some other, more enjoyable use. Here's how:

1. **Click at the beginning of the page where you want the watermark to first appear.**

2. **Choose Insert➪Watermark.**

   A dialog box appears, asking whether you want to create Watermark A or B. You can create two watermarks per page (A and B), and you can create multiple sets of A and B watermarks. For example, you can create two watermark pages for a document, one with watermarks for a left-hand page in a bound book and a second with watermarks for a right-hand page. Pick the watermark you want to create and click Create. WordPerfect displays a blank page, and the Property Bar displays buttons related to formatting your watermark, as shown in Figure 22-6.

3. **Add the text and graphics for the watermark.**

   Type your text and add your graphics as you would on a normal WordPerfect document page. Chapters in Part II tell you everything you need to know. Most, but not all, of the normal WordPerfect commands are available when you're creating a watermark.

4. **Adjust the shading.**

   You can make the watermark darker or lighter by clicking the Shading button on the Property Bar, which opens the Watermark Shading dialog box. The dialog box offers two controls, one for adjusting the text shading and another for adjusting the shading of graphics. Click OK after adjusting the values.

5. **Click the Placement button to choose which pages get the watermark.**

   The Placement dialog box, shown in the middle of Figure 22-6, appears. You can put the watermark on odd pages, even pages, or every page. Click OK after you select one of the radio buttons.

6. **Click the Close Watermark button.**

   You're returned to your normal WordPerfect document window. You can see the watermark if you work in Page view (View➪Page), but not in Draft view.

To edit a watermark, click anywhere on a page that uses the watermark and choose Insert➪Watermark. Choose the watermark that you want to edit (A or B) and click Edit. The watermark window appears, as when you initially created your watermark. To edit a different watermark of the same type (A or B), just click the Previous Watermark or Next Watermark buttons on the Property Bar.

If you get sick of seeing a watermark, click on the page where you want to turn the watermark off, choose Insert➪Watermark, select the watermark, and click Discontinue.

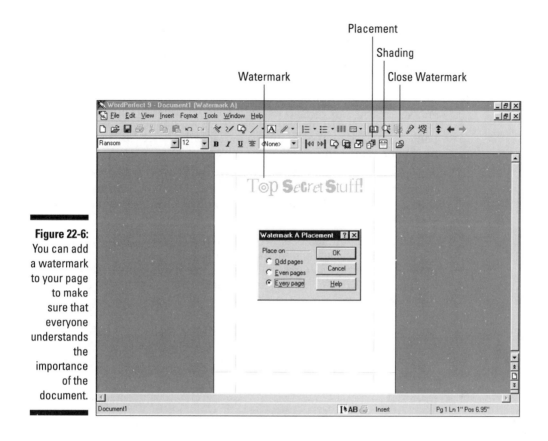

Figure 22-6:
You can add
a watermark
to your page
to make
sure that
everyone
understands
the
importance
of the
document.

Play with PerfectExpert Templates

For still more fun adventures, click the PerfectExpert icon on the DAD bar. Or choose Programs➪WordPerfect Office 2000➪Corel New Project from the Windows Start menu. The PerfectExpert dialog box appears. Click the Create New tab to see a listing all the available PerfectExpert templates (formerly known as QuickTasks and now sometimes called Experts).

As discussed in Chapter 3, the templates create most or all of the text and graphics for certain common documents. You can edit the documents to customize them as you see fit. (I recommend that you turn on the PerfectExpert Help feature, also covered in Chapter 3, when using the templates.) Some of my favorite PerfectExpert documents are:

✔ **Award:** Available if you select the WordPerfect 9 category from the drop-down list in the Corel New Project dialog box, this template helps you create an official-looking certificate, perfect for proclaiming yourself Employee of the Month.

✔ **Handwriting practice paper:** This template, available from the Education category, creates pages with those solid and dashed lines for practicing your penmanship. All you need is a big, fat crayon and the scent of an open jar of paste to take you right back to your preschool days.

✔ **Recipe card:** Joking aside, here's one that I actually use often. Select this template from the Home and Family category to type your recipes on pages formatted to fit on standard recipe cards. Your cards can even have your name and a graphic if you like.

✔ **Hangman game sheet:** Tired of wasting time playing computer games? Print a hangman game sheet and waste some time the old-fashioned way! You can find this template, along with another for creating Tic Tac Toe game sheets, in the Home and Family category.

✔ **Gift tag:** When you don't care enough to buy the very best, use this template, also available in the Home and Family category, to create a homemade gift tag to adorn that cheap present you bought. Really, you just can't say "I celebrate the wonderful person you are" any better than this.

Some PerfectExpert templates use graphics stored on the WordPerfect Office 2000 CD-ROM. So, if you see a dialog box complaining that the PerfectExpert can't access a required file, slip the CD into your CD-ROM drive and try again.

Chapter 23

Ten Shortcuts You Can Use All the Time

*W*hen I was a kid, I was fascinated by the notion that Samantha Stevens, the magical mom of TV's *Bewitched,* could do her household chores simply by twitching her nose. I thought that if I concentrated hard enough, I, too, could make my bed, clean my room, and do other tedious tasks by wrinkling my nose. Alas, I never acquired the touch, or should I say, the twitch.

Imagine my delight, then, when I discovered that computers have built-in shortcuts that enable you to perform certain jobs in one quick step instead of working your way through menu after menu to dig out the commands you want. This chapter shares some of the keyboard shortcuts and buttons you can use in WordPerfect, Quattro Pro, and Presentations to get your work done faster and with less effort. It's not magic, mind you, but then again, you don't have to worry about the side effects that so often plagued the Stevens household, where people were forever getting turned into barnyard animals because of a glitch in a twitch.

Several of the shortcuts presented in this chapter also work inside CorelCentral, Corel Print Office, Corel Photo House, and many other Windows programs. Not all programs offer all the toolbar buttons shown in this chapter, however. Keep in mind that some programs enable you to create your own toolbar button for a command or feature that you use frequently, as I explain in Chapter 24.

Creating and Opening Documents

 To create a new document, press Ctrl+N or Alt+F, N (hold down Alt+F while pressing N) or click the New Document button.

 To open an existing document, press Ctrl+O or Alt+F, O. Or, if you prefer clicking to pressing keys, click the Open Document button.

Closing the Current Document

 To close the current document, just click the Close button for the document window. You can also press Ctrl+F4 or Alt+F, C. Regardless of how you go about issuing the close command, you're prompted to save your document if you haven't already done so.

Moving Around Documents and Dialog Boxes

To jump quickly to the end of your WordPerfect document, press Ctrl+End. To jump to the beginning of the document, press Ctrl+Home. Press Home to move to the beginning of the current line and press End to move to the end of the current line. These shortcuts also work in most other word-processing programs.

In Quattro Pro, pressing Ctrl+Home moves you to the first cell on the first worksheet in the notebook; pressing Home moves you to the first cell in the current worksheet.

To move from one option to the next inside a dialog box, press Tab or press Alt plus the underlined letter in the option name. To move to the previous option in the dialog box, press Shift+Tab.

Cutting, Copying, and Pasting Data

 To make a copy of some text or a graphic, select it and then press Ctrl+C or click the Copy button. The copy trots off to the Windows Clipboard, where it stays until the next time you choose the Copy or Cut command.

 To cut data from one spot and move it to the Windows Clipboard, press Ctrl+X or click the Cut button. The data remains on the Clipboard until you choose Cut or Copy again.

 To paste the contents of the Clipboard into your document, click the spot where you want to put the data and press Ctrl+V or click the Paste button. (If you want to paste the contents from one program into another as an OLE object, as explained in Chapter 21, choose the Paste Special command from the Edit menu instead.)

 You can paste the Clipboard contents in multiple places if you want; just keep clicking the location where you want to paste the data and pressing Ctrl+V.

Printing Documents

 To print the current document, press Ctrl+P or Alt+F, P. Or click the Print button.

Saving Your Work

 To save the current document to disk, press Ctrl+S or Alt+F, S or click the Save button. The first time you save, a Save File dialog box appears, and you're asked to give the document a name, specify a file type, and choose where you want to store the document. The next time you press Ctrl+S or click the Save button, the document is saved using the same Save settings; the dialog box doesn't appear. If you want to save the document using different settings, choose File⇨Save As, press F3, or press Alt+F, A.

Undoing Mistakes

 Screw up big time? You can erase all evidence of your mistake by pressing Ctrl+Z, or pressing Alt+E, U, or clicking the Undo button. Undo can reverse most, but not all, actions; you can't undo saving a file, for example.

If you change your mind about that Undo, you can choose the Redo command, which reverses your Undo. Press Ctrl+Shift+Z in WordPerfect and Quattro Pro; press Ctrl+Shift+R in Presentations. In all three programs, you can also press Alt+E, R or click the Redo button to undo your Undo. Choose Redo *immediately* after you choose Undo, though, or this feature may not work.

Making Text Bold, Italic, or Underlined

 If your data's looking dull, give it some flair by applying character formatting. First, select the text you want to format. Then press Ctrl+B to make it bold, Ctrl+I to italicize it, and Ctrl+U to underline it. Or click the **B**, *I*, and U buttons on the Property Bar. Press the shortcut or click the button again to turn the formatting off.

Getting Help

If you're stumped as to how a particular feature works, press F1 to display the Help window. See Chapter 3 for information about how to find the information you need in the Help window.

In WordPerfect, Quattro Pro, and Presentations, you can also click the PerfectExpert button or choose Help⇨PerfectExpert to display the PerfectExpert window, a special Help feature explained in Chapter 3. Be sure to click the button that's on the toolbar, not the DAD icon on the Windows taskbar. Clicking the DAD icon displays the PerfectExpert dialog box, the starting point for creating documents based on PerfectExpert templates.

 Some dialog boxes include a question mark button. Click the button and then click a dialog box option to find out more about that specific option. Or click the button labeled Help to get information about the dialog box contents in general.

Quitting a Program

When you've had all you can take of this computing business, press Alt+F4 or Alt+F, X to shut down the current program. Or simply click the program's Close button. If you have any open documents, you're prompted to save them before you exit the program.

Chapter 24

Ten Ways to Save Time

*T*ick tick tick tick . . . Recognize that sound? It's not a bomb — at least, I don't think so, unless you offended a mobster lately or something like that. No, that sound is the clock on the wall, reminding you that there are only so many minutes in a day, and you haven't even begun to accomplish all the tasks slated for this day's minutes.

With so much to do and so little time, what you need is a way to make your computer work faster. (Certainly *you're* already going as fast as you can go.) With that thought in mind, this chapter continues Chapter 23's time-saving theme by bringing you ten more ways to speed things up. Put these tips into practice, and you may even make up for all that time you spend tooling around the Internet when no one's looking.

Click Once instead of Twice

Whenever possible, avoid hunting through menus to access commands. Instead, choose a command by clicking its toolbar button, selecting it from a Property Bar drop-down list or button, or pressing its keyboard shortcut. (Chapter 23 provides a rundown of buttons and shortcuts for the most frequently used commands.)

You can also save yourself some time by right-clicking to access QuickMenus, which contain commands related to the text, graphic, or other element you right-clicked.

Create Your Own Toolbar and Property Bar Buttons

Many programs enable you to customize your toolbar or Property Bar by adding buttons for commands that you use often. The following steps show you how to create a button in WordPerfect 9. The command names for creating and editing buttons may vary slightly in other programs; you should find specifics in the Help system for the program you're using if that program offers customizable toolbars.

1. **Right-click the toolbar or Property Bar you want to change and choose <u>E</u>dit from the QuickMenu.**

   The Property Bar Editor dialog box, as shown in Figure 24-1, appears. (If you right-clicked the toolbar, the dialog box is named Toolbar Editor instead, but works the same.) When you open the dialog box, the Features tab should be showing. If it isn't, click the tab to display it.

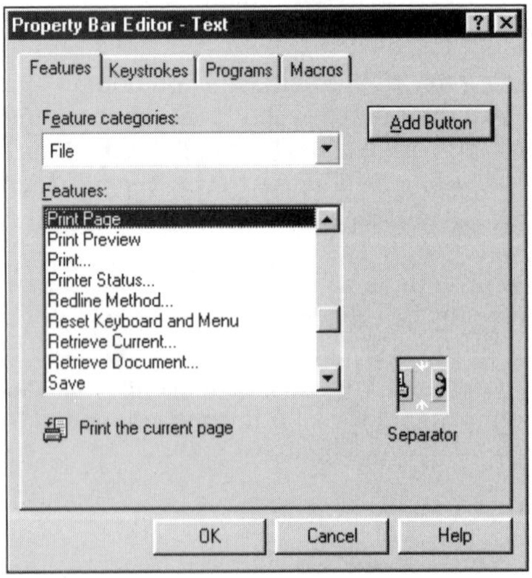

Figure 24-1: Create your own toolbar and Property Bar buttons for commands you use often.

2. **In the <u>F</u>eatures list box, click the command you want to turn into a button.**

   Commands are organized by menus; you can switch to a different menu by selecting it from the Feature Categories drop-down list.

3. **Drag the highlighted command to the toolbar or Property Bar.**

    You can also click Add Button or double-click the command to add the button to the end of whichever bar you right-clicked in Step 1 (toolbar or Property Bar).

4. **Click OK to make your addition permanent.**

To remove a button from the toolbar or Property Bar, press Alt as you drag the button off the bar. You can also rearrange buttons and move buttons by holding down Alt and dragging them.

If you don't like the button face that WordPerfect assigns to a command, you can change it. With the Property Bar or Toolbar Editor dialog box open, double-click the button you want to change. You see a dialog box in which you can change the name of the button and specify what QuickTip text you want to see when you pause the mouse cursor over the button. Click the Edit button to display a dialog box that lets you edit the colors and design of the button.

Use Quick Thinking and Templates

WordPerfect Office 2000 offers several speed-it-up features that begin with the word Quick: QuickCorrect, QuickWords, and so on.

Using QuickCorrect, for example, you can correct typing errors on-the-fly inside WordPerfect, as explained in Chapter 6. And with QuickWords, covered in Chapter 9, you can tell WordPerfect to automatically type a long phrase or name whenever you type a certain abbreviation.

Different programs offer different Quick commands, so browse through the menus looking for commands related to the project you're doing. Be sure to also right-click around the screen to display different QuickMenus, which are mini-menus containing commands related to whatever you right-click.

On another front, PerfectExpert templates help you blaze your way through various routine tasks, such as creating fax cover sheets. The templates provide the basic building blocks for documents, handling formatting and entering some text and graphics automatically. You can then edit the document to customize it to your needs. For more on using templates, see Chapter 3.

Work in Style

Especially in WordPerfect, you can save yourself a great deal of time by using *styles* to format documents. Styles enable you to automatically apply many different formatting attributes at once, instead of choosing them one by one from various menus. Using styles also ensures that the different components of your document — headlines, body text, and so on — have a consistent look.

For more information about using styles in WordPerfect, flip back to Chapter 9. Chapter 11 tells you how styles work in Quattro Pro. For information about using styles in another program, check out the Help index in the program.

Keep Automatic Backup Turned On

Most programs offer a feature that automatically saves your document every so often to protect you from losing all your work should the power to your computer go out unexpectedly. But, in many cases, you have to turn this automatic backup feature on before it can do its job.

Where you activate automatic backup depends on the program:

✔ In WordPerfect, choose Tools➪Settings, click the Files icon, click the Document tab, and make sure that the Timed Document Backup Every check box is selected.

✔ In Presentations, use the same steps as just described, but click the Backup tab instead of the Document tab to find the backup options.

✔ In Quattro Pro, choose Tools➪Settings and click the File Options tab of the resulting dialog box to find the automatic backup option.

✔ To locate the option in another program, consult the program's Help system.

Don't set the backup interval too low. Some users report that if they set the backup interval to less than 10 minutes, their systems don't always successfully recover the backup file from a crash. Also, automatic backup *is not* a substitute for saving your document on a regular basis. For an explanation of why this is so, see Chapter 5.

Teach Your Programs How to Share Data

Don't re-create the same data over and over again; create it once and then use OLE commands or the normal Cut, Copy, and Paste commands to copy and move it into other documents. If you want, you can use OLE to create copies that automatically get updated when you update the original data. You can find out more about these options in Chapter 21 and also in the editing sections of chapters discussing individual programs in the suite.

Practice the Art of Drag and Drop

If you want to copy or move data, you can select the data, choose the Cut or Copy command, click the spot where you want to place the data, and then choose the Paste command. Or you can make life easy by simply selecting the data and dragging it to its new home using your mouse.

You can drag and drop data within the same document, between two open documents in the same program, and, in some cases, between two open documents in different programs.

 In most programs, you drag to move data between documents and press Ctrl while dragging to copy data. For more information, see Chapters 6 and 13. You can use the techniques presented there to drag and drop stuff in most programs.

When you drag data between programs, the data is embedded as an OLE object, as explained in Chapter 21.

Seek Out Online Help

Corel Corporation maintains a site on the World Wide Web at www.corel.com. This site is a great place to find out about the latest Corel products and programs and access technical support. See Chapter 3 for information about how to access different online help resources from within WordPerfect Office 2000 programs.

You may also want to post a message in one of the discussion groups related to the WordPerfect Office 2000 programs. You can find links to some of these groups at the Corel Web site.

Don't Be Shy about Calling for Help

I can't tell you how many hours I lost trying to research and solve my own computer headaches before I finally wised up to the benefits of calling tech support. In some cases, I would have never been able to find a solution myself because the problem was related to some software or hardware bug known only to the folks at tech support.

So, if you encounter a problem that you just can't seem to solve, don't waste endless hours trying to track down a solution on your own. Instead, pick up the phone and call the technical support department for the software or hardware that's causing you fits. (Corel lists its support telephone numbers in the Help files of its programs; look for the Technical Support entry in the Help system index.)

In some cases, you may pay a small surcharge for technical support — and you may have to wait on hold for some time before you get to speak to a real, live person. But if you weigh those drawbacks against all the time you lose if you try to fix things yourself, you almost always come out ahead.

When All Else Fails . . .

Many people seem to feel that they should be able to install and use a new piece of software just like that, with no instruction and no information about how the program works. They refuse to read the manual that came with the program or any other references, such as this book. As a result, they never learn to use the program to even a bazillionth of its capacity — which means they plunk down a lot of money for a meager return. They also spend much more time than necessary getting things done because they don't know how to put the program's power to work for them.

Of course, I know that *you* don't fall into this category because you bought this book. But just in case the book was a gift (or was anonymously put on your desk by someone who was tired of hearing you yell at your computer), understand that it is no reflection on your intelligence that you can't learn how computer programs work by osmosis. Heck, you didn't learn how to tie your shoes by osmosis, did you? (Oh . . . is that why you're wearing loafers?) So swallow your pride and let this book show you how to use WordPerfect Office 2000. If you spend just five minutes a week reading, you can pick up techniques and tricks that will save you hours in the future.

Appendix

Installing WordPerfect Office 2000

•••

*I*nstalling the programs in WordPerfect Office 2000 is relatively painless — the setup program walks you through the entire process. But just in case you're new to installing programs, this appendix offers some additional guidance.

If the steps you see here don't mesh exactly with what you see on-screen, don't panic. Software manufacturers sometimes alter the installation routine when they make minor updates to their programs or when they customize programs for a particular audience (such as a computer vendor). Follow the on-screen instructions, and you'll be fine.

Installing the Core Programs

To install the core components of WordPerfect Office 2000, whether you own the Standard or Voice-Activated Edition, follow these steps:

1. **Put the WordPerfect Office 2000 program CD into your CD-ROM drive.**

   If you have your CD drive's autoplay feature enabled, the WordPerfect CD-ROM screen appears.

   If the screen doesn't appear, click the Windows Start button and click Run. In the Open dialog box, enter **D:\Setup.exe** and click OK. (This instruction assumes that drive D is your CD-ROM drive; if the drive is assigned some other letter, substitute that letter for D.)

2. **Click WordPerfect Office 2000 Setup.**

   The Corel Setup Wizard dialog box appears.

3. **Click the Release Notes button.**

   The Help system cranks into gear. In the Help window, you find documents that provide last-minute installation notes. (For an explanation of how to navigate a Help window, see Chapter 3.) After you scan the notes, click the little X button in the upper-right corner of the Help window to close it.

4. **Click Next.**

   A dialog box appears, asking you whether you agree to the terms of the software licensing agreement.

5. **Click Accept to signal that you're A-Okay with the terms of the agreement.**

6. **Enter your name and company name (optional) and then click Next.**

7. **Enter the program serial number and click Next.**

   You can find the serial number on the product registration card.

8. **Choose an installation type and click Next.**

   You have three installation options:

   - **Typical** performs a standard installation and requires about 177MB of empty hard drive space. I recommend this option unless you're short on disk space, in which case I recommend the Custom option.

   - **Compact** installs the minimum components required to run the suite. It takes about 117MB of free hard drive space, but you won't be able to take advantage of some program features.

   - **Custom** lets you pick and choose which components you want to install. The amount of disk space required depends on how many components you install.

   Selecting the CD-ROM Based check box lets you install just some of the program files on your hard disk and access the rest from the program CD-ROM. This option requires less hard drive space, but your programs run really, really slowly. Also, you must have the WordPerfect Office 2000 CD in the CD-ROM drive to run programs. I don't recommend this option.

   If you selected the Typical or Compact installation option, skip to Step 11.

9. **Select the components you want to install and click Next.**

   A check mark next to a component means that component will be installed. A gray, shaded check box means that only some parts of a program will be installed. Click the plus sign to the left of the check box to display all the associated files or tools that you can install. Again, put a check mark next to those you want to install; click to remove the check mark from options you don't want to install. Any components that have a red check mark are required.

   By default, all the Reference Center manuals (electronic manuals for suite programs) are installed on your hard drive. If you're short on disk space, deselect all the boxes for the Reference Center except the Program Files box. You can access the manuals from the CD anytime as long as you install the Program Files option.

As you decide which options to install, keep in mind that you can always go back later and install additional components.

10. Choose your conversion filters and click Next.

Conversion filters enable you to work with different types of files in your programs. Click the plus sign next to the Conversion File Types check box to see the available filter sets. Click the plus sign next to a filter set to see what file types are included, and select the filters for the types of files you use.

11. Select your language and click Next.

This option controls the language used for the suite's dictionaries, spell checkers, and other writing tools. The default is English. To install additional languages, select them from the list.

If you're doing a Typical install, skip now to Step 13.

12. Select which fonts you want to install and click Next.

The default font group should give you more than enough fonts to use. Keep in mind that each additional font sucks up more disk space. Too many installed fonts can slow your system down, too.

13. Choose a destination folder and click Next.

The destination folder is the location where your program files will be installed. Chances are, the default is fine. But if you want to install to some other location, enter it in the Destination Directory option box.

14. Specify a shortcut folder and click Next.

Here, the default option is fine.

15. Click Install.

Or, if you want to make any changes to the installation options, click the Back button to work your way back through the installation screens.

When the installation is finished, the Setup program invites you to register your copy of the program via modem. If you want to do so, click Next and follow the on-screen instructions. Otherwise, click Register Later. The installer begs you to reconsider; click Yes to send it packing. You, thereafter, get a reminder every two weeks to register. The installer then presents a dialog box saying that installation is complete. Click OK. The installer notifies you that it was kidding earlier — the installation won't *really* be complete until you restart your computer. Click Yes to restart and wrap things up for good.

If you installed CorelCentral, you're asked upon the system restart whether you want CorelCentral to run each time you start your computer. Click Yes or No, depending on your feelings. (You can always change the setting later; see Chapter 18 for information.)

Adding and Removing Components

After you do the initial suite installation, you can go back at any time and install additional components. Follow Steps 1 and 2 of the normal installation process, choose the Add New Components option in the initial setup window, and then follow Steps 9, 10, 11, 12, and 15.

To remove a program, first close any open suite programs, including DAD and CorelCentral Day Planner and Alarms. Then click the Windows Start button and choose Programs➪WordPerfect Office 2000➪Setup & Notes➪ Corel Remove Program. The Corel Uninstaller window appears. Click Next and select the programs you want to remove. Click Next and then click Next again.

Installing Adobe Acrobat

If you want to view the Reference Center electronic manuals, you must install Adobe Acrobat. Take Step 1 of the installation instructions presented earlier. In the WordPerfect CD-ROM window, click Adobe Acrobat Reader Setup. Click Yes when asked if you want to install the program. Then follow the on-screen prompts, accepting the default options that are presented.

Installing the Voice-Activated Edition

To install the main components of the Voice-Activated Edition, follow the same steps outlined for installing the Standard Edition. Dragon Naturally Speaking and Corel Print Office each come on a separate CD and must be installed separately.

To install either program, put the program CD into your CD drive. If the installation screen doesn't appear after a few moments, click the Windows Start button and then click Run. In the Open option box, enter **D:\Setup.exe** and click OK. (If your CD drive is set to a letter other than D, substitute that letter.)

Follow the on-screen prompts to complete the installation. For Dragon NaturallySpeaking, accept the default installation options. If you're upgrading from a previous version of the program, be sure to accept the option that enables you to save your existing speech files so that you don't have to completely retrain the program to recognize your voice. (See Chapter 19 for more information.)

When installing Print Office, I suggest that you choose the Custom installation option and then deselect the option that installs Corel Colleagues and Contacts, which duplicates many of the functions provided by CorelCentral. (If you don't see this component, don't worry about it — your version of the program may not include Colleagues and Contacts.)

Index

• *Numbers* •

3-D depth, adding to objects, 363
3-D spreadsheets, described, 159

• *A* •

absolute address, worksheet formulas, 181
absolute tabs, described, 92–93
accent marks, creating, 111–113
Action menu, finding/replacing text, 138
actions, undoing last (Ctrl+Z/Alt+Backspace),
    76, 138, 199, 251
active cell, described, 153
Active Cells dialog box
    alignment options, 175–176
    color/background options, 228–229
    numeric format editing, 172–173
    resizing columns/rows, 203–204
Active Notebook dialog box, described, 157
Active Sheet dialog box
    described, 157–158
    enabling/disabling gridlines, 226
    line/border options, 226–228
active vocabulary, Dragon NaturallySpeaking,
    316
Address Book
    adding addresses to, 303–304
    creating, 303
    customizing, 302–303
    deleting addresses, 305
    described, 290, 300–305
    editing addresses, 305
    information field types, 302
    inserting address into a WordPerfect docu-
        ment, 146
    MAPI (Messaging Application
        Programming Interface) support, 302
    moving addresses, 305
    starting, 301
    summary view, 301
    tree view, 301
    uses, 300
    window elements, 301
Address⇨New Entry command, 303

addresses
    adding to Address Book, 303–304
    inserting into documents, 146
Adobe Acrobat
    installing, 382
    Reference Center document viewing, 33–35
advance modes, slide shows, 276–277
Alarm dialog box, CorelCentral 9, 296–297
alarms, CorelCentral 9 sounds, 296–297
alignment
    text formatting, 99–101
    worksheet cell options, 174–176
Alignment button, Quattro Pro 9, 174–175
All justification, described, 100
Alt key, keyboard shortcuts, 17
animations, slide show inclusion, 279
Application Bar
    content editing, 45
    described, 19
    hiding/displaying, 44
    insertion marker location display, 41
appointments
    alarms, 296–297
    Calendar/Day Planner scheduling, 292–295
arguments, functions, 185–186
Arrange⇨Group (Ctrl+G) command, 333
Arrange⇨To Background (Ctrl+End)
        command, 325
Arrange⇨To Foreground (Ctrl+Home) com-
        mand, 325
Arrange⇨Ungroup (Ctrl+G) command, 333
artistic text
    editing, 330–331
    Print Office creation, 328
Ask the PerfectExpert, described, 28–29
asterisk (*) character, appearance in
        worksheet cells, 167
As-You-Type, QuickCorrect features, 78–80
at (@) symbol, built-in function indicator, 185
attributes, font editing, 85–86
audiences, custom slide show creation,
        282–283
Auto Replace, when to use, 141
automatic backups, advantages, 376
Autoscrolling, described, 56–57
@AVG function, uses, 193
axes, chart labeling, 219

• B •

• C •

(continued)

(continued)

FREE GIFT!

FREE

IDG Books/PC WORLD CD Wallet

and a Sample Issue of

PC WORLD

THE #1 MONTHLY COMPUTER MAGAZINE
How to order your sample issue and FREE CD Wallet:

✉ Cut and mail the coupon today!

☎ Call us at 1-800-825-7595 x434
Fax us at 1-415-882-0936

☞ Order online at
www.pcworld.com/resources/subscribe/BWH.html

...For Dummies is a registered trademark under exclusive license to IDG Books Worldwide, Inc., from International Data Group, Inc.

ORDER TODAY!

✂

FREE GIFT/SAMPLE ISSUE COUPON

Cut coupon and mail to: PC World, PO Box 55029, Boulder, CO 80322-5029

YES! Please rush my FREE CD wallet and my FREE sample issue of PC WORLD! If I like PC WORLD, I'll honor your invoice and receive 11 more issues (12 in all) for just $19.97—that's 72% off the newsstand rate.

NO COST EXAMINATION GUARANTEE.
If I decide PC WORLD is not for me, I'll write "cancel" on the invoice and owe nothing. The sample issue and CD wallet are mine to keep, no matter what.

PC WORLD

Name

Company

Address

City   State   Zip

Email

Offer valid in the U.S. only. Mexican orders please send $39.97 USD. Canadian orders send $39.97, plus 7% GST (#R124669680). Other countries send $65.97. Savings based on annual newsstand rate of $71.88.   7B587

YOUR ONLINE RESOURCE

WWW.DUMMIES.COM

Discover *Dummies*™ Online!

The *Dummies* Web Site is your fun and friendly online resource for the latest information about *...For Dummies*® books on all your favorite topics. From cars to computers, wine to Windows, and investing to the Internet, we've got a shelf full of *...For Dummies* books waiting for you!

Ten Fun and Useful Things You Can Do at www.dummies.com

1. Register this book and win!
2. Find and buy the *...For Dummies* books you want online.
3. Get ten great *Dummies Tips*™ every week.
4. Chat with your favorite *...For Dummies* authors.
5. Subscribe free to *The Dummies Dispatch*™ newsletter.
6. Enter our sweepstakes and win cool stuff.
7. Send a free cartoon postcard to a friend.
8. Download free software.
9. Sample a book before you buy.
10. Talk to us. Make comments, ask questions, and get answers!

Jump online to these ten fun and useful things at **http://www.dummies.com/10useful**

WWW.DUMMIES.COM

For other technology titles from IDG Books Worldwide, go to **www.idgbooks.com**

Not online yet? It's easy to get started with *The Internet For Dummies*®, 5th Edition, or *Dummies 101*®: *The Internet For Windows*® *98*, available at local retailers everywhere.

Find other *...For Dummies* books on these topics:

IDG BOOKS WORLDWIDE

Business • Careers • Databases • Food & Beverages • Games • Gardening • Graphics • Hardware
Health & Fitness • Internet and the World Wide Web • Networking • Office Suites
Operating Systems • Personal Finance • Pets • Programming • Recreation • Sports
Spreadsheets • Teacher Resources • Test Prep • Word Processing

IDG BOOKS WORLDWIDE
BOOK REGISTRATION

We want to hear from you!

Register This Book and Win!

Visit **http://my2cents.dummies.com** to register this book and tell us how you liked it!

- ✔ Get entered in our monthly prize giveaway.

- ✔ Give us feedback about this book — tell us what you like best, what you like least, or maybe what you'd like to ask the author and us to change!

- ✔ Let us know any other ...*For Dummies*® topics that interest you.

Your feedback helps us determine what books to publish, tells us what coverage to add as we revise our books, and lets us know whether we're meeting your needs as a ...*For Dummies* reader. You're our most valuable resource, and what you have to say is important to us!

Not on the Web yet? It's easy to get started with *Dummies 101*®: *The Internet For Windows*® *98* or *The Internet For Dummies*®, 5th Edition, at local retailers everywhere.

Or let us know what you think by sending us a letter at the following address:

...*For Dummies* Book Registration
Dummies Press
7260 Shadeland Station, Suite 100
Indianapolis, IN 46256-3917
Fax 317-596-5498

™
...FOR DUMMIES

BESTSELLING BOOK SERIES